in a basement with a wooden floor. I remember it
was a Sunday. It was raining ...be
I am now transcribing this in
from notes I wrote in a house where ...   e
is a large lake. Four nights ago (from my
notes it is two) we had a covering of snow
on each of the flat and angled rooftops
near to us. The house is number 907 on a street
that looks north.

This house somehow helps me to remember you and I
Not from the first time but a time when I saw you
again, later. I sat with you and stayed with you
I like to be near as I can't see very well. we were
indoors in one of those places that has molding
around it's ceiling and a large wooden door at
one end. You and I could leave if needed to go
outside, to go outdoors. It was in october. The

elt rotated flinging each one outdoors — into
a nightime. (long strings of wires, cables,
bits of bodies crumpled into digitized (coding)
we can see them... we can see them!...)
"I am laughing, she is laughing, we are all laughin
We can see them coming through on the screen.
Yet I saw them leave.
Now they are in another space. we sat
watching in this old molded building — In this
museum they allowed us to see them on a wall
in their part scifi, part boys bedroom, part
outdoor/indoor display case, part museum set.
All I still seem to remember is laughing, and
laughing — laughing so hard — yet now all I
seem to remember is how sad they left,
why did they escape, how fragile they

THE MAKING OF A MEMORY

10 years of Gob Squad remembered in words and pictures
10 Jahre Gob Squad erinnert in Wort und Bild

Edited by/Herausgegeben von
Gob Squad & Aenne Quiñones

Synwolt Verlag Berlin

CONTENTS
INHALT

photo: Manuel Reinartz

Gob Squad: The Making of a Memory

How performance is remembered, documented and archived has been continually debated throughout its long history. Just as a slideshow of holiday snaps fails to capture the essence of being there and often ends up boring friends and family to tears, it is widely believed that photographs, video and writing about performance can never capture a work´s "liveness" and that attempts to do so only serve to highlight the "in the moment" quality of performance.

Our tenth year together has provided us with a milestone from which to look back on our work. Having produced nearly 30 different performances, installations, radio pieces and other artworks we were curious to know how much people actually remembered of our fleeting activities. Which moments had survived time and live on in peoples minds?

To answer this question we asked a wide range of people to remember specific performances that they had a special relationship to. The contributors to this book come from a variety of backgrounds and include artists, theatre producers, project funders, academics and audience members. Some are professional writers, some aren't. The documentation of performance is a contradiction in terms, setting out to commodify or objectify something that is by its very nature impossible to capture.

Wie Performance erinnert, dokumentiert und archiviert werden kann, wurde im Laufe ihrer Geschichte viel diskutiert. So wie eine Dia-Show von Schnappschüssen niemals das Wesentliche eines Ferienaufenthalts einfängt und Freunde und Familie oft zu Tode langweilt, herrscht der Konsens, dass Fotografien, Videos und Texte über Performance niemals die Unmittelbarkeit eines Werks einfangen können und dass Versuche in diese Richtung nur die flüchtige Qualität von Performance unterstreichen.

Mit unserem zehnten gemeinsamen Jahr haben wir einen Meilenstein erreicht, von dem aus wir auf unsere Arbeit zurückschauen. Wir haben fast 30 verschiedene Performances, Installationen und andere Arbeiten produziert und waren neugierig, wieviel davon in Erinnerung geblieben ist. Welche Momente haben die Zeit überlebt und leben in den Köpfen weiter?

Um diese Frage zu beantworten, haben wir einige Wegbegleiter gebeten, einzelne Performances, zu denen sie einen besonderen Bezug hatten, zu erinnern. Die Menschen, die zu diesem Buch beigetragen haben, kommen aus verschiedenen Kontexten, sie sind Künstler, Kuratoren, Produzenten, Theoretiker oder Zuschauer. Manche sind professionelle Autoren, andere nicht.

The contents of this book are subjective. Our contributors were encouraged to be open to the fragmentary nature of memory in the recalling of images, moments, smells and feelings from our work. The various submissions are not intended as reconstructions of our works. They are personal, lost in thought, incomplete or focused on a detail. Sometimes they are incorrect, blurring different events together, describing things that never happened and quoting lines that have never been said.

Looking back over the many different responses we received, it appears that sometimes the elements that we labored over during the working process became unimportant details over time. As the names or faces of performers, the images, actions and choices of words or music dissipated what survived in peoples' memories were the emotional responses we provoked.

We have called this book "The Making of a Memory". We hope you like it.

Die Dokumentation von Performance ist in sich ein Widerspruch, weil sie zu verdinglichen oder zu objektivieren versucht, was im Wesentlichen nicht einzufangen ist. Der Inhalt dieses Buchs ist subjektiv. Unsere Mitarbeiter waren angehalten, sich auf das fragmentarische Wesen der Erinnerung einzulassen, wenn sie sich Bilder, Momente, Gerüche und Gefühle unserer Arbeit ins Gedächtnis riefen. Die verschiedenen Beiträge sind nicht als Rekonstruktionen unserer Stücke gedacht. Sie sind persönlich, gedankenverloren, unvollständig oder detailfixiert. Manchmal sind sie unkorrekt, vermischen unterschiedliche Ereignisse miteinander, beschreiben Dinge, die nie geschehen sind, und zitieren Worte, die nie gesagt wurden. Wenn man auf die vielen verschiedenen Reaktionen schaut, die wir erhalten haben, dann scheint es, dass die Elemente mit denen wir im Arbeitsprozess zu kämpfen hatten, mit der Zeit zu unwichtigen Details geworden sind. Namen oder Gesichter von Performern, Bilder, Aktionen, Worte oder Musik verloren sich, doch was in der Erinnerung überlebte, waren Gefühle, die wir hervorgerufen hatten.

Wir haben dieses Buch „The Making of a Memory" genannt. Wir hoffen, dass es Euch gefällt.

Foreword by/Vorwort von
Aenne Quiñones (Volksbühne am Rosa-Luxemburg-Platz, Berlin, D)

Is it really only 10 years ago that we met in a furniture show-room in Nottingham? For me in 1996 there was so much to discover in British cities such as London, Bristol, Manchester, Nottingham and Cardiff. Live Art was emerging which ignited the interest of performers and theatregoers alike both in the UK and across Europe. After my first meetings with Gob Squad and others involved in the UK Live Art scene such as Tim Etchells, Lois Keidan and Blast Theory I drove back to Berlin feeling inspired and motivated. I had found something that connected with me. These performers and writers analysed their everyday life and placed their own experiences at the centre of their work, drawing energy directly from it that was both convincing and inspiring. This attitude resulted in a search for new forms of expression and mistrust of high culture, as the points of reference were now popular music, film, new media and one's own day-to-day life experiences and absolutely not theatre in the traditional sense. It is no coincidence that Gob Squad, rather than going on stage opted to play in a house, an office or a shopping centre. The stage came later but even then as with all their other projects the definition of the spectator/participant relationship was negotiated.

Dann sind es also noch nicht mal 10 Jahre, seit wir uns begegnet sind, damals, 1996, in Nottingham, im Möbel-discounter? Zu dieser Zeit gab es für mich viel Neues zu entdecken in Städten wie Nottingham, London, Bristol, Manchester oder Cardiff. Live Art war im Kommen und wie eine Initialzündung für viele Theaterleute und Performer, auch in „mainland Europe". Nach dieser ersten Begegnung mit Gob Squad und vielen anderen aus der britischen Live-Art-Szene wie z.B. Tim Etchells, Lois Keidan oder Blast Theory fuhr ich zurück nach Berlin, inspiriert und motiviert. Hier war mir etwas begegnet, was auch mit mir zu tun hatte. Leute, die ihren Alltag „durchleuchteten", ihre eigenen Erfahrungen ins Zentrum stellten und daraus eine unmittelbare Energie zogen, die überzeugte und begeister-te. Selbstverständlich ergab sich aus dieser Haltung die Suche nach neuen Formen und erst einmal ein Misstrauen gegen jegliche Form von „Hochkultur". Bezugspunkte waren eher Musik, Film, neue Medien und die eigenen Alltags-erfahrungen, und schon gar nicht das Theater im traditionellen Sinne. Und so war es kein Zufall, dass Gob Squad, statt auf die Bühne zu gehen, ein Wohnhaus, ein Büro oder ein Einkaufszentrum bespielten. Die Bühne kam später auch mal vor. Dann ging es aber darum, wie auch in allen

Recently, whilst working on *Prater Saga 3 (In diesem Kiez ist der Teufel eine Goldmine/In this Neighbourhood the Devil is a Gold Mine)* they consistently pursued their own vision, reconfiguring the stage and its possibilities by leaving the theatre during the show and encouraging passers-by to enter the performance space to enact René Pollesch's text.

Gob Squad undertake the challenge of collective work again and again. This indicates the presence of respect, consideration, mutual interest, self-assurance and humour, qualities that are appreciated as a colleague or as a spectator in the knowledge that they are difficult to achieve and maintain. One wishes urgently for more and seeks to ensure that the next project can take place as soon as possible. Whenever I am in one of the unmistakeable Gob Squad shows it seems to me as if we've known each other forever. They are always a little like coming home.

Working together with Gob Squad is always an intensive and inspiring process. We are especially happy that they have found an artistic home for their urban interventions at Prater/Volksbühne as they continue to work for and against theatre, searching to make connections between inside and outside. So, onward and Happy Birthday Gob Squad!

anderen Projekten, die jeweilige räumliche Situation zu thematisieren und das Verhältnis Zuschauer/Akteur immer wieder neu zu definieren. Wie jetzt auch im dritten Teil der Prater-Saga *In diesem Kiez ist der Teufel eine Goldmine*, wo sie konsequent ihren Weg weitergehen und die Bühne nun auch anderen, von draußen, überlassen, um in diesem konkreten Falle Texte von René Pollesch von Passanten sprechen zu lassen.

Gob Squad stellt sich immer wieder der Herausforderung kollektiver Arbeit. Das setzt einiges voraus – z. B. Respekt, Aufmerksamkeit, gegenseitiges Interesse, Souveränität und Humor. Alles Dinge, die man auch als Kollege oder Zuschauer zu schätzen weiß, schon deshalb, weil die heutzutage nicht mehr so einfach zu haben sind. Um so dringlicher wünscht man sich und tut auch was dafür, dass das nächste Projekt so bald wie möglich stattfindet. Bin ich dann in einer dieser unverwechselbaren Gob-Squad-Shows, kommt es mir so vor, als würden wir uns schon ewig kennen und es ist irgendwie immer ein bisschen wie „coming home".

Die Zusammenarbeit mit Gob Squad ist jedesmal wieder ein intensiver und inspirierender Prozess. Deshalb freut es uns ganz besonders, dass sie mittlerweile im Prater der Volksbühne eine künstlerische Heimat gefunden haben, für ihre urbanen Interventionen auf der Suche nach einer Verbindung von drinnen und draußen, gegen und für das Theater. Also weiter so und Happy Birthday, Gob Squad!

Foreword by/Vorwort von
Gordana Vnuk (Kampnagel, Hamburg, D)

Gob Squad is a group whose progress I have followed for many years. In my capacity as a producer and programmer I have been instrumental in showing their work at Chapter Arts Centre in Cardiff, Eurokaz Festival in Zagreb and now at Kampnagel in Hamburg. In Zagreb and Hamburg I have shown Gob Squad in the context of so-called "iconoclastic theatre" alongside such artists as BAK-Truppen, Showcase Beat le Mot, PME and L&O who represent a special form of iconoclasts. It was always important to me that these works were suitable framed.

After the first generation of iconoclasts (Soc. Raffello Sanzio, Goat Island, Forced Entertainment, BAK-Truppen), Gob Squad can already be counted as members of the second. Numerous younger artists have adopted the specific stylistic characteristics of iconoclastic theatre. Inherent is the denial of the usual concepts of "good theatre" and the renouncement of actorly virtuosity in favour of attempting to achieve a purer presence on stage. Spending time with one another, bizarre combinations, worn out signs and shabby equipment, "noble dilettantism" as a style of representation, the staging of emptiness and so on. These artists, that have strongly positioned themselves against visual theatre and the ideo-

Gob Squad ist eine der Gruppen, die ich seit vielen Jahren begleitet und in den Theatern und auf den Festivals, bei denen ich in den letzten Jahren tätig war, präsentiert habe: das Chapter Arts Centre in Cardiff, das Eurokaz Festival in Zagreb und jetzt auf Kampnagel in Hamburg. Zweimal (in Zagreb und in Hamburg) habe ich Gob Squad im Kontext des so genannten „Ikonoklastischen Theaters" gezeigt – zusammen mit Künstlern wie den BAK-Truppen, Showcase Beat le Mot, PME, L&O, die eine ganz besondere Form der „Bilderstürmer" darstellen –, da es mir immer wichtig war, ihrer Arbeit einen geeigneten Rahmen zu geben.

Nach einer ersten Generation von „Ikonoklasten" (wie zum Beispiel Soc. Raffello Sanzio, Goat Island, Forced Entertainment, BAK-Truppen) kann Gob Squad bereits zur zweiten Generation der „Bilderstürmer" gezählt werden. Aber auch zahlreiche jüngere Künstler haben die spezifischen stilistischen Charakteristika des „ikonoklastischen" Theaters übernommen. Dazu gehört beispielsweise die Verweigerung gegenüber den gängigen Vorstellungen von „gutem Theater", der Verzicht auf schauspielerische Virtuosität, reine Anwesenheit auf der Bühne, das Verbringen von Zeit miteinander, bizarre Kombinationen, abgenutzte Zeichen und schäbige

logy of the image offer open, fluid structures in which the wishes enjoy themselves, without aiming at an object of desire or a product (Deleuze/Guattari).They develop a specific kind of "play" which combines high entertainment value with a relaxed social atmosphere that mixes artists and the public. The theatre of the iconoclasts releases the energy of the unconscious. It confounds the expectations of the spectator and questions the conventions of perception.

Kampnagel is one of the largest and most important independent production houses and venues in Europe. Over the last four years it has strengthened and developed the claim to create contexts that highlight the basis of the artistic work and likewise its position in an historical context alongside contemporary developments in the dance and theatre world. I see Kampnagel's commitment to the realisation of 'The Making of a Memory' as part of this ongoing research.

I hope that Gob Squad continues to develop their engaging performance aesthetics as consistently and successfully for the next decade as they have for the previous one.

Ausstattung, „nobler Dilettantismus" als Darstellungsstil, Inszenierung der Leere etc. Diese Künstler, die sich stark gegen ein visuelles Theater und die Ideologie des Bildes positioniert haben, bieten offene, sich im Fluss befindliche Strukturen, in denen die Wünsche sich selbst genießen, ohne auf ein Objekt des Begehrens oder ein Produkt zu zielen (Deleuze/Guattari). Sie entwickeln eine spezifische Art des „Spiels", bei dem Unterhaltung und entspannte Atmosphäre im sozialen Miteinander von Künstlern und Publikum einen hohen Stellenwert haben. Das Theater der Bilderstürmer setzt Energien des Unbewussten frei, es irritiert die Erwartungen der Zuschauer und stellt die Wahrnehmungskonventionen in Frage.

Kampnagel, eine der größten und bedeutendsten freien Produktions- und Spielstätten in Europa, hat in den letzten vier Jahren verstärkt den Anspruch entwickelt, Kontexte zu ermöglichen, in denen sich Gründe und Zweck einer künstlerischen Arbeit ebenso zeigen wie ihre Position in der Theatergeschichte und den aktuellen Entwicklungen der Tanz- und Theaterwelt. Ich sehe es als Teil dieser Recherchearbeit, dass Kampnagel dazu beiträgt, dieses Buch zu realisieren.

Gob Squad wünsche ich für das nächste Jahrzehnt ihres Bestehens, dass sie ihre eigene, engagierte Performance-Ästhetik so konsequent und erfolgreich weiterentwickeln wie in den ersten zehn Jahren!

Foreword by/Vorwort von
Andrew Caleya Chetty (artistic director of the NOW Festival 1995–2001, Nottingham, UK)

Gob Squad. A Personal View/Gob Squad. Eine persönliche Ansicht.

Writing this makes me feel bloody old. 10 years on from *House* and I have watched the Gob Squad get better. There was something happening in 1994 in the UK. Its cultural landscape was being steered by the e-generation and we were just about to feel the heat of e-culture. Nottingham was jumping with a fantastic generation of artists, performance and dance makers, underground musicians, DJs, producers and novelists and playwrights all doing it because they had to get it out there. Their work was clearly informed by the music they listened to, the films and TV they watched, the technology they played with and the drugs that they took, not just what they were taught, very well, at university.

At some time in 1994 I went to an event housed within a council house in Forest Fields. It was a performance installation by a group of ex-Nottingham Trent University students and their German collaborators, the new-formed Gob Squad. In the house they took over they put surprises around every corner, poetics unfolding as doors opened and closed and

Verdammt alt fühle ich mich, während ich dies schreibe. 10 Jahre sind seit *House* vergangen, und ich konnte beobachten, wie Gob Squad immmer besser wurde. 1994 geschah etwas in Großbritannien. Die Kulturlandschaft wurde von der E-Generation gelenkt, und wir begannen ihren Einfluss zu spüren. Nottingham war voll von Performern und Choreografen, Underground-Musikern, DJs, Produzenten, Romanautoren und Dramatikern, eine Künstler-Generation, die sich ihrer Tätigkeit verschrieb, weil sie etwas zu sagen hatte. Ihre Arbeit war beeinflusst von der Musik, die sie hörten, den Filmen und Fernsehsendungen, die sie sich ansahen, der Technologie, mit der sie spielten, und den Drogen, die sie nahmen, und nicht nur durch das, was man ihnen sorgfältig an der Universität beigebracht hatte.

Irgendwann 1994 ging ich mir eine Veranstaltung in einem Sozialwohnungsbau in Forest Fields ansehen. Es war eine performative Installation einer Gruppe ehemaliger Studen-

the quirky performances happened everywhere you looked. A fantastic immersive experience in the tradition of artist groups like The People Show, Lumiere & Son and even Fine Rats.

For me a sign of a good relationship with artists is when you can programme them blind, being able to say 'yes' even before you know anything about the project. That is how the NOW Festival worked with Gob Squad. It was 4 years since I last saw their work and I was happy to see The Public programming *Super Night Shot* as the centrepiece to *Weekend Break* in June 2004. It was like being taken back 10 years, standing in *Work* or *Close Enough To Kiss* or *Calling Laika* or *Say It Like You Mean It* but better, much better. All the telltale hallmarks were still there, the performance style, the interaction with the real world the audience involvement, and of course the humour. I smiled, laughed and was amazed by their incredible craftsmanship (you need to see it to understand that comment). In writing this and thinking about their work the best way of describing my 10 years of experiencing Gob Squad would be absolute enjoyment.

ten der Trent University und ihrer deutschen Partner, die sich gerade unter dem Namen Gob Squad gegründet hatten. In dem Haus, das sie übernommen hatten, sorgten sie hinter jeder Ecke für Überraschungen, Poesie entfaltete sich, wo sich Türen öffneten und schlossen, und die gewitzte Performance fand überall statt, wo man hinsah. Eine fantastische, einnehmende Erfahrung in der Tradition von Künstler-Gruppen wie The People Show, Lumière & Son und sogar Fine Rats.

Für mich ist es ein Zeichen einer guten Beziehung mit Künstlern, wenn man sie „blind" einladen kann, wenn man ja sagen kann, bevor man irgendwas über das Projekt weiß. So arbeitete das NOW Festival mit Gob Squad. Vier Jahre war es her, dass ich zuletzt eine ihrer Arbeiten sah, und ich freute mich, als The Public *Super Night Shot* im Juni 2004 an zentraler Stelle ins Programm von *Weekend Break* nahm. Es war, als würde man 10 Jahre zurückgeführt, zu *Work* oder *Close Enough to Kiss* oder *Calling Laika* oder *Say It Like You Mean It*, aber besser, viel besser. Alle Markenzeichen waren noch da, der Darstellungsstil, die Interaktion mit der realen Welt, die Einbeziehung des Publikums und natürlich der Humor. Ich lächelte, lachte und war verblüfft über ihre unglaubliche handwerkliche Fertigkeit (man muss die Arbeit sehen, um diesen Kommentar zu verstehen). Während ich dies schreibe und über ihre Arbeit nachdenke, müsste die beste Beschreibung für meine 10-jährige Erfahrung mit Gob Squad wohl absolutes Vergnügen lauten.

Gob Squad, 2004. photo: Manuel Reinartz

Peter Laudenbach:
For me the new century began with a Gob Squad performance
Für mich hat das neue Jahrhundert mit einer Gob-Squad-Inszenierung begonnen

1.

For me the new century began with a Gob Squad performance. I was the only spectator. There were a few hundred or even a thousand performers, none of whom had any idea that they were part of a typical Gob Squad situation. For me it became clear when I saw Liane and Alex in the Berlin nightclub WMF in the middle of all the unfamiliar people plunging with somnambulist hysteria into the first day of the New Year.

As always, Liane and Alex were the most courteous people one can imagine and as always they took note of their surroundings with the utmost, unshakeable matter-of-factness. The exhilarated and the wasted, the confused nightlife with the broken people, the lucky one, the communication overload and the autism. All of this suddenly had space and dignity within the Gob Squad installation. Individual perception as with residual social perception, works within a grid of inclusivity/exclusivity. This individual perception was suddenly permeable when one entered this social situation as defined by Gob Squad and continued to echo alongside a

1.

Für mich hat das neue Jahrhundert mit einer Gob-Squad-Inszenierung begonnen. Ich war der einzige Zuschauer, es gab einige hundert oder tausend Performer, und keiner von ihnen ahnte, dass sie gerade Teil einer typischen Gob-Squad-Situation waren. Und mir wurde es auch erst klar, als ich Liane und Alex zwischen all den fremden Menschen sah, die sich im Berliner WMF in einer Art somnambuler Hysterie in den ersten Tag des neuen Jahres stürzten.

Wie immer waren Liane und Alex die höflichsten Menschen, die man sich vorstellen kann, und wie immer nahmen sie ihre Umgebung mit größter, durch nichts zu erschütternder Selbstverständlichkeit zur Kenntnis. Die Aufgekratzten und die Weggetretenen, das Nachtleben-Durcheinander mit den Kaputten, den Glücklichen, dem Kommunikations-Überschuss und dem Autismus, das alles hatte innerhalb der Gob-Squad-Installation plötzlich Raum und Würde. Die eigene Wahrnehmung, die genau wie die Wahrnehmung der anderen mit Inklusions-Exklusions-Rastern arbeitet, wird plötzlich enorm durchlässig, wenn man in eine von Gob Squad de-

developing feeling of shame about one's own preconditioned ideas of social truth and perception.

It was long after midnight on 1st January 2000 and the atmosphere in WMF had a beauty often found in Gob Squad pieces: a kind of attentiveness and natural politeness that, in a veritable mass of utterly unknown people allowed the sharing of states of euphoria, distraction, affection or acquiescence without having to fear that personal boundaries would shift against the desire of the participants. The most wonderful school of mass social communication imaginable. I thought for a moment that this scene in WMF, the nocturnal party people, this club world I knew as an infrequent but therefore appreciative visitor was all a Gob Squad installation. As I knew that this was nothing more than a pleasant club night that I was experiencing, a club night that Liane and Alex had coincidentally landed in and because I thought these things simultaneously a kind of double exposure happened. Everything was simultaneously a set-up that took me amicably by the hand as a guest and led me through the evening and at the same moment not a set-up but life filled with confusion. It is exactly these two moments, the casual school of a wide-open social communication and the double exposure between set-up and life, real time this constitutes the art of Gob Squad for me.

finierte soziale Situation gerät. Was dann später als Echo wie eine Art Schamgefühl über die eigenen Praktiken soziale Wirklichkeit und ihre Wahrnehmung zu sortieren, nachwirkt.

Es war lange nach Mitternacht am 1. Januar 2000 und die Stimmung im WMF war von einer Schönheit, wie sie einem in Gob-Squad-Inszenierungen öfter begegnet: eine Art von Aufmerksamkeit und selbstverständlicher Höflichkeit, die es erlaubt, in einer dichten Menge mit lauter völlig unbekannten Menschen Zustände von Euphorie, Verstörtheit, Zuneigung oder Entäußerung zu teilen, ohne befürchten zu müssen, dass sich Distanzgrenzen auf eine andere Weise als von den beteiligten Personen gewünscht verschieben. Die denkbar wunderbarste Schule sozialer Kommunikation. Weil ich für Momente dachte, diese Szenerie im WMF, die Nachtlebenkreaturen, diese Club-Welt, die ich nur als seltener Gast kenne, all das sei eine Gob-Squad-Installation, und weil ich natürlich gleichzeitig wusste, dass es nichts als eine angemehme Clubnacht ist, was ich da gerade erlebe, eine Clubnacht, in der Liane und Alex zufällig auch gelandet waren, weil ich beides gleichzeitig dachte, entstand eine Art Doppelbelichtung. Alles war gleichzeitig eine Inszenierung, die mich als Gast freundlich an die Hand nahm und durch den Abend führte und im selben Moment war es nicht inszeniert, sondern Leben, also Durcheinander. Genau diese beiden Momente, die beiläufige Schule einer sehr weit geöffneten sozialen Kommunikation und die Doppelbelichtung zwischen Inszenierung und Leben, Echtzeit, macht für mich die Kunst von Gob Squad aus.

2.

What is it about if, as a theatre spectator I am allowed to watch people in boxes full of rubbish and I see how they eat, sleep, kiss each other, play with cheap toys, argue, make a din, talk and doze, if it is not about models of living together, consensual perception, tact and giving your all? I watch them living thus, condensed into this box with no other narrative than that of people occupying their own biosphere and imposing their own reality on it. If Berit Stumpf, dressed as a rock star runs across the stage shouting something it is not about the statement of being a rock star nor about how good one can imitate one but in each moment it is about the construction of the 'rock concert' demonstrating how through such an environment the construction of the fiction can be asserted. What is great is that on the one hand you see through the game and draw pleasure from this deciphering (you may also call it deconstruction) yet on the other you naturally rock out.

The production that I remember best turned the intimate situation of visiting people in their private box inside out. In the theatre space we watched projected images of live TV. An imaginary pursuit or a detective hunt, an adventure in the urban space of Berlin with its never-ending vastnesses blah... Ever since seeing this show, whenever I am waiting for an underground train or want to shoot a rude taxi driver, I always hope that somewhere a Gob Squad camera watches. This would make me better inured to the social disorder and would fill me with the desire to present a better example,

2.

Um was, wenn nicht um Modelle und Schulen des Zusammenlebens, der gegenseitigen Wahrnehmung, des Taktgefühls und um die gute alte Verausgabung geht es, wenn ich als Theaterzuschauer Leuten in vollgemüllten Boxen dabei zusehen darf, wie sie essen, schlafen, sich küssen, mit billigem Spielzeug spielen, sich streiten oder Krach machen, reden oder dösen, wenn ich ihnen also beim Leben zusehe, das sich in diesen Boxen auf einer Bühne verdichtet, aber keine Geschichte erzählt außer der von Menschen, die ihr eignes Biotop mit dem, was ihre Wirklichkeit ist, besetzen. Wenn in einem Stück Berit Stumpf als Selfmade-Rockstar über die Bühne rennt und irgendwas schreit, geht es in keinem Augenblick um die Behauptung, ein Rockstar zu sein oder das auch nur gut imitieren zu können, und in jedem Moment um die Konstruktion des Settings „Rockkonzert". Beziehungsweise darum, vorzuführen, wie so ein Setting behauptet wird, die Konstruktion der Fiktion. Was toll ist, weil man das Spiel einerseits durchschaut und aus diesem Durchschauen (Du darfst auch Dekonstruktion dazu sagen) den Genuss zieht. Und andererseits natürlich abrockt.

Die Inszenierung, an die ich mich am besten erinnere, hat die Intimsituation, Menschen in der Privatbox zu besichtigen, nach außen gestülpt. Drinnen, im Theaterraum, verfolgen wir über Live-TV auf der Leinwand eine imaginäre Verfolgungsjagd oder eine Detektiv-Suche. Abenteuer im Stadtraum, Berlin, unendliche Weiten, bla ... Seitdem hoffe

to be more polite for instance.
Berlin as a Gob Squad stage set is more beautiful than Berlin without the fiction that everything is only a game.

3.

I don't know if something like punk in the theatre exists. If punk in the theatre means being sick on the public like Iggy Pop then I'd rather go to an Iggy Pop concert. Anyway I was never a punk. I was, at sixteen, and still am a kind of messed up, educated, middle-class kid. I was lucky though because there was a wonderful punk scene going on in Pforzheim, the small town where I lived. No one said it better than Greil Marcus when he talked about the effect that concerts by Moloko Plus, Magi Razzo, Rhythmus Radikal and the Lennons had on those with small town upbringings and his thoughts have long echoed in my adult life. Marcus described punk as a movement from which "the participants emerged changed. One of these changes manifests as permission to throw a fleeting view on life, one rich and full of promises. A place it becomes possible to speak to everyone about everything. When this instance – that perhaps lasts a week, a month, a year – is over, these people find out that normal life doesn't satisfy them any more, that it works like a fraud, more like a video screen than something real. They look back on this one moment in which the world seemed to change and try to find out what happened." There is precious little in theatre to compare to the punk feeling but Gob Squad performances often have this power. I have forgotten

ich immer, wenn ich auf die U-Bahn warte oder einen unhöflichen Taxi-Fahrer am liebsten erschießen will, dass irgendwo eine Gob-Squad-Kamera zuschaut. Und sofort wäre ich erstens besser aufgehoben im sozialen Durcheinander und zweitens vom Wunsch erfüllt, ein besseres Bild abzugeben, bzw. höflicher zu sein. Berlin als Gob-Squad - Bühnenbild ist schöner als Berlin ohne die Fiktion, dass das alles nur ein Spiel ist.

3.

Ich weiß nicht, ob es so etwas wie Punk auf dem Theater gibt, und wenn Punk auf dem Theater bedeutet, wie Iggy Pop ins Publikum zu kotzen, gehe ich lieber gleich in ein Iggy-Pop-Konzert. Ich war nie Punk, ich war immer eine Art verkrachter Bildungsbürger, schon mit sechzehn, aber ich hatte Glück. Als ich sechzehn war, gab es in Pforzheim, der Kleinstadt, in der ich lebte, eine wunderbare Punkszene. Niemand hat es besser als Greil Marcus gesagt, was die Konzerte von Moloko Plus, Magi Razzo, Rhythmus Radikal und der Lennons für meine Kleinstadtjugend und als lang anhaltendes Echo für mein erwachsenes Leben bedeutet haben. Greil Marcus beschreibt Punk als Bewegung, aus der „die Beteiligten verändert hervorgingen. Eine der Arten von Veränderung ist dabei, einen flüchtigen Blick auf ein Leben werfen zu dürfen, das reich ist und voller Versprechen. Wo es möglich wird, mit allen über alles zu sprechen. Wenn dieser Augenblick – der vielleicht eine Woche, Monate, Jahre dauert – verflogen ist, haben diese Leute herausge-

individual scenes just as I have forgotten the songs of Rhythmus Radikal. I don't know the details any longer and yet I know precisely what they released in me, for example the feeling of freedom.

funden, dass das normale Leben sie nicht mehr befriedigt. Dass es wie ein Betrug wirkt. Eher wie ein Bildschirm als irgendwas, das real ist. Sie schauen zurück auf diesen einen Moment, in dem die Welt sich zu verändern schien, und versuchen herauszufinden, was passiert war." Es gibt wenig im Theater, was man damit vergleichen kann. Gob-Squad-Auftritte, deren einzelne Szenen ich genauso vergessen habe wie die einzelnen Nummern von Rhythmus Radikal, haben öfter diese Kraft. Ich weiß nichts mehr von den Details, aber ich weiß noch sehr genau, was das in mir ausgelöst hat. Zum Beispiel das Gefühl von Freiheit.

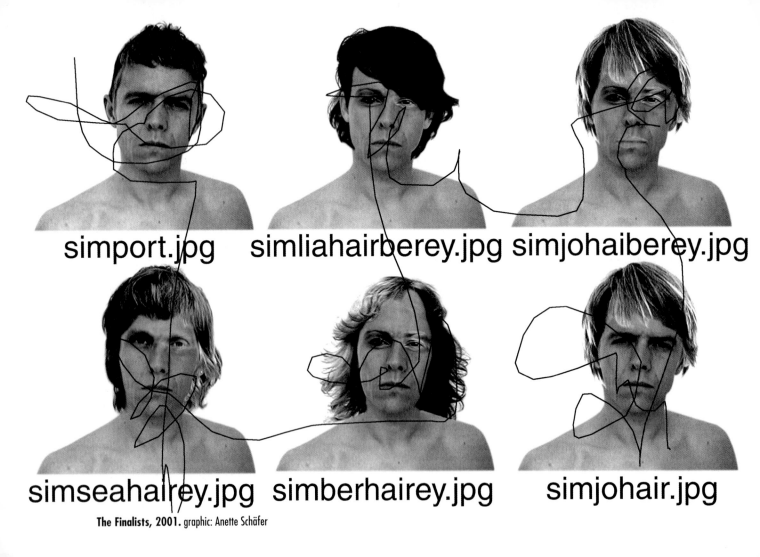

simport.jpg   simliahairberey.jpg   simjohaiberey.jpg

simseahairey.jpg   simberhairey.jpg   simjohair.jpg

The Finalists, 2001. graphic: Anette Schäfer

Till Müller-Klug:
Us Ltd / Die Wir-AG

The word collective makes me think of endlessly debating Dungarees. Or about the Borg, an evil insatiable Cyborg organism from Star Trek that attempts to assimilate everything that it can get its hands on. Or even Gob Squad.

In the 70s, collectives were widespread but today they have become a rare species. Instead, millions of mini-bosses populate the working world, their staff reduced to one single person, namely themselves. Being one's own Boss is being a temp with open prospects, it is unforgiving and masochistic, the choice of victims for workplace bullying not exactly copious. Like the hero in the film 'Fight Club' who punches himself upstairs, the self employed creature tries to claw his own way up the ladder of success or at least cling on to the current rung. In light of this contemporary societal phenomenon and business environment, groups like Gob Squad should really be swamped with job applications and lots of similar collectives should be founded.

Sarah said to me once that one reason to join a group is to assuage the fear of having to make and then perform something on ones own. In contrast if the outcome of a piece of group work is not so great one can always say, "Oh well, I was great but the others didn't quite pull it off". Such statements stem of course from an early phase of assimilation where the individual and collective brain cannot be clearly differentiated a borderline that became increasingly vague during the collectivisation process of both the Borg and Gob Squad. Today, in place of this, complex and unmanageable meshes of life and work relations blink and proliferate. Kilometres of cable, ten years of know-how, their own hi-tech equipment, several hundredweights of group-owned junk (Gob Squad's cellar at Podewil was a unique, involuntary installation), pictures of couples, of new lives and the whirring gyration of human satellites from circles of friends and acquaintances to which I too belong.

I was once absorbed into the group core from my personal orbit. Together we developed the live sound piece *Little White Lies* in 1999 for the Akademie der Künste in Berlin. I experienced a temporary assimilation for three weeks. Firstly it struck me that the hedonistic aspect was not as forthcoming as I had thought (and perhaps hoped) it would be. To put it another way: we worked on it a lot, from early morning until sometimes late at night and all this on an equally poor wage for everyone.

Later it was clear to me that most of the Gob Squaddies did not see it that way at all, because for them the division between work and private life had long since been blurred. Because I had been less entangled in the amorphous collective organism, I initially rated the time together in the

arbeit am Ende nicht so toll wird, ließe sich immer sagen: „Tja, ich war klasse, aber leider haben's die Anderen nicht gebracht."

Solche Statements stammen natürlich aus einem frühen Stadium der Assimilation, wo zwischen Einzel- und Gruppengehirn noch klar getrennt werden kann. Eine Abgrenzung, die sich bei den Borg wie auch bei Gob Squad im weiteren Kollektivierungsprozess zunehmend verliert. An ihrer Stelle blinkt und wuchert heute ein unüberschaubares Geflecht aus Arbeits- und Lebensbeziehungen, Kilometern von Kabeln, zehnjähriger Projekterfahrung, einzelner Hi-Tech-Geräte und zentnerweise Gerümpel im Gruppenbesitz (der Gob-Squad-Keller im Podewil war eine einzigartige, unfreiwillige Installation), Pärchenbildungen, neuem Leben und den umherschwirrenden menschlichen Satelliten der Freundes- und Bekanntenkreise, zu denen ich auch gehöre.

Einmal wurde ich aus meiner Umlaufbahn eingesogen in den Gruppenkern. Zusammen erarbeiteten wir das Live-Hörspiel *Little White Lies* in der Berliner Akademie der Künste 1999. Ich machte also für drei Wochen die Erfahrung einer temporären Assimilation. Als Erstes fiel mir auf, dass der hedonistische Aspekt nicht so ausgeprägt war, wie ich vermutet und vielleicht auch erhofft hatte. Anders ausgedrückt: Es wurde sehr viel gearbeitet, von vormittags bis manchmal spät in die Nacht. Und das bei gleich schlechter Bezahlung für alle.

rehearsal room as work in the old fashioned sense.

From day to day I was ensnared ever more in the collective pattern of production and life. I was convinced that the greater part of the working time actually consisted of productively hanging out with each other, especially at the early stage of the project. We talked about this and that drank tea and beer, had barbeques, listened to music, watched videos, rummaged through flea markets, collections of old clothes and tinkered around with technical equipment and bits of junk. It would always return to the project but in the beginning it was never focused in the sense of a master plan because in Gob Squad, there is no master. Similarly, I cannot remember placing votes or other nominally democratic rituals of decision-making.

It proceeded seemingly without a plan. Everyone threw in whatever occurred to him or her during the rehearsals. If someone ran out of ideas, he or she would say less for a couple of hours or for a day only to resume again sometime later. Naturally at times there was tension but it was rarely about work decisions. Absolutely no skirmishes arose about how much text or scenes someone should play, that was self regulated. I only remember one isolated, familial moan over the question of someone mothering too much. On the whole it proved to be a shining example of British manners in hindrance of conflict and furtherance of communication.

Without a boss or initial plan and apparently casually, an astonishingly precise product finally arose. That was a fasci-

Später wurde mir klar, dass die meisten Gob Squadies das gar nicht so empfanden, weil für sie die Trennung zwischen Arbeit und Privatleben längst aufgeweicht war. Da ich aber weniger als die anderen mit dem amorphen Gesamtorganismus verwachsen war, stufte ich die gemeinsam im Probenraum verbrachte Zeit zunächst ganz altmodisch als Arbeit ein.

Von Tag zu Tag wurde ich tiefer in die kollektivistische Produktions- und Lebensweise verstrickt. Ich stellte fest, dass ein großer Teil der Arbeitszeit eigentlich in einem produktiven gemeinsamen Rumhängen bestand, besonders in der Anfangsphase des Projekts. Wir redeten über dies und das, tranken Tee und Bier, grillten und hörten Musik, sahen Videos, durchstöberten Flohmärkte und Altkleidersammlungen und bastelten an technischen Geräten und Gerümpel rum. Immer wieder ging es auch um das Projekt, aber anfangs nie gezielt im Sinne eines Master Plans, denn bei Gob Squad gibt es keinen Master. Genauso wenig kann ich mich an Abstimmungen erinnern oder an andere basisdemokratische Rituale der Entscheidungsfindung.

Es ging ziemlich planlos zu. Alle warfen ihr Input in den Probenraum, was ihnen gerade so einfiel. Wenn jemandem mal nichts einfiel, sagte die oder der ein paar Stunden oder Tage lang weniger und irgendwann wieder mehr. Natürlich gab es auch manchmal Stress. Der bezog sich aber selten auf konkrete Arbeitsentscheidungen. Es entstand überhaupt kein Gerangel darum, wer wie viele Texte oder Szenen spie-

nating experience. There was never the feeling that the performance was the result of compromise. Instead of which I found "my" ideas realised, multiplied with those of the others and in the end standing together on the stage.

With their decentralised nervous system, Gob Squad and the Borg are extremely adaptable, toughened, capricious creative organisms. On their 10th birthday we experience the tender beginnings of their global and intergalactic dissemination.

len soll, das ergab sich wie von selbst. Ich erinnere mich bloß an ein vereinzeltes, familienmäßiges Gemaule über die Frage, wer wen zuviel bemuttert. Generell erwies sich der hohe Standard der britischen Umgangsformen als ausgesprochen konfliktlindernd und kommunikationsfördernd.

Ohne Boss und ohne Anfangsplan ist dann scheinbar ganz nebenbei am Ende ein erstaunlich präzises Produkt entstanden. Das war ein faszinierendes Erlebnis. Es gab dabei nicht das Gefühl, die Aufführung sei ein Ergebnis von Kompromissen. Stattdessen fand ich „meine" Ideen verwirklicht, multipliziert mit denen aller anderen und am Ende standen wir damit gemeinsam auf der Bühne.

Mit ihrem dezentralen Nervensystem sind Gob Squad und die Borg äußerst zähe, zugleich widerstands- und anpassungsfähige, unberechenbar kreative Organismen. An ihrem zehnten Geburtstag erleben wir die zarten Anfänge ihrer globalen und intergalaktischen Ausbreitung.

Gob Squad, 2003

HOUSE (1994)

Home home on the range
Where the deer and the antelope play
Where seldom is heard a discouraging word
And the skies are not cloudy or grey
(Traditional folk song/Volkslied)

Where: a disused suburban home
Who: a woman swinging aggressively on a swing watching telly; a woman reading a book on "How to have a small nervous breakdown"; a man and a woman in synchronized swimmer outfits practising holding their breath; a sleepless couple, covered in snow; a woman dressed up in a ball gown training a dressed-up Rottweiler; a ballerina in a cupboard curtseying; 7 very assertive door-to-door salesmen; a beautiful voice (as a guide)
What: a front room (floor covered in raffle tickets); a kitchen (icing sugar on cakes, walls, cupboards and windows); a bathroom (rose-print wallpaper merging into real flowers); a toilet (dried smelly fish pinned to walls); a bedroom (fake snow has fallen and Scalextric cars race round a bed); a bedroom (laid out with real grass); a cupboard (playing a tune when you open the door); chalk writing on the walls (listing everything that is missing); dictaphones; "Only you" (sung by Elvis)
How long: 40 minutes

Wo: ein leerstehendes Wohnhaus in einem Vorort
Wer: eine Frau, die in einem Buch nachliest, „Wie man einen kleinen Nervenzusammenbruch hat"; ein Mann und eine Frau in Synchronschwimmerkostümen in der Badewanne; ein schneebedecktes, schlafloses Paar; ein rausgeputzter Rottweiler; eine knicksende Ballerina in einem Wandschrank; 7 Handelsvertreter, die sich vom Garten dem Haus nähern; eine beruhigende Stimme (zur Sicherheit)
Was: ein Wohnzimmer (der Boden bedeckt mit Lottoscheinen); eine Küche (Puderzuckerornamente auf Kuchen, Wänden, Schränken und Fenstern); ein Bad (dessen Tapetenmuster in echte Rosen übergeht); eine Toilette (in der getrocknete, stinkende Fische die Wände verzieren); ein Schlafzimmer (in dem Carrera-Autos um ein Bett rasen); ein Schlafzimmer (mit Gras ausgelegt); ein Wandschrank (beim Öffnen, erklingt eine Melodie); Kreideschrift an den Wänden (alles aufzählend, was fehlt); Diktiergeräte; „Only you" (gesungen von Elvis)
Wie lange: 40 Minuten

Miriam Dreysse:

One of the first site-specific live installations I had seen was in 1995 when I entered a house in North Giessen that was occupied and fitted out by Gob Squad. The theatre world was still under the influence of the 'return to the proscenium arch' tendency of the 80s. Even the post-dramatic theatre of this time took place to a large extent in traditional theatre buildings. Also the temporal framing and the role of the spectator were usually of the conventional kind: the public sat down in the places intended for them, watched, and applauded at the conclusion.

In Gob Squad's *House* however, one moved independently through the entire house. One found one's own way, thus in the long run, each spectator experienced a performance to which he contributed. The actions in separate rooms had an enduring nature. In a bedroom a woman lay on the bed sleeping – or was she on the telephone? Wasn't someone in a cupboard somewhere? Was there a kind of fencing competition in the living room? Other areas were without a performer, like a toilet with tinned sardines – or was it raw eels – like the ones Angela Winkler stuffed herself with on the toilet in the "Tin Drum"?

Concrete details remained less in my memory than the method of the work´s delivery, which was new for me. My wandering through the house was just like at an exhibition, an easy, absent-minded attention which latches itself again

Miriam Dreysse:

Als ich 1995 ein Haus in der Gießener Nordstadt betrat, das von Gob Squad eingerichtet und bespielt wurde, war dies eine der ersten ortsspezifischen Live-Installationen, die ich sah. Das Theater war noch geprägt von der ‚Rückkehr auf die Guckkastenbühne' der 80er Jahre, selbst das postdramatische Theater dieser Zeit spielte sich weitgehend in traditionellen Theaterbauten ab. Auch die zeitliche Rahmung und die Rolle des Zuschauers waren meist konventioneller Art: Das Publikum setzte sich auf die für es bestimmten Plätze, schaute zu und klatschte am Schluss.

In *House* von Gob Squad hingegen bewegte man sich selbstständig, durch das gesamte Haus. Man suchte seinen eigenen Weg, jeder Zuschauer erlebte so eine Performance, die er selbst mitbestimmte. Die Aktionen in einzelnen Räumen hatten dauerhaften Charakter. In einem Schlafzimmer lag eine Frau auf dem Bett, schlief – oder telefonierte sie? War nicht irgendwo jemand in einem Schrank? Gab es eine Art Fechtkampf im Wohnzimmer? Andere Räume waren ohne Performer gestaltet, so eine Toilette mit Ölsardinen – oder waren es doch rohe Aale, wie sie Angela Winkler in der „Blechtrommel" auf der Toilette in sich reinstopft?
Konkrete Einzelheiten sind mir weniger in Erinnerung geblieben als die mir damals neue Rezeptionshaltung. Mein Flanieren durch das Haus ähnlich wie durch eine Ausstellung, eine leicht zerstreute Aufmerksamkeit, die sich immer wieder an einzelnen Details, Objekten, Bildern bün-

SPONGE
NOSE CLIPPERS
CIGARETTE DISPENSER
PLAYING CARDS
BAMBOO BLIND
X-RAY GLASSES
PACEMAKER
DUMBELL
A LITTLE SMILE
CONTACT LENSE
HANKERCHEIF
TEA TOWEL
HALF A PEG
PETROLEUM JELLY
WAGON WHEEL
SHOWER GEL
PAMPASS GRASS
NOVELTY KEYRING
SUNGLASSES
LEGO
CROSSWORD PUZZLE
HAIR MOUSSE
ANGEL DELIGHT
TRAVEL PILLOW
CUSTARD TART
T.V. GUIDE
PRINT TRAY
SANITARY TOWEL
PLASITCKNIFE
SUN CREAM
TOY SOLDIER
NEEDLE
CHALK
MARKER PEN
FIVE GOLD RIN
EASTER EG
CALCULATO
HUMIDIFYE
TORCH
FLOWER BU
FILM CANIST

CHEESE SLICER
APPRECIATIVE AUDIENCE
RAINCLOUD
TOMATO KETCHUP
SOUP LADLE
BOLT OF LIGHTENING
FILOFAX
FEATHER BOA
MICROPHONE
MY LITTLE PONY
STORMTROOPER
POSTCARD
BASKET OF FLOWERS
CLOCKWORK MOUSE
CATFOOD
LOOSE CHANGE
A FRIENDLY VOICE
FROG
ICECUBE
AXE
GIRLFRIEND
SIDEBURN
SIDE SALAD
WAX CRAYON
SKATEBOARD
ONE TO LISTEN
EST GATEAU
RUBBER DUCK
CAR
SQUASH
GAMMON
WHISK
AMIN PILL
DADDY LONGLEG
CANDY FLOSS

FRUIT BASKET
MUESLI
LIGHT SWITCH
SPANISH DOLL
ICE CREAM
BUCKLE
BIONIC ARM
FLYING DUCK
LASER GUN
LASOO
CARTOON
SILLY PARTY H
EMBARASSING
POSTER
BUTTER DISH
FISH FINGER
DISTANT VO
PICTERESQUE
YO-YO
MUSIC CENTRE
ICE LOLLY
EAR MUFFS
BANDAGE
TIME MACHINE
STICKY TOFFE
SHOULDER P
ALIEN

STOP WATCH
FAG PACKET
SEVEN INCH RECORD
HAIR DYE
FLYING OBJECT
TENSION
ENT
CALL

and again onto individual details, objects, pictures or is interrupted by banal, scurrilous, funny or surprising live moments. One experienced the oscillation between the private and the public with which *House* played, a corporeal feeling at times like an illicit voyeur, at times as in a childhood fantasy in which one is transformed so that one can curiously explore a dolls house.

The familiarity of the spaces – living room, kitchen, bath, bedroom – intersects with its artistic configuration as the everyday activity of a house visit combined with the attention and the heightened awareness of the art lover who, as with ready-mades sees familiar things in a new way.

delt oder von banalen, skurrilen, witzigen, überraschenden Live-Momenten unterbrochen wird. Man bekam das Schwanken zwischen Privatheit und Öffentlichkeit, mit dem House spielte, am eigenen Leibe zu spüren, fühlte sich mal als unerlaubter Voyeur, mal wie in einer Kindheitsfantasie versetzt in ein Puppenhaus, das man neugierig erkundet.

Die Gewöhnlichkeit der Räume – Wohnzimmer, Küche, Bad, Schlafzimmer – kreuzte sich mit ihrer künstlerischen Gestaltung, die Alltäglichkeit einer Hausbesichtigung mit der Aufmerksamkeit, dem anderen Blick des Kunstbetrachters, der wie beim Ready Made Altbekanntes auf neue Weise sieht.

WORK (1995)

I've never been a ballerina. I've never stood on stage in white and had roses thrown at me. I've never been thrown by one man to be caught by another. I've never been a cowboy. I never shot a man. I've ridden a horse but not with the sun setting behind me. I've never eaten beans in a tin round a campfire.

If we all wanted to grow up to be ballerinas and spacemen, where did we go so wrong?

Where: an office in the centre of town (with people in neighbouring buildings hard at work)
Who: 7 people dressed in their best interview suits (sometimes caught in a loop of repetitive tasks, sometimes asleep in a pile on the floor, sometimes dancing with filing cabinets - always tired by the end of the day)
What: 6 desks, 6 office chairs, 5 filing cabinets (to file DREAMS, FEARS, HOPES, WORRIES and QUESTIONS); 1 computer (with Kudos job research programme); 1 telephone (used to interview the public about their jobs); 1 photocopier (where faces are reproduced and renamed); 3 walls covered with photocopied clocks (showing the passing of time by the minute); surveillance cameras and 2 monitors; 1 door with a bright shining light (where every now and then a spaceman or an ice skater appears); pencils, party hats, heaps of shredded paper.
How long: 40 hours, the length of a working week (9 to 5 from Monday to Friday)

Wo: ein Büro im Stadtzentrum
Wer: 7 Menschen, seriös gekleidet wie für ein Vorstellungsgespräch (manchmal gefangen in repetitiven Arbeitsabläufen, manchmal in einem Haufen auf dem Boden schlafend, manchmal mit Aktenschränken tanzend – immer müde am Ende des Tages)
Was: 6 Schreibtische, 6 Bürostühle, 5 Aktenschränke (um TRÄUME, ÄNGSTE, HOFFNUNGEN, SORGEN und FRAGEN zu ordnen); 1 Computer (mit Berufsfindungsprogramm); 1 Telefon (um die Öffentlichkeit nach ihren Berufen zu befragen); 1 Fotokopierer (auf dem Gesichter vervielfältigt und neu beschrieben werden); 3 Wände, behängt mit den Fotokopien einer Uhr (das Verstreichen der Zeit auf die Minute genau festhaltend); Überwachungskameras und 2 Monitore; 1 Tür mit gleißend hellem Licht (aus dem hin und wieder ein Astronaut oder eine Eiskunstläuferin treten); Bleistifte, Partyhüte, Haufen von vernichteten Akten
Wie lange: 40 Stunden, die Dauer einer Arbeitswoche (Montag bis Freitag von 9 bis 17 Uhr)

Ange Taggart:

At the time I was a support worker in a family centre, child-care was my profession. I remember the daydreams of the workers struck a chord with me. The fantasy of being a space-man, the dancing filing cabinets and the sense of individual lives lost and living in their work daydreams what they really wanted to be. I stayed a long time. There wasn't much space for the audience and it felt like I was being greedy and shouldn't have stayed so long. I left feeling like I wanted more. So inspired by *Work* I turned my own daydream into a reality. I left my 'work', got into university, and graduated in Contemporary Art in 2000 and have been performing ever since.

Mieke Matzke:

Tuesday evening – perhaps 4.45 pm

I had travelled from Giessen to Nottingham in order to see *Work*, a one-week performance about work taking place every day from 9 to 5. Our train was delayed in Coventry and therefore I only managed to catch the last minutes of Tuesday's performance, just before going home time. With my rucksack still on my back I stormed into the office. There were two benches for the audience on one side and opposite them six tables, each with a computer, fax, telephone, filing cabinet, a photocopier at the back and a door (to the kitchen?). On the walls were innumerable photocopies of clocks. The door opened – a backlit entrance. All performers wore suits or twin sets, their hair strictly made up, a smart

Ange Taggart:

Ich arbeitete damals als Sozialarbeiterin in einem Fami-lienzentrum, von Beruf war ich Erzieherin. Ich erinnere mich, dass die Tagträume der Angestellten eine Seite in mir zum Klingen brachten. Die Fantasie, ein Raumfahrer zu sein, die tanzenden Aktenschränke und das Gefühl, dass sie ihr Leben verloren gaben, während sie bei der Arbeit ihren Tagträumen nachhingen, darüber, was sie eigentlich sein wollten. Ich blieb lange. Es gab nicht viel Platz für die Zuschauer, und ich fragte mich anschließend, ob ich zu gie-rig gewesen war und nicht so lange hätte bleiben sollen. Ich ging mit dem Gefühl, mehr zu wollen. Ich war so inspiriert von *Work*, dass ich meine eigenen Tagträume wahr machte. Ich verließ meine „Arbeit", schrieb mich an der Universität ein, schloss 2000 das Kunst-Studium ab und bin seither Performance-Künstlerin.

Mieke Matzke:

Dienstag Abend – vielleicht 16 Uhr 45

Ich war von Gießen nach Nottingham gefahren, um *Work* zu sehen: eine einwöchige Performance über Arbeit, jeden Tag von 9 bis 17 Uhr. Unser Zug hatte in Coventry Verspätung und deshalb schaffte ich es gerade noch so, die letzten Minuten des Dienstags mitzubekommen. Kurz vor Feier-abend. Noch mit dem Rucksack auf dem Rücken stürmte ich ins Büro: zwei Zuschauerbänke auf der einen Seite, gegenüber sechs Tische mit Computer, Fax und Telefon, Aktenschränke, hinten ein Kopierer und eine Tür (zur Tee-

smile on their lips. They came to us as if on a catwalk, turning around to easy listening music. Everyone was introduced through their professional experiences: waiters, car washers, letter sorters. Berit got the most laughs for the fact that she had been a showgirl for Mercedes Benz. I sat there and thought about my work experiences. As a student, my life at that time was far removed from the regular office day and, if I am honest, it is the same today. I was completing my studies, and had doubts about what my future occupation would be. My occupational aspiration to be a 'performer' confronted me with insecurities and confusions – how do you explain to your grandparents what kind of work it is, if you don't know yourself? Is it work at all? Can one call artistic pursuit work in any way?

Within the contemporary performance and dance scene there is a lot of work about artistic work, how this work corresponds to voluntary self-exploitation in a globalised society and how artistic work can be evaluated and remunerated. In 1995 all that seemed very far away, even though it actually concerned our social environment directly. It is here that *Work* applied itself. What made Gob Squad's performance so special at that time (and still pertinent today) was the way in which art as work became tangible and comprehensible right in front of our eyes for 8 hours a day, forty hours a week. It was not only concerned with the office as location, but with the context within which work takes place. Gob Squad 'performed' work and over its duration the performance became work in all its facets: as a utopian blue-

küche?). An den Wänden: unzählige Kopien von Uhren. Dann ging die Tür auf, ein Auftritt im Gegenlicht. Alle Darsteller trugen Anzüge oder Kostüme, die Haare streng zurechtgemacht, ein smartes Lächeln auf den Lippen. Wie auf einem Catwalk kamen sie auf uns zu, drehten sich zu Easy-Listening-Musik. Jeder wurde mit seinen Berufserfahrungen vorgestellt: Kellnern, Autowaschen, Briefesortieren. Die meisten Lacher bekam Berit dafür, dass sie Showgirl bei Mercedes Benz gewesen war. Ich saß da und dachte über meine Arbeitserfahrungen nach. Als Studentin war mir damals nichts ferner als ein regelmäßiger Bürotag, und wenn ich ehrlich bin ist er es mir heute noch. Ich war gerade dabei, mein Studium abzuschließen, und zweifelte selbst daran, was mein zukünftiger Beruf sein würde. Mein Berufsziel ‚Performerin' stieß in meiner Umgebung auf Zweifel und Irritationen – wie erklärt man seinen Großeltern, was das für eine Arbeit ist, wenn man es selbst nicht weiß. Ist es überhaupt Arbeit? Kann man künstlerisches Handeln überhaupt als Arbeit bezeichnen?

In der aktuellen Performance- und Tanzszene gibt es eine Menge Arbeiten über die künstlerische Arbeit, darüber, wie diese Arbeit der freiwilligen Selbstausbeutung in einer globalisierten Gesellschaft entspricht, wie künstlerische Arbeit bewertet und entlohnt werden kann. 1995 schien das alles noch weit entfernt, obwohl es eigentlich direkt unser Lebensumfeld betraf. Und hier setzte *Work* an. Was Gob Squads Performance damals so besonders machte – und letztlich auch heute noch so aktuell –, war die Art und Weise, wie hier

photo: Simon Cunningham

print of the self or a possibility for self implementation, work as dumb occupation in order to make a living or as part of social life and unemployment with its accompanying lack of self definition.

Wednesday – approximately 12 o'clock
I went to the office about three hours after the performers. They had been at it for three hours while I was still lying in bed, having breakfast. I was annoyed, 3 hours missed, the whole of Monday missed and nearly all of Tuesday. I felt behind with my work as a spectator. In the office, not much was happening. Was it lunchtime? Is there such a thing in a performance? I started to think about how they ate during the day: in the back? In the kitchen? I asked myself what it would mean if the performance comprised of not only two hours (a special time-out) but became everyday life with all its necessities and needs?

Later on Wednesday – about 4 pm
In the meantime I also had to go out and eat something. When I returned the back door opened. Johanna stood back-light in a sailor suit. She swayed back and forth, as if on a ship and saluted in our direction. The others swayed as well, behind their desks. The sentence on the flyer occurred to me again, '...when we all wanted to be spacemen, engine drivers and pop stars...' I don't know any longer exactly how it continued, but I know that at that time I thought for a long time about what I wanted to be when I grew up: beautician, attorney, psychologist and now performance artist? How we

Kunst als Arbeit wirklich erfahrbar und nachvollziehbar wurde – vor unseren Augen, acht Stunden am Tag, vierzig Stunden die Woche. Es ging nicht nur um den Ort des Büros, sondern um die Situation, in der Arbeit stattfindet. Gob Squad performte Arbeit und über die Dauer wurde die Performance selbst zur Arbeit mit all ihren Facetten: als utopischer Selbstentwurf oder Möglichkeit zur Selbstver-wirklichung, Arbeit als stupide Beschäftigung, um den Le-bensunterhalt zu verdienen, Arbeit als Anteil am gesell-schaftlichen Leben und Arbeitslosigkeit einhergehend mit einer fehlenden Selbstdefinition durch die Arbeit.

Mittwoch – ungefähr 12 Uhr
Ich kam ca. drei Stunden nach den Performern ins Büro. Sie waren schon drei Stunden dabei, während ich noch im Bett lag und frühstückte. Und dennoch ärgerte ich mich: drei Stunden verpasst, den ganzen Montag verpasst und fast den ganzen Dienstag. Ich fühlte mich hinterher mit meiner Arbeit als Zuschauerin. Im Büro war nur wenig los – Mit-tagspause? Gibt es so etwas bei einer Performance? Ich fing an darüber nachzudenken (ich hatte ja gerade gefrühstückt), wie die es wohl hinbekommen, den Tag über zu essen? Hin-ten in der Teeküche? Ich fragte mich, was es bedeutet, wenn die Aufführung nicht mehr nur zwei Stunden umfasst – eine besondere Auszeit sozusagen –, sondern zum Alltag wird mit all seinen Notwendigkeiten und Bedürfnissen?

sketch a picture of ourselves, in which we imagine ourselves in occupations, and whether it is at all possible to find your dream job because real work is usually, however, completely different to the preconception you have of it.

A little later, Johanna sat on a chair just one metre in front of us. From both sides a camera was directed towards her, so that we could see her video image above, on monitors on the wall. She began to list her abilities, 'I can speak German', (I can too, I thought), 'I can speak English' (ok, I can, but not as well as you) Further skills and abilities followed, which I can hardly remember. I immediately started to compare my own abilities and scrutinise whether they are true at all. All this reminded me of a job interview: See here, these are my strengths and these are my abilities! The camera and the monitors served to reinforce this impression. How can I talk about my abilities and be as authentic as possible? The scene resembled an experimental set-up that Johanna had constructed, in which she focused the cameras and composed the image. Who examined who was not evident. What most impressed me was her claim that she could apply lipstick without a mirror. I planned to try it for myself that evening.

Thursday – perhaps 10 am
I actually wanted to be in the office early that morning, but of course I didn't manage it. I still had one day.
Berit was on the telephone carrying out an interview with someone, asking whether or not he had work, if he was con-

Später am Mittwoch – so circa 16 Uhr
Inzwischen musste auch ich mal raus und etwas essen. Als ich wiederkam, ging hinten die Tür auf. Johanna stand in einem Matrosenanzug im Gegenlicht. Sie schwankte hin und her, als stände sie auf einem Schiff. Salutierte in unsere Richtung. Die anderen schwankten mit, hinter ihren Schreibtischen. Der Satz auf der Einladungskarte fällt mir wieder ein: Wenn wir alle Raumfahrer, Lokführer und Popstars werden wollten ... ich weiß nicht mehr genau, wie es weiterging, aber ich weiss dass ich darüber nachdachte, was ich früher werden wollte: Kosmetikerin, Rechtsanwältin, Psychologin, und nun Performancekünstlerin? Wie wir ein Bild von uns selbst entwerfen, in dem wir uns in Berufen vorstellen. Und ob es überhaupt möglich ist, seinen Traumberuf zu finden, da die wirkliche Arbeit doch meist ganz anders ist als die Vorstellung, die man sich von ihr gemacht hat.

Und dann – kurze Zeit später – saß Johanna vorne auf einem Stuhl, nur einen Meter vor uns. Von jeder Seite war eine Kamera auf sie gerichtet, so dass wir ihr Videobild auch in den Monitoren oben an der Wand sehen konnten. Sie begann Fähigkeiten aufzuzählen: I can speak German. (Kann ich auch, dachte ich.) I can speak English. (O.k. kann ich schlechter als du.) Es folgten weitere Kenntnisse und Fähigkeiten, an die ich mich kaum erinnern kann. Sofort fing ich an, meine eigenen Fähigkeiten abzugleichen und manche Behauptungen zu hinterfragen, ob sie überhaupt stimmen. Das Ganze erinnerte mich an ein Vorstellungsgespräch: Hier seht hin, das sind meine Stärken, das sind meine Fähigkeiten! Die Kamera

photo: Simon Cunningham

tented with the work and what he had wanted to be as a child. Sarah stood up and went to the photocopier. She opened the flap, pressed her face to the glass and made a copy. The copy presented her distorted face, the nose and lips were flat, the hair stuck to the glass. Over a monitor you could see how she labelled the copy, "Me as the Queen Mum". She took the copy and hung it on the wall with a lot of others. Throughout the week the walls filled with these self-portraits. New self-projections were constantly added. Each job defines the worker who does it. Work is not only the possibility of self-definition; it forces definitions upon you as well. Perhaps that is the special thing about artistic work: that it can play with these definitions – and add new ones.

Friday – about 11 am
I had missed my last chance to get to the office in the morning. I still discovered new things whilst watching: voices came from the filing cabinets at the back by the wall if you opened them. The office spoke and the filing cabinets started to dance and the whole office started to move. I only went out once, briefly, to drink tea, otherwise I remained for the whole of Friday on my bench, in order to get as much as possible. I noticed how I became tired – and thought I could also notice it in the performers – but nevertheless I looked forward to sitting there on the bench again, and watching the familiar, to have a regular occupation, to know that it carried on. The space had become ever more real for me over the days. I had nevertheless spent three days here –

und die Monitore verstärkten diesen Eindruck: Wie schaffe ich es, von meinen Fähigkeiten zu sprechen und dabei möglichst authentisch zu wirken? Die Szene glich einem Versuchsaufbau, den Johanna selbst einrichtete, indem sie die Kameras fokussierte und den Bildausschnitt festlegte. Wer hier wen prüfte, war allerdings nicht ersichtlich. Am meisten beeindruckte mich die Behauptung, sie könne Lippenstift ohne Spiegel auftragen. Ich nahm mir vor, das abends selbst zu überprüfen.

Donnerstag – vielleicht 10 Uhr
Eigentlich wollte ich schon morgens mit den Performern im Büro sein, aber natürlich hatte ich es nicht geschafft. Einen Tag hatte ich noch. Berit saß am Telefon und führte ein Interview mit jemandem: Ob er Arbeit habe, ob er mit der Arbeit zufrieden sei, was er als Kind werden wollte? Sarah stand auf und ging zum Kopierer. Sie öffnete die Klappe, presste ihr Gesicht auf die Glasfläche und machte eine Kopie. Die Kopie gab das Gesicht verzerrt wieder: Die Nase und Lippen waren platt gedrückt, die Haare klebten an der Scheibe. Über einen Monitor war zu sehen, wie sie die Kopie beschriftete: „Me as Queen Mum". Sie nahm das Blatt und hängte es zu einer Vielzahl bereits gemachter Kopien an die Wand. Über den Verlauf der Woche füllten sich die Wände mit diesen Selbstporträts. Immer neue Selbstprojektionen kamen hinzu. Jede Arbeit definiert auch den Arbeitenden, der sie tut. Arbeit ist nicht nur Möglichkeit zur Selbstdefinition, sondern sie zwingt auch Definitionen auf. Vielleicht ist das das Besondere an der künstlerischen Arbeit, dass sie mit die-

perhaps 17 hours. 17 real hours. Perhaps herein lies the characteristic of *Work*, the fact that it isn't just site specific and reinterprets real space as theatrical space, but really fills it again with work. It becomes clear that work also always means life, time that must be filled, time that must be found, time in which one does something that is defined. To this extent *Work* is not only site specific but also time specific. In this way the performance not only raised the condition and distribution of work for discussion but also made it experiential. *Work* does not only play with the contexts and structures of the working world, but shows concretely the influence that work (as well as a lack of it) has. I asked myself at the end of the week whether an artist could actually be unemployed because artistic work is the embodiment of self-determined work, and is said to be free from all expedience. Someone told me later that in England most artists finance themselves through unemployment benefit, which seen in this way, constitutes the largest portion of cultural subsidy.

sen Definitionen spielen kann – immer wieder neue hinzufügen.

Freitag – so um 11 Uhr

Meine letzte Chance, morgens mit den Performern ins Büro zu kommen, hatte ich verpasst. Immer noch entdeckte ich Neues beim Schauen: Aus den Aktenschränken hinten an der Wand kamen Stimmen, wenn man sie öffnete. Das Büro sprach und die Aktenschränke fingen an zu tanzen – das ganze Büro kam in Bewegung. Ich ging nur einmal kurz raus, um einen Tee zu trinken. Ansonsten blieb ich den ganzen Freitag, um möglichst noch alles mitzubekommen. Ich merkte wie ich müde wurde – und glaubte es auch den Performern anzusehen – und trotzdem freute ich mich, auf meiner Bank zu sitzen, Bekanntes wiederzusehen, eine regelmäßige Beschäftigung zu haben, zu wissen, dass es immer weiterging. Der Raum war über die Tage für mich immer realer geworden. Immerhin hatte ich hier drei Tage und vielleicht 17 Stunden verbracht. Reale 17 Stunden. Vielleicht liegt hier die Besonderheit von *Work*, dass es nicht nur site-specific ist und den realen Raum als theatralen inszeniert, sondern ihn real wieder mit Arbeit füllt. Dabei wird deutlich, dass Arbeit auch immer Lebenszeit bedeutet: Zeit, die gefüllt werden muss, Zeit, die aufgebracht werden muss, Zeit, in der man etwas tut, die definiert ist. Insofern ist *Work* nicht nur site-specific, sondern auch „time-specific". Die Aufführung thematisiert so nicht nur Arbeitsbedingungen und -verteilung, sondern macht sie erfahrbar. *Work* spielt nicht nur mit den Inszenierungen und Strukturen der Arbeitswelt, sondern zeigt ganz real den Einfluss, den die Arbeit (auch die fehlende) auf den Einzelnen hat. Ich fragte mich am Ende dieser Woche, ob ein Künstler eigentlich arbeitslos sein kann, denn künstlerische Arbeit ist doch der Inbegriff selbst bestimmter Arbeit, die von jeder Zweckmäßigkeit befreit sein soll. Später erzählte mir dann jemand, dass sich in England die meisten Künstler über Arbeitslosenunterstützung finanzieren würden, die so gesehen den größten Anteil an Kultursubventionen ausmache.

photos: Simon Cunningham

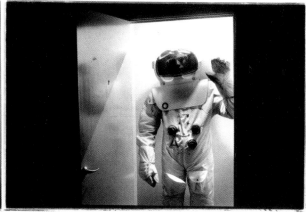

SHOW AND TELL (1996) / CLOSE ENOUGH TO KISS (1997)

I am 17
I am a natural blond
I am afraid of flying
I am the next big thing
I am a non-smoker
I am a Virgo
I am a liar
I am taking my time
I am a class 'A'
I am very photogenic
I am cold
I am good with children
I am looking at you right now

Where: a dead-end corridor made of 2-way mirrored perspex
Who: audience wandering round the corridor, deciding on viewing distance; 6 perfomers checking their appearance in the mirror; a man making an entrance through a door (again and again); a woman on a stool pretending to talk about herself; a woman flying on an ironing board; a princess singing "Fly me to the Moon" in a thin voice; a man on a toy telephone, spraying his face with water; a blindfolded woman, trapped in a corridor full of junk
What: lighting (changing the mirror effect from inside to out-

Wo: ein Gang aus beidseitig verspiegeltem Glas, der in einer Sackgasse endet
Wer: Zuschauer, die um den Gang wandern und über ihre Blickdistanz selbst entscheiden; 6 Darsteller, die ihre Erscheinung im Spiegelbild überprüfen; ein Mann, der (wieder und wieder) durch eine Tür auftritt; eine Frau auf einem Hocker, die so tut, als spräche sie von sich; eine Frau, die auf einem Bügelbrett fliegt; eine Prinzessin, die mit dünner Stimme „Fly me to the Moon" singt; ein Mann an einem Spielzeugtelefon, der sein Gesicht mit Wasser besprüht; eine Frau,

side and back again); the gaze of both performers and audience; reflections in the mirror; slow motion movement; white noise; a beat; 6 people posing; a sound which makes things disappear; various props (1 red lipstick, 1 Marilyn Monroe dress, 1 magnifying glass, 1 camera, 6 dog masks, 1 box of soap flakes, 1 fan, 1 piece of wood print wall paper, 1 piece of red brick wallpaper, 1 cherry tree backdrop, 1 carpet of fake grass, 1 butterfly on a stick, 3 white fluffy bunnies, 1 hula-hula chain, 1 cow mask, 1 sheep mask, a clock, a plate printed with a beautiful landscape, 2 pair of high heel shoes for men, 1 LED display board full of confessions, hand written signs describing smells and sounds,1 bubble machine)

How long: 60 minutes

Gerald Siegmund:
Protheses of Fantasy

It must have been in July. In any case it was warm. July 1996, as an old program, from the Theater am Turm (TAT for short) in Frankfurt am Main has it. On the left of the rehearsal stage, as you enter the foyer, an image. A young lad in a white suit sits just so on the edge of a chair, relaxed and casual, right lower arm supported by the thigh. His head turning effortlessly away from me, he looks into emptiness. A strange frame, a kind of cage, covered with mirror foil, surrounds him. I see him, but he cannot see me. Wasn't there, in this narrow tube that served as a reflective surfa-

der die Augen verbunden sind, gefangen in einem zugemüllten Korridor voller Ramsch

Was: Licht (das den Spiegeleffekt von innen nach außen und wieder zurück kehrt); die Blicke der Darsteller und Zuschauer; Spiegelbilder; Bewegung in Zeitlupe; Rauschen; ein Rhythmus; 6 Menschen, die posieren; ein Geräusch, das Dinge verschwinden lässt; eine Anzahl von Requisiten (1 roter Lippenstift, 1 Marylin-Monroe-Kleid, 1 Vergrößerungsglas, 1 Fotoapparat, 6 Hundemasken, 1 Schachtel Seifenflocken, 1 Ventilator, 1 Stück Tapete mit Holzaufdruck, 1 Stück Tapete mit Backsteinmaueraufdruck, 1 Kirschbaumblüten-Hintergrund, 1 Kunstgras-Teppich, 1 Schmetterling am Stab, 3 weiße Hasen, 1 Hula-Hula-Kette, 1 Kuhmaske, 1 Schafsmaske, eine Wanduhr, ein Teller mit dem Aufdruck einer schönen Landschaft, 2 Paar hochhackige Schuhe für Männer, 1 LED-Laufband voller Geständnisse, handgeschriebene Schilder, die Gerüche und Geräusche beschreiben, 1 Seifenblasenmaschine)

Wie lange: 60 Minuten

Gerald Siegmund:
Prothesen der Fantasie

Es muß im Juli gewesen sein. Auf jeden Fall war es warm. Juli 1996, so will es ein alter Programmzettel des Theaters am Turm, kurz TAT, in Frankfurt am Main. Auf der Probebühne zur Linken, wenn man das Foyer betritt – ein Bild.

ce, an ironing board as well? Didn't someone try to iron a shirt in order to go out? Hadn't the bloke combed his hair before? There were no roles or characters behind which the young man and his fellow combatants could hide themselves, only a few gestures, stances, poses and attitudes, which were constantly tested. Enter, exit, and enter again: does the shirt sit right, is this stance better? How do I come across?

I also remember this image because the bloke looked sexy. However, the image radiated a certain coldness. The mirror isolated the actors, who regarded themselves in narcissistic self-reflection, without being able to respond to me there outside. I could regard the actors from all sides. They had to feel my gaze. When I came closer to the cage it seized them from everywhere but they could not locate it. The walls and the light conspire to ensure that our gazes never meet. In this way I was shut out, but my gaze was what it depended on. This caused an uncanny feeling and revealed expectations and projections, however that which was immediately visible played no part in them. The actors behind the mirror invented themselves, as we have to invent ourselves daily. We never know how glances fall upon us because we can never be sure where we stand.

The mirrored wall presented the actors to me as if in aspic, or like garish butterflies, skewered and pinned to a velvet background. The image also had something clichéd about it. And why not? In the end a cliché is nothing other than the

Ein junger Typ im weißen Anzug sitzt gerade mal so auf der Kante eines Stuhls, lässig und locker, den rechten Unterarm auf den Oberschenkel gestützt. Den Kopf leicht von mir abgewandt, blickt er ins Leere. Er ist umgeben von einem merkwürdigen Gestell, einer Art Käfig, der mit einer Spiegelfolie bezogen ist. Ich sehe ihn, aber er kann mich nicht sehen. Gab es in diesem engen Schlauch, der als Spielfläche diente, nicht auch ein Bügelbrett? Versuchte nicht jemand, ein Hemd zu bügeln, um sich ausgehfertig zu machen? Hatte der Typ sich vorher nicht gekämmt? Es gab keine Rollen oder Figuren, hinter denen sich der junge Mann und seine Mitstreiter und Mitstreiterinnen verstecken konnten. Ein paar Gesten nur, Gänge, Posen und Haltungen, die ständig erprobt wurden. Auftreten, abgehen, noch einmal auftreten: Sitzt das Hemd, ist der Gang so besser? Wie komme ich rüber?

Ich erinnere mich auch an das Bild, weil der Typ sexy wirkte. Das Bild strahlte jedoch eine gewisse Kälte aus. Der Spiegel isolierte die Darsteller, die sich in narzisstischer Selbstbespiegelung selbst betrachteten, ohne auf mich da draußen eingehen zu können. Ich konnte die Akteure von allen Seiten aus betrachten. Sie mussten meinen Blick spüren, vor allem wenn ich nahe an den Käfig herantrat. Er erfasste sie von überall, ohne dass sie ihn allerdings lokalisieren konnten. Die Wand und das Licht leiteten und inszenierten unsere Blicke regelrecht aneinander vorbei. So war ich zwar ausgeschlossen, doch auf meinen Blick kam es an. Über weite Strecken der Inszenierung war kein gegenseitiges Aner-

photo: Simon Cunningham

photo: Simon Cunningham

clotted sum of experiences that we have again and again, repeating whether you want them to or not. They are formulas and empty phrases that give us the permission on the one hand to position ourselves. However, by making this possible they can also quietly reduce us and make us immovable. I expect I must have smirked a lot during that evening, because I felt recognized. Suddenly the light in the cage diminished. The mirror foil released the view of the outside to the inside. Now we could see ourselves but the spell was broken, the charm past, the gaze disappointed. Everything was just the prosthesis of fantasy. I recognized myself and saw the nullity and futility of my self-production. Gob Squad creates this moment in *Show and Tell, Close enough to Kiss* and *What Are You looking At?* and also in their later work. It remains central to their work and serves as memento mori of the vanity, the loss and the transience. We have to live with it.

Perhaps there never was a scene with the young man in the white suit. Perhaps I built it up in my memory from other pictures like a cover memory behind which different memories hide themselves. I do not know. But that's not what it's about anyway; it's not about seeking out the truth. What I make of this image is much more important to them. How it lives on in me and imprints itself onto my experiences and my life. How I put it to use (perhaps unconsciously) as I prepare to go out, standing before the mirror in order to give my appearance the final touch. It is then that it is present. My image does not belong to me at all, because it belongs

kennen Auge in Auge möglich. Das Medium der Spiegelwand ließ das nicht zu. Es war verantwortlich für dieses Fehlschlagen, das ein unheimliches Gefühl auslöste, welches wiederum einen Raum der Erwartungen und Projektionen eröffnete, in dem das, was wirklich zu sehen war, keine Rolle mehr spielte. Die Akteure hinter dem Spiegel erfanden sich wie wir uns täglich erfinden müssen, weil wir nie wissen, von wo aus der Blick des Anderen uns trifft, weil wir nie sicher sein können, wo wir stehen.

Die Spiegelwand lieferte mir die Akteure wie in Aspik. Oder wie farbenfrohe Schmetterlinge, die auf einem Untergrund aus Samt aufgespießt und festgepinnt wurden. Das Bild hatte auch etwas Klischiertes. Warum nicht. Schließlich ist ein Klischee auch nichts anderes als die geronnene Summe von Erfahrungen, die man immer wieder und wieder auf die gleiche Art und Weise macht, ob man will oder nicht. Es sind Formeln und Floskeln, die es uns einerseits erlauben, uns zu positionieren. Indem sie genau das ermöglichen, stellen sie uns andererseits aber auch still, reduzieren uns und machen uns unbeweglich. Ich muss wohl viel geschmunzelt haben an diesem Abend, denn ich fühlte mich erkannt. Plötzlich erlosch das Licht im Käfig. Die Spiegelfolie gab den Blick von innen nach außen frei. Jetzt konnten wir uns gegenseitig sehen, doch der Bann war gebrochen, der Zauber vorbei, der Blick enttäuscht. Alles nur Prothesen der Fantasie. Ich erkannte mich und sah die Nichtigkeit und Vergeblichkeit meiner Inszenierung. Der Moment, den Gob Squad in *Show and Tell, Close Enough To Kiss* und *What Are You Looking*

to everyone, because it is part of our cultural experience. It shows us how we treat, and traverse within, our culture. It also refers to our dislocation from it, because it cannot answer individuals' questions about love and happiness. It seems to me that upon reflection with *Show and Tell* and other pieces Gob Squad use theatre to ask this question.

Ina Kaifi:
She is standing in a box made of glass. At the end of the performance she begins to sing. The thick pane absorbs her voice. It sounds strange, as if a glass was pressed on one's mouth. Somehow airless. She spreads her arms out like a politician, who wants to embrace the whole world. I think she wears a pink dress. Which song was it? I only remember the muffled voice.

When I saw my brother for the first time my mother stood behind a pane of glass with him. I had so looked forward to seeing him. I so wanted to hold him, show and explain everything to him. Finally he was outside. And now just this helplessness. Before the birth I could feel his movements if I lay my face on my mother's belly. I imagined how he was floating in a bubble, like an astronaut in space, entirely free.

At? kreieren und der in zahlreichen ihrer späteren Arbeiten als leitende Idee von zentraler Bedeutung bleibt, ist auch ein Memento mori der Eitelkeit, des Verlusts und der Vergänglichkeit. Damit müssen wir leben.

Vielleicht hat es die Szene mit dem jungen Mann im weißen Anzug so nie gegeben. Vielleicht habe ich sie in meiner Erinnerung aus anderen Bildern zusammengesetzt wie eine Deckerinnerung, hinter der sich nur wieder andere Erinnerungen verbergen. Ich weiß es nicht. Doch darum geht es ohnehin nicht. Nicht um das Aufspüren der Wahrheit kreist das Theater von Gob Squad. Was ich aus diesem Bild mache, ist ihnen viel wichtiger. Wie es in mir weiterlebt und sich in mein Leben, meine Erfahrungen einprägt. Wie ich es gebrauche, vielleicht sogar unbewusst wiederhole, jedes Mal wenn ich mich zum Ausgehen fertig mache, wenn ich vor dem Spiegel stehe, um meinem Aussehen den letzten Schliff zu geben. Dann ist es da. Mein Bild, das mir gar nicht gehört, weil es allen gehört, weil es Teil unserer kulturellen Erfahrung ist. Es zeigt uns, wie wir uns in unserer Kultur bewegen, wie wir mit ihr umgehen. Dadurch verweist es aber auch auf unser Unbehaustsein in ihr, weil sie die großen Fragen nach der Liebe und dem Glück für jeden ganz individuell nicht beantworten kann. Um diese Frage zu stellen, gibt es, so will es mir in der Erinnerung an *Show and Tell* und all die anderen Stücke scheinen, für Gob Squad das Theater.

Janine Schulze:

One of the performers lies on an ironing board, arms spread out to the sides, simulating a weightless flight. In addition, a projection provides the perfect illusion of floating. The difficult, somewhat impoverished, almost sad ironing board reality and the emergent dream of flying come together in an affecting and whimsical way. Perhaps almost a prototypical scene for the theatre of Gob Squad: the bringing together of the simplest of props and perfectly controlled media technology.

Ina Kaifi:

Sie steht in einem Kasten aus Glas, und jetzt am Ende der Aufführung fängt sie an zu singen. Die dicke Scheibe dämpft ihre Stimme. Das klingt merkwürdig. Als würde man sich ein Glas auf den Mund pressen. Irgendwie luftleer. Sie breitet die Arme aus wie ein Politiker, der alle Welt umarmen will. Ich glaube, sie trägt ein rosafarbenes Kleid. Welches Lied? Ich erinnere nur noch die gedämpfte Stimme.

Als ich meinen Bruder das erste Mal gesehen habe, stand meine Mutter mit ihm hinter einer Scheibe. Ich hatte mich so auf ihn gefreut. Ich wollte ihn so gerne mal halten, ihm alles zeigen und erzählen. Endlich war er draußen. Und nun diese Hilflosigkeit. Vor seiner Geburt konnte ich seine Bewegungen spüren, wenn ich mein Gesicht auf den Bauch meiner Mutter legte. Ich stellte mir vor, wie er in einer Blase schwebte wie ein Astronaut im All. Vollkommen frei.

Janine Schulze:

Eine der Darstellerinnen liegt auf einem Bügelbrett, die Arme zur Seite ausgebreitet und einen schwerelosen Flug simulierend. Eine Kamera liefert dazu auf einem Bildschirm die perfekte Illusion des Schwebens. Die harte, fast ein wenig ärmliche Bügelbrett-Realität und der bildgewordene Traum vom Fliegen fallen hier auf rührende, aber auch skurrile Art und Weise zusammen. Vielleicht geradezu eine „Ur-Szene" für das Theater von Gob Squad: die Verbindung von simpelsten Requisiten und perfekt beherrschter Medientechnik.

AN EFFORTLESS TRANSACTION (1996)

Welcome! come on in! there are hundreds of excited young sofas and tables inside waiting to meet their new families!

Where: a furniture shop at the cheap end of a big shopping centre

Who: performed sales assistants (with pink suits and white ties); real sales assistants (with grey suits and blue ties); audience laden with shopping bags; gangs of bored teenagers trying to disrupt the proceedings

What: easy listening muzak with hidden subversive messages; countless "Hurry Buy Now!" stickers; free balloons for the kids printed with the words "Shopping Is A Feeling"; loud waltz music; LED display board (text: true confessions of former sales assistants); hundreds of sofas, armchairs, pouffes and occasional tables in materials from floral easy-wash to fake mahogany, all with tassles, valances, pelmets and 3 year no-quibble guarantees; every half hour a musical scene in a different seating arrangement (as long as it hasn't been sold in the meantime)

How long: opening hours of the shop (10am-5pm) every Saturday for a month

Wo: ein Möbelgeschäft in der Ramschecke eines Einkaufszentrums

Wer: Darsteller als Verkäufer (in rosa Anzügen und weißen Krawatten); echte Verkäufer (in grauen Anzügen und blauen Krawatten); Zuschauer beladen mit Einkaufstüten; Gruppen gelangweilter Teenager, die versuchen, ins Geschehen einzugreifen

Was: Easy-listening-Musik mit versteckten subversiven Botschaften; unzählige „Jetzt zuschlagen! Solang der Vorrat reicht!"-Aufkleber; Luftballons als Kundengeschenke, bedruckt mit den Worten „Shopping Is A Feeling"; laute Walzermusik; ein LED-Band (Text: die wahren Geständnisse eines ehemaligen Verkäufers); hunderte von Sofas, Sessel und Beistelltische – von geblümt und leicht abwaschbar bis hin zu Mahagony-Imitat, alle mit Fransen, Volants und „Geld zurück-Garantie"; jede halbe Stunde eine Musicalszene in wechselnden Sitzgruppen (sofern sie nicht in der Zwischenzeit verkauft wurden)

Wie lange: Ladenöffnungszeiten (von 10 bis 17 Uhr) an vier Samstagen

Aenne Quiñones:

I mingled with the customers and regarded the shapeless, monstrous furniture, arranged as different living areas in the showroom. What did it have to do with me? I became aware of a few people dressed completely in pink, wearing white curly wigs and suddenly the different arrangements of beds, settees, tables and chairs became the strange setting for a play about dreams, ideas, longing and an imaginary life which could be gladly accepted as a free gift whilst shopping for furniture.

Sean told me later that one of the salesmen had thanked them after the project ended. For him it was the most exciting and entertaining time he had experienced since he began working there. You couldn't have asked for a better compliment.

Paul Fraser:

I sat in a furniture store four times a day for a week dressed in grey trousers and shirt with a matching grey wig, watching Gob Squad perform on the edge of the space (I operated some technical gadgets). The only negative was the endless hours spent trying to offer an explanation to the bemused staff. To be involved with a group who offer no pretentiousness and raise genuine smiles was a real joy, my alcoholism left me for a week. There was something quite beautiful watching art in location devoid of any creativity (a furniture store in the middle of a shopping centre). If I had been offer-

Aenne Quiñones:

Ich mischte mich unter die Kunden und betrachtete die unförmigen, monströsen Möbel, die in verschiedenen Wohnsituationen arrangiert waren. Was hatte das mit mir zu tun? Aber dann waren da ein paar Leute ganz in Rosa und mit weißen Lockenperücken und plötzlich wurden die verschiedenen Arrangements von Betten, Sesseln, Tischen und Stühlen zu merkwürdigen Kulissen für ein Spiel über Träume, Vorstellungen, Sehnsüchte und ein Leben, das man sich, als eine Art Werbegeschenk, beim Möbelkauf gern gleich noch gratis mit abgeholt hätte.

Später erzählte mir Sean, dass sich einer der Verkäufer nach Beendigung des Projektes besonders bei ihnen bedankt hatte: Für ihn war es die aufregendste und unterhaltsamste Zeit, seit er in diesem Laden arbeitete. Ein besseres Kompliment hätte man sich eigentlich nicht wünschen können.

Paul Fraser:

Eine Woche lang saß ich viermal täglich in einer grauen Hose und Hemd mit passender grauer Perücke in einem Möbelhaus und sah Gob Squad dabei zu, wie sie am anderen Ende des Raums performten (ich bediente einige technische Geräte). Das einzig Negative waren die stundenlangen Diskussionen, in denen wir versuchten, den Angestellten Erklärungen abzuliefern. Mit einer Gruppe zu arbeiten, die sich nicht verstellt und echtes Lächeln provoziert, hat mich für eine Woche von meinem Alkoholismus befreit. Es lag

ed money I would have gladly done this for the rest of my life. Their effortless beauty became their trademark (I remain a passing beauty within their body of work).

sehr viel Schönes in dem Vorgang, Kunst an einem Ort zu sehen, dem jegliche Kreativität fehlt (ein Möbelhaus mitten in einem Einkaufszentrum). Wenn man mir Geld angeboten hätte, hätte ich das gerne für den Rest meines Lebens gemacht. Ihre mühelose Schönheit wurde zu ihrem Markenzeichen (ich dagegen blieb eine flüchtige Schönheit innerhalb ihres Werks).

15 MINUTES TO COMPLY (1997)

Where would you like to be right now?
In a garden surrounded by walls, in a town by the fountain of
free champagne where all the people rest on sun beds
You have all the time in the world

Where: an underground platform (graffiti, bins, 3 advertising billboards, 2 platforms, tunnels each side)

Who: 8 people waiting to move on; 2 men waiting for a train; a girl and a woman falling over to drum n'bass music (again and again); a couple about to meet (when snow is falling); a lady wearing nothing but a towel (her back to the wall); a man with a briefcase (walking towards a light in parallel with a happy dog running home); a voice (announcing the minutes remaining)

What: 3 video projectors; 3 billboards used as projection screens; fast-forward motion in video images, sound and lights; a series of images from idealised places; a Sony Playstation; a handful of fake snow per performer; tannoy announcements; arrows pointing at people, predicting their future; drum'n'bass music; eerie musical choirs; 1 garden fountain for each bin in the station; a model train running the length of the platform; an underground train coming to take the performers away

How long: 15 minutes

Wo: eine U-Bahnstation (Graffiti, Mülleimer, 3 Plakatwände, 2 Bahnsteige, Tunnel zu beiden Seiten)

Wer: 8 Wartende, die weiterwollen; ein Mädchen und eine Frau, die zu Drum-'n'-Bass-Musik hinfallen (wieder und wieder); ein Paar, das kurz davor ist, sich zu begegnen (während es schneit); eine Frau, nur mit einem Handtuch bekleidet (mit dem Rücken zur Wand); ein Mann mit einem Aktenkoffer, der einem Licht entgegenläuft (gemeinsam mit einem Hund); eine Stimme, die die verbleibenden Minuten ansagt

Was: 3 Videoprojektoren; 3 Plakatwände als Projektionsleinwände; schnelle Vorwärtsbewegung in Videobildern, Sound und Licht; eine Bildserie paradiesischer Orte; eine Sony Playstation; eine Handvoll Kunstschnee pro Darsteller; Lautsprecheransagen; Pfeile, die auf Menschen zeigen und deren Zukunft vorhersagen; Drum-'n'-Bass-Musik; feenhafte Chöre; 1 Gartenspringbrunnen pro Mülleimer in der Station; eine Modelleisenbahn in der Länge des Gleises; eine einfahrende U-Bahn, die die Darsteller davonträgt

Wie lange: 15 Minuten

Till Briegleb:

When it is suddenly revealed how rarely we as individuals represent complete personalities, art makes me happy. What is interesting about humans are their fears, shame and the courageous moments when these are consciously shown because I guess that only through these over comings can alluring and suprising images and embraces be created. Take for example, the dog. In a desperate video loop he ran repeatedly over a meadow as if the bestial hunt were the embodiment of bliss. In front were all the lonely people and their various dress codes – from young to square – who tried to throw themselves into the social flux of approval in an at-tempt to find something beautiful, only to find themselves sitting alone in the dirt of a draughty underground tram stop with the diesel smell of time, practicing the crowning discipline of fear: waiting.

As participants in their longing we stood on the opposite platform, a tourist party from Catherine David and Tom Stromberg's Kassel Avantgarti Tours and felt collectively exhausted by various attempts to recognise content and meaning in the transience of a promenade theatre event that last for many hours. During the course of this intellectual wine tasting, one was informed about the Baader-Meinhof Gang, art, the body, the Romans, burning telephone boxes and contemporary music. One soon began to busy oneself with one's fellow travellers, to speak to one or other of one's acquaintances then trail off or look at women and sort out coded messages of curiosity or disinterest. This

Till Briegleb:

Wenn sich plötzlich offenbart, wie wenig wir Menschen als Einzelfiguren vollständige Persönlichkeiten bilden, bin ich in der Kunst glücklich. Interessant am Menschen sind seine Ängste, seine Scham und die mutigen Momente, wo er diese bewusst zeigt. Denn vermutlich entstehen nur aus diesen Überwindungen Bilder und Umarmungen, die helfen, locken, überraschen. Zum Beispiel dieser Hund. In einem verzweifelten Video-Loop rannte er immer wieder über eine Wiese, als sei das tierische Jagen ein Inbegriff von Glückseligkeit. Davor diese Einsamen, die mit diversen Dresscodes – von jung bis bieder – versuchten, sich in einen gesellschaftlichen Fluss von Anerkennung zu werfen, um irgendetwas Schönes für sich zu finden, die aber dann doch nur alleine im Dreck einer unterirdischen zugigen Straßenbahnhaltestelle saßen und mit dem Benzingeruch der Zeit in der Nase die Königsdisziplin der Angst betrieben: das Warten.

Als Teilhaber ihrer Sehnsucht standen wir auf dem Bahnsteig gegenüber, eine Reisegruppe der Kassler Avantgarti-Tours von Catherine David und Tom Stromberg, und fühlten uns kollektiv erschöpft von verschiedenen Versuchen, in der Flüchtigkeit eines vielstündigen Theater-Parcours richtig Gehalt- und Bedeutungsvolles zu erkennen. Über die RAF, die Künste, die Körper, die Römer, brennende Telefonzellen und die zeitgenössische Musik wurde man bei dieser intellektuellen Weinprobe unterrichtet. Man begann bald, sich mit den Mitreisenden zu beschäftigen, den einen oder an-

feeling was met by *15 Minutes to Comply*. There were written messages and demanding signs but seven years later I don't remember them. Slogans are simply transient – but solitude, hope and an intense atmosphere of expectation are things that never occur under the auspices of world analysis, especially when they retain a sense of humour. And this dog was just simply very funny.

However, watching waiting people and their foibles (that arguably influence our perception of other people more than we are aware of) is hardly a dramatic concept. It took a hormonal outlay brought on by loud music and wild dancing to entangle the stories of these people that were broadcasting their individual stories a safe distance from one other. The threshold of embarrassment, which needs to be transgressed in order to affect others, is here so touchingly and simply broken. Even an uptight person such as the theatre critic Gerhard Stadelmeier, who simply cannot relate to the concept of aesthetics as the morals of surface experienced some seconds of release.

Perhaps it was all totally different, but that is how it is buried in the memory. The tram arrived and took us away from the again lifeless Sleeping Beauties of everyday capitalism and we were left with the feeling of recovery. They stayed in isolation and waited until the end of the world for another moment when the prince of euphoric music will take them back to the feelings of disembodiment. Sometimes a quarter of an hour is sufficient to perceive the contemporary

deren Bekannten zu sprechen und wieder zu verlieren oder Frauen anzusehen und verschlüsselte Nachrichten von Neugier oder Desinteressen zu sortieren. Und dieses Gefühl fand dann *15 Minutes To Comply*. Auch hier gab es irgendwelche Textbotschaften und Zeichen mit Anspruch, aber die erinnere ich sieben Jahre später nicht mehr. Parolen sind halt so vergänglich – aber Einsamkeit, Hoffnung und eine intensive Atmosphäre des Erwartens, das sind Dinge, die niemals in die Reichsacht der Welterklärung fallen. Zumindest, wenn sie sich ihren Humor bewahren. Und dieser Hund war schon einfach super komisch.

Doch nur Menschen mit kleinen Maröttchen – die unsere Wahrnehmung von anderen Menschen wohl stärker bestimmen, als wir selber merken – beim Warten zuzusehen ist natürlich noch kein dramatisches Konzept. Also brauchte es eine Hormonausschüttung mit lauter Musik und wildem Tanz, um die Geschichten dieser Menschen, die da in sicherer Distanz vom anderen ihre Geschichte ausstrahlten, zu verknäulen. Die Schwelle der Peinlichkeit, die überschritten gehört, wenn man andere berühren möchte, wurde hier so rührend einfach genommen, dass selbst ein so verbiesterter Mensch wie Gerhard Stadelmeier, der mit dem Konzept von Ästhetik als Moral der Oberfläche so gar nichts anfangen kann, einige Sekunden Gelöstheit erlebte.

Vielleicht war das alles auch ganz anders, aber so ist es in der Erinnerung vergraben. Als die Straßenbahn einfuhr und uns wegnahm von den wieder erschlafften Dornrös-

photo: Friedemann Simon

whilst other established artists chase their tails like a dog.

Jens Hoffmann:

One detail that stayed in my mind over the many years revolved around a small element in one of Gob Squad earlier performances. It was a little, very discretely placed destination sign on a subway train that they used for one of their most stunning pieces *15 Minutes to Comply*. All the sign said was "Somewhere Else."

Since seeing the performance I have always hoped that one day some train that I take will bring me to this unknown destination. I imagine that Gob Squad would hijack the train and take me to wherever this "Somewhere Else" is. The journey would take many days but it would not matter since I would not perceive time anymore the way I used to. One day would feel like an hour and an hour would feel like a day.

I cannot imagine what "Somewhere Else" would ultimately look like. I do not want to know. I want to be taken there by that train and be surprised, be overwhelmed and shocked at the same time. The attraction comes from not knowing what this place will look like but being certain that it must be so much better than any of the other destinations that we are all usually heading for. With Gob Squad it is always about this destination. Destination: "Somewhere Else."

chen des kapitalistischen Alltags, die dort in ihrer Isolation zurückblieben und bis an das Ende aller Tage auf den nächsten Moment warten würden, wo der Prinz der euphorischen Musik sie zurück in das Spüren von Entkörperlichung führen würde, blieb das Gefühl der Erholung. Manchmal reicht eben eine Viertelstunde zum Erkennen von Gegenwart, wo Stunden der Großkunst nur rennen wie ein Hund.

Jens Hoffmann:

Ein Detail, das mir in den langen Jahren, in denen ich das Glück hatte, Gob Squad zu kennen, in Erinnerung geblieben ist, dreht sich um ein ziemlich kleines Element in einer ihrer frühen Performances. Es war eine kleine, sehr diskret platzierte Fahrtrichtungsanzeige auf einem U-Bahn-Wagen, den sie für eines ihrer großartigsten Stücke *15 Minutes to Comply* benutzten. Auf dem Schild stand nur „Somewhere Else".

Seit ich die Performance gesehen habe, habe ich immer gehofft, dass mich irgendwann ein Zug, in den ich einsteige, zu diesem unbekannten Ziel bringen wird. Ich stelle mir vor, dass Gob Squad den Zug kidnappen und mich dorthin fahren, wo immer dieses Anderswo auch ist. Die Fahrt würde einige Tage dauern, aber das wäre egal, weil ich Zeit nicht mehr so wahrnehmen würde wie bisher. Ein Tag würde sich wie eine Stunde anfühlen und eine Stunde wie ein Tag.

Ich kann mir nicht vorstellen, wie „Somewhere Else" letztlich aussehen würde. Ich will es gar nicht wissen. Ich will

Daniel Haaksman:

It was an exceptional summer, the summer of 1997. The sun shone in July and August without a break and it was hot all the way through. Sean said several times that as a student he'd read about the art world event *documenta* and could hardly believe that here he was participating in it. Princess Diana had had a fatal accident in a Paris motorway underpass, Bellin's "Samba de Janeiro" was pumping out of every radio, Drum n' Bass was the new, exciting sound in the clubs, and I was in love.

In the middle of this summer the performance *15 Minutes To Comply* took place. A 15-minute long daydream: People waiting for trains collided with music and video projections. Hurtling through life at high speed then left isolated again to board their trains. It was 15 minutes of exciting theatre.

My calendar from the year 1997 shows in the notes for 6th September 'Kassel – documenta', and in small writing underneath 'c/o Desch, 7 Juliusstein'. This address was the house in which Gob Squad and some of their guests stayed during their rehearsals for *documenta*. It was a mansion owned by couple of academics that had gone on holiday and left their house for the use of artists in the festival. Shortly before the performance of *15 Minutes to Comply* there were a dozen or so people staying there. Strangely, the couple came back from their holidays earlier than expected. Sean and Berit met them on the doorstep with the couple's video recorder under their arms, which they wanted to borrow for *15 Minutes*

von diesem Zug dorthin gebracht und überrascht werden, überwältigt und geschockt zugleich. Die Anziehung kommt daher, dass man nicht weiß, wie dieser Ort genau aussehen wird, und doch ist man sicher, dass er viel besser ist als alle anderen Fahrtziele, die man normalerweise ansteuert. Bei Gob Squad geht es immer um dieses Ziel, das Fahrtziel „Somewhere Else".

Daniel Haaksman:

Es war ein ziemlicher Spitzensommer, der Sommer von 1997. Die Sonne schien im Juli und August ohne Pause, und es war durchweg warm. Sean sagte mehrmals, dass er es kaum glauben könnte. Als Student hätte er immer nur über die Welt-Kunst-Ausstellung *documenta* gelesen und nun wäre er selbst Teilnehmer dort. Prinzessin Diana verunglückte in einer Pariser Autobahnunterführung tödlich, Bellins „Samba de Janeiro" lief im Radio rauf und runter, Drum´n´Bass war der neue, aufregende Sound in den Clubs, und ich war verliebt.

Mitten in diesem Sommer fand die Aufführung von *15 Minutes To Comply* statt. Ein 15-minütiger Tagtraum: Menschen warten auf den Zug und werden durch Musik- und Videoprojektionen im Hintergrund aufeinander gestoßen, durchrasen im Schnelldurchlauf ein Leben, um dann, wieder vereinzelt, in den Zug zu steigen und wegzufahren. Es waren 15 Minuten aufregendes Theater.

to Comply. The hosts were not amused especially when it became clear that friends and friends of friends of Gob Squad were also staying there. They were furious and wanted everybody out. I thought they overreacted and because I was so angry about it I nicked a book from their library. The book is still lying about at my place today and, if I pick it up, it takes me back to my memories of the summer of '97, those days in Kassel and *15 Minutes to Comply*.

Mein Kalender aus dem Jahr 1997 zeigt in den Notizen vom 6. September: Kassel documenta, klein darunter c/o Desch, Am Juliusstein 7. Diese Adresse war das Haus, in dem Gob Squad und einige ihrer Gäste für die Zeit ihrer Proben bei der documenta untergebracht waren. Es war die Villa eines Akademikerpärchens, das in den Urlaub gefahren war und das ihr Haus Künstlern der documenta überlassen hatte. Kurz vor der Aufführung von *15 Minutes To Comply* waren dort bestimmt ein Dutzend Leute untergebracht. Komischerweise kam das Akademikerpärchen früher als geplant zurück aus dem Urlaub. Als sie erfuhren, dass in ihrem Haus auch die Freunde und Freundesfreunde von Gob Squad wohnten, machten sie Ärger und wollten alle rausschmeißen. Übertriebenermaßen, wie ich fand, und weil ich mich darüber so aufregte, klaute ich ein Buch aus ihrer Bibliothek. Das Buch liegt noch heute bei mir herum und jedes Mal, wenn ich es in die Hand nehme, führt es mich zurück in die Erinnerungen des 97er Sommers, die Tage in Kassel und an *15 Minutes To Comply*.

CALLING LAIKA (1998)

Here are 10 sounds I am sending to you:
1. The silence that you hear after watching bad television
2. A Nintendo game boy with a list of games
3. Marvin Gayes "What's going on?"
4. The sound of a baby crying
5. 180 beats per minute
6. A list of the world's dirtiest swear words
7. I'm sending you the sound of a busy city street to get a feeling of how many of us there are on this big planet
8. I'm sending you the Starwars trilogy just because it's such a good story
9. A tape recording of two people having an argument, trying to work it out
10. The sound of a man who doesn't know who he is anymore

Where: a car park (full of gravel and rubbish, the city skyline behind it, the open sky above)
Who: the male voice of a radio host; the female voice of a cosmic guide; 10 people in similar coats (falling over to the sound of gunshots again and again); a man in a polar bear costume, trying to plant a flag somewhere (holding the bear head under his arm like an astronauts helmet); 3 couples in ballroom gowns (waltzing in the cold); a woman holding a white balloon (refusing to let go of a lost lover); a woman driving a car (trapped in the circle, caught in the rain); a man doing a handbrake turn; a naked man being dumped from a driving car (with a plastic bag on his head and the word

Wo: ein Parkplatz (Kies und Dreck, die Skyline der Stadt in der Ferne, der Nachthimmel über einem)
Wer: die männliche Stimme eines Radiomoderators; die weibliche Stimme eines kosmischen Führers; 10 Leute in ähnlichen Mänteln (die wieder und wieder zu dem Geräusch von Schüssen zusammenbrechen); ein Mann in einem Eisbärenkostüm, der versucht eine Flagge zu setzen (den Bärenkopf wie einen Astronautenhelm unter dem Arm haltend); 3 Paare in Ballkleidern (die in der Kälte Walzer tanzen); eine Frau, die einen weißen Ballon hält (und eine verlorene Liebe nicht loslässt); eine Frau, die ein Auto fährt (eingeschlossen im Kreis, verloren im Regen); ein Mann,

"heretic" painted on his back); a stupid old man wearing an alien mask (trying to scare people)

What: 30 cars parked in a circle (audience sitting in them, watching through the windscreen); a radio station (broadcasting the soundtrack across town, car radios tuned in); a snow machine; a fork-lift truck; a strong water hose (to produce rain); dozens of aircraft landing lights, pyrotechnic effects, confetti bombs and fireworks (to send signals out into the night); strong searchlights (to chase people escaping from cars); sound samples from Spielberg movies; countdowns and recurring waltzes; adverts for missing people; several billboard signs (reminders to stay in touch)

How long: 60 minutes

Miriam Dreysse:

Meeting other spectators in the cars from *Calling Laika* is for me a setting that still remains unsurpassed to this day. I was struck by the homely intimacy of the cars in contrast to the large parking lot at night. This urban non-place, in which nobody normally lingers, carried at the same time a promise of progression in itself. The lost-ness of the individual actors in the car park evokes film images of the American desert with people hoping to make connection. This lostness of the individual in the world with their hope for something out there that could cancel out or at least console the lost ness. It is always bordering on kitsch but at the same time repeatedly broken by irony or by use of the most everyday activities. For example instructions transferred over the

der mit quietschenden Reifen bremst; ein nackter Mann, der aus einem fahrenden Auto geworfen wird (eine Plastiktüte über dem Kopf und das Wort „Ketzer" auf dem Rücken); ein dummer alter Mann mit Alienmaske (der versucht, die Leute zu erschrecken)

Was: 30 in einem Kreis geparkte Autos; das Publikum, das in den Autos sitzt und durch die Windschutzscheiben zuschaut; eine Radiostation (die den Soundtrack in die Stadt und zu den Autoradios sendet); eine Schneemaschine; ein Gabelstapler; ein Wasserschlauch mit starkem Wasserdruck (um es regnen zu lassen); Dutzende von Landebahnsignallichtern, pyrotechnische Effekte, Konfettibomben und Feuerwerk, um Signale in die Nacht zu schicken; Suchlichter (um aus den Autos fliehende Leute zu verfolgen); Soundsamples aus Spielberg-Filmen; Countdowns und wiederkehrende Walzermusik; Vermisstenanzeigen; diverse Plakate (Mahnungen, in Kontakt zu bleiben)

Wie lange: 60 Minuten

Miriam Dreysse:

Das Zusammentreffen mit anderen Zuschauern in den Autos von *Calling Laika* ist bis heute als Setting für mich fast unübertroffen. Die heimelige Intimität in den Autos im Kontrast zu dem großen Parkplatz bei Nacht, diesem urbanen Nicht-Ort, an dem sonst niemand verweilt, der zugleich ein Versprechen von Fortkommen in sich trägt. Dann die Verlorenheit der einzelnen Akteure auf diesem Parkplatz, der plötzlich Filmbildern amerikanischer Wüsten gleicht, in denen man

car radio ask us 'please turn on the headlights three times' which immediately takes one back to the miserable car park floor in Frankfurt.

The exhibited longing for an establishment of contact, which could be a salvation, is contrasted by the situation inside the cars: You sit together with other spectators you have never seen before within the intimate confines of a car and experience the performance together. As the establishment of contact with the outside or transcendent world remains unsuccessful, so the establishment of contact between people in the smaller world of the individual cars is increasingly successful. This constant reinvention of the artist/spectator relationship is one of the many aspects that make up the Live Art of Gob Squad. It is this memory that stays with me. This communal experience of brief encounters and the relationships between people, as fleeting as they might be.

Kontakt aufnimmt, die Verlorenheit des Einzelnen in der Welt mit seiner Hoffnung auf irgendetwas da draußen, das die Verlorenheit aufheben oder zumindest trösten könnte, immer nah an der Grenze zum Kitsch, zugleich wieder ironisch gebrochen oder mit den profansten Mitteln – z.B. der über das Autoradio übertragenen Anweisung, doch bitte dreimal aufzublenden – auf den Boden des tristen Parkplatzes in der Frankfurter City zurückgeholt.

Der inszenierten Sehnsucht nach einer Kontaktaufnahme, die eine Rettung sein könnte, wird die konkrete Situation in den Autos gegenübergestellt: Man sitzt zusammen mit anderen Zuschauern, die man vorher nie gesehen hat, in einem Auto, in der Intimität dieses kleinen Raumes, und erlebt die Aufführung gemeinsam. So erfolglos die Kontaktaufnahme mit einem Außer- oder Überweltlichen bleibt, so erfolgreich ist die zwischenmenschliche Kontaktaufnahme im Kleinen, in den einzelnen Autos. Und dies ist ein Aspekt der Live Art von Gob Squad und ihrem immer wieder neuen Spiel mit der Zuschauersituation, der mir von vielen ihrer Aufführungen in Erinnerung geblieben ist: kurze Begegnungen und zwischenmenschliche Beziehungen im gemeinsamen Erleben, so flüchtig sie auch sein mögen.

photo: Simon Cunningham

Albrecht Kunze:
Re-calling Laika

I remember:
Firstly and above all a stage of light.
A circle of cars whose headlights formed a further circle,
which became the stage, visible because they were of light,
but not graspable.

I remember:
I thought how alone the actors are, who, in the midst of the
light, called into the dark sky, from which nothing echoed
back. Alone in the light, but, on the other hand:
This is the title of a book, which I bought only recently.
Thus, to have this thought years after I thought it.

I remember that THE moment for me in *Calling Laika* was
the search for the place of death.
Of Laika, who perished in orbit, and with that of all those
who died in the air.
Perhaps on their way home (in order to die there)
Just as Wooster Group member Ron Vawter, whose illness
was well known and who, as everyone knew he was dying,
provided probably the most touching moment in the history
of the Frankfurt TAT (where I also saw *Calling Laika*) with the
parting monologue from Chekov's *Three Sisters;*
'Mascha, I have to go now...'
Ron Vawter who died on a flight back to New York.
His death was just as placeless as Laika's

Albrecht Kunze:
Re-calling Laika

Ich erinnere mich:
zuerst und vor allem, an – eine Bühne aus Licht.
An einen Kreis von Autos, deren Scheinwerfer einen weiteren Kreis bildeten, der zur Bühne wurde – die, weil aus
Licht: sicht-, aber nicht greifbar war.

Ich erinnere mich: daß ich dachte – wie allein die Akteure
sind, die, inmitten des Lichts, in den dunklen Himmel riefen, aus dem nichts zurückschallte: Allein im Licht, aber –
andererseits:
ist dies der Titel eines Buches, das ich mir erst kürzlich
kaufte. Also: Jahre nachdem ich dachte, dies gedacht zu
haben.

Ich erinnere mich, daß der DER Moment in *Calling Laika* für
mich war:
die Suche nach dem Ort des Todes.
Von Laika, die auf ihrer Umlaufbahn verendete, und damit:
von allen, die auch in der Luft gestorben sind. Vielleicht: auf
ihrem Weg nach Haus (um dort zu sterben).
So wie Ron Vawter, Mitglied der Wooster Group, von dessen
Krankheit alle wußten, und der, im gemeinschaftlichen
Wissen seines Sterbens, mit dem Abschiedsmonolog aus
Tschechows *Drei Schwestern* für den wohl ergreifendsten Mo-
ment in der Geschichte des Frankfurter TAT (wo ich auch
Calling Laika sah) gesorgt hatte: Mascha, I have to go now ...

And he is someone you look for as well when you look and call for Laika,
Although you find neither.
However that is actually a bit of a comfort:
Both of them have a place in you, if only because you look and call for them, and so:
You visit them for one instant – if you call after them.
A place within those who look and call for them, desire them, where for one moment this desire is greater and stronger than death.
A place where there is so little to grab on to, like a stage of light.

Elisabeth Schweeger:

What theatre can still achieve in our times is to make experiences possible and attempt to do this in a "now-time" as Walter Benjamin expressed it, a unity of past, present and future. I remember... Gob Squad... *Calling Laika*. The first creature sent into space was Laika, a Russian dog. Who remembers that? Gob Squad sent us on that journey again.

We had to get thirty cars at that time in the Marstall in Munich. The delivery alone of these cars was already an event in itself. Concentrated technology to serve mankind's urge to move forward. The spectators sat in cars that formed a circle and recollection took place. A poetic fantasy on the boundlessness of humans, their longing to want to reach for the stars and also to culpably neglect every now and then

Ron Vawter, der auf dem Flug zurück nach New York gestorben ist. Dessen Tod also: genauso ortlos ist wie der von Laika, und:
den man ebenso sucht,
wenn man nach Laika sucht und ruft – und keinen der beiden findet.
Aber:
und das ist ein wenig tröstlich:
die beide einen Platz in einem selber haben, gerade weil man nach ihnen sucht und ruft, und so:
sie für einen Augenblick besucht – wenn man nach ihnen ruft.
Einen Platz, oder: einen Ort – in denen, die nach ihnen suchen und rufen. Sie also: begehren, und – für einen Moment – dieses Begehren größer und: stärker ist als der Tod.
Ein Ort, der so wenig zu greifen ist wie eine Bühne aus Licht.

Elisabeth Schweeger:

Was Theater in dieser Zeit noch vollbringen kann, ist, Erfahrungen möglich zu machen und den Versuch zu unternehmen, in einer „Jetzt-Zeit", wie Walter Benjamin es formulieren würde, Vergangenes, Gegenwärtiges und Zukünftiges zu vereinen. I remember – Gob Squad – *Calling Laika*.
Das erste Wesen, das in den Weltall geschickt worden ist: Laika – eine russische Hündin. Wer erinnert sich schon daran? Gob Squad schickte uns noch einmal auf diese Reise.

photo: Simon Cunningham

the humanitarian principle. If we remember, Laika never came back. And let us also remember: humans need contact, communication and look for exchange.

As tender as these images were, they were also shocking and stayed in your head. Mankind technologising his habitat dismisses humanity in the loneliness of amnesia.

Tom Stromberg:
Why make theatre on the stage? Gob Squad makes theatre under the stars. The light scans the sky. We call Laika, the Russian dog, who was shot into space never to be seen again. We call all the missing persons of this world. Longing... for what there is in the darkness above us? Loneliness... with *Are you lonesome tonight?* melting the snow. A NASA polar bear plants a flag in vain. Laika would have howled at the moon and I would have gladly been the polar bear.

Dreißig Autos mussten wir damals im marstall/München besorgen. Die Anlieferung allein dieser Autos war schon ein Ereignis für sich, geballte Technik allein für den Fortbewegungsdrang des Menschen.
Der Zuschauer saß im Auto, im Kreis, den die Autos bildeten, und Erinnerung fand statt. Eine poetische Fantasie zur Maßlosigkeit des Menschen, zu seinen Sehnsüchten, nach den Sternen greifen zu wollen und dabei mitunter auch das humanitäre Prinzip sträflich zu vernachlässigen. erinnern wir uns, Laika kam nie wieder zurück. Und Erinnern wir uns auch: Der Mensch braucht den Kontakt, braucht die Kommunikation, sucht den Austausch.

Wie zärtlich diese Bilder auch waren, so erschreckend bleiben sie einem auch im Kopf. Der Mensch, der sich immer technoisierter seinen Lebensraum gestaltet, entlässt den Menschen in die Einsamkeit seiner Erinnerungslosigkeit.

Tom Stromberg:
Warum Theater auf der Bühne machen? Gob Squad macht Theater ... zum Beispiel unter den Sternen. Das Licht sucht den Himmel ab. Wir rufen Laika, die russische Hündin, die auf Nimmerwiedersehen ins All geschossen wurde. Wir rufen alle Vermissten dieser Welt. Sehnsucht ... Was ist dort im Dunkel über uns? Einsamkeit ... Mit „Are you lonesome tonight?" schmilzt der Schnee. Ein NASA-Eisbär setzt vergeblich Flagge. Laika hätte den Mond angeheult und ich wäre zu gern der Eisbär gewesen.

I CAN (1998)

I can curl my hair (£18)... I can make dinner for 30 people (£320)... I can bake bread (£3.50)... I can cry like a baby (£65)... I can talk shit (£120)... I can walk backwards (£35)... I can fix computers (£20)... I can put lipstick on without looking in the mirror (£38)... I can fall in love ($1,000,000)

Where: an art gallery
Who: 6 people listing all the things they can do
What: 6 monitors with 6 talking heads; shopping channel graphics; soothing music; subtle choreography (2 people blowing their noses at the same time while 3 people scratch their chins); the sound of people thinking; a telephone; a sales catalogue; a customer service team following up placed orders
How long: 60 minute loop

Tashi Iwaoka (ordered 2000, delivered 2001:
What I remember about *I Can* is that I was sitting on a wooden horse-like object whilst waiting for Gob Squad to arrive. I remember that I arrived in Podewil a little earlier than the appointment. I was very curious to see how they appeared and from where.

I think at least one year had passed since the *I Can* exhibition in Angel Row gallery, Nottingham where I had ordered my performance. I was very excited when I was told I was the

Wo: eine Galerie
Wer: 6 Menschen, die alle ihre Fähigkeiten aufzählen,
Was: 6 Monitore mit 6 sprechenden Köpfen; TV-Shopping-kanal-Grafik; beruhigende Musik; subtile Choreographie (2 putzen sich die Nase, während 3 andere sich das Kinn kratzen); das Geräusch von Menschen, die nachdenken; ein Telefon; ein Verkaufskatalog; ein Kundenbetreuungsteam, das eingehende Bestellungen bearbeitet
Wie lange: 60-minütiger Loop

Tashi Iwaoka (bestellt 2000, Lieferung empfangen 2001):
Woran ich mich bei *I Can* zunächst erinnere, ist, dass ich auf einem hölzernen, einem Pferd ähnelnden Objekt saß, während ich auf die Ankunft von Gob Squad wartete. Ich erinnere mich, dass ich etwas früher als verabredet im Podewil eintraf. Ich war sehr neugierig zu sehen, wie und woher sie auftauchen würden.

Es war mindestens ein Jahr vergangen seit der *I Can*-Ausstellung in der Angel Row Gallery in Nottingham, wo ich

first person who had actually purchased an *I Can*. My friend had also ordered an *I Can* for her friend's birthday but for some reason it wasn't possible to deliver it on that day, so she cancelled her order.

Two of Gob Squad appeared from the stairs looking smart (maybe in black? This memory is not sure). I think it was around £3. I told them I had forgotten to change DM into pounds but they were prepared for that situation (how professional!) and said it was OK to pay in DM. I think I asked them if I was able to get my money back just to pull their legs. They said if I wasn't satisfied they would do it again. (It was something like sticking a pen up her nose..? Where's my memory?) I did not claim my money back. The whole

meine Bestellung aufgegeben hatte. Ich war sehr aufgeregt, als ich erfuhr, ich sei die erste Person, die tatsächlich ein *I Can* erstanden hatte. Meine Freundin hatte ebenfalls ein *I Can* zum Geburtstag ihrer Freundin bestellt, aber aus irgendeinem Grund war es nicht möglich gewesen, es an dem Tag zu liefern, deshalb stornierte sie ihre Bestellung.

Zwei von Gob Squad erschienen auf der Treppe, sie sahen schick aus (vielleicht in Schwarz? Bei dieser Erinnerung bin ich mir nicht sicher.) Ich glaube, es kostete so um die 3 Pfund. Ich sagte ihnen, ich hätte vergessen, DM in Pfund umzutauschen, aber darauf waren sie vorbereitet (wie professionell!), und es war in Ordnung, in DM zu zahlen. Ich glaube, ich fragte sie noch, ob es eine Möglichkeit gäbe,

thing (what should it be called? A performance? A purchase? A business?) did not take very long and I remember the picture was supposed to be sent to me via e-mail. Was it? (my memory is not so reliable) If so, where has it gone? I'm still waiting for it.

mein Geld zurückzubekommen, nur um sie auf den Arm zu nehmen. Sie sagten, wenn ich nicht zufrieden sei, würden sie es nochmal wiederholen. (Es war irgendwas in der Art wie, sich einen Stift in die Nase zu stecken ...?) Ich verlangte mein Geld nicht zurück. Das ganze Ding (wie sollte man das nennen? Eine Performance? Einen Kauf? Ein Geschäft?) dauerte nicht lang. Und ich erinnere mich, ich sollte das Bild dann per E-Mail bekommen. (War das so? Mein Gedächtnis ist nicht besonders verlässlich.) Wenn es so war, wo ist es dann hingekommen? Ich warte immer noch darauf.

WHAT ARE YOU LOOKING AT? (1998)

I can always find someone
To say they symphatize
If I wear my heart out on my sleeve,
But I don't want some pretty face
To tell me pretty lies
All I want is someone to believe
Honesty is such a lonely word
Everyone is so untrue,
Honesty is hardly ever heard
And mostly what I need from you.
(song lyrics by/Liedtext von Billy Joel)

Where: A room made of two-way mirrored perspex. Audience (outside) can see in; performers (inside) only see their own reflections
Who: A gang of Goths or Ravers setting up a fondue; American teenagers dressed up for the prom, off their faces on something illegal; the local tennis club having a right knees-up; a bunch of black polo-necked intellectuals singing along to Britney; a group of performers working out what to do next
What: 1 record player; a huge stack of records (anything and everything from Elton John to Public Enemy to Black Sabbath to Sugababes); an unhealthy quantity of booze (lager, wine, gin, absinth, you name it...); heartfelt singing; party games

Wo: ein Raum aus beidseitig verspiegeltem Glas. Publikum (außen) kann reinschauen; Darsteller (innen) sehen nichts als ihr eigenes Spiegelbild
Wer: eine Gang von Gruftis oder Ravern, die ein Fondue zubereiten; amerikanische Teenager, angezogen für den Prom-Ball, vollgepumpt mit irgendwas Illegalem; der örtliche Tennis-Verein, der eine Sause hat; eine Gruppe Intellektueller in schwarzen Rollkragenpullovern, die lautstark Britney-Spears-Songs mitsingen; eine Gruppe von Darstellern, die sich überlegen, was sie als Nächstes tun sollen
Was: 1 Plattenspieler; ein großer Stapel Platten (alles von Elton John über Public Enemy, Herbert Grönemeyer bis hin

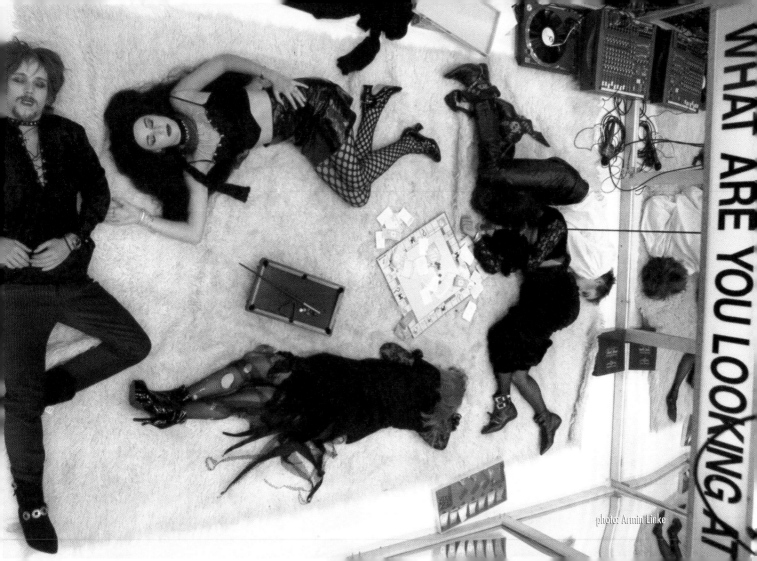

WHAT ARE YOU LOOKING AT

photo: Armin Linke

(twister, charades, boules, strip poker); 2 mics, 1 effects box set to "Reverb: large cathedral"; 18 pulsing light bulbs; 1 Mobile phone; 1 TV; videos for a night in with the boys (Predator 2, Lethal Weapon 3, Asian Babes 4); magazines for a night in with the girls (Take A Break, Hello, Gala); 1 illuminated "What Are You Looking At?" sign; a comfy rug; living room or garden furniture; various props and nicknacks (assorted tennis rackets, plastic flowers, party poppers, filthy ashtrays, bowls of peanuts, disposable cameras, Christmas decorations, cakes, plates of cheese, pens, beer-stained cushions, broken glasses); stupid dance routines, a séance, a holiday slide show; someone asleep behind the sofa
How long: 4–6 hours

Nikola Duric:

Sean Patten once said that it would have been completely sufficient if Gob Squad had just made the piece *What Are You Looking At?* As nearly every modern festival and performance venue from Baghdad to Baden Baden wanted to have this piece. *What Are You Looking At?* was performed until finally Simon Will during a get out in 2002, chucked the screws (which had held the glass cage together and were worn to stumps) into the corner

In 1998 everyone who wanted to have anything to do with Pop Theory was running around in the Berlin Biennale congress. In the club, Turntable Terranova was playing records,

zu Black Sabbath and Sugababes); eine ungesunde Menge an alkoholischen Getränken (Bier, Wein, Gin, Absinth, was auch immer du willst …); Mitsingen (aus vollem Herzen); Partyspiele (Twister, Scharade, Boules, Strip Poker); 2 Mikrophone, 1 Effektgerät (eingestellt auf „Hall: große Kathedrale"); 18 pulsierende Glühbirnen; 1 Mobiltelefon; 1 TV; Videos für eine Nacht mit den Jungs (Predator 2, Lethal Weapon 3, Heiße Girls in der Karibik 4); Zeitschriften für einen Abend mit den Mädchen (Gala, Brautmoden, Strickmuster); 1 erleuchtetes Schild mit der Aufschrift „What Are You Looking At?"; ein gemütlicher Teppich; Wohnzimmer- oder Gartenmöbel; diverse Requisiten und Nippes (eine Auswahl von Tennisschlägern, Plastikblumen, Partyknaller, dreckige Aschenbecher, Erdnüsse, Einwegkameras, Weihnachtsdekoration, Kuchen, Käseteller, Stifte, bierbefleckte Kissen, kaputte Gläser); alberne Tänze, eine Geisterbeschwörung, eine Diashow; jemand, der eingeschlafen ist hinter dem Sofa
Wie lange: 4–6 Stunden

Nikola Duric:

Sean Patten sagte einmal, dass es völlig ausreichend gewesen wäre, wenn Gob Squad nur das Stück *What Are You Looking At?* gemacht hätten. Fast jedes moderne Festival und viele Aufführungsorte wollten dieses Stück haben. Von Bagdad bis Baden-Baden. *What Are You Looking At?* wurde gespielt, bis Simon Will schließlich beim Abbau 2002 die stumpf gewordenen Spaxe, die den Glaskäfig zusammengehalten hatten, Richtung Müllecke pfefferte.

holding each one up in the air that was a success on the dance floor. Screams. Rewind. Again.

In a somewhat hidden part of the foyer, Gob Squad had built a mysterious glass room. At approximately 11 o'clock the lights came on inside and the magic began. The lighting technician, Hagen Gottschalck from Giessen, had seen a documentary film just before the production about a Berlin inventor who had found the formula for an everlasting light bulb. Out of fear about turnover losses no large company wanted to give this invention a patent, and so its inventor had to get thousands of light bulbs made somewhere in the East, before dying in dubious circumstances. His lighting design was an homage to this man. From the ceiling of the glazed room large transparent light bulbs hung at different heights, their tungsten spirals visible, distributing warm light. The task, which Gob Squad now achieves with a video and sound mixing-desk, was at that time fulfilled by the light bulbs and used as a dramaturgical instrument and instigator of overall rhythm. They flickered, changed their light intensity and seemed to have a life of their own. Again and again when a scene reached its high point it came to a complete blackout and the lights came on in the auditorium. For a few seconds the exterior of the glass case became reflective and the voyeurs saw themselves. Afterwards, the light seeped once more into the box, and the performers suddenly stood very near the panes of glass, now transparent again, close enough to kiss but nevertheless far away from the world that they observed.

1998, Berlin Biennale. In der schwangeren Auster liefen alle rum, die etwas mit Pop-Theorie zu tun haben wollten. Im Club legten gerade Turntable Terranova auf und hielten das Cover jeder Platte, die auf der Tanzfläche gut ankam, in die Luft. Geschrei, Backspin, noch mal.

In einem etwas versteckten Teil des Foyers hatten Gob Squad einen geheimnisvollen Glasraum aufgebaut. Um etwa 23 Uhr gingen darin die Lichter an und der Zauber begann. Der Lichttechniker, Hagen Gottschalck aus Gießen, hatte kurz vor der Produktion einen Dokumentarfilm über einen Berliner Erfinder gesehen, der die Formel für eine ewig leuchtende Glühbirne errechnet hatte. Aus Angst vor Umsatzverlusten wollte keine große Firma dieses Patent in Produktion geben, und so ließ ihr Erfinder einige tausend Birnen irgendwo im Osten fertigen, bevor er unter dubiosen Umständen verstarb. Sein Lichtdesign war eine Hommage an diesen Mann. Von der Decke des verglasten Raumes hingen auf unterschiedlicher Höhe große durchsichtige Glühbirnen mit sichtbaren Wolframspiralen und verbreiteten warmes Licht. Die Aufgabe, die heute bei Gob Squad das Video- und Tonmischpult als dramaturgisches Instrument und Rhythmusgeber innehat, erfüllten damals die Glühbirnen. Sie flackerten, änderten ihre Lichtstärke und schienen ein gewisses Eigenleben zu führen. Und immer wieder, wenn eine Szene ihrem Höhepunkt entgegenstrebte, kam es zu einem vollständigen Black und im Zuschauerraum ging das Licht an. Für Sekunden war die Außenseite des Glaskastens verspiegelt und die Voyeure sahen sich selbst.

The action happening in the glass case used the costumes as a starting point. There was the high school graduation party, the conspiratorial meetings of existentialist artists or a hard rock fest in leathers and chains. When the clothes seemed to reinforce the stereotypes, Gob Squad were always careful to disrupt them through the introduction of unusual material. In the high school scene a porno video was playing on small monitor in the background. The dolled up hard rocker danced to Josh Wink's raucous anthem "Higher State of Consciousness" rather than to guitar excesses.

In 2002 I was allowed to take part in two shows. Another basic element (aside from the commentarial light and costumes) was a sort of simple karaoke machine. The action in the glazed space was interrupted again and again by the actors playing a favourite record and singing along to it. I had underestimated this aspect of the evening and totally disgraced myself with Wham's "Wake Me Up Before You Go-Go". Later, when the atmosphere was jollier, I tried the Chicks on Speed version of "Kaltes Klares Wasser" (cold clear water). Simple German lyrics, but still too few words in order to really sing along with. So I poured a whole bottle of Evian over my head. I suggested, "Who Let the Dogs Out?" as a last song. To the barking on the record, Johanna, Sarah, Sean, Simon and I all threw ourselves onto all fours, sniffed the others, then in the chaotic finale we bit through the record cover, gulped down the punch or pissed on the mixing desk.

Anschließend schlenderte das Licht wieder in die Box, und die Performer standen plötzlich ganz nah an den nun abermals durchsichtigen Scheiben, close enough to kiss and doch weit weg von der sie betrachtenden Welt.

Das Handlungsgeschehen im Glaskasten selbst wurde von den Kostümen aus entwickelt. Es gab High-School-Abschlussfeste, verschwörerische Treffen von existenzialistischen Künstlern oder Hard-Rock-Gelage in Leder und Ketten. Immer waren Gob Squad jedoch darauf bedacht, mit den Vorgaben, welche die Kleidung vorzuschreiben schien, zu brechen und stilfremde Mittel einzusetzen: In der High-School-Szenerie liefen en passant Porno-Videos auf einem kleinen Monitor. Die aufgebrezelten Hard-Rocker tanzten eher zu Josh Winks Sägezahn-Hymne „Higher State of Conciousness" als zu Gitarren-Eskapaden.

2002 durfte ich in zwei Shows mitmachen. Ein weiteres tragendes Element, neben dem kommentierenden Licht und den Kostümen, war eine Art simple Karaoke-Maschine. Immer wieder wurde die Handlung im Glasraum unterbrochen. Die Akteure legten eine Lieblingsplatte auf und sangen dazu. Ich hatte diesen Aspekt des Abends unterschätzt und blamierte mich bei Whams „Wake Me Up Before You Go-go" bis auf die Knochen. Später, bei ausgelassenerer Stimmung, versuchte ich mich noch an der Chicks on Speed Version von „Kaltes klares Wasser". Einfacher, deutschsprachiger Text, aber eben dann doch zu wenig Worte, um richtig mitzusingen. Also schüttete ich mir eine ganze Evian-Flasche über

What Are You Looking At? managed to be simple like a party, amusing like a child's birthday and at the same time as serious and sublime as a piece of beautiful choreography. The spectators never knew what would happen next, and frequently it was the same for the performers. In this way it was also an exciting piece for the actors. Like the telephone call of a stranger, who, dialling the wrong number and without prompting, tells great stories off the cuff. *What Are You Looking At?* was a seductive mixture of private and public, normality and sensationalism. It was everyday life as state of emergency and therefore exactly what reality shows fail at all the time because they only show permanent competition, the worst part of everyday life.

Gob Squad do not only create and reflect upon the present they also let the world outside penetrate unfiltered into their universe. The evenings that Gob Squad make are equal in quality to the contemporary cinema films showing during their rehearsal phases. If the Euro Top Ten rocks in an unusual way at the moment, that is the best time for a good Gob Squad production. What the sun and the rain are to a good wine, the music charts, magazines, cinema, literature and sometimes perhaps the performances of their friends She She Pop and Showcase Beat Le Mot are to Gob Squad shows.

den Kopf. Als letzten Song hatte ich „Who Let the Dogs Out?" vorgeschlagen. Zu dem Hundegebell auf der Platte warfen wir uns, Johanna, Sarah, Sean, Simon und ich, auf alle Viere, beschnupperten die anderen, um dann im chaotischen Finale Plattencover zu zerbeißen, die Bowle auszuschlürfen oder ans Mischpult zu pinkeln.

What Are You Looking At? schaffte es, einfach zu sein wie eine Party, amüsant wie ein Kindergeburtstag und gleichzeitig ernst und erhaben wie eine schöne Choreografie. Die Zuschauer wussten nie, was als Nächstes passieren würde, und häufig ging es den Akteuren genauso, deshalb war es auch ein spannendes Stück für die Darsteller selbst. Wie der Telefonanruf eines Fremden, der sich verwählt hat, aber ungefragt gute Geschichten aus dem Ärmel schüttelt. *What Are You Looking At?* war eine attraktive Mischung aus Privatem und Inszeniertem, Normalität und Sensation. Es war der Alltag als Ausnahmezustand, und damit genau das, was Reality-Show-Macher ein ums andere Mal verfehlen, weil sie nur den schlechtesten Teil des Alltags, den permanenten Konkurrenzkampf, zur Schau stellen.

Gob Squad erzeugen und reflektieren die Gegenwart nicht nur, sie lassen die Welt da draußen auch ungefiltert in ihr Universum eindringen. Die Abende von Gob Squad sind immer so gut, wie die parallele Qualität von gerade laufenden Kinofilmen während ihrer Probephasen. Rockt gerade die Euro-Top-Ten auf ungewöhnliche Weise, so ist das die beste Zeit für eine gute Gob-Squad-Produktion. Was für

photo: Bettina Blümner

Uta Schnell/Alf Thum:

At the turn of the century, on the occasion of a world exhibition in a town in Lower Saxony a problem arose due to the fact that all countries were participating except for one, the United States of America. It had reserved a not inconsiderable plot but then did not come. The organisers' hectic thinking began: what should be there? With 150 days to comply?

Tom Stromberg was at that time a culture boss and wanted to be a problem solver. He suggested showing a Mega-size, XXL 150 day version of *What Are You Looking At?* Gob Squad submitted a project description and budget (150 days in a mirrored box, 6 performers, 8 hours daily, a shift system, a record player, a refrigerator, a kitchenette) to the world exhibition. Absolutely fitting. Absolutely world class the only problem was that they were looking at being in the box for five months. We were worried.

It was not realized. It was allegedly too expensive. On the plot they placed a mobile Mongolian yurt. A sort of antique central Asian caravan.

einen guten Jahrgangswein die Sonne und der Regen sind, das sind für Stücke von Gob Squad die Charts, die Zeitschriften, das Kino, die Literatur und vielleicht ein bisschen auch die anderen Theaterstücke ihrer Freunde von She She Pop oder Showcase Beat Le Mot.

Uta Schnell/Alf Thum:

Um die Jahrtausendwende, anlässlich einer Weltausstellung in einer niedersächsischen Kleinstadt, ergab sich das Problem, dass alle Länder teilnahmen bis auf eines: die Vereinigten Staaten von Amerika. Man hatte eine nicht unbeträchtliche Fläche reserviert, aber sie kamen nicht. Bei den Funktionären setzte ein hektisches Nachdenken ein: was soll dahin – 150 days to comply?

Stromberg war damals Kulturchef und wollte Problemlöser sein. Er schlug vor, eine Ultramaximum XXL-150-Tage-Version von *What Are You Looking At?* zu zeigen. Gob Squad reichten dafür Konzept und Kalkulation ein. 150 Tage im Spiegelkasten, 6 Performer, 8 Stunden täglich, Schichtsystem, Plattenspieler, Kühlschrank, Kochnische – auf der Weltausstellung. Absolut passend, absolutes Weltniveau – nur, dass die fünf Monate im Kasten sitzen. Da haben wir uns Sorgen gemacht.

Es ist nicht realisiert worden, da angeblich zu teuer. Auf der Fläche wurde eine fahrbare mongolische Riesenjurte, quasi ein antiker zentralasiatischer Caravan, hingestellt.

SAFE (1999)

I'm on my way now...
I've left everything behind, everything. I've left my boyfriend, my car, my flat, my cat. All my records, my books, my shoes... and my shower curtain.
And there are these people in front of me, smiling. And they're so beautiful. Their hair, it's so silky... and their skin, so soft and smooth. And their fingernails...
their nails are just perfect. These people really are angels, not from this world. And somehow — I don't know why, they make me feel really... really... safe.

Where: a stage
Who: 6 wannabes; a comic pilot; a reassuring stewardess; a beauty queen "Miss Catastrophe" (several costume changes); a cocktail shaking barman; a drummer who has lost her sense of rhythm; a man in a bunny costume, faking a guitar solo; a man discovering the meaning of rock; 6 air stewards playing air guitars
What: 1 Electric Guitar, 1 Bass, 1 Drum kit, 1 Synthesizer, 2 verses, 1 chorus of "We Will Rock You", 2 verses, 2 choruses of "Rocking All Over The World", 2 choruses, 2 verses of "Über den Wolken" (Heavy Metal version), 2 choruses, 2 verses of "I Believe I Can Fly"; 1 bar with various alcoholic drinks, cocktail umbrellas; semicircular steps that light up when you step on them; a frame of showbiz lights; 1 big projection screen, a continuous projected backdrop (free fall, disaster movie montages, fireworks, tropical beaches, anxious Bunnies, applauding crowds, open hearts and explosions); 1 energetic dance routine; 40 fake plastic flowers placed under audience seats to throw on stage; 3 staged

Wo: eine Bühne
Wer: 6 Möchtegern-Rockstars; ein komödiantischer Pilot; eine beruhigende Stewardess; eine Schönheitskönigin „Miss Katastrophe" (mehrere Kostümwechsel); ein cocktail-shakender Barmann; eine Schlagzeugerin, die ihr Rhythmus-gefühl verloren hat; ein Mann in einem Hasenkostüm, der ein Gitarrensolo vortäuscht; ein Mann, der die Bedeutung von Rock entdeckt; 6 Flugbegleiter, die Luftgitarre spielen
Was: 1 E-Gitarre, 1 Bass, 1 Schlagzeug, 1 Synthesizer, 2 Stro-phen und 1 Refrain von „We Will Rock You", 2 Strophen und 2 Refrains von „Rocking All Over The World", 2 Refrains, 2 Strophen von „Über den Wolken" (Heavy Metal-Fassung), 2 Refrains, 2 Strophen von „I Believe I Can Fly"; 1 Bar mit di-versen alkoholischen Getränken und Cocktailschirmchen; halbrunde Treppen, die aufleuchten, wenn man auf sie tritt; ein Rahmen aus Showbizlichtern; 1 große Projektions-leinwand; ein ständiger Hintergrund aus projizierten Bil-dern (freier Fall, Katastrophenfilmcollagen, Feuerwerk, tro-pische Sandstrände, ängstliche Hasen, applaudierende

It feels good to relax

photo: Christina von Haugwitz

"band deaths"; 1 Hal Hartley film quote; model cars, houses, farmyard animals, people and planes; 3 cans of hairspray, stupid sunglasses, black PVC trousers and miniskirt, 1 Hawaiian shirt, 1 brown velvet suit, 1 dress which looks like a garden
How long: 75 minutes

Jordan McKenzie:

... safe and sound ...safe as houses ... safe as a butcher´s dog... Apparently there had been some kind of war (possibly nuclear, but then again it could have been the destruction of the death star by Luke, who knows ...) It was a long time ago, on a forgotten planet in a distant universe, but even if I had seen the Gob Squad's production of *Safe* yesterday I would still have walked away with that same feeling of fragmentation, that disturbing feeling of cultural vertigo that the Gobs manage to achieve even in the setting of a traditional theatre space. My memory recalls the piece as if I have a theatrical remote control and the screen (stage, performers) is constantly flipping through its channels. Bad REM, Scissor Sisters pop band ... a distraught fairy running after a stage light willo' the wisp ... Jimi Hendrix air stewards ... I believe I can fly ... other stuff ...

The reason why I enjoyed *Safe* so much was because it wasn't afraid to trip itself up, to poke fun, to attempt to sing R Kelly without irony. It's as if they are saying, look, we know that we can present critiques of popular culture, talk about

Massen, offene Herzen und Explosionen); 1 energetischer Tanz; 40 Plastikblumen unter den Sitzen der ersten Reihen, um sie auf die Bühne zu werfen; 3 inszenierte „Tode" der Band; 1 Zitat aus einem Hal-Hartley-Film; Spielzeugautos, Häuser, Bauernhoftiere, Menschen und Flugzeuge; 3 Dosen Haarspray, alberne Sonnenbrillen, schwarze PVC-Hosen und 1 Minirock, 1 Hawaiihemd, 1 brauner Samtanzug, 1 Garten als Kleid
Wie lange: 75 Minuten

Jordan McKenzie:

... sicher ist sicher ... im sicheren Hafen ... sicher wie in Abrahams Schoß... Anscheinend hatte es irgendeine Art Krieg gegeben (vielleicht einen nuklearen, aber, wer weiß, es hätte auch die Zerstörung des Todessterns durch Luke Skywalker sein können...) Es war vor langer Zeit, auf einem vergessenen Planeten in einem entfernten Universum, aber selbst wenn ich Gob Squads Produktion *Safe* erst gestern gesehen hätte, hätte ich sie mit demselben Gefühl von Fragmentierung verlassen, diesem verstörenden kulturellen Schwindelgefühl, das die Mitglieder von Gob Squad sogar im Rahmen eines traditionellen Theaterraums erzeugen können.
In meiner Erinnerung ist das Stück, als ob ich eine theatrale Fernbedienung habe, und der Bildschirm (die Bühne, die Performer) schaltet unablässig durch die Kanäle. Die schlechte REM-, Scissor-Sisters-Pop-Band ... eine verstörte Fee, die hinter einem irrlichternden Bühnenspot herläuft

hegemony, deliver socially and artistically aware messages about globalisation … but this is our culture and we are not apart from it, we take it on, with all its beauty and faults.Gob Squad take on the areas of popular culture that other parts of the worthier performance art world are too afraid of.

OK … maybe I can put it another way … seeing *Safe* was a bit like the ending of the *Truman Show* where he bumps into the horizon … but what the Gob Squad do is show you the door and the horizon both at the same time but the major difference is – unlike the film – the door is no more 'real' than the sky … they ask you to believe in both.
I believe I can fly … watch me running through that open do or or …

Johan Reyniers:
I remember the line from *Safe*: "You may not know the words, but I'll sing them for you." I noted it down at the time.

Philip Bither:
My memories of *Safe*: Post-apocalypse disaster – scenes of kitsch and carnage and a run-down bar illuminated only by the glaring light of a survivor's flashlight, revealing, piece by piece, fragments of this wrecked world. Moving back in time to the alternating ludicrous and poignant lives of these over-blown wannabe rock stars. Slow-mo air guitar on video played by musicians turned airline stewardess/stewards in an erie, empty air terminal. Fake flowers thrown by the

… Jimi-Hendrix-Flugbegleiter … I believe I can fly … und anderes Zeug …

Safe gefiel mir so gut, weil es keine Angst hatte, sich selbst ein Bein zu stellen, sich lustig zu machen, zu versuchen, R Kelly ohne Ironie zu singen. Es ist so, als würden Gob Squad sagen, wir wissen, dass wir zeitgenössische Kritik von Populärkultur präsentieren, über Hegemonie sprechen und sozialkritische, künstlerische Botschaften über Globalisierung abliefern können … aber das hier ist unsere Kultur, und wir sind nicht davon abgetrennt, wir nehmen sie an mit all ihrer Schönheit und ihren Fehlern. Sie widmen sich Bereichen der populären Kultur, vor denen andere Teile der anständigeren Performance-Kunst zurückschrecken.

Okay … vielleicht kann ich es anders ausdrücken … *Safe* zu sehen war ein bisschen wie das Ende der *Truman Show*, wo er an den Horizont stößt, aber was Gob Squad machen, ist, dir die Tür und den Horizont zugleich zu zeigen, der Hauptunterschied ist allerdings – anders als im Film –, die Tür ist nicht „realer" als der Himmel … du bist aufgefordert, an beides zu glauben.
I believe I can fly … watch me running through that open do or or …

Johan Reyniers:
Ich erinnere mich an den Satz aus *Safe*: „You may not know the words, but I'll sing them for you." Habe ich damals auch aufgeschrieben.

band out to the audience, landing on our feet. A critique of our popular and shallow culture, yet understanding and empathetic of the ecstasy and adrenaline that parts of that culture can give us.

Philip Bither:

Meine Erinnerung an *Safe:* Eine post-apokalyptische Katastrophe – Szenen von Kitsch und Gewalt und eine runtergekommene Bar, beleuchtet vom blendenden Licht der Taschenlampe eines Überlebenden, die, Stück für Stück, Fragmente dieser zerstörten Welt enthüllt. Die durch die Zeit zurückführt zu den mal lächerlichen, mal eindringlichen Lebensgeschichten dieser überzeichneten Möchtegern-Rockstars. Luftgitarre in Zeitlupe auf Video, gespielt von Musikern, die sich in Stewards/Stewardessen einer Fluglinie verwandelten in einem unheimlichen, verlassenen Flughafen-Terminal. Künstliche Blumen, die die Band ins Publikum warf und die zu unseren Füßen landeten. Eine Kritik unserer seichten Populärkultur, und doch verständig und einfühlsam gegenüber der Ekstase und dem Adrenalinrausch, in die sie uns manchmal versetzt.

SAY IT LIKE YOU MEAN IT (2000)

Ladies and Gentlemen, tonight we're going to claim back our emotions. I woke up this morning and I thought, "Today I'm going to live life to the max" and I felt a bit cheesy because "live life to the max" is a slogan for Pepsi. But now that the world has ended, that doesn't matter anymore

Where: a large white marquee (deep within a fictional forest populated by wolves and bears …or a theatre)
Who: a team of post-apocalypse survivalists, dressed in wellies and white suits
What: 6 bottles of the cheapest vodka you can lay your hands on, 1 bottle of Grenadine, 3 large measures of coconut liqueur, 2 cartons of orange juice, 90 plastic cups with "trust us" written on them; 1 very long loud explosion; 1 garden arch, 1 "Hollywood Swing", 1 small paddling pool with water fountain and smoke pellets (the genesis project); 9 Swiss Rolls, marzipan, icing sugar, various cake decorations; tin foil, 12 small rolls of sellotape, 8 rolls of large sellotape, approximately 24 rolls of wallpaper (various), lots of used cardboard boxes, chalk, felt tips, ribbon, toilet roll, balloons, cotton wool; 5 rousing speeches; 1 continuous soundtrack starting with 60s hits, ending with 90s hits and organised so that the beats per minute increase throughout the night; 14 chinese paper lanterns with lights on a chaser sequence; 1 made up song, sang without accompaniment to the tune of Ave Maria; 12 Headphones, 12 peepholes, 1 cordless mic, one inside-out commentary; various secret messages; 1

Wo: ein großes, weißes Festzelt (… tief im Herzen eines imaginären Waldes, der von Wölfen und Bären bewohnt wird … oder in einem Theater)
Wer: ein Team von Überlebenden in weißen Anzügen und Gummistiefeln
Was: 6 Flaschen des billigsten Wodkas, den man finden kann, 1 Flasche Grenadine, 3 große Einheiten Kokosnusslikör, 2 Packungen Orangensaft, 90 Plastikbecher, mit der Aufschrift „Trust us" („Vertrau uns"); 1 sehr lange und laute Explosion; 1 Laubenbogen, 1 Hollywood-Schaukel, 1 Planschbecken mit Springbrunnen und Rauchtabletten (das "Genesis-Projekt"); 9 Biskuitrollen, Marzipan, Puderzucker, diverse Kuchendekorationen; Alufolie, 12 kleine Rollen Tesafilm, 8 große Rollen Tesafilm, ungefähr 24 Rollen Tapete (verschiedene Muster), viele leere Pappkartons, Kreide, Filzstifte, Geschenkband, Toilettenpapier, Luftballons, Wattebälle; 5 bewegende Reden; 1 Soundtrack, der mit Hits der 60er beginnt und mit Hits der 90er endet und dessen Beats per minute sich kontinuierlich steigern; 14 große, pulsierende Reisball-Lampen; 1 erfundenes Lied, das ohne Begleitung zu der Melodie von Ave Maria gesungen wird; 12 Kopfhörer,

made up ritual, 1 made up pledge; 1 group photograph of everyone there, 1 video printer; 1 video camera to playback stills of the night

How long: 90–120 minutes

Matt Watkins:

Having been invited into a tent in the middle of "a forest" populated by ghetto blaster wolves and walkman birds, we meet the Gob Squad in their usual, "we really want you to like us" mode. Welcoming us all in. Inviting us to join a party (drinks provided). Asking you to help by putting out chairs and tables and generally putting you at ease making you feel like you're part of something sweet and fun.

The theme of camping, of everybody mucking in for the common good seems to be a recurring feature of Gob Squad's work, but as everybody knows camping is always a mixture of Famous Five jolly japes and Nuts in May nightmares. There are always dark clouds forming over that game of swing ball and the Dr Who special effects bubbling in Gob Squad's paddling pool are a vital clue.

A huge barrage of sound and visuals creates the most visceral and unnerving end of the world scenario I've ever experienced. The sounds of metal shearing off combined with explosions that seemed to layer painfully over each other. Playing just that little bit to long and loud to leave any of the assembled a party in any doubt that this is serious,

12 Sehschlitze, 1 drahtloses Mikrofon, ein Live-Kommentar; diverse heimliche Botschaften; 1 erfundenes Ritual, 1 erfundener Schwur; 1 Gruppenbild von allen Anwesenden, 1 Videodrucker; 1 Videokamera, die Fotos aufnimmt und als Diashow wiedergibt

Wie lange: 90–120 Minuten

Matt Watkins:

Eingeladen in ein Zelt mitten in einem „Wald", bevölkert von Ghettoblaster-Wölfen und Walkman-Vögeln, treffen wir auf Gob Squad in ihrer gewohnten „Wir möchten, dass ihr uns gern habt"-Manier. Sie heißen uns willkommen. Laden uns ein zu einer Party (Getränke inbegriffen). Bitten uns, beim Aufbauen von Stühlen und Tischen zu helfen und versetzen uns ganz allgemein in das wohlige Gefühl, Teil von etwas Nettem und Lustigem zu sein.

Das Camping-Credo „Alle mit anpacken für die gemeinsame Sache!" scheint ein wiederkehrendes Motiv im Werk von Gob Squad zu sein. Aber bekanntlich ist Camping eine Mischung aus fröhlichen Streichen mit den *Fünf Freunden* und *Nuts-In-May-Albträumen*[1]. Immer brauen sich dunkle Wolken über dem Federballspiel zusammen, und die Spezialeffekte von Dr. Who, die in Gob Squads Planschbecken Blasen schlagen, lassen das schon erahnen.

Ein gewaltiger Schwall aus Ton und Bild erzeugt das emotionalste und enervierendste Weltuntergangs-Szenario, das

that they mean it.

It's easy to be glib and knowing about something so clichéd but there wasn't a single sly wink or attempt to make light of an immense soundscape. Everything stops and I'm reprogrammed ready for phase 2.

In a state of shock it's back to Gob Squad's after the bang party. Encouraged by some to build weapons of mass destruction and others to create more peaceful tools, we are transplanted to a naïve world of cardboard tubes and sellotape where we build our world anew, even though dark forces haunt the outside of our tent.

There something about a sort of enforced playtime in the aftermath of such a sensory assault which is faintly ridiculous but great at the same time. You feel part of it. You are surrounded by performers and audience alike who seem to be the only people left. Even if it is just for now and you know that Friday night is still going on out there and this is all primary school make believe. But for now let's pretend. You can't be sure in all the chaos that they has still got a grip on what's going on but you like it and that shoddiness draws you in further, until you almost forget that Sean is not Sean, Berit is not Berit, Johanna is not Johanna.

I have probably made it clear that I like this piece by now, and I do. It will always feel like one of the most rewarding performance events I've been to, because you never knew exactly where it all begins and ends. And like the class

ich jemals erlebt habe. Das Geräusch von berstendem Metall kombiert mit Explosionen, die sich schmerzhaft überlagern schienen währt genau so viel zu lang und zu laut, um in der versammelten Party-Gesellschaft niemanden mehr im Unklaren zu lassen, dass es ernst ist, dass sie es ernst meinen. Es ist schlau und abgehoben zu sein mit etwas so Klischeehaftem, aber es gab kein einziges Blinzeln oder den Versuch, die gewaltige Tonebene abzuschwächen. Alles stoppt, und ich bin umprogrammiert, bereit für Phase 2.

Noch im Schockzustand, finden wir uns wieder auf Gob Squads Weltuntergangs-Party. Einige rufen uns zur Herstellung von Massenvernichtungswaffen auf, andere zur Anfertigung friedlicherer Werkzeuge. Wir werden in eine naive Welt aus Pappe und Tesafilm versetzt, woraus wir unsere Welt neu erbauen, obwohl draußen vor unserem Zelt dunkle Mächte lauern.

Es ist etwas Lächerliches, aber zugleich auch Großartiges an dieser Art erzwungener Spiel-Zeit unter den Nachwirkungen einer solchen sensorischen Attacke. Man nimmt Anteil. Man ist gleichsam umgeben von Performern und Zuschauern, die die letzten Überlebenden zu sein scheinen. Auch wenn es nur für den Augenblick ist und man weiß, dass die Freitagnacht da draußen weitergeht und das alles nur Kindergarten-Spiele sind: Lasst uns für den Moment so tun als ob. In dem ganzen Chaos kann man nicht sicher sein, dass Gob Squad noch irgendwas im Griff hat, aber es ist liebenswert und das Flickwerk zieht einen immer weiter

photos: Friedemann Simon

photo we recieve as we leave, it's all slightly fuzzy and indistinct, stupid and meaningful at the same time and it stays with you. A bit like a great night at a club or a festival where you feel (and this is usually something to do with the drugs, but not totally) that you did something with a group of people half of whom you never spoke to, but you felt like you all contributed to a shared moment of madness.

I still keep my memento and my scars in the form of a favourite shirt ruined with streaks of packing tape glue, completely resistant to all washing powders. The result of Simon Will inspired bravado, an arm mounted cardboard bazooka or something.

Mark Waugh:
The memory of *Say It Like You Mean It* is still spinning in the fragmented light of that apocalyptic disco. For me the show began with an idea. What would it be like if the millennium party you attended ended up as an end of the world party?

In the queue I met with Steve Slater whom I have known since the late 80's but I hadn't seen him in about 5 years. It was great to see him but he seemed troubled. He told me his mother was critically ill. There were other people we both knew there and I think the support and empathy of friends was what he needed.

rein, bis man fast vergisst, dass Sean nicht Sean ist, Berit nicht Berit und Johanna nicht Johanna.

Es ist inzwischen wohl schon klar geworden, dass ich dieses Stück sehr mag. Es wird für mich immer eines der bereicherndsten Performance-Erlebnisse bleiben, weil man nie genau wusste, wo das anfängt und wo es endet. Und wie das Klassenfoto, das man zum Abschied bekommt, ist alles ein bisschen verschwommen und unscharf, albern und bedeutsam zugleich. Es bleibt einem im Kopf. So ähnlich wie eine tolle Clubnacht oder ein Festival, wo man den Eindruck zurückbehält (und das hat oft was mit Drogen zu tun, aber nicht nur), man hat etwas mit einer Gruppe von Leuten erlebt, und mit der Hälfte hat man vielleicht nicht mal gesprochen, aber man fühlt sich, als ob alle zu einem gemeinsamen Moment des Wahnsinns beigetragen haben.

Meine Erinnerung und meine Narben bewahre ich in Form eines Lieblingshemdes auf, das mit Klebstoff-Streifen von Paketband versaut wurde, die absolut resistent sind gegen jedes Waschpulver. Spuren eines durch Simon Will inspirierten Bravados, ein tragbares Maschinengewehr aus Pappe oder so was Ähnliches.

1 „Nuts In May" ist ein komischer und in seiner genauen Beobachtung schmerzhafter Film von Mike Leigh (1976), in dem ein Pärchen campen geht und herausfindet, daß es nicht einfach ist, tolerant zu sein, wenn andere nicht die gleichen Überzeugungen teilen.

But it did seem to bizarrely mix into the concept of the show. We went inside a tent that was totally ready to rock. Inside the 'performance space' we were invited to dress up for a party using assorted props provided and I remember Steve using the sellotape to wrap and distort his face, an image which perfectly captured his emotional turmoil. That some people are very good with plastic, glitter and crepe paper is another lesson I learnt that evening. The environment was VIP chill out deluxe with sounds and solos thrown in just to make sure the energy was always edging into the danger zone. Then someone asked had I been outside the tent and I naively said no and got up to have a look. Along the side of the tent there was a series of peep holes with headphones. Some members of the audience were already hooked up and addicted to the twisted postmodern commentary that was being improvised over the soundtrack by the performers. Suddenly the show was inside out and the audience and performers had switched roles by inadvertently getting too involved with expressing themselves. Club culture is always at its best when the clubbers take control and direct the ambience and intensity of a night. This was the first performance group in the art world who seemed to have any real grasp on this ecology.

Mark Waugh:

Die Erinnerung an *Say It Like You Mean It* dreht sich noch immer im gebrochenen Licht dieser apokalyptischen Disko. Für mich begann die Show mit einer Idee. Was wäre, wenn sich die Millenniumsparty, auf der du zu Gast bist, als Party zum Weltende herausstellt?

Während ich in der Schlange stand, traf ich Steve Slater, den ich seit den späten 80ern kannte, den ich aber seit etwa fünf Jahren nicht mehr gesehen hatte. Es war schön, ihn wiederzusehen, aber er schien besorgt. Er erzählte mir, seine Mutter sei schwer krank. Es waren noch andere Leute da, die wir beide kannten, und ich glaube, Unterstützung und Mitgefühl von Freunden war genau das, was er brauchte. Tatsächlich schien sich auf bizarre Weise mit dem Konzept der Show zu vermischen.

Wir betraten ein Zelt, das bereit war zu rocken. Innen im „Bühnenraum" wurden wir aufgefordert, uns unter Verwendung bereitgestellter Requisiten für eine Party „hübsch zu machen", und ich erinnere mich, dass Steve sein Gesicht ganz mit Tesafilm umwickelte und verzerrte – ein Bild, das seinen inneren Aufruhr perfekt zum Ausdruck brachte. Dass manche Leute wirklich gut mit Plastik, Glitter und Krepp-Papier umgehen können, ist eine weitere Erkenntnis, die ich aus diesem Abend zog. Das Set war die Luxus-Ausgabe einer VIP-Chill-Out-Lounge, und die eingestreuten Sounds und Solos hielten den Abend immer am Rand der Gefahrenzone. Dann wurde ich gefragt, ob ich schon drau-

Alexander Kelly:

Sean leads my group – he shines a torch at a huge brick chimney – look how big that tree has grown, he says. We cross a bridge (plank) over a stream (tape player playing a recording of flowing water), enter a forest (antiques market) and are led into a big marquee (a big marquee). I remember two pieces of paper (still stuck into a notebook somewhere) pressed into my palm: your words are being transmitted to a secret website; break on through to the other side. The joy of cardboard ears and antlers attached to headphones, which recast silhouetted audience members as 'animals' from the 'forest'. I remember the video recap taking us up to the moment we watched it (the seed of a later work?).

Anthony Rizzi:

I remember most of all thinking wow these guys have big balls when I went to see the show that started like a safari tour and ended with a party. I felt like I was on an field trip with school, sneaking out of the tent to smoke some grass. And then to watch a slide show out of the event at the end was amazingly touching. I have never felt so connected with my fellow audience members before.

ßen vor dem Zelt gewesen sei, und ich sagte ganz unschuldig nein und ging raus, um mich umzusehen. Entlang der Außenseite des Zeltes war eine Reihe von Sehschlitzen mit Kopfhörern. Einige Zuschauer waren bereits gefangen und geradezu süchtig nach dem verdrehten, postmodernen Kommentar, der auf der Tonspur von den Performern improvisiert wurde. Plötzlich hatte sich die Show von innen nach außen gekehrt, und die Zuschauer hatten mit den Performern die Rollen getauscht, indem sie sich versehentlich zu sehr darein vertieft hatten, sich selbst darzustellen. Club-Kultur ist immer dann am besten, wenn die Beteiligten die Kontrolle übernehmen und die Atmosphäre und Intensität einer Nacht selbst bestimmen. Das war die erste Performance-Gruppe in der Kunstszene, die wirklich Ahnung von dieser Ökologie zu haben schien.

Alexander Kelly:

Sean führt meine Gruppe – er leuchtet mit einer Taschenlampe an einem riesigen Backstein-Schornstein entlang – Seht mal, wie hoch dieser Baum gewachsen ist, sagt er. Wir überqueren eine Brücke (Planke) über einen Fluss (ein Kassettenrekorder spielt eine Aufnahme von fließendem Wasser), wir betreten einen Wald (Antiquitäten-Markt) und werden in ein großes Zelt (ein großes Zelt) geführt. Ich erinnere mich an zwei Stück Papier, die ich in die Hand gedrückt bekam (und die immer noch irgendwo in einem Notizbuch kleben): *Deine Worte werden auf eine geheime Website übertragen; Break on through to the other side.* Die Freude an Papp-Ohren und Geweihen, die an Kopfhörern befestigt waren und die Silhouette von Zuschauern zurückwarfen als „Tiere" des „Waldes". Ich erinnere mich, dass die später abgespielten Videostills uns bis zu dem Moment führten, den wir betrachteten (die Saat für eine weitere Arbeit?).

Anthony Rizzi:
Ich erinnere mich vor allem daran, dass ich dachte, wow, die trauen sich was, als ich mir die Show ansah, die wie eine Safari-Tour begann und mit einer Party endete. Ich fühlte mich wie auf einem Schulausflug, wo man sich aus dem Zelt schleicht, um heimlich Gras zu rauchen. Und dann eine Dia-Show von dem Ereignis anzusehen war erstaunlich berührend. Ich habe mich nie zuvor mit anderen Zuschauern so verbunden gefühlt.

photo: Armin Linke

WHERE DO YOU WANT TO GO TO DIE? (2000)

There's no time for us
There's no place for us
What is this thing that builds our dreams yet slips away
From us
Who wants to live forever
Who wants to live forever...?
There's no chance for us
It's all decided for us
This world has only one sweet moment set aside for us
Who wants to live forever
Who wants to live forever?
(Songlyrics by/Liedext von Brian May/Queen)

Where: a minibus
Who: 7 friends
What: a minibus journey; summer nights; the city of Berlin (everywhere from Brandenburg Gate to near the bins at the back of a shopping mall); the sound of a radio; ghosts made from sheets, squashed strawberries, silly string, talcum powder, champagne, a bag of flour, water, a pile of clothes, ketchup; reckless abandon; 1 video projector
How long: 53 minute loop

Wo: ein Mini-Reisebus
Wer: 7 Freunde
Was: eine Minibusreise; Sommernächte; die Stadt Berlin (vom Brandenburger Tor zu den Mülltonnen auf der Rückseite der Einkaufszentren); ein Radio; Gespenster aus Bettlaken, zerdrückte Erdbeeren, „Silly String", Babypuder, eine Flasche Sekt, eine Packung Mehl, Wasser, ein Haufen Kleider, Ketchup; haltlose Selbstaufgabe; 1 Videoprojektor
Wie lange: 53-minütiger Loop

Tatjana Turanskyj:
The last romantics

To write about "the authentic" in relation to Gob Squad, would surely be interesting because that was a term often used at premieres although fortunately, nobody knows what "the authentic" actually is. It is something (incomprehensible to me) that moves people and I noted that this apparent lack of separation between the private and the public, between friendship and work, life and show, probably contributes to the linking of Gob Squad with this term. Of course that is also rubbish and doesn't describe it at all. The opposite is the case. The best work of Gob Squad is in the realm of the surface. I would even say that they work continually at the surface. The surface, the image is their subject. Maybe it is the desire for beauty, for sugar and the resulting great happiness that propels them to give this desire an expression. Their shows are full of images of longing. They work with longing, they are romantics and fighters for what I, because I am so kitsch, call "the wonderful world".

In the video installation *Where Do You Want to Go to Die?* you learn how to die with Gob Squad. Like nearly all their performances, this video installation operates as test apparatus. Subject: the celebration of nightlife. One disco after another. The condition between the parties. The way there. The excitement. Driving together through the city. The expectation always being better than the party. The group drives in a car apparently "in private" through the streets of Berlin. They

Tatjana Turanskyj:
Die letzten Romantiker

Über das „Authentische" bei Gob Squad zu schreiben wäre sicher interessant, denn das ist einer der Begriffe gewesen, der auf Premieren gerne gefallen ist, obwohl ja zum Glück niemand weiß, was „das Authentische" eigentlich ist. Aber es ist – aus mir unverständlichen Gründen – etwas, was die Leute bewegt und ich möchte dazu nur bemerken, dass die scheinbare Nichttrennung von Privatheit und Öffentlichkeit, Freundschaft und Arbeit, Leben und Show, vermutlich dazu beigetragen hat, Gob Squad mit diesem Begriff zu versehen. Aber das ist natürlich Quatsch und trifft gar nichts. Das Gegenteil ist der Fall. Die besten Arbeiten von Gob Squad bewegen sich an der Oberfläche. Ich würde sogar sagen, dass sie sich an der Oberfläche abarbeiten, die Oberfläche – also das Bild – ihr Thema ist. Dass es der Wunsch nach Schönheit, nach Zucker, nach dem ganz großen Glück ist, der sie antreibt. Diesem Wunsch einen Ausdruck zu geben, vielleicht. Ihre Shows sind voll von Bildern der Sehnsucht. Sie sind Sehnsuchtsarbeiter. Romantiker und Kämpfer für das, was ich, verkitscht wie ich bin kurz, „The wonderful world" nenne.

In der Videoinstallation *Where Do You Want to Go to Die?* konnte man mit Gob Squad sterben lernen. Wie fast alle ihre Performances ist auch diese Videoinstallation eine Versuchsanordnung. Thema: Celebration nightlife. Eine Disko nach der anderen Disko. Der Zustand zwischen den Partys. Der

drink, they talk. They address each other by their real names. A recurring style element and perhaps one of their best secrets is the knowledge that we are here and you are not with us, although we know that you would like to be.

After the first short journey, a performer steps out of the car, in the place in which he or she has selected to die, or rather where the ultimate performance takes place. We see their concept of the end performed to us. The end is here, the exit from the collective, the distance in space from the others. But through this visual change of perspective, something else takes place as well, as we, the spectators also see the person who will soon die. This finally makes us a part of the group and very happy for a moment. Perhaps this moment in which one is allowed to take a place is the most beautiful moment in this installation. This shift of perspective and reference to the fact that everything is only a question of viewpoint and always can and will be different. These are the moments of hope and happiness. I could enumerate many moments of happiness like this one because Gob Squad are always producers of happiness. It is what they always do, they always say YES. Perhaps it is this oblivious, stubborn YES that agitates one and makes one happy.

Each of the performers dies in their individual way. Berit Stumpf pours flour in her hair and head-bangs. Some 80s hit accompanies. After her performance the car drives on as if nothing had happened and leaves a small white ghost

Weg dahin. Die Aufregung. Gemeinsam durch die Stadt fahren. Die Erwartung – immer besser als die Party. In der Installation fährt die Gruppe scheinbar „privat" im Auto durch die Straßen. Sie trinken, sie reden. Sie sprechen sich mit ihren realen Namen an etc. Ein wiederkehrendes Stilelement und vielleicht eines ihrer besten Geheimnisse. Dieses Wissen: Wir sind hier und ihr seid nicht dabei, obwohl wir wissen, dass ihr jetzt gern dabei wärt.

Nach kurzer Fahrt steigt der erste Performer aus dem Auto aus, an dem Ort, den er oder sie zum Sterben gewählt hat, oder besser, wo die eigentliche Performance stattfindet. Wir sehen seine vorgestellte Vorstellung vom Ende. Das Ende ist hier der Raustritt aus dem Kollektiv. Die räumliche Distanz zu den anderen. Aber durch diesen visuellen Perspektivwechsel findet auch noch etwas anderes statt: Auch wir Zuschauer sehen die Person, die gleich sterben wird. Das macht uns endlich zum Teil der Gruppe und man ist für einen Moment sehr glücklich. Vielleicht ist dieses Moment des Platz-einnehmen-Dürfens der schönste Moment in dieser Installation. Die Blickverschiebung. Oder überhaupt der Verweis darauf, dass alles nur eine Frage des Blicks ist. Oder, dass alles immer auch anders sein und werden kann. Das sind die Momente der Hoffnung und des Glücks. Ich könnte viele solcher Momente des Glücks aufzählen, denn Gob Squad sind immer auch Glücksproduzenten. Was immer sie tun, sie sagen immer JA. Vielleicht ist es dieses unbeirrte trotzige JA, dass einen rührt und glücklich macht.

ready to live on in limbo. And so it goes on until all the performers of the group die in a place of their choosing. Simon Will dies glamorously at a petrol station, pouring champagne over his head, Sarah Thom sprays a kind of liquid foam stuff on her naked body and transforms slowly into a rigid angel. Sean Patten simply disappears, dancing into the nothing of a clearing.

You are almost a bit annoyed because it is all so simple. But it isn't. Gob Squad celebrate the longing. Since the longing must remain unfulfilled, this sadness always surfaces in their work. Under the mirror smooth surface of a successful Gob Squad show sadness always lurks. And this sadness is the real moment in Gob Squad's work. It is a bittersweet sadness. Perhaps wistfulness is a more suitable word. After another journey through the city, Liane Sommers is the last to get out of the car. The car stops, she stands before it and looks at us all through the windshield. A blurred picture develops, because water squirts onto the pane and the windshield wipers start. She doesn't do anything. She just looks at us. Then you suddenly see she is crying.

Jeder der Performer stirbt auf seine individuelle Art und Weise. Berit Stumpf schüttet sich zum Beispiel Mehlstaub ins Haar und macht Headbanging. Dazu läuft irgendein 80er Hit. Nach ihrer Performance fährt das Auto weiter, als wäre nichts passiert, und lässt sie als kleines weißes Gespenst zurück, bereit, im Zwischenreich weiterzuleben. So geht das, bis alle Performer der Gruppe an einem Ort ihrer Wahl gestorben sind. Simon Will stirbt glamourös an einer Tankstelle und schüttet sich Champagner über den Kopf, Sarah Thom sprüht sich eine Art Flüssigschaumstoff auf den nackten Körper und verwandelt sich langsam in einen starren Engel. Sean Patten verschwindet einfach tanzend ins Nichts einer Lichtung.

Fast ist man dann ein bisschen sauer. Weil das alles so *simple* ist. Ist es aber dann doch nicht. Gob Squad feiern die Sehnsucht. Da die Sehnsucht unerfüllt bleiben muss, kommt in ihren Arbeiten immer auch das Traurige zum Vorschein. Unter der spiegelglatten Oberfläche einer gelungenen Gob-Squad-Show lauert immer auch Trauer. Und diese Trauer ist das reale Moment in Gob-Squad-Arbeiten. Es ist eine bittersüße Traurigkeit. Vielleicht ist Wehmut das passendere Wort. Nach einer weiteren Fahrt durch die Stadt steigt Liane Sommers als Letzte aus dem Wagen. Der Wagen hält, sie stellt sich vor ihn und schaut uns alle durch die Windschutzscheibe an. Ein verschwommenes Bild entsteht, weil Wasser an die Scheibe spritzt, die Scheibenwischer gehen an. Sie macht nichts, sie schaut uns nur an. Dann kann man plötzlich sehen, dass sie weint.

Gareth Howell:

In the Japanese film *Afterlife*, the recently dead are given the chance to make a film depicting the most important memory of their lives, which is then filmed as the one thing they can take with them to the other side/oblivion (they never say which). One of the last scenes is of a cinema gradually emptying as one by one, the dead watch their films until there is no-one left.

Where Do You Want to Go to Die? has stayed with me ever since I first saw it and still when I watch it, I think it is one of the most emotive and evocative pieces Gob Squad have made.

When we are first in the van with them, there is the familiar comfort of driving at night; the mumbling voices, chuckling, nothing really being said. It's a thing we see over and over again, the driving at night thing, but it never fails to get to me. There's something about it, however schmaltzy and

Gareth Howell:

In dem japanischen Film *Afterlife* bekommen die kürzlich Verstorbenen die Möglichkeit, einen Film zu machen von der wichtigsten Erinnerung ihres Lebens. Dieser Film ist das einzige, was sie auf die andere Seite oder ins Vergessen (es wird nie genau gesagt, was es ist) mit hinübernehmen dürfen. Eine der letzten Szenen zeigt ein Kino, das sich nach und nach leert, während sich die Toten einer nach dem anderen ihre Filme ansehen, bis niemand mehr übrig ist.

Where Do You Want to Go to Die? ist mir im Kopf geblieben, seit ich es das erste Mal gesehen habe, und jedesmal, wenn ich es wieder sehe, denke ich, es ist das gefühlvollste und bewegendste Stück, das Gob Squad je gemacht hat.
Zunächst, wenn man mit ihnen im Auto ist, erlebt man die tröstliche Vertrautheit einer Nachtfahrt; die gedämpften Stimmen, das leise Lachen, Gespräche, die um nichts kreisen. Man sieht sie wieder und wieder, diese Nachtfahrten, aber

nostalgic, that can't help but put me in the back seat of a Vauxhall Astra on a rainy drive home from Poynton in October, some time in the late Seventies.

The journey is broken up by stops, where one by one the members of Gob Squad get out of the van and perform a parting gesture, of defiance or desperation or pure abandonment, lit by the headlights. The van reverses away, leaving the performer watching or lost in their action. By the end of the film there will be no-one left. In the final stop, Liane gets out of the van, and is followed by ghosts. They are Charlie Brown's Halloween ghosts; sheets with eyeholes cut out of them. As they dance around, she breaks down into uncontrollable slow motion tears, sobbing hysterically. In the background, Freddie Mercury is singing "Who wants to live forever?". It goes on for ages. It breaks my heart.

Where Do You Want to Go to Die? is about memory and time. Throughout our lives we drop people off, and retain a lasting image of them. Not a real image, but an image of who they were and how they made us feel. Gangs break up and friendships fade. The gang you smoked Bensons with outside Spar aren't the same people you spend weekends barbecuing with and discussing mortgages with. They probably won't be the same people you discuss your grandchildren with, but you will keep them with you, because right now they are everything.

sie verfehlen nie ihre Wirkung auf mich. Irgendwas daran, wie kitschig und nostalgisch es auch sein mag, versetzt mich zurück in einen Vauxhall Astra auf einer regnerischen Heimfahrt von Poynton im Oktober, irgendwann in den späten 70er Jahren.

Die Fahrt ist unterbrochen von Stationen, an denen die Mitglieder von Gob Squad einer nach dem anderen aus dem Kombi steigen und, beleuchtet von den Autoscheinwerfern, eine Geste des Abschieds zeigen, eine trotzige Geste, eine verzweifelte oder eine Geste reiner Selbstaufgabe. Der Kombi setzt zurück und entfernt sich vom Performer, der dem Auto hinterherschaut oder verloren ist in seiner Aktion. Am Ende des Films wird niemand mehr übrig sein. Beim letzten Halt steigt Liane aus dem Wagen und wird von Geistern verfolgt. Es sind Charlie Browns Halloween-Gespenster, Leinentücher mit ausgeschnittenen Augenhöhlen. Während sie um sie herumtanzen, bricht sie in Zeitlupe in unkontrollierbare Tränen aus, in hysterisches Schluchzen. Im Hintergrund singt Freddy Mercury „Who Wants to Live Forever?" Es geht ewig. Es bricht mir das Herz.

Where Do You Want to Go to Die? handelt von Erinnerung und Zeit. Unser ganzes Leben hindurch lassen wir Leute zurück und bewahren dabei ein dauerhaftes Bild von ihnen. Kein wirkliches Bild, aber ein Bild davon, wer sie waren, und wie wir uns mit ihnen gefühlt haben. Cliquen brechen auseinander, und Freundschaften vergehen. Die Clique, mit der du vor Spar gestanden und geraucht hast, das sind nicht dieselben

Where Do You Want to Go to Die? is the Gob Squad's cover of "Yesterday Once More", by The Carpenters. It can really make me cry.

Leute, mit denen du am Wochenende Grillen gehst und über Hypotheken diskutierst. Sie werden wahrscheinlich nicht dieselben sein, mit denen du über deine Enkelkinder redest, aber du wirst dich an sie erinnern, weil sie jetzt im Moment alles sind.

Where Do You Want to Go to Die? ist Gob Squads Cover-Version von „Yesterday Once More" von den Carpenters. Es rührt mich zu Tränen.

THE GREAT OUTDOORS (2001)

- Excuse me, do you know how to get out?
- Yes. Best take the train.
- And then I'm out?
- Well, that'll get you out of town.
- No ... I mean how do I really get out of here?
- Grünau for example. There you really are out... It's really nice there.
- Really? Then I'm really out? Out of everything?
- Right. So that's what you mean. Well, I suppose there's only one possibility ...
You'll have to throw yourself right under the train. Then you'll be really out of everything.
(Conversation with a stranger)

Where: a theatre, city streets
Who: 4 people in one tent; a man singing a musical song dedicated to "The Great Outdoors", who leaves the theatre to explore the city (sights, houses, cars, wastelands); a woman feeling numb, who leaves the theatre in order to feel real; a woman who leaves the theatre in order to find a way out; a lonely man taking calls (dressed as an explorer about to go on an expedition); a sad woman in a bath (singing sea shanties into a phone); the abandoned audience
What: 1 tent; 1 path made from gravel leading to the exit doors; 1 picnic table with telephone, sandwiches and souvenir tea mugs; numerous empty tripods; 2 video screens; 5 farewells; 4 mobile phones; a number of surveillance and

Wo: ein Theater, die Straßen der Stadt
Wer: 4 Menschen in einem Zelt; ein Mann, der einen Musical-song singt und das Theater verlässt, um die Welt zu entdecken (Sehenswürdigkeiten, Häuser, Autos, Niemandsland); eine Frau, die nichts spürt und das Theater verlässt, um sich echt zu fühlen; eine Frau, die das Theater verlässt, um einen Ausweg zu finden; ein einsamer Mann, der Anrufe entgegennimmt (gekleidet als Pionier, der auf Expedition gehen wird); eine traurige Frau in der Badewanne, die Seefahrerlieder in ein Telefon singt; das verlassene Publikum
Was: 1 Zelt; 1 Kiespfad, der vom Zelt zur Ausgangstür führt; 1 Picknick-Tisch mit Telefon, belegten Broten und Souvenir-Bechern; leere Stative, 2 Videoleinwände; 5 Abschiede,

video cameras; doodles on video; 1 big weather balloon; conversations with strangers in the city; the view back from space; a phone on stage that eventually stops ringing
How long: 90 minutes

Arnd Wesemann:

There were only a few tents on a stage and a telephone. In a flash, the participants came out of the tent, sang a song, had a fried egg for breakfast, slung a rucksack over their shoulder and disappeared out of the emergency exit door, one after the other. The rest we believed through cameras: Sean Patten at the Brandenburg Gate, Johanna Freiburg at Rosa Luxemburg Platz, Berit Stumpf at Zoo Station and Sarah Thom in a bath. Only Simon Will stayed on stage a while keeping in telephone contact with his friends. Then he was off too.

Berit Stumpf disbelievingly asked, the handle to the escape route door still in her hand, "For me it does not go any further. [To the audience] And you, are you are staying in here forever?" Where does she want to go? Back to reality. Johanna Freiburg asks an older married couple on the street to touch her. When they refuse she is triumphant, "I knew it, you are not real, you are all just in your own world." On the street, they come across so much autism that it cannot possibly fit into a theatre. People embrace reality gladly but they fear that their faintheartedness in reality comes across as more fainthearted than one could ever character-

4 Mobiltelefone, eine Anzahl von Überwachungs- und Video-kameras; Kritzeleien auf Video; 1 großer Ballon; Gespräche mit Fremden in der Stadt; ein Blick zurück aus dem All; ein Telefon auf der Bühne, das schließlich aufhört zu klingeln
Wie lange: 90 Minuten

Arnd Wesemann:

Es standen nur ein paar Zelte auf einer Bühne und ein Tele-fon. Im Nu waren die Akteure raus aus dem Zelt, haben ein Lied gesungen, ein Spiegelei gefrühstückt, den Rucksack geschultert, und einer nach dem anderen ist zur Notaus-gangstür verschwunden. Den Rest machten uns Kameras glauben: Sean Patten am Brandenburger Tor, Johanna Freiburg am Rosa-Luxemburg-Platz, Berit Stumpf am Bahn-hof Zoo, Sarah Thom in einer Badewanne. Nur Simon Will hielt auf der Bühne noch eine Weile Telefonkontakt zu sei-nen Freunden. Dann war auch er weg.

Ungläubig fragte Berit Stumpf, die Türklinke zum Flucht-weg noch in der Hand. „Für mich geht's hier nicht mehr weiter. (Zum Publikum:) Und ihr, ihr bleibt hier drin bis ewig?" Wohin sie will? Zurück in die Realität. Johanna Freiburg bittet auf der Straße ein älteres Ehepaar, sie anzu-fassen. Als es sich weigert, triumphiert sie: „Ich wusste doch, ihr seid nicht echt, ihr seid alle nur in eurem eignen Film." Auf der Straße begegnet ihnen so viel Autistisches, dass es unmöglich in ein Theater passt. Zwar wollen Men-schen gern in die Wirklichkeit, aber haben Angst, dass ihr

ise on stage. And so Gob Squad found the street, but no people. And for exactly that reason the stage remains empty up here in the theatre. On the table the telephone rings. Nobody in the audience dares to go up to it. There could be someone there.

Mark Jeffery:
It was Karen who reminded me when I first told her what I was doing – tracing birds from a cut out newspaper article. "Ornithologists in the dark about mysterious decline of British owls" and "Bird decline halted but worries remain". "Can't you remember", she said. "They were all stuck in the tent and we were all sitting in the audience waiting. The promoters had decided to wait until one show was over before they could start. I think we had to wait over half an hour before the show started."
"Ah yes", I said.
"I remember, they were all zipped in the tent writing with their fingers on a keyboard. We could see the confused, questioned words they were typing on the computer screen being typed on a wall, outside the tent."
"Yes," she said, "that's right, they were wondering why they were waiting."

We laughed, I laughed, she laughed, then and now. At the time I don't think we could stop laughing. I remember feeling a space of a warmth, of a familiar, as if I had stored the Enid Blyton tales of a faraway place in my head – where

Kleinmut dort noch viel kleinmütiger wirkt als ihn die Bühne je karikieren könnte. So fand Gob Squad zwar die Straße, aber keine Menschen. Und genau deshalb bleibt hier oben im Theater die Bühne leer. Auf dem Tisch klingelt das Telefon. Niemand wagt im Publikum, an den Apparat zu gehen. Es könnte ja jemand dran sein.

Mark Jeffery:
Es war Karen, die mich wieder daran erinnerte, als ich ihr erzählte, womit ich gerade beschäftigt war – Vögel abzeichnen von einem Artikel, den ich aus der Zeitung ausgeschnitten hatte: „Ornithologen im Dunkeln über mysteriösen Rückgang des Bestands britischer Eulen" und „Vogelschwund gestoppt, doch die Sorge bleibt".
„Erinnerst du dich", fragte sie, „Sie steckten alle in dem Zelt, und wir saßen im Publikum und warteten. Die Veranstalter hatten beschlossen, mit dem Beginn der Show zu warten bis eine andere vorüber war. Ich glaube, wir mussten über eine halbe Stunde warten, bis ihre Show anfing."
„Ach ja", sagte ich. „Ich erinnere mich, wie sie da alle in dem Zelt eingeschlossen blieben, mit den Fingern auf einem Keyboard schrieben – wir konnten die verwirrten, fragenden Worte, die sie tippten, auf der Wand über dem Zelt sehen."
„Ja, genau", sagte sie, „Sie fragten sich, warum sie warteten."

Wir lachten, ich lachte, sie lachte, damals und jetzt. Damals konnten wir gar nicht aufhören zu lachen. Ich erinnere mich,

things were 'super good' and 'super fun', where there was a definite need for bread and lovely toast, especially the red headed lady said so.

The present that we knew had just the previous month fallen down in front of us on many TV screens. What they yearned in their departures we could see. This is somewhat where we wanted. To go back to a before land. To recover and put back toether the fallen down land. We were there because we were attempting an aftermath. They seemed to be there to leave us, to depart to report from a REMOTE in leaving through a wooden door. Along a thread like stream each one reported back live from the nighttime city on what could have seen/been.

A static fuzz as the game show conveyer belt rotated flinging each one outdoors into a nighttime (long strings of wires, cables, bits of bodies crumpled into digitized coding). We can see them … we can see them! … (I am laughing, she is laughing, we are all laughing.) We can see them coming through on the screen. Yet I saw them leave. All I still seem to remember is laughing, and laughing – laughing so hard – yet now all I seem to remember is how sad they left, why did they escape, how fragile they all were in their lost outdoors of discovering. Their attempt to find a new space of zero gravity, in going outdoors, in going outside.

I remember in the gut a celebration. Deep in the gut that allows a release of a trapped bird to escape into the night-

dass ich eine Wärme und Vertrautheit spürte, als hätte ich einen Zugang zu einem entfernten Speicher in meinem Hirn voll mit Enid-Blyton-Geschichten entdeckt, wo alles „supergut" oder „superlustig" war, und wo man einen ausdrücklichen Wunsch nach einem leckeren Brot verspürte – wie von der rothaarigen Frau gesagt.

Die Gegenwart, wie wir sie kannten, war erst im vergangenen Monat auf vielen Bildschirmen vor uns zusammengebrochen. Was sie sich von ihren Aufbrüchen ersehnten, konnten wir sehen. Dorthin wollten irgendwie auch wir. Zurückgehen in ein Vorher-Land. Gesund werden und das zusammengebrochene Land wieder zusammensetzen. Wir waren dort, weil wir nach einer Nachwirkung suchten. Sie schienen da zu sein, um uns zu verlassen, aufzubrechen, um von einem FERN zu berichten, indem sie durch eine Holztür gingen. Entlang eines lebendigen Stroms und seinem eigenen Faden folgend, erstattete uns jeder von ihnen einen Live-Bericht aus der nächtlichen Stadt, darüber, was es zu sehen/zu erleben geben könnte.

Begleitet von konstantem Schneetreiben, rotierte das Gameshow-Förderband und schleuderte jeden einzeln ins Freie – hinaus in die Nacht (lange Leitungen, Kabelrollen, Ausschnitte von Körpern, zerknittert durch digitalisierte Kodierungen) – wir können sie sehen … wir können sie sehen! … (Ich lache, sie lacht, wir alle lachen.) Sie erscheinen auf der Leinwand. Und doch habe ich sie gehen sehen. Alles, woran ich mich noch zu erinnern scheine, ist, dass ich lachte und lachte –

sky. A smiling toothed mouth released into the nightsky. An escape. Upwards, mobile, away. UP. UP. AWAY. Yet now I wish to cry, to cry, to cry, to cry, to cry, to cry, to cry, to cry, to cry, to cry, to cry, to cry, to cry, to cry, to cry.

Christiane Kühl:
I've experienced some very beautiful catastrophes with Gob Squad. During two of them the world ended. The first time they wanted it in *Say It Like You Mean It*, the second time, with *The Great Outdoors* I wanted it to happen and so did the spirit of the world. In both cases I was glad to have been there.

It is obvious that Gob Squad are no apocalyptic troupe. On the contrary, Gob Squad are not afraid, Gob Squad don't moan. Gob Squad are simply always there. *Say It Like You Mean It* celebrated the apocalypse with dramatic consideration. It is rich in images, sensational, and along the way gives rise to the possibility of putting together a new version of the universe entirely from one's personal preferences. *Say It Like You Mean It* was a big party in 2000 and gave grown people the permission to celebrate a wild children's carnival without embarrassment, because with Gob Squad being in the moment and at the same time subtly commenting upon it, operate side by side.

Two years later, when *The Great Outdoors* came out, the situation was fundamentally different because in the meantime the world had really gone under. Aircraft had exploded into the

so viel lachte –, und doch erinnere ich mich, wie traurig sie fortgingen, warum sie flüchteten, wie verletzlich sie waren in ihrer verloren gegangenen Außenwelt des Entdeckens. Ihr Versuch, einen neuen schwerelosen Raum zu finden, indem sie ins Freie traten, indem sie nach draußen gingen.

Ich erinnere tief in den Eingeweiden eine Feier, die einen gefangenen Vogel in den nächtlichen Himmel entkommen ließ. Einen lächelnden Mund voller Zähne, entlassen in den nächtlichen Himmel. Ein Entkommen. In die Höhe, beweglich, fort. HOCH. HOCH. DAVON. Und doch ist mir jetzt zum Weinen, zum Weinen, zum Weinen, zum Weinen, zum Weinen, zum Weinen, zum Weinen, zum Weinen, zum Weinen, zum Weinen, zum Weinen, zum Weinen, zum Weinen, zum Weinen, zum Weinen.

Christiane Kühl:
Mit Gob Squad habe ich einige sehr schöne Katastrophen erlebt. Zweimal ging dabei die Welt unter. Das erste Mal wollten sie es so – *Say It Like You Mean It* –, das zweite Mal, bei *The Great Outdoors*, wollte ich es und der Weltgeist auch. In beiden Fällen bin ich froh, dabei gewesen zu sein.

Selbstverständlich ist Gob Squad keine Weltuntergangstruppe. Im Gegenteil, Gob Squad fürchtet nicht, Gob Squad jammert nicht, Gob Squad ist einfach immer schon da. *Say It Like You Mean It* feierte die Apokalypse aus dramatischen

World Trade Centre, the Taliban terrorised the earth from their unassailable caves and on the perceived scales of threat, a third world war looked imminent. Presumably Gob Squad did not deal with this in their working process but to re-enter the Podewil for one night with them, with the memory of their jolly end-of-the-world party still so present, it was a real shock to see their meagre, inhospitable tent-landscape with the lonely microphone stand like a leafless tree rising in the scenery sky. I had just returned from New York where everyone told their versions of the 11th September and their wishes to leave the city despite the economic and emotional impossibilities of really doing so. I could not help interpreting the emptiness before me with the camping stove and the isolated figures as a picture of our imminent future. And so what did Gob Squad do? They left. One after another they left the theatre, running with cameras through Berlin at night like a private Homeland Security Patrol and throwing the audience back onto its own paranoia. The outside was there against all expectation. And this moment of bafflement, the inversion of inside and outside, in which it was almost casually made clear that the theatre no longer reflected the world but projected into the world, was a great moment.

On the screen as I followed the performers still laden with my apocalyptic anxiety, they urgently asked the nocturnal passers-by for "the way out." The Berliners were Berliners and had the answer: "The best way is to take the train." So easy. That is theatre.

Erwägungen: Sie ist bilderreich, hat tolle Knalleffekte und gibt nebenbei die Gelegenheit, eine Neuversion des Universums ganz nach persönlichen Vorlieben zu basteln. *Say It Like You Mean It* war 2000 eine große Party und ließ erwachsene Menschen ausgelassen Kinderfasching feiern. Ganz ohne Peinlichkeiten, denn dabei sein und subtil kommentieren funktioniert bei Gob Squad synchron.

Zwei Jahre später, als *The Great Outdoors* herauskam, war die Situation eine grundlegend andere, denn zwischendurch war die Welt wirklich untergegangen. Flugzeuge waren im World Trade Center explodiert, die Taliban terrorisierten die Erde aus uneinnehmbaren Höhlen heraus, und auf der gefühlten Bedrohungsskala stand der dritte, asymmetrische Weltkrieg ganz unmittelbar bevor. Vermutlich hat das Gob Squad bei ihrer Arbeit nicht konkret bekümmert, aber 2002 wieder für eine Nacht mit ihnen das Podewil zu betreten, wo die Erinnerung an die lustige Weltuntergangsparty noch so präsent war, und nun die karge, unwirtliche Zeltlandschaft mit einsamen Mikroständern zu sehen, die wie laublose Bäume in den Bühnenhimmel ragten, war ein echter Schock. Ich war gerade aus New York zurückgekehrt, wo jeder seine Version vom 11. September erzählte, vom Wunsch, die Stadt zu verlassen und von der ökonomischen wie emotionalen Unmöglichkeit, es wirklich zu tun, und konnte nicht anders, als die Leere vor mir mit dem Campingkocher und den vereinzelten Figuren als Bild unserer nahen Zukunft zu interpretieren. Und was machten Gob Squad? Sie gingen. Einer nach dem anderen verließen sie das Theater, liefen mit Kameras durch das nächtliche Berlin wie eine private Home-

photo: Miles Chalcraft

land Security Patrol und warfen das Publikum auf die eigene Paranoia zurück. Das Draußen fand nämlich wider Erwarten noch statt. Und dieser Moment der Verwirrung, des Umstülpens von Innen und Außen, der fast nebenbei klar machte, dass das Theater nicht mehr die Welt spiegelt als vielmehr Vorstellungen in die Welt hineinprojiziert, war ein großer Moment.

Auf der Leinwand waren weiter die mit meiner Weltuntergangsangst aufgeladenen Performer zu verfolgen, die die nächtlichen Passanten drängend nach dem „Weg hier raus" fragten. Der Berliner war Berliner und hatte Antwort: „Da nehm` Se am besten die S-Bahn." So einfach. Das ist Theater.

ROOM SERVICE – Help Me Make It Through the Night (2003)

Here I am in my hotel room and I can do anything I want. I could...
... start a fire in my wastepaper basket and open the window and shout FIRE FIRE until a fireman comes and rescues me
... deliberately bankrupt myself by ringing up room service and asking them to charge every drink bought in the bar tonight to my Visa card
... unscrew the paintings from the walls and turn them upside down and see if the cleaners notice
I could save up all the free packets of shower gel and resell them on the internet from my laptop
... change the "Do Not Disturb" sign on my door to read "Please do disturb every hour with violent beatings"
and then complain to the manager if they don't fulfill my wishes

Where: a hotel (a conference room for the audience, 4 identical hotel rooms for the performers)
Who: 2 women, 2 men
In the conference room: 300 m of video cables, 700 m of sound cables, 4 old computers; 4 big monitors; 1 telephone; 1 hotel bar; comfortable cushions to spend the night on
In the hotel rooms: 4 cameras; some costumes (7 coats, 12 suits, 14 dresses, 22 shirts, 8 nighties, 4 dressing gowns, 9 pairs of pyjamas, various bras, pants, ties); some props (9 wigs, 2 fake beards, "Freddy Krueger" mask, glow-in-the-dark hands, briefcase, business magazines, trashy novels, toothpaste); pop songs to sing; games to play; everything which comes with the hotel room; a phone to call someone watching (and the hope that someone cares to answer)
How long: A sleepless night

Wo: ein Hotel (ein Tagungsraum für die Zuschauer, 4 identische Hotelzimmer für die Darsteller)
Wer: 2 Frauen und 2 Männer
Im Tagungsraum: 300 m Videokabel, 700 m Soundkabel, 4 alte Computer; 4 große Monitore; 1 Telefon; 1 Hotelbar; bequeme Kissen, um die Nacht zu verbringen
In den Hotelzimmern: 4 Kameras; eine Anzahl von Kostümen (7 Jacken, 12 Anzüge, 14 Kleider, 22 Hemden, 8 Nachthemden, 4 Morgenmäntel, 9 Pyjamas, diverse BHs, Unterhosen, Krawatten); eine Anzahl von Requisiten (9 Perücken, 2 falsche Bärte, 1 „Freddy Krueger"-Maske, Aktenkoffer, Kitschromane, Zahnpasta); Popsongs zum Singen; Spiele zum Spielen; alles, was zum Hotelmobiliar gehört; ein Telefon, um jemanden anzurufen, der einem zuschaut (und die Hoffnung, daß jemand abnimmt)
Wie lange: eine schlaflose Nacht

Emina Visnic:

A (Wo)man/performer/individual is alone in his/her room and he/she is only able to communicate with others by using mediating tools such as a telephone, audio-visual systems or even a letter.

Everything that is (not) happening is in the neutral spaces of hotel rooms. These (non) events, (non) happenings are placed next to entertaining songs or other reference points that are familiar to all of us as consumers and products of the global westernisation of culture. Room Service is slapstick, a soap opera, an ad, a drama and a reality show. It is live and it is mediated. It comes to you personally and addresses all of us in the same way as an "Orbit Winterfresh" advert.

Using technology as a tool *Room Service* is successful (despite the clearly defined physical barrier) in establishing creative contact. Paradoxically as long as the performer that tries to communicate with audience stays behind the screen the canal is open. As long as the one who has the power to start and finish the communication process stays behind the plasma wall with his or her movements, words and gestures being shown and hidden at the same time the audience is willing to occupy two positions: to feel relatively secure in the darkness of the conference room (public gathering place) and enjoy the advantages of a voyeuristic view but also to be ready to answer a phone to dance under the mask or to give him- or herself "for ever".

Emina Visnic:

Eine Frau/ein Mann/ein(e)PerformerIn/eine Person ist allein in seinem/ihrem Hotelzimmer, und kann nur mit medialen Hilfsmitteln wie Telefon, audiovisuellen Systemen oder Briefen kommunizieren.

Alles was (nicht) passiert, geschieht in den neutralen Räumen von Hotelzimmern. Diese (Nicht-)Ereignisse stehen neben unterhaltsamen Song-Einlagen oder anderen Referenzpunkten, die uns als Konsumenten und Produkte der globalen Verwestlichung der Kultur vertraut sind. Es richtet sich persönlich an dich und wendet sich doch an uns alle wie ein Werbespot für „Orbit Winterfresh".

Room Service setzt Technologie erfolgreich als Mittel ein, um einen kreativen Kontakt herzustellen (trotz der klar definierten physischen Barriere). Paradoxerweise ist der Kanal offen, solange der Performer, der mit dem Publikum zu kommunizieren versucht, hinter dem Bildschirm bleibt. So lange derjenige, der den Kommunikationsprozess beginnen und beenden kann, hinter der Plasma-Wand bleibt, seine Bewegungen, seine Worte und Gesten also zugleich ausgestellt und versteckt sind, sind die Zuschauer bereit, zwei Positionen zu besetzen: sich relativ sicher zu fühlen im Dunkel des Konferenzzimmers (einem öffentlichen Versammlungsort) und die Vorzüge einer voyeuristischen Perspektive zu genießen, aber auch bereit, einen Telefonanruf anzunehmen, unter einer Maske zu tanzen oder sich selbst „für immer" hinzugeben.

The performers apply the domino principle in their vivid game with the audience. If one of the performers is trying to talk by phone with a member of the audience other spectators get involved directly or indirectly. Everybody and anybody there in the conference room of Hotel Laguna, Zagreb could have become part of Gob Squad's lucid entertainment. Right here, Right now. One person's inconvenient, provocative situation could become at any moment, somebody else's or everybody's. This provides continuous, particular tension. Will I have to (or could I) answer the "call for help" from the other side of screen? Will I be able to perform my personality in front of the audience? Who will help me to do that? Will I be able to play the game and which role will I have to play? Although at first sight the process of this theatrical performance can seem accidental, a more careful spectator/participant will soon realise that this piece is very precisely structured and composed. Fiction is here all the time but it

In ihrem lebhaften Spiel mit dem Publikum wenden die Performer das Domino-Prinzip an. Wenn einer der Performer versucht, mit einer Person aus dem Publikum zu telefonieren, werden andere Zuschauer direkt oder indirekt einbezogen. Alle und jeder dort im Konferenzzimmer des Hotels Laguna, Zagreb, konnte Teil von Gob Squads klarsichtigem Entertainment werden. Right here, Right now. Die unbequeme, ausgestellte Situation eines Zuschauers konnte sich jederzeit auf jemand anderen oder auf alle übertragen. Das schafft eine ständige, besondere Spannung. Muss ich (oder kann ich) auf den „Hilferuf" von der anderen Seite des Bildschirms reagieren? Kann ich mich vor dem Publikum darstellen oder ausdrücken? Wer wird mir dabei helfen? Kann ich dieses Spiel spielen, und welche Rolle wird mir dabei zufallen?

is not able to overcome the present so as they interweave throughout the show they involve the audience in a strange but adorable game.

Tobias Dusche:

The eye is the monitor to the soul. The soul is a strange quagmire. Dodgy. Funny. Despairing. Mean. Moving. Sexy. Revolting. Great. The soul celebrates its birthday and overdoes it. It puts itself to bed and mother is a monster. It is a pop star and trashes the place. It asks itself questions, which no one answers. It answers questions that no one answers and poses for absent foreigners. Fortunately, the soul stays where it is. It only calls sometimes. Hello? The soul wants to play. Sometimes someone plays along. The collective soul contradicts and fights itself. It gets spots and disintegrates into a thousand moments. The cinema connects everything. Projection. Beneficial power of an all-loving love. Gob Squad is a hotel rented by the hour.

Kathrin Tiedemann:

The strongest impression that you leave me with is the unusual devotion with which you meet your spectators. Memories of unforgettable moments of extreme intensity and a close proximity to the performers run through all of your work. This can only be inadequately described by the terms interaction or public participation. For me you are the masters of creating situations full of passion and big emotions as

Obwohl der Verlauf dieser theatralen Performance auf den ersten Blick zufällig erscheinen mag, wird dem aufmerksameren Zuschauer/Teilnehmer bald deutlich, dass dieses Stück sehr genau komponiert und strukturiert ist. Überwiegend herrscht die Fiktion, sie kann jedoch die Gegenwart nie ganz verdrängen. Während sie sich die gesamte Show hindurch miteinander verflechten, ziehen sie uns in ein merkwürdiges und liebenswertes Spiel hinein.

Tobias Dusche:

Das Auge ist der Monitor zur Seele. Die Seele ist ein komischer Sumpf. Vertrackt. Witzig. Verzweifelt. Fies. Ergreifend. Sexy. Eklig. Toll. Die Seele feiert Geburtstag und treibt es zu wild. Sie bringt sich zu Bett und Mutter ist ein Monster. Sie ist ein Popstar und zerlegt das Mobiliar. Sie stellt sich Fragen, die keiner beantwortet. Sie beantwortet sich Fragen, die keiner beantwortet, und posiert für abwesende Fremde. Die Seele bleibt zum Glück, wo sie ist. Sie ruft nur manchmal an. Hello? Die Seele will spielen. Manchmal spielt einer mit. Die kollektive Seele widerspricht sich und bekriegt sich. Sie kriegt Pickel und zerfällt in 1000 Momente. Das Kino fügt alles zusammen. Projektion. Heilsame Macht einer alles liebenden Liebe. Gob Squad ist ein Stundenhotel.

well as many smaller ones.

On the border between fiction and reality a space for seduction, in which everything seems possible, opens up for one moment. An event between two people, incalculable and open-ended. Only those who play along draw pleasure from the special thrill contained within these live situations. Dreams, longing, friendship, happiness, heartache, disappointment, weaknesses, the many small inadequacies of the individual and eternal failure are the material from which Gob Squad adventures are made. Again and again situations in which the right moment remains unrecognised and the borders uncrossed elapse unused. But the play always continues somehow. Just as in life, only more intensive, wild and romantic.

'We aim to please' you once said and you wanted to change the world with your art. An equal commitment to Pathos and Pop does not have to be a contradiction and this for me is the beauty of Gob Squad.

Kathrin Tiedemann:

Der stärkste Eindruck, den Gob Squad bei mir hinterlassen hat, ist die außergewöhnliche Hingabe, mit der Ihr Euren Zuschauern begegnet. Durch alle Eure Arbeiten hindurch zieht sich die Erinnerung an unvergessliche Momente äußerster Intensität und Nähe zu den PerformerInnen. Das lässt sich mit den Begriffen Interaktion oder Publikumspartizipation nur unzureichend beschreiben. Für mich seid Ihr Meister im Herbeiführen von Situationen voller Leidenschaft und kleiner wie großer Gefühle.

Auf der Grenze zwischen Fiktion und Realität eröffnet sich für einen Moment ein Raum der Verführung, in dem alles möglich scheint. Ein Ereignis zwischen zwei Menschen, unberechenbar und offen im Ausgang. Nur wer mitspielt, kommt in den Genuss dieses besonderen Nervenkitzels, den die Live-Situation bereithält. Träume, Sehnsüchte, Freundschaft, Glück, Liebeskummer, Enttäuschungen, die vielen kleinen Unzulänglichkeiten der eigenen Person, Schwächen und das ewige Scheitern sind der Stoff, aus dem die Gob-Squad-Abenteuer sind. Und immer wieder Situationen, in denen es nicht gelingt, die Gunst des Augenblicks zu erkennen und die Grenze zu überschreiten. Er verstreicht ungenutzt. Doch das Spiel geht immer irgendwie weiter. Wie im Leben – nur intensiver, wilder und romantischer.

We aim to please, habt Ihr mal gesagt, und dass Ihr mit Eurer Kunst die Welt verändern wollt. Dass das kein Widerspruch sein muss, ein Bekenntnis zu Pathos und Pop gleichermaßen, das ist für mich die Schönheit von Gob Squad.

SUPER NIGHT SHOT (2003)

Each of us is just one in a million, easy to replace and easy to forget in a city that doesn't really need us. But don't worry. We're going to change all that. We've got a plan. This city will need us and this film will be our witness

Where: the city streets, a theatre laid out like a cinema
Who: a hero; a casting-agent; a promoter; a location-scout; all the people on the street that night
What: 4 video cameras set to super night shot shoot-in-the-dark mode; a room with a screen and 4 video projectors; a map of the city; 8 digital watches; 4 camouflage suits; 4 animal masks; chalk; posters and flyers; a lot of charm to convince strangers; some synchronised moments; a long screen kiss; a hero's welcome (sparklers, streamers, "The End"- banner)
How long: the length of a video tape (60 minutes)

Georg Diez:
Gob Squad and *Super Night Shot* was the end as beginning, it was party poppers and fairy lights and a corridor of people who didn't know what they were cheering for (and in the end they were happy not to have understood this beginning because understanding in its anticipatable form is not how the world presents itself or offers itself for decoding, and it is also not the way Gob Squad shows this world.)

Wo: die Straßen der Stadt, ein Theater als Kino
Wer: ein/e HeldIn; ein/e Casting-AgentIn; ein Promoter; ein Location-Scout; die Passanten der Nacht
Was: 4 Videokameras eingestellt auf Super Night Shot, einen Modus, mit dem man im Dunkeln filmen kann; ein Raum mit einer Projektionsleinwand und 4 Videoprojektoren; ein Stadtplan; 8 digitale Uhren; 4 Kampfanzüge; 4 Tiermasken; Kreide; Poster und Flyer; ausreichend Charme, um Fremde überzeugen zu können; eine Anzahl synchronisierter Momente; ein langer Filmkuss; ein Empfang für 4 Helden in Unterwäsche (Wunderkerzen, Luftschlangen, „The End"- Transparent)
Wie lange: die Länge einer Videokassette (60 Minuten)

Georg Diez:
Gob Squad und *Super Night Shot*, das war das Ende als Anfang, das waren Luftschlangen und Leuchtkerzen und ein Spalier von Leuten, die nicht wussten, was sie da bejubeln (und am Ende waren sie glücklich, diesen Anfang nicht verstanden zu haben, denn das Verstehen in seiner erwartbaren Form

Gob Squad and *Super Night Shot* was four actors and two languages. It was faces that were reassuring and, in their own way, beautiful and exciting (even if that is a stupid word).

Gob Squad and *Super Night Shot* was the reversal of the fictionalising of the world. It was not how the street, the night, and life, enraptures through the ubiquity of the media and how our perception is modified through films, television and the Internet. Rather it was a completely modern fairy-tale in which the Princes were pale and average and knew nothing of their fortune when it happened to them, and quite possibly had no suspicion later on of what kind of possibility they had just missed (it was a kind of enchantment, a worldly one, that we vacant and sated big-city dreamers can only dare to imagine for ourselves).

Gob Squad and *Super Night Shot* was the theatre, how it played cinema but nevertheless was so much faster and nearer to the dreams, the contradictions, the cowardice, the head-over-heels rush, the desired worlds, the hero worship, the wavering, the waiting and the hoping for this one moment. Much closer to the people, waiting on a corner, crossing the road looking almost unconcerned whether a tram or good fortune runs them down (because they have stopped hoping but not for too long. We soon observe from our seats someone kindle the flame of hope that more than hunger or thirst or war or love constitutes us, as it constitutes all humans. The hope …bah).

ist nicht die Art, wie sich die Welt präsentiert und entschlüsseln lässt, und also auch nicht die Art, wie Gob Squad diese Welt zeigt).

Gob Squad und *Super Night Shot*, das waren vier Schauspieler und zwei Sprachen, das waren Gesichter, die beruhigend waren und auf ihre Weise schön und spannend (auch wenn das ein dummes Wort ist).

Gob Squad und *Super Night Shot*, das war die Umkehrung der Fiktionalisierung der Welt, das war nicht die Straße, die Nacht, das Leben, wie es entrückt wird durch die Allgegenwart der Medien und unsere Wahrnehmung, die so verändert wird durch Filme, Fernsehen, Internet, das war vielmehr eine ganz moderne Märchenstunde, in der die Prinzen blass waren und durchschnittlich und nichts von ihrem Glück wussten, als es ihnen passierte, und womöglich auch später nichts davon ahnten, was für eine Möglichkeit sie gerade verpaßt hatten (es war eine Art von Verzauberung, aber auf die weltlichste Weise, die wir leergefegten und vollgestopften Großstadtsehnsüchtler uns vorzustellen wagen).

Gob Squad und *Super Night Shot*, das war das Theater, wie es Kino spielte und doch so viel schneller war und näher dran an den Träumen und den Widersprüchen, an der Mutlosigkeit und dem Hals-über-Kopf, an den Wunschwelten und der Heldenverehrung, an dem Zaudern und dem Warten und dem Hoffen auf diesen einen Moment, viel näher dran an diesen Menschen, die an der Ecke lehnen und dann über

Gob Squad and *Super Night Shot* was people as images as people. It was the dramaturgy of our world because it was tragedy as comedy as happens in everyday life and devouring everything. It is everything that politics, history and longing absorb (a collective sponge).

Gob Squad and *Super Night Shot* was a romance that was not, a promise that was not, luck that was not, love that was not, life as it could be, the step we never take, an attempt, nothing more, one hour and then that was the end of it, an end we already knew. (A deathly sad evening basically, but nevertheless as bright as the clear day.)

Gob Squad and *Super Night Shot* was a true moment, manufactured not by a director or a stage designer or a dramatist but by strength from outside. This strength that connects and separates people, which people curse but need. A true moment under the only law that really applies, coincidence (with hindsight, even the party poppers and the sparklers, even coincidence makes sense.)

Emily Shenston:
I attended the viewing of *Super Night Shot* – a film created just one hour before it is viewed and shot in my home town of West Bromwich. I have lived in West Bromwich for 21 years – my whole life. I played on the same streets as a child that I now walk each day to the office. For me, the film captured this, my everyday routine which Gob Squad injected with a

die Straße gehen und denen es fast schon egal zu sein scheint, ob sie jetzt von der Trambahn überfahren werden oder vom Glück überrollt (weil sie aufgehört haben zu hoffen, aber nur so lange, das sehen wir, auf unseren Sitzen, vor diesen Bildern, bis jemand diese Flamme entfacht, die mehr als der Hunger oder der Durst oder der Krieg oder die Liebe uns ausmacht, als Menschen ausmacht, die Hoffnung, puh).

Gob Squad und *Super Night Shot*, das waren Menschen als Bilder als Menschen, das war die Dramaturgie unserer Welt, weil es die Tragödie als Komödie war, wie sie im Alltag stattfindet und doch alles verschlingt und alles ist, was die Politik und die Geschichte und die Sehnsucht aufsaugt (ein kollektiver Schwamm).

Gob Squad und *Super Night Shot*, das war eine Romanze, die keine war, das war ein Versprechen, das keines war, das war das Glück, das keines war, das war die Liebe, die keine war, das war das Leben, wie es sein könnte, das war der Schritt, den wir nie tun, das war ein Versuch, mehr nicht, das war eine Stunde, und das war das Ende, das wir schon kennen (ein todtrauriger Abend, im Grunde, und doch heiter wie der lichte Tag).

Gob Squad und *Super Night Shot*, das war ein wahrer Moment, der hergestellt war, nicht von einem Regisseur oder einem Bühnenbildner oder einem Dramatiker, sondern von einer Kraft dort draußen, die die Menschen verbindet und trennt, die die Menschen verfluchen und die sich brauchen, ein

whole new dimension. The cracked paving slabs, the traffic, the neon take-away signs against the cold grey concrete. This unedited and beautifully realistic piece made me realise just how much I see but fail to observe.

Super Night Shot worked because it was real ... and reality is what affects every one of us, every day of our lives. I became lost in my own reality ... in the raw and gritty beauty of it all. I left feeling special, thankful and with an overwhelming feeling of self awareness.

Robin Arthur:

OK, it goes something like this: there are four of them and one is the Hero (although later on he decides to be the Villain), one is the Location Scout, one is the Publicity Agent, and one is the Casting Director, and it all starts at the end, when you're in the bar before the show has really started and you get given these sparklers and streamers and you're asked to welcome the performers back into the theatre. And you wave them about a bit as they come through the bar and disappear into the theatre.

You take your seat and opposite from where you are sitting is a screen that is divided into four sections, they light up and there is a lot of confused talking, some people appear to be getting ready to do something and some of them sound a little bit nervous, and at a certain point they all say something like 'Synchronise watches', although I think in fact they say something else, but that's the gist of it.

wahrer Moment unter dem einzigen Gesetz, das wirklich gilt, dem des Zufalls (und vom Ende her betrachtet, da machen sogar die Luftschlangen und die Lichtkerzen, da macht sogar der Zufall Sinn).

Emily Shenston:

Ich besuchte Vorstellung von *Super Night Shot* – einem Film, der erst eine Stunde vor seiner Aufführung entstand und in meiner Heimatstadt West Bromwich gedreht worden ist. Ich lebe seit 21 Jahren in West Bromwich – mein ganzes Leben lang. Als Kind spielte ich auf denselben Straßen, durch die ich heute zum Büro gehe. Für mich hat der Film meine tägliche Routine eingefangen und gleichzeitig hat Gob Squad darin eine ganz neue Dimension eingeführt. Die rissigen Pflastersteine, der Verkehr, die Neonschilder der Take-Aways gegen den kalten grauen Zement. Dieses ungeschnittene und wunderschön realistische Stück hat mir vor Augen geführt, wie viel ich sehe, ohne es zu betrachten.

Super Night Shot funktionierte, weil es echt war ... und Wirklichkeit ist das, was uns betrifft, jeden von uns, an jedem Tag unseres Lebens. Ich verlor mich in meiner eigenen Realität ... in ihrer rauen, ungeschminkten Schönheit und ging mit dem Gefühl, besonders zu sein, dankbar für das überwältigende Gefühl, mir meiner selbst bewusst zu sein.

And then it begins.

Or at least what I mean to say is that then the bit of it that lies in the centre of the piece begins, because of course it all began back there in the bar with the bit that will actually turn out to be the end. And it begins with them all going out of the theatre, and the cameras are mostly pointed at the floor and swinging about a lot, but if you know the venue then you recognise that they are walking towards Kastanienallee, although of course it doesn't have to be there, it could be somewhere else, but on this night (which is a cold night, a fucking cold night in Berlin in December), that's where they are. In my head it's all a bit confused what happens next, but for sure they all split up. They are no longer all in the same vicinity, and the cameras start not to point just at the floor but up at the protagonists:

1. Simon as the Hero going up to people and asking them if they have anything heroic they'd like him to do, and somebody letting him carry them across the road.
2. Sean as the Location Scout hanging around in a lot of ill-lit alley ways complaining that they're not the right place.
3. Berit as the Press Agent, putting up posters with Simon's face on, and announcing the appearance of a hero to the bemused looking passers by.
4. Elyce as the Casting Agent trying to persuade people that they'd like to be in a film, and not having much luck, and eventually getting so frustrated that she flags down a rather confused looking guy on a bicycle and asks him if he'll give her a lift, and him rather uncertainly agreeing,

Robin Arthur:

Okay, es geht ungefähr so: Sie sind zu viert, und einer von ihnen ist der Held (obwohl er sich später entscheidet, der Schurke zu sein), einer ist der Location Scout, einer ist der Presse-Agent und einer ist der Casting-Agent, und es beginnt alles am Ende, wo man in der Bar ist, bevor die Show anfängt, und man bekommt diese Wunderkerzen und Luftschlangen ausgehändigt und wird gebeten, die Performer, die gerade ins Theater zurückkehren, willkommen zu heißen. Und man winkt ihnen ein bißchen hinterher, während sie durch die Bar kommen und im Theater verschwinden. Man nimmt seinen Platz ein, gegenüber ist eine Leinwand, die in vier Teile aufgeteilt ist, die Projektion beginnt, und dann wird viel durcheinander geredet. Ein paar Leute scheinen sich auf irgendwas vorzubereiten, und einige klingen ein bißchen nervös, und an einem bestimmten Punkt sagen alle sowas wie „Uhren synchronisieren", obwohl, ich glaube, in Wirklichkeit sagen sie was anderes, aber es geht in die Richtung.

Und dann fängt es an.

Oder zumindest beginnt dann der Teil, der den Mittelpunkt des Stücks bildet, weil natürlich alles schon draußen in der Bar begonnen hat mit dem, was sich dann als Ende herausstellen wird. Es beginnt also damit, dass sie alle das Theater verlassen, und die Kameras sind vor allem auf den Boden gerichtet und schwenken viel hin und her, aber wenn man den Veranstaltungsort kennt, dann erkennt man, dass sie auf die Kastanienallee rauslaufen, obwohl es natürlich nicht da sein müsste, es könnte auch woanders sein, aber an

photo: David Baltzer

although looking a bit concerned when he asks her 'Where to?', and she says 'Anywhere'.

I'm being thrown effortlessly backwards and forwards between these narratives by the way in which the sound is being edited, and I feel as though I have been invited into a very strange place indeed, although it is still mostly recognisable as the area around Kastanienallee. Elyce is in middle of trying to explain to this guy with the bike that she'd like him to be in this film she's making, and that he'd have to kiss someone, and that he looks just a little bit disappointed when she explains that this someone is not going to be her. The hallucinatory quality is upped just a little bit more as all of the screens begin to show the same image, or the same action, or more precisely, on all four screens the cameras are circling the protagonists, who are standing still in the middle of the picture, and at this point the piece goes somewhere else, because now you understand that although this piece is in love with the random events of the city at night, it is also a kind of dance, a strangely imposed symmetry, where the chance encounter is given a shape and a consequence. In a strange way I'm reminded of *A Midsummer Night's Dream*, although, of course, this is Midwinter Night, or near as dammit, and the woods outside Athens have been exchanged for the streets of Prenzlauer Berg. And as we are all watching these four rotating cameras we are happy. You can feel this still sometimes in what I will persist in calling the theatre.

diesem Abend (der ein kalter, verdammt kalter Abend in Berlin im Dezember ist), sind sie dort. In meinem Kopf geht alles ein bißchen durcheinander, was als Nächstes passiert, aber sicher ist, dass sich alle trennen. Sie sind jetzt nicht mehr in nächster Nähe zueinander und die Kameras richten sich nicht mehr auf den Boden, sondern auf die Protagonisten:

1. Simon als der Held geht auf Leute zu und fragt sie nach etwas Heroischem, das er für sie tun könnte, und einer lässt sich von ihm über die Straße tragen.
2. Sean als Location Scout hängt viel in schlecht beleuchteten Gassen herum und beschwert sich, dass sie nicht geeignet sind.
3. Berit als Presse-Agentin hängt Poster mit Simons Bild auf und kündigt erstaunten Passanten das Erscheinen eines Heldes an.
4. Elyce als Casting-Agentin versucht jemanden zu überzeugen, in einem Film mitzuwirken, hat dabei nicht viel Glück und wird irgendwann so frustriert, dass sie einen ziemlich verwirrten Typ auf einem Fahrrad ranwinkt und ihn fragt, ob er sie mitnimmt, und er etwas verunsichert einwilligt, und dann doch ein bisschen betroffen guckt, als er fragt „Wohin?", und sie antwortet „egal".

Durch die Art, wie der Ton gemischt wird, werde ich mühelos zwischen den Erzählungen hin und her geworfen, und ich fühle mich, als wäre ich an einen sehr merkwürdigen Ort eingeladen worden, obwohl es immer noch größtenteils

It goes on:

5. Simon rejects the role of Hero and adopts that of Villain. 'Internet is over,' he shouts in an internet café, 'Why don't you get out and talk to real people?' – 'Because I spent $700 on phone calls home last month' replies a pissed off customer.
6. Elyce is chatting with her cyclist in his apartment. He seems to be coming round to the idea that he could do this film thing.
7. Berit is in a tram, warning people not to approach Simon the villain. People are looking a bit bewildered.
8. Sean has put a wolf's head mask on and is howling. (Did this really happen, or am I making it up?)

There's a kind of menace in the air. I am increasingly concerned that this piece will end with some kind of violence (I mean, is it really sensible to go back to the apartment of somebody you don't know at all? When will somebody punch Simon? What the fuck is Sean doing? How often can you rail at people in a tram before some conscientious citizen calls the police?) And it's at this point that the mechanism behind the piece swings into action, that the form asserts itself and we find ourselves pulled back from the edge. The moment we have been waiting for all through the piece has happened, and in many ways it's not much – a man embraces another man wearing a rabbit head. In other ways it feels like an epiphany – a moment beyond time, the construction of something from nothing, the triumph of a persistent kind of hope

erkennbar ist als die Gegend um die Kastanienallee. Elyce ist dabei, dem Typ mit dem Fahrrad zu erklären, dass sie ihn in dem Film haben will, den sie gerade dreht, und dass er darin jemanden küssen müsste, und er sieht ein bisschen enttäuscht aus, als sie erklärt, dass dieser jemand nicht sie sein wird. Die halluzinierende Qualität steigert sich noch, als alle Leinwände anfangen, das gleiche Bild zu zeigen, oder die gleiche Handlung, oder genauer gesagt, auf allen vier Leinwänden umkreisen die Kameras die Protagonisten, die im Mittelpunkt des Bildes unbewegt stehen, und an diesem Punkt nimmt das Stück eine andere Wendung, weil man jetzt versteht, dass, obwohl das Stück verzaubert ist von den willkürlichen Ereignissen der Stadt bei Nacht, es doch auch eine Art Tanz ist, eine merkwürdig täuschende Symmetrie, in der die zufällige Begegnung eine Form und eine Konsequenz erhält. Merkwürdigerweise fühle ich mich an den *Sommernachtstraum* erinnert, obwohl das natürlich ein Winternachtstraum ist, oder beinahe, verdammt noch mal, und die Wälder außerhalb von Athen haben sich in die Straßen von Prenzlauer Berg verwandelt. Und während man diesen vier rotierenden Kameras zusieht, ist man glücklich. Man kann das in dem, was ich hartnäckig das Theater nenne, manchmal immer noch spüren.

Es geht weiter:

5. Simon weist die Rolle des Helden von sich und nimmt die des Schurken an. „Internet ist Vergangenheit", schreit er in einem Internet-Café. „Warum geht ihr nicht raus und

over a brittle adversity. Like a bad teller of jokes I'm left with the same line – 'you had to be there to understand it'. Not perhaps such a bad thing to say about a show, something live, something not reducible to text.

And then there's the aftermath. Bodies pile into a car. There is something that threatens to be a final crash, but is thrown away, and lastly, the performers enter the bar to their deservedly triumphant greeting. And you do look. You do look to make sure that you're there in that crowd of sparkler-waving streamer-throwing people, just to be sure that no tricks have been played, that this hour was a real hour, and of course you pick yourself out on the screen.

Tarkovsky titled his critical autobiography *Sculpting in Time*, and I was constantly reminded of this phrase during *Super Night Shot*. A piece of time shaped and made good. But time is an ephemeral medium, and memory is poor paper. That was *Super Night Shot*, fading slowly in my mind, but strangely present still, and destined to remain there all my life.

redet mit echten Leuten?" – „Weil ich letzten Monat 700 $ für Telefonanrufe nach Hause ausgegeben habe", antwortet ein verärgerter Kunde.

6. Elyce plaudert mit ihrem Radfahrer in seiner Wohnung. Er scheint langsam auf den Geschmack zu kommen, bei dieser Film-Sache mitzumachen.

7. Berit ist in der Straßenbahn und warnt die Leute, sich von Simon, dem Schurken, fernzuhalten. Die Leute sehen leicht bestürzt aus.

8. Sean hat sich eine Wolfsmaske aufgesetzt und heult den Mond an. (Ist das wirklich passiert, oder denk ich mir das aus?)

Eine Art Bedrohung liegt in der Luft. Meine Sorge wächst, dass dieses Stück auf irgendeine Weise in Gewalt enden wird. (Ich meine, ist es etwa vernünftig, mit jemandem nach Hause zu gehen, den man überhaupt nicht kennt? Wann wird jemand Simon eine reinhauen? Was zum Teufel macht Sean? Wie lang kann man Leute in der Straßenbahn anschreien, bevor irgendein gewissenhafter Bürger die Polizei ruft?) Und genau an diesem Punkt fängt der Mechanismus hinter dem Stück an zu greifen, die Form erfüllt sich, und wir fühlen uns vom Abgrund zurückgerissen. Der Augenblick, auf den wir das ganze Stück lang gewartet haben, findet statt, und irgendwie passiert nicht viel – ein Mann küsst einen anderen Mann, der eine Hasenmaske trägt. Andererseits ist es wie eine Erleuchtung – ein Moment jenseits der Zeit, das Erschaffen von etwas aus dem Nichts, der Triumph einer hartnäckigen Art von Hoffnung über jede

photo: David Baltzer

spröde Widrigkeit. Wie ein schlechter Witze-Erzähler, bleibt mir nur dieser Satz – „Man muss dabei gewesen sein, um es zu verstehen". Vielleicht nicht das Schlechteste, was man über eine Show sagen kann, etwas das live ist, das man nicht auf Text reduzieren kann.

Und dann kommt das Nachspiel. Körper drängen sich in ein Auto. Es gibt etwas, das eine finale Kollision zu sein droht, und schließlich betreten die Performer die Bar zu ihrer verdient triumphalen Begrüßung. Und man schaut hin. Man schaut genau hin, um sicherzugehen, dass man da in der Menge von Wunderkerzen schwenkenden, Luftschlangen werfenden Leuten steht, nur um sicher zu sein, dass da kein Trick war, dass diese Stunde eine wirkliche Stunde war, und natürlich findet man sich auf der Leinwand wieder.

Tarkowsky hat seiner kritischen Autobiografie den Titel Sculpting In Time („Die versiegelte Zeit") gegeben, und während *Super Night Shot* fühlte ich mich ständig an diese Formulierung erinnert. Ein Stück Zeit gestaltet und zu etwas Gutem gemacht. Doch Zeit ist ein ephemeres Medium, und Erinnerung ist nur armseliges Papier. Das war *Super Night Shot*, welches langsam in meinem Hirn verblasst, doch immer noch merkwürdig präsent ist und dort für immer bleiben wird.

Something To Believe In

Selected Photographs/Auswahl an Fotografien

Gob Squad, 2004. photo: Manuel Reinartz

Gob Squad, 1997

Gob Squad, 2001

House

House

Work. photo: Simon Cunningham

An Effortless Transaction. photo: Simon Cunningham

An Effortless Transaction. photo: Simon Cunningham

An Effortless Transaction. photo: Simon Cunningham

Close Enough To Kiss

Close Enough To Kiss. photo: Simon Cunningham

15 Minutes To Comply. photo: Wonge Bergmann

15 Minutes To Comply.

Calling Laika. photo: Wonge Bergmann

Calling Laika. photo: Wonge Bergmann

What Are You Looking At?

What Are You Looking At? photo: Armin Linke

Safe. photo: Arno Declair

Safe. photo: Arno Declair

Say It Like You Mean It. photo: Armin Linke

Say It Like You Mean It. photo: Christian Brox

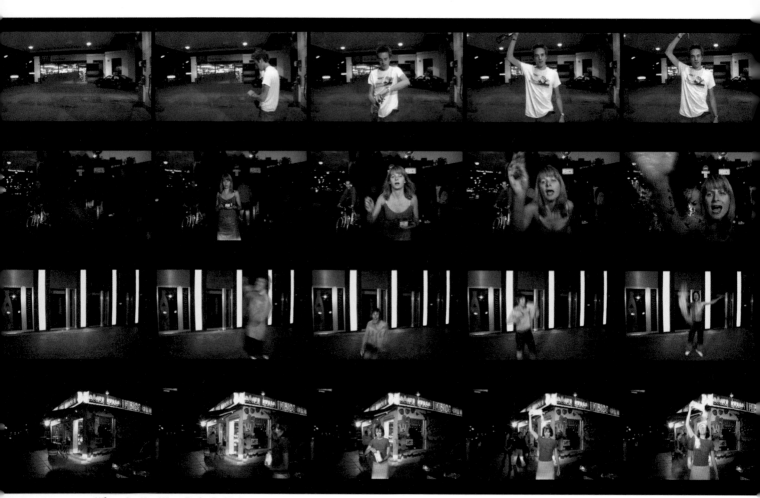

Where Do You Want To Go To Die?

Where Do You Want To Go To Die?

Where Do You Want To Go To Die?

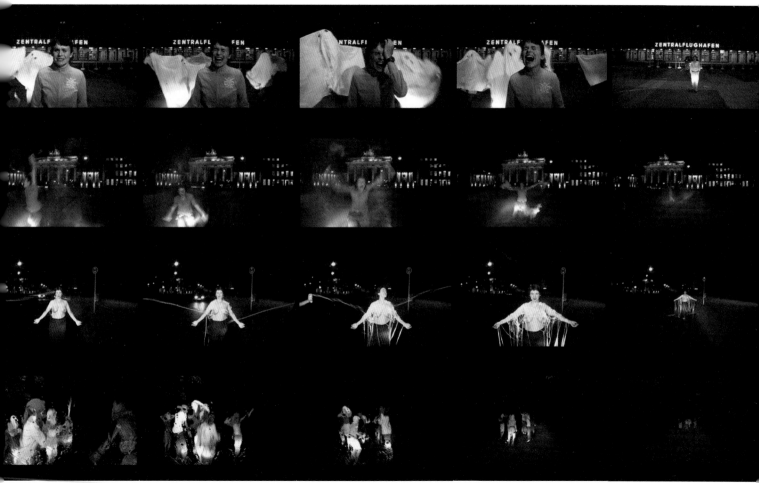

Where Do You Want To Go To Die?

The Great Outdoors. photo: Miles Chalcraft. drawing: Mark Jeffery

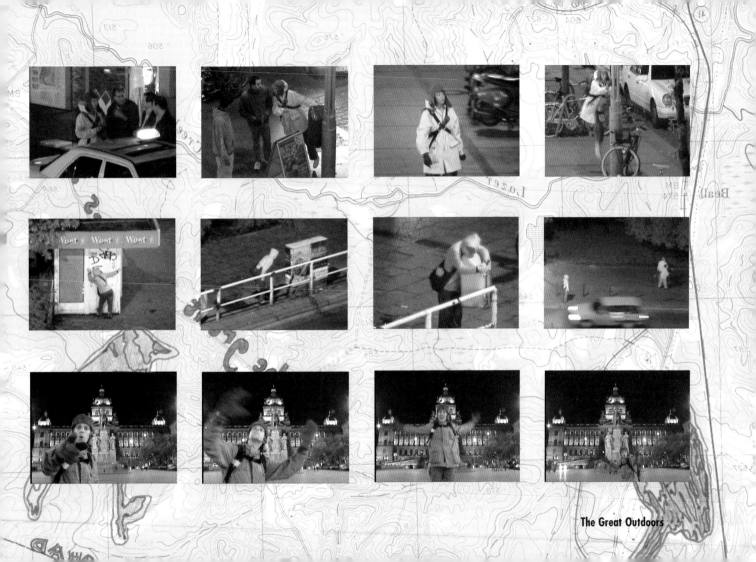

The Great Outdoors

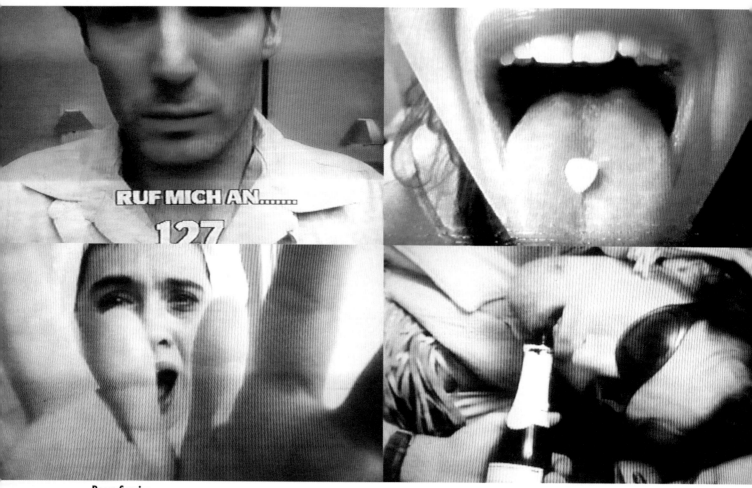

RUF MICH AN.......
127

Room Service

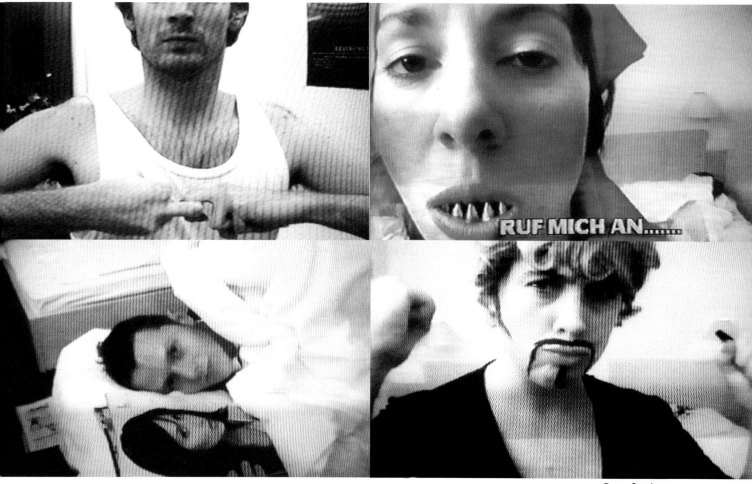

RUF MICH AN.......

Room Service

Super Night Shot. photo: David Baltzer

Super Night Shot. photos: David Baltzer/Gob Squad

Daniel Brine:
Things from my collection/Dinge aus meiner Sammlung

On a shelf at home I display a small collection of perform-ance memorabilia. It consists of little things I've been given or picked up as part of performances – a packet of turnip seeds, a small box of sand, a few grains of rice, a bar of hotel soap, a security pass, a vinyl single, a couple of polar-oids, some badges, an acorn, etc. Some of these things are mementos of performances I've enjoyed or are linked to people I admire or represent projects I have worked on or are just nice objects. It's sentimental, I know, but some-times it's nice to prompt memory.

These things are part of my collection:

A Christmas greeting from Gob Squad on a small slip of paper
The piece of paper is very small and I can't remember if it came inside a party popper or not. I do remember that it was accompanied in an envelope by some glitter that stuck around for months. Printed in the centre of the slip is a photo of the Gob Squad members wearing white tuxedoes and long party frocks, and red 'Santa' hats with white fluffy trim and pom-poms. To the left of Gob Squad are instruct-ions:

Auf einem Regal bei mir zu Hause habe ich eine kleine Sammlung von Performance-Andenken ausgestellt. Sie be-steht aus Dingen, die ich bekommen oder aufgesammelt habe als Bestandteil von Performances – eine Packung Tulpen-samen, eine kleine Schachtel mit Sand, ein paar Reiskörner, ein Stück Hotelseife, ein Sicherheitsausweis, eine Vinyl-Single, ein paar Polaroid-Fotos, einige Anstecker, eine Eichel etc. Manche dieser Sachen sind Erinnerungsstücke von Perfor-mances, die mir besonders gefallen haben, oder sie sind mit Leuten verbunden, die ich bewundere, oder stehen für Pro-jekte, an denen ich beteiligt war, oder es sind einfach schöne Gegenstände. Es ist sentimental, ich weiß, aber manchmal ist es gut, dem Gedächtnis auf die Sprünge zu helfen.

Folgende Dinge gehören zu meiner Sammlung:

Ein Weihnachtsgruß von Gob Squad auf einem kleinen Streifen Papier
Das Stück Papier ist sehr klein, und ich kann mich nicht ent-sinnen, ob es aus einem Knallbonbon kam oder nicht. Ich erinnere mich aber, dass es in einem Umschlag war zusam-men mit etwas Glitter, der monatelang überall hängenblieb. In der Mitte des Papierstreifens ist ein Foto der Gob-Squad-Mitglieder in weißen Smokings und langen Abendkleidern

gather a small crowd.
generate an atmosphere of seasonal excitement.
release the christmas spirit (do not point at eyes).

On the right there is a warning:
party poppers can sometimes be a little disappointing!

A photo that looks like a bad school photo but it isn't

I can't actually recognise myself because the print quality is low and the image has faded. But I know I'm standing in the back row wearing a tall crown/hat and a bib that I made to shield myself from radiation. The photo was taken as part of the climax of *Say It Like You Mean It*.

A Gob Squad business card

I don't know if someone handed me this card or if it came in the post. On one side is the Gob Squad address. On the other side is a picture of two wide-eyed kittens standing upright wearing dresses and aprons. One of the kittens is standing in front of an ironing board. The text, under the image, reads: *it doesn't always make sense.*

mit roten Nikolaus-Hüten mit flauschigem weißem Pelzrand und Bommel. Links von Gob Squad steht eine Gebrauchsanweisung:

Versammeln Sie eine kleine Gesellschaft.
Erzeugen Sie eine Atmosphäre festlicher Vorfreude.
Setzen Sie die Weihnachtsstimmung frei. (Nicht auf die Augen richten.)

Rechts ist ein Warnhinweis:
Knallbonbons können manchmal etwas enttäuschend sein!

Ein Foto, das wie ein schlechtes Schulfoto aussieht, aber keines ist

Ich weiß, dass es keines ist, weil ich Teil der Gruppe bin. Ich kann mich selbst nicht wirklich erkennen, weil die Druckqualität schlecht ist und das Bild verblichen. Aber ich weiß, dass ich in der letzten Reihe stehe, eine hohe Krone/Hut trage und einen Latz, den ich mir zum Schutz vor Strahlung gemacht habe. Das Foto wurde aufgenommen als Teil des Höhepunkts von *Say It Like You Mean It*, aber ich bin mir nicht mehr sicher, ob es vor oder nach der Prozession durch die Liebeslaube gemacht wurde.

Eine Visitenkarte von Gob Squad

Ich weiß nicht, ob mir jemand diese Karte gegeben hat oder ob sie mit der Post kam. Auf einer Seite ist die Gob Squad-Adresse. Auf der anderen Seite ist ein Bild von zwei großäugigen Kätzchen, die aufrecht stehen und Kleider und Schürzen tragen. Eines der Kätzchen steht vor einem Bügelbrett. Der Text unter dem Bild lautet: Es macht nicht immer Sinn.

Gob Squad:
The Unauthorised Biography/Die wahre Geschichte

Part One: The Early Years

1992: A bunch of long-haired students at Nottingham Trent University's Creative Arts course make up a performance to get into Glastonbury festival for free. The piece is hailed as wonderfully entertaining nonsense by the Glastonbury revellers and a sharp Marxist critique of the class system by their tutors back at college. Taking their name from a mixtape playing in the van on the way to Somerset, they call themselves "The Gob Squad". They go on to make 4 further Glastonbury shows, all in exchange for free tickets.

Part Two: From Rags To Riches

1994: The group graduate from university and make their first professional piece of work, *House*, performed in a Nottingham council house. Sean Patten, Sarah Thom and visiting Gießen "theatre science" student Berit Stumpf get the project started and are later joined by Theatre Design graduate Liane Sommers, fellow Gießen student Johanna Freiburg and "rocket artist" Miles Chalcraft. Alex Large plays a duster salesman in the back garden. The project is com-

Teil Eins: Die frühen Jahre

1992: Eine Gruppe langhaariger Studenten des Kunststudiengangs an der Trent University, Nottingham macht eine Performance, um umsonst beim Glastonbury-Festival dabeisein zu können. Das Glastonbury-Festival ist das größte Pop/Rockfestival in Europa – das englische Woodstock (3 Tage, 3 Nächte; 100.000 Leute schlafen in Zelten; viele Bands, viele Drogen). Das Stück wird vonseiten der Partygänger in Glastonbury als großartig unterhaltsamer Unsinn begrüßt und vonseiten ihrer Dozenten am College als scharfe marxistische Kritik des Klassensystems. Sie nennen sich „The Gob Squad" nach einer Mix-Kassette, die sie im Transporter nach Somerset spielten. Sie werden 4 weitere Shows für Glastonbury produzieren, alle im Tausch gegen Festival-Freikarten.

Teil Zwei: Auf dem Weg nach oben

1994: Die Gruppe schließt ihr Studium an der Universität ab und macht ihre erste professionelle Arbeit *House* in einem Sozialwohnungsbau der Stadt Nottingham. Sean Patten,

Alex Large
1994-2001

Sarah Thom
1994-?

Sean Patten
1994-?

Liane Sommers
1994-2001

Johanna Freiburg
1994-?

Simon Will
1999-?

Berit Stumpf
1994-?

Bastian Trost
2003-?

Nottingham, 1992. Alex Large emblazons the company logo on a hired van. Alex Large appliziert das Gruppenlogo auf einen geliehenen Transporter.

missioned by young arts producer Simon Will for Expo 94 with a total production budget of £400. The group make their first TV appearance, a 3 minute slot on "East Midlands Today".

1995: Patten and Thom spend their entire earnings from a bit of teaching work on a PC. They become the first people on their (admittedly run-down) street to own a computer and write the concept for *Work* on it, enthusiastically handing it in personally to NOW festival director, Andrew Chetty. Later

Sarah Thom und Berit Stumpf, Theaterwissenschafts-Studentinnen aus Gießen, bringen das Projekt auf den Weg, dem sich später auch Liane Sommers (studierte Bühnenbildnerin), die Gießener Studentin Johanna Freiburg und der „Raketenkünstler" Miles Chalcraft anschließen. Alex Large spielt im Garten einen Staubwedel-Vertreter. Das Projekt wird von dem jungen Kurator Simon Will für die Expo 94 mit einem Gesamtbudget von 400 Pfund in Auftrag gegeben. Die Gruppe erhält zum ersten Mal die Aufmerksamkeit der Medien: ein 3-Minuten-Feature in der Lokalsendung „East Midlands Today".

1995: Ihren gesamten Verdienst aus ein bißchen Lehrtätigkeit geben Patten und Thom für einen Computer aus. Sie sind die ersten in ihrer (zugegebenermaßen runtergekommenen) Straße, die einen Computer besitzen, schreiben darauf das Konzept zu *Work* und übergeben es begeistert dem Leiter des NOW Festivals, Andrew Chetty. Später in diesem Jahr wird *Work* eine Arbeitswoche lang täglich 9 – 17 Uhr aufgeführt. Diejenigen, die für die nächsten 5 Jahre Kernmitglieder der Gruppe sein sollten, arbeiten zusammen an dem Projekt: Freiburg, Large, Patten, Sommers, Stumpf, Thom. Miles Chalcraft arbeitet ebenfalls mit. Das Produktionsbudget beträgt mehr als das 10fache von *House*. Nach der Hälfte des Arbeitsprozesses kauft sich die gesamte Gruppe neue Klamotten im Trend-Bezirk Hockley. Miles Chalcraft tritt die nächsten 9 Jahre nicht mehr mit Gob Squad auf.

that year, *Work* is performed in Nottingham from 9-5 each day for a working week. The core membership of the group for the next 5 years all work on the project: Freiburg, Large, Patten, Sommers, Stumpf, Thom. Miles Chalcraft also collaborates. The production budget is over 10 times greater than for *House*. Half way through the process the entire group buys themselves some new clothes from the trendy Hockley district. Miles Chalcraft doesn't perform again with Gob Squad for another 9 years.

1996: Now working collectively on the concept, design, devising and performing of their projects, the group produce *An Effortless Transaction*, performed in a furniture shop in Nottingham's Broadmarsh shopping centre. Despite trauma and relationship turmoil within the group, the piece is actually quite good. The shop has since closed down.

1997: *15 Minutes to Comply* presented in an underground station at Documenta X. The group asks for the use of a train on the technical list. Their request is granted. However, it is politely explained that artists "don't get paid" to be in Documenta, so they learn the lesson that fortune doesn't necessarily follow fame relatively early in their careers. The first Gob Squad office opens in Nottingham. Wages for admin work start to be paid at a rate of £1.25 per hour. First website and business cards produced. Alex Large edits first company promotional video. *Close Enough To Kiss* tours UK and Germany. First company computer purchased: Apple Performa 5400. The word "The" is dropped from the group's official title.

1996: Die Gruppe, die jetzt im Kollektiv an Konzept, Ausstattung, Planung und Ausführung ihrer Projekte arbeitet, produziert *An Effortless Transaction*, das in einem Möbelgeschäft im Broadmarsh-Einkaufszentrum in Nottingham aufgeführt wird. Trotz Krise und Beziehungsproblemen innerhalb der Gruppe ist das Stück letztendlich ziemlich gut. Der Laden hat seither zugemacht.

1997: *15 Minutes to Comply* wird in einer unterirdischen Straßenbahn-Haltestelle auf der *documenta* X präsentiert. Die Gruppe beantragt die Benutzung einer U-Bahn auf der Technikliste. Dem Antrag wird stattgegeben. Allerdings erklärt man ihnen freundlich, dass Künstler für ihren Auftritt bei der *documenta* „nicht bezahlt werden", so lernen sie relativ früh in ihrer Karriere, dass Reichtum nicht notwendig auf den Ruhm folgt. Das erste Gob-Squad-Büro öffnet in Nottingham. Das Gehalt für administrative Arbeit beginnt bei einem Stundenlohn von 1,25 £ (umgerechnet 1,80€). Die erste Website und Visitenkarten werden hergestellt. Alex Large produziert das erste Werbevideo der Company. *Close Enough to Kiss* tourt durch England und Deutschland. Die Company kauft ihren ersten Computer: einen Apple Performa 5400. Das Wort „The" wird aus dem offiziellen Titel der Gruppe gestrichen.

Part Three: Fame And Fortune

1998: Gob Squad moves to a new, but damp office with just a wood-burning stove for heating. Important documents start to go mouldy but are burnt for warmth. Martin Cooper, a sound technician recently thrown out of a band for putting too many annoying samples into the mix, is enlisted to work on the soundtrack for *Calling Laika*. The project is produced at TAT, Frankfurt under the watchful eyes of theatre impresario Tom Stromberg. The group starts flying with BA instead of driving a van to Germany. Backpacks from student days wear out and are replaced by suitcases. *What Are You Looking At?* premieres at Berlin Biennale and for a few heady days Gob Squad is the talk of the town. Matt Adams, part-time lecturer in German philosophy, becomes first company administrator. Admin wage increases to £1.87 per hour.

1999: Simon Will stops climbing the arts administration career ladder and joins the group instead. They start taking music lessons during the rehearsal process for *Safe*. After weeks of effort, "Rockin' All Over The World" is played at the Kampnagel premiere in Hamburg. Thanks to a little nepotism, Safe is presented at the Edinburgh Fringe, courtesy of Armstrong Vinyl Flooring.
The majority of the group now lives in Berlin, and become artists-in-residence at the Podewil Centre for Contemporary Art at the invitation of theatre curator Aenne Quiñones. Christina Runge, fresh out of a cultural management course, takes over as administrator and achieves a rare under-

Teil Drei: Ruhm und Reichtum

1998: Gob Squad zieht in ein neues, aber feuchtes Büro um, das nur einen Holzofen zum Heizen hat. Wichtige Dokumente verschimmeln, werden aber noch zum Heizen verwendet. Martin Cooper, ein Tontechniker, der kurz zuvor aus einer Band geworfen wurde, weil er zu viele nervige Samples im Mix verwendete, wird angeworben, am Soundtrack von *Calling Laika* zu arbeiten. Das Projekt wird am TAT Frankfurt unter den wachsamen Augen des Impresarios Tom Stromberg produziert. Die Gruppe reist von nun an mit British Airways, anstatt mit einem Kleinbus nach Deutschland zu fahren. Rucksäcke aus Studenten-Tagen sind mittlerweile abgetragen und werden durch Koffer ersetzt. *What Are You Looking At?* hat auf der *berlin biennale* Premiere, und für ein paar turbulente Tage ist Gob Squad Stadtgespräch. Matt Adams, Teilzeit-Dozent für deutsche Philosophie, wird der erste Administrator der Company. Der Stundenlohn für administrative Tätigkeiten steigt auf 1.87 £ (umgerechnet 2,70€).

1999: Simon Will gibt es auf, die Karriereleiter des Kunstbetriebs hinaufzusteigen und tritt stattdessen der Gruppe bei. Während des Probenprozesses zu *Safe* nehmen die Mitglieder Musikunterricht. Nach wochenlangen Mühen wird „Rockin' All Over the World" auf der Kampnagel-Premiere in Hamburg gespielt. Vetternwirtschaft ist es zu verdanken, daß *Safe* auf dem Edinburgh Fringe Festival gezeigt werden kann („Mit freundlicher Unterstützung von Armstrong Vinyl Fußbodenbeläge"). Der Großteil der Gruppe lebt jetzt in Berlin

Kampnagel, Hamburg, 1999. The "structure wall" takes shape during rehearsals for *Safe*. Action, Text, Sound, Video and the Emotions Graph are mapped out from left to right. / Die „Dramaturgie-Wand" füllt sich während der Proben für *Safe*. Handlung, Text, Sound, Video und Emotionsschwankungen werden von links nach rechts graphisch fixiert.

standing of the workings of the German tax system, earning her the nickname "Miss Moneypenny", *Little White Lies*, a one-off performance for live audience and radio broadcast is presented at Akademie der Künste. At the after-show party, Alex Large's bag, containing all photo and video documentation of the piece, is stolen, never to be seen again.

Portland, 2001. Our name in lights

2000: In spite of last-minute help from sound designer Sebastian Bark, *Say It Like You Mean It* premieres to a mixed response. Several important critics and promoters chat, smoke and even sleep through the performance then say their goodbyes. A video installation, *Where Do You Want To Go To Die?* is made for Expo 2000, Hannover and installed outside the German pavillion. Soon after opening, the piece is closed down by the

und wird auf Einladung der Kuratorin Aenne Quiñones Artist-In-Residence im Podewil, Zentrum für zeitgenössische Kunst. Christina Runge, frisch vom Kulturmanagement-Seminar kommend, übernimmt die Administration und erwirbt ein außergewöhnliches Verständnis des deutschen Steuersystems, welches ihr den Spitznamen „Miss Moneypenny" einbringt. *Little White Lies*, eine einmalige Performance für Live-Publikum und Radio-Übertragung, wird an der Akademie der Künste präsentiert. Auf der Party nach der Show wird Alex Larges Tasche mit der gesamten Foto- und Video-Dokumentation des Stücks gestohlen und taucht nie wieder auf.

2000: Trotz Hilfe in letzter Minute durch Sounddesigner Sebastian Bark ruft *Say It Like You Mean It* bei der Premiere gemischte Reaktionen hervor. Mehrere wichtige Kritiker und Veranstalter schwätzen, rauchen und schlafen während der Performance, um sich im Anschluss auf Nimmerwiedersehen zu verabschieden. *Where Do You Want To Go To Die?*, eine Video-Installation, wird für die *Expo 2000 Hannover* produziert und auf dem Gelände vor dem Deutschen Pavillon aufgebaut. Kurz nach der Eröffnung wird das Stück von den Organisatoren abgesetzt, aus Angst vor schlechter Publicity, nachdem ein Besucher im Gebäude zu Tode gestürzt ist. Der Stundenlohn für administrative Tätigkeiten steigt auf 10 Deutsche Mark.

organisers who fear bad publicity after a member of the public falls to his death inside the building. Admin wage increases to 10 Deutschmarks (£3.30) per hour.

Part Four: Ch... Ch... Changes

2001: The year they broke America... and America almost broke them. Safe tours the US and the group are pleasantly surprised to find that a piece sometimes reviewed as "superficial and shallow" in Germany was thought of as "deep, dark" and "far-out" in the States. However, these were to be the final performances of Safe as Liane Sommers and Alex Large decide enough is enough and leave the group to pursue solo careers in the music video industry. The unflappable Eva Hartmann supersedes Christina Runge as company administrator. The remaining members are rejoined by Miles Chalcraft and take a new direction, working with internet, phone and video technology to make *The Great Outdoors*.

2002: The average age of the group is now distinctly over 30. Journalists have ceased referring to the collective as "young" artists. Group members now live in Hamburg, Nottingham and Berlin. Some have children, some are pregnant and some are in therapy. It seems impossible to draw up a rehearsal schedule which meets everyone's needs. Everyone agrees Room Service will be Gob Squad's make-or-break project. The group asks film/TV actor, Bastian Trost and

Teil Vier: „Ch... Ch... Changes" (Veränderungen)

2001: Das Jahr, in dem sie es bis nach Amerika schafften... und Amerika sie fast zerbrach. *Safe* tourt durch die USA, und die Gruppe ist angenehm überrascht, dass ein Stück, das in Deutschland zuweilen als „oberflächlich und seicht" rezensiert wurde, in den Vereinigten Staaten für „tiefgründig", „düster" und „abgedreht" befunden wird. Trotz alledem sollen dies die letzten Aufführungen von *Safe* sein, da Liane Sommers und Alex Large entscheiden, genug ist genug, und die Gruppe verlassen, um Solo-Karrieren in der Musikvideo-Industrie zu verfolgen. Die unerschütterliche Eva Hartmann übernimmt von Christina Runge die Administration der Company. Die übrigen Mitglieder schließen sich erneut mit Miles Chalcraft zusammen und schlagen eine neue Richtung ein, sie arbeiten mit Internet-, Telefon- und Video-Technologie an *The Great Outdoors*.

2002: Das Durchschnittsalter der Gruppe liegt jetzt deutlich über 30. Journalisten haben aufgehört, das Kollektiv als „junge Künstler" zu bezeichnen. Die Gruppenmitglieder leben jetzt in Hamburg, Nottingham und Berlin. Manche haben Kinder, manche sind schwanger und manche sind in Therapie. Es scheint unmöglich, einen Probenplan zu erstellen, der allen Bedürfnissen gerecht wird. Alle sind sich einig, dass *Room Service* entweder den Durchbruch oder das Ende von Gob Squad bedeuten wird. Die Gruppe fragt den Film- und Fernsehschauspieler Bastian Trost und die amerikanische Performance- und Videokünstlerin Elyce Semenec, an

Leuven, Belgium, 2001. On the road. photo: Falk Hoysack

Podewil, Berlin, 2004. Backstage at Lust Lies Art & Fashion.

American performance/video artist Elyce Semenec to collaborate on the project. Sound designer Jeff McGrory also works with Gob Squad for the first time. Rehearsals get underway in an erotic photo-studio in Berlin and despite an outbreak of scarlet fever, group morale is restored and *Room Service* is judged a great success.

Part Five: A World Without Frontiers

2003: Podewil loses both funding and artistic direction and the Gob Squad office moves to a disused perfume shop in central Berlin. As the year planner gradually fills up with *Room Service* gigs, Gob Squad is sued for 6000€ by a hotel chain

dem Projekt mitzuwirken. Auch Sounddesigner Jeff McGrory arbeitet zum ersten Mal mit Gob Squad. Die Proben beginnen in einem Erotik-Fotostudio in Berlin, und trotz eines Ausbruchs von Scharlachfieber ist die Moral der Gruppe wiederhergestellt, und *Room Service* wird als großer Erfolg verzeichnet.

Teil Fünf: Welt ohne Grenzen

2003: Das Podewil verliert sowohl seine Förderung als auch seine künstlerische Leitung, und das Gob-Squad-Büro zieht in einen ehemaligen Parfüm-Laden in Berlin-Mitte um. Wegen eines Tropfens Theaterblut auf einem Teppich wird Gob Squad von einer Hotelkette auf einen Schadensersatz von 6000€ verklagt. Gleichzeitig füllt sich der Kalender nach und nach mit *Room Service*-Gastspielen. Die Gruppe verbringt die beiden heißesten Wochen, die Großbritannien seit Jahrzehnten erlebt hat, auf den mit Wodka, Gewalt und Erbrochenem gepflasterten nächtlichen Straßen von Nottingham. Leicht bekleidet, mit Video-Kameras in der Hand, machen sie improvisierte Filme mit Passanten. Diese Ausbeute wird sich später zu *Super Night Shot* entwickeln, dessen Premiere im Prater der Volksbühne Berlin im eiskalten Dezember stattfindet. Bastian Trost tritt der Gruppe bei und wird das erste Gob-Squad-Mitglied, das jemals eine Schauspielschule besucht hat.

after a drop of fake blood is spilled on a carpet. The group spend the two hottest weeks Britain has seen for decades on the vodka, vomit and violence-strewn streets of night-time Nottingham, walking around half-dressed with video cameras making improvised films with passers-by. These exploits were to evolve into *Super Night Shot*, premiered at the Volksbühne, Berlin in sub-zero December. Bastian Trost joins the group and becomes the first Gob Squad member to have been to drama school.

2004: Oh la la! Having toured Germany, Britain and most of Europe for years, it is now time to conquer the final frontier: France. Festivals all over the country take an interest in the company's work. Those members who got better than grade C at school start learning their French lines ostentatiously in an effort to wind up those who have to stay behind. Back-stage at *Art Rock* in Brittany, Bastian Trost chats to the drummer from Franz Ferdinand's girlfriend just as Jane Birkin walks past. Nina Thielicke joins as assistant administrator. Work begins on *Prater-Saga 3: In diesem Kiez ist der Teufel eine Goldmine*. During a performance, an outraged audience member heckles Berit Stumpf and shouts "Watch out for your soul! You will pay for this! You will all die!" before walking out. Gob Squad end the year with a 10th birthday party and a huge cake. Admin wage is now 9€ per hour.

2004: Oh là là! Nachdem sie jahrelang durch Deutschland, Großbritannien und einen Großteil Europas getourt sind, ist nun die Zeit gekommen, die letzte Grenze zu erobern: Frankreich. Festivals überall im Land zeigen Interesse an den Arbeiten der Company. Diejenigen Gruppenmitglieder, die in der Schule besser als Drei benotet wurden, fangen ostentativ an, ihre französischen Texte zu lernen, nur um damit diejenigen zu nerven, die zu Hause bleiben müssen. Backstage bei *Art Rock* in der Bretagne plaudert Bastian Trost mit der Freundin des Drummers von Franz Ferdinand, als gerade Jane Birkin vorbeiläuft. Nina Thielicke kommt als Administrationsassistentin hinzu. Die Arbeit an *Prater-Saga 3: In diesem Kiez ist der Teufel eine Goldmine* beginnt. Während einer Aufführung fällt ein aufgebrachter Zuschauer Berit Stumpf ins Wort und ruft: „Gebt acht auf eure Seele! Ihr werdet dafür bezahlen! Ihr werdet alle sterben!" und verlässt den Saal. Gob Squad beendet das Jahr mit einer Party zum zehnjährigen Jubiläum und einer riesigen Torte. Der Stundenlohn für administrative Tätigkeiten liegt jetzt bei 9€.

Complete overview of work (in chronological order)
Übersicht aller Arbeiten (in chronologischer Reihenfolge)

House
site-specific performance
ortsspezifische Performance

Where: a disused suburban home
How long: 40 minutes

Wo: ein leerstehendes Wohnhaus
Wie lange: 40 Minuten

The audience explores a suburban home room by room, peeping into every cupboard. Basic household activities like sleeping, having a bath and cooking become bizarrely abstracted as the performers search for beauty in the every-day and mundane.

Das Publikum ist eingeladen, ein Wohnhaus Raum für Raum bis hin zur letzten Schublade zu entdecken. Einfache häusliche Tätigkeiten wie Schlafen, Baden und Kochen werden zu bizarren Bildern auf der Suche nach Schönheit im Alltäglichen.

Performed and devised by/Gespielt und inszeniert von: Miles Chalcraft, Johanna Freiburg, Trina Furre and Milly the dog, Sean Patten, Liane Sommers, Berit Stumpf, Sarah Thom, Anja von Steht
With/Mit: James Flower, Gareth Howell, Alex Large, Bobby Singh, Stewart Smith, Matt Watkins, Stephen Watson
Voiceover/Stimme: Rigley Riley
Commissioned by/Im Auftrag von: Expo 94, Nottingham, UK
First performance/Uraufführung: 13.11.1994 (Expo 94, Nottingham, UK)
Further performances/Weitere Aufführungen: Diskurs Festival, Gießen, D (1995)

Way Out West
street performance
Freilichtperformance

Where: outdoors
How long: 20 minutes

Wo: im Freien
Wie lange: 20 Minuten

Dressed in oversized cardboard costumes and lip-synching to a soundtrack sampled from hundreds of films, clichéed Western characters deliver a gag per minute to an audience who are mostly on drugs.

Western-Pappfiguren agieren lippensynchron zu einem Soundrack aus Filmschnipseln und liefern einem Publikum, das überwiegend auf Droge ist, einen Gag pro Minute

Performed and devised by/Gespielt und inszeniert von: Alex Large, Sean Patten, Liane Sommers, Leanne Price, Stephen Watson
Commissioned by/Im Auftrag von: Glastonbury Festival of Contemporary Performing Arts, UK
First performance/Uraufführung: 23.6.1995 (Glastonbury Festival, Glastonbury, UK)
Further performances/Weitere Aufführungen: Nottingham Spring Extravaganza, UK (1995); Nottingham Riverside Festival, UK (1995); Lincoln Street Theatre Festival, UK (1995)

Work

site-specific and durational performance
ortsspezifische Performanc und Live-Installation

Where: a city centre office
How long: 40 hours, the length of a working week (Monday to Friday from 9am-5pm)

Wo: ein Büro im Stadtzentrum
Wie lange: eine 40-Stunden-Woche (Montag bis Freitag von 9 bis 17 Uhr)

Dressed in their best interview suits, Gob Squad spend a full working week in an office, photocopying and filing each precious minute, disturbed only by the brief appearance of astronauts and iceskaters.

Gob Squad verbringt eine gesamte Arbeitswoche in einem Büro und fotokopiert jede Minute ihrer kostbaren Zeit. Nur das kurze Erscheinen von Astronauten und Eiskunstläuferinnen kann ihren Arbeitseifer stören.

Way out West

Performed and devised by/Gespielt und inszeniert von: Miles Chalcraft, Johanna Freiburg, Alex Large, Sean Patten, Liane Sommers, Berit Stumpf, Sarah Thom
Commissioned by/Im Auftrag von: NOW Festival, Nottingham, UK
First performance/Uraufführung: 13.11.1995 (NOW Festival, Nottingham, UK)

Getting from A to B (and things we might learn along the way)

site-specific performance lecture
ortsspezifischer performativer Vortrag

Where: natural history museum
How long: 60 minutes

Wo: Naturkundemuseum
Wie lange: 60 Minuten

Four museum attendants lead a tour in the darkness of a deserted museum. Looking as dusty as the artefacts they look after, they try and explain life, the universe, and everything, drawing tenuous logic from exhibits such as stuffed badgers and bird skeletons.

Vier Museumsführer leiten eine Tour durch die Dunkelheit eines verlassenen Museums. Genauso verstaubt wie die Ausstellungsobjekte, versuchen sie mit fadenscheiniger Logik das Leben, das Universum und überhaupt alles zu erklären. Ausstellungsstücke wie ausgestopfte Dachse und Vogelgerippe dienen zur Anschauung.

Performed and devised by/Gespielt und inszeniert von: Alex Large, Sean Patten, Liane Sommers, Sarah Thom
Commissioned by/Im Auftrag von: Worcester City Museum, Worcester, UK
First performance/Uraufführung: 19.9.1996 (Worcester City Museum, Worcester, UK)

Show and Tell

theatre-based performance
Performance für einen Theaterraum

Where: a corridor made of two-way mirrored perspex
How long: 30 minutes

Wo: ein Gang aus beidseitig verspiegeltem Glas
Wie lange: 30 Minuten

Show and Tell is Gob Squad's first work for a theatre space. Applying the site specific approach to the theatre, the performers cage themselves inside a two way mirrored corridor of never-ending reflections. Ever aware of their own gazes and those of the voyeurs watching them on the outside, the performers play with different identities.

Show and Tell ist Gob Squads erste Arbeit für einen Theaterraum. Den situationsspezifischen Ansatz auf das Theater übertragend, schließen sich die Darsteller in einen verspiegelten Gang unendlicher Reflektionen ein. In diesem Raum der Selbst- und Fremdbeobachtung spielen sie mit verschiedenen Identitätsentwürfen.

Performed and devised by/Gespielt und inszeniert von: Johanna Freiburg, Alex Large, Sean Patten, Liane Sommers, Berit Stumpf, Sarah Thom
Producer/Produzent: TAT Frankfurt/Main, D
First performance/Uraufführung: 28.6.1996 (Bunter Abend 5, TAT Probebühne Daimlerstraße, Frankfurt/Main, D)

An Effortless Transaction

site-specific performance
ortsspezifische Performance

Where: a furniture shop
How long: shop opening hours every Saturday for a month (10 to 5 pm)

Wo: ein Möbelgeschäft
Wie lange: Geschäftsöffnungszeiten an vier Samstagen eines Monats (10 – 17 Uhr)

Gob Squad's heaven-sent sales assistants work alongside the regular staff of a furniture shop and gently subvert the mundane atmosphere of the store, searching for the inherent beauty and humanity in every nest of tables and 3 piece suite.

Sechs dem Himmel entsandte Verkäufer arbeiten neben dem regulären Personal in einem Möbelgeschäft und untergraben die Normalität des Geschäfts. Unermüdlich zeigen sie ihren Glauben an die Schönheit und Humanität jeder Gruppe von Beistelltischen und Polstermöbelgarnituren im Angebot.

Performed and devised by/Gespielt und inszeniert von: Suna Imre, Alex Large, Sean Patten, Henry Platt, Liane Sommers, Sarah Thom
Voiceover/Stimme: Rigley Riley, Dan Jones
Technicians/Techniker: Matt Adams, Paul Fraser
Producer/Produzent: NOW Festival, Nottingham, UK
Financial assistance/Mit finanzieller Unterstützung von: East Midlands Arts, UK
First performance/Uraufführung: 19.10.1996 (Wades, Broadmarsh Centre/NOW Festival, Nottingham, UK)

15 Minutes To Comply

site-specific performance
ortsspezifische Performance

Where: an underground station
How long: 15 minutes

Wo: eine U-Bahnstation
Wie lange: 15 Minuten

Audience and performers face each other across the tracks of an underground station. Eight people wait to move on, dreaming of another place, a better place. Video, sound and light scan the length of the space sketching a feeling of motion.

Publikum und Darsteller stehen sich auf zwei Bahnsteigen gegenüber. Acht Menschen, die weiterwollen, träumen von einem anderen, einem besseren

Ort. Video, Sound und Licht durchlaufen die Länge des Raumes und suggerieren ein Gefühl der Bewegung und Rastlosigkeit.

Concept/Konzept: Gob Squad/Stefan Pucher
Performed and devised by/Gespielt und inszeniert von: Thorsten Eibeler, Johanna Freiburg, Alex Large, Sean Patten, Stefan Pucher, Liane Sommers, Berit Stumpf, Sarah Thom
Voice over/Stimme: Rigley Riley
Video: Gob Squad/Stefan Pucher
Sound: Gob Squad/Stefan Pucher
Lighting Design/Lichtgestaltung: Hagen Gottschalck
Assistant/Assistenz: Thorsten Eibeler
Producer/Produzent: documenta X, Kassel, D
First performance/Uraufführung: 5.9.1997 (Theaterskizzen, documenta X, Kassel, D)

Close Enough to Kiss
theatre-based performance
Performance für einen Theaterraum

Where: a corridor made of two-way mirrored perspex
How long: 60 minutes

Wo: ein Gang aus beidseitig verspiegeltem Glas
Wie lange: 60 Minuten

Full length version of *Show and Tell*. the performers cage themselves inside a two way mirrored corridor of never-ending reflections. Ever aware of their own gazes and those of the voyeurs watching them on the outside, the performers play with different identities.

Abendfüllende Fassung von *Show and Tell*. Eingesperrt in einem verspiegelten Gang unendlicher Reflexionen schaffen die Darsteller einen Raum der Selbst- und Fremdbeobachtung und spielen mit verschiedenen Entwürfen von Identität.

Performed and devised by/Gespielt und inszeniert von: Johanna Freiburg, Alex Large, Sean Patten, Liane Sommers, Berit Stumpf, Sarah Thom
Lighting Design/Lichtgestaltung: Matti Fischer
Musical consultants/Musikalische Beratung: Johnny C, Daniel Haaksman
Sound Operator/Soundtechniker: Jason Simpson
Co-commissioned by/Im Auftrag von: NOW Festival, Nottingham, UK and Nottinghamshire New Arts Work, UK
Financial assistance/Mit finanzieller Unterstützung von: East Midlands Arts; The Arts Council of England, UK
Supported by/Mit Unterstützung von: MAERSK Air (a British Airways company/einem British Airways Unternehmen); Vink Plastics, UK; Link Agent, UK
First performance/Uraufführung: 24.10.1997 (SpielArt-Festival München, D)
Further performances/Weitere Aufführungen: „Live Art. New Theatre for the 90s" Podewil, Berlin, D (1997); NOW Festival, Nottingham, UK (1997); Chapter Arts Centre, Cardiff, UK (1998); Theaterhaus Gessnerallee, Zürich, CH (1998); Festival a/d Werf, Utrecht, NL (1998); Exciting Neighbours Festival, Marburg, D (1998); Diskurs Festival, Gießen, D (1998); The Junction, Cambridge, UK (1998)

Calling Laika – a secret meeting under the stars
site-specific performance and live radio broadcast
ortsspezifische Performance und Hörspiel

Where: a carpark
How long: 60 minutes

Wo: ein Parkplatz
Wie lange: 60 Minuten

Watching from a circle of 30 cars, the audience participate in a seance beneath the stars and listen to a soundtrack broadcast across the city to their car radios. This is a place for calling Laika, for calling anyone or anything out there.

Aus dem Inneren von 30 Autos in eine Arena blickend, nimmt das Publikum an einer Séance unter dem nächtlichen Sternenhimmel Teil und empfängt den Soundtrack über das Autoradio. Wir rufen Laika und jeden und alles, was sonst noch da draußen ist.

Performed and devised by/Gespielt und inszeniert von: Johanna Freiburg, Alex Large, Sean Patten, Liane Sommers, Berit Stumpf, Sarah Thom
With/Mit: Miles Chalcraft, Matti Fischer, Anette Schäfer, children of the/ Kinder der Carnarvon School Nottingham
Voice over/Stimme: Rigley Riley, Barry Smith
Soundtrack production/Soundtrackumsetzung: Martin Cooper
Musical consultants/Musikalische Beratung: Johnny C, Tony G., Daniel Haaksman
Lighting Design/Lichtgestaltung: Hagen Gottschalck
Special Effects: Städtische Bühnen Frankfurt/Main, D
Artistic Design Doggy Bags/Künstlerische Gestaltung Doggy Bags: Miles Chalcraft
Producer/Produzent: Theater am Turm, Frankfurt/Main, D
Financial assistance by/Mit finanzieller Unterstützung von: Siemens Kulturprogramm, The British Council
Supported by/Mit Unterstützung von: MAERSK Air (a British Airways company/ einem British Airways Unternehmen), UK; Turtle Rent car rental agency/ Turtle Rent Autovermietung, D; Radio X Frankfurt/Main, D
First performance/Uraufführung: 26.3.1998 (TAT, Frankfurt/Main, D)
Further performances/Weitere Aufführungen: Festival a/d Werf Utrecht, NL (1998); UK Open-Festival Neues Theater & Marstall München, D (1998); radio version broadcast by / als Hörspiel gesendet von DeutschlandRadio Berlin, D (1999 & 2000)

Stars And Their Pies

Stars And Their Pies

street performance
Freilichtperformance

Where: outdoors
How long: 20 minutes

Wo: im Freien
Wie lange: 20 Minuten

Based on the TV show Stars In Their Eyes, a bunch of no-hopers sing for their supper – tasty pies!

Basierend auf dem TV-Format einer bekannten Castingshow, singt eine Gruppe Talentloser für ihr Abendbrot: leckere Teigtaschen!

Performed and devised by/Gespielt und inszeniert von: Mat Hand, Gareth Howell, Alex Large, Sean Patten, Liane Sommers, Berit Stumpf
Commissioned by/Im Auftrag von: Glastonbury Festival of Contemporary Performing Arts, UK
First performance/Uraufführung: 26.6.1998 (Glastonbury Festival, Glastonbury, UK)

I Can

video installation
Videoinstallation

Where: an art gallery
How long: 60 minute loop

Wo: eine Galerie
Wie lange: 60-minütiger Loop

Gob Squad's first work for the art market puts the sum of Gob Squad members' abilities up for sale on their very own shopping channel. By calling a number an order can be placed which will be fulfilled by the artists at a later date.

Gob Squads erste Arbeit für den Kunstmarkt bietet auf einem eigenem TV-Shopping-Kanal die Fähigkeiten der einzelnen Mitglieder zum Verkauf an. Per Anruf kann eine Bestellung aufgegeben werden, die von den Künstlern zu einem späteren Zeitpunkt erfüllt wird.

Performed and devised by/Gespielt und inszeniert von: Johanna Freiburg, Alex Large, Sean Patten, Liane Sommers, Berit Stumpf, Sarah Thom
Video/Graphics: Alex Large
Commissioned by/Im Auftrag von: „Berlin Berlin"/berlin biennale, Berlin, D
First exhibited/Erstmals ausgestellt: 18.6.1998 (Sean Kelly Gallery, New York, USA)
Further exhibited/Weitere Ausstellungen: „Berlin Berlin"/berlin biennale, Berlin, D (1998), Trampoline, Nottingham, UK (1998); Site Gallery, Sheffield, UK (1999); Venlo, NL (1999); Angel Row Gallery (2000); "Living On Video – 10 years of Gob Squad"; Volksbühne im Prater, Berlin, D (2005)

What Are You Looking At?
durational performance
Live-Installation

Where: a 3 metre square box made of 2-way mirrored perspex
How long: 4-6 hours

Wo: eine 6m² grosse Box aus beidseitig verspiegeltem Glas
Wie lange: 4–6 Stunden

Sealed in a two-way mirrored box, five revellers loose themselves in reckless abandon. Amusing and boring themselves with food, drinks, records, slide shows, porn, video and party games, the apparent chaos occasionally freezes into the stillness of a photograph. A sign illuminates with the words "What Are You Looking At?".

Eingeschlossen in einer beidseitig verspiegelten Box, verlieren sich fünf Partygänger in rücksichtsloser Selbstaufgabe. Sie amüsieren und langweilen sich mit Getränken, Essen, Schallplatten, Dias, Pornos, Videos und Partyspielen. Das scheinbare Chaos gefriert von Zeit zu Zeit zum Gruppenbild, und ein Schild mit den Worten „What Are You Looking At?"

leuchtet auf (übersetzt: „Worauf blickst du?", aber auch „Was glotzt du so?").

Performed and devised by/Gespielt und inszeniert von: Johanna Freiburg, Alex Large, Sean Patten, Liane Sommers, Berit Stumpf (in 1999 joined by/gemeinsam mit Sarah Thom from/ab 1999, Simon Will from/ab 2000)
Lighting Design/Lichtgestaltung: Hagen Gottschalck
Technical Assistant/Technische Assistenz: Stephan Trümper
Producer/Produzent: congress 3000/berlin biennale, Berlin, D
Financial assistance by/Mit finanzieller Unterstützung von: Arts Council of England, UK (UK Touring)
First performance/Uraufführung: 1.10.1998 (berlin biennale, Berlin, D)
Further performances/Weitere Aufführungen: Diskurs-Festival Gießen, D (1998); Trampoline, Nottingham, UK (1998); Künstlerhaus Mousonturm Frankfurt/Main, D (1999 + 2001); Fondation Cartier pour l'art contemporain Paris, F (1999); Home & Away-Festival/Expo Hannover, D (1999); reich & berühmt Festival Berlin, D (2000); European Media Festival, Osnabrück, D (2001); ICA, London, UK (2001); Kampnagel, Hamburg, D (2001); Warwick Arts Centre, UK (2002); DIGIart Festival, Århus, DK (2002); „10 Jahre Podewil", Berlin, D (2002); Colchester Arts Centre, UK (2002); NOW Festival, Nottingham, UK (2002); Kunsthalle Baden-Baden, D (2002); Fierce! Festival, Coventry, UK (2003)

Safe
theatre-based performance
Performance für einen Theaterraum

Where: a stage
How long: 75 minutes

Wo: eine Bühne
Wie lange: 75 Minuten

Unable to play any instruments, Gob Squad have formed a band. Performing against a continuous backdrop of video imagery, their attempts to rock are thwarted by arguments, power cuts and stage fright. *Safe* is a concert of frustrated desire, blurring the distinctions between image and real life.

Unfähig, irgendwelche Instrumente zu spielen, gründen Gob Squad eine Band. Gegen eine Flut von Videobildern anspielend, scheitern ihre Rock-Versuche an Streit, Stromausfällen und Lampenfieber. *Safe* ist ein Konzert voller frustrierter Sehnsucht, das die Grenze zwischen Bild und echtem Leben verwischt.

Performed and devised by/Gespielt und inszeniert von: Johanna Freiburg, Alex Large, Sean Patten, Liane Sommers, Berit Stumpf, Simon Will
Video: Alex Large, Leigh Haas
Slide Projections/Diaprojektionen: Leigh Haas
Sound: Martin Cooper
Musical consultants/Musikalische Beratung: Daniel Haaksman, Johnny C, DJ Tilman
Lighting Design/Lichtgestaltung: Hagen Gottschalck
Rock band tuition/Rock Mentoren: Ingo Bousa, Sophie Fishwick
Technical Management/Technische Leitung: Hagen Gottschalck (from/seit 2000 Susanne Weber)
Technical Assistant/Technische Assistenz: Stephan Trümper
Assistant/Assistenz: Arnd Heuwinkel
Co-producers/Koproduzenten: Kampnagel Hamburg, D; Podewil Berlin, D;
Funded by/Gefördert von: Kulturbehörde der Freien und Hansestadt Hamburg, D
Financial assistance/Mit finanzieller Unterstützung von: East Midlands Arts, UK
Supported by/Mit Unterstützung von: The British Council
US tour preparation and -management/US-Tourvorbereitung und -management: Christina Runge
First performance/Uraufführung: 3.3.1999 (Kampnagel, Hamburg, D)
Further performances/Weitere Aufführungen: Podewil Berlin, D (1999); Nottingham Playhouse, Nottingham, UK (1999); Künstlerhaus Mousonturm, Frankfurt/Main, D (1999); Edinburgh Fringe Festival, UK (1999); Kaaitheater, Brussels, B (1999), „4 Days" Festival, Praha, CZ (1999), Festival BIG, Torino, I (2000); Stadttheater Konstanz, D (2000); Eurokaz-Festival, Zagreb, HR (2000); „Neue Szene", Salzburg, A (2000); Walker Art Center, Minneapolis, USA (2001); On the Boards, Seattle, USA (2001); Pica, Portland, USA (2001)

Little White Lies
live radio play
live produziertes Hörspiel

Where: a stage with audience seated on two sides
How long: 60 minutes

Wo: eine Bühne mit Publikum auf zwei Seiten
Wie lange: 60 Minuten

An event takes place before the public and is transmitted live over the radio. The spectators attending will become, in the course of the evening, participants and eyewitnesses of a fictitious event and differentiate themselves in this respect to the listeners at home. What actually takes place, what is the simple assertion?

Eine Veranstaltung vor Publikum wird live im Radio übertragen. Die anwesenden Zuschauer werden im Lauf des Abends zu Teilnehmern und Augenzeugen eines fiktiven Events und unterscheiden sich in dieser Hinsicht von den Zuhörern zu Hause. Was findet tatsächlich statt, was ist bloße Behauptung? *Little White Lies* sind harmlose Lügen, Lügen, die man anwendet, um niemandem wehzutun.

Performed and devised by/Gespielt und inszeniert von: Johanna Freiburg, Alex Large, Till Müller-Klug, Sean Patten, Liane Sommers, Berit Stumpf, Sarah Thom
Text: Gob Squad/Till Müller-Klug
Soundtrack production and Live sound mix/Soundtrackumsetzung und Live Sound-mischung: Martin Cooper
Musical consultant/Musikalische Beratung: Daniel Haaksman
Co-producers/Koproduzenten: DeutschlandRadio Berlin, D; Bayerischer Rund-funk, D
First performed and broadcast/Uraufführung und Erstausstrahlung: 20.11.1999 (Akademie der Künste Berlin, D)
Further broadcasts/Weitere Ausstrahlungen: HR2 (1999), Deutschlandfunk (1999)

Say It Like You Mean It

interactive party performance

interaktive Partyperformance

Where: a marquee set up in a theatre
How long: 90-120 minutes

Wo: ein Festzelt in einem Theater
Wie lange: 90 bis 120 Minuten

Say It Like You Mean It creates a make-believe environment in a tent set deep in an imaginary forest. Gob Squad announce the end of the world and ask the remaining survivors to build a new future out of sellotape and cardboard. People are invited to 'let go' in order to be 'in the moment'. At the same time, participants are encouraged to step out and view the situation from outside the marquee through special eyeholes while listening to a live commentary on the event.

Say It Like You Mean It schafft eine spielerische Atmosphäre in einem Zelt, das in einem imaginären Wald aufgeschlagen wurde. Gob Squad erklärt das Ende der Welt und bittet die Überlebenden, eine neue Zukunft aus Tesafilm und Pappe zusammenzubasteln. Eingeladen, „loszulassen", um „im Moment" zu sein, werden die Teilnehmer gleichzeitig animiert, auch eine andere Rolle einzunehmen, denn es ist möglich, das Geschehen von außen durch Sehschlitze zu betrachten, während man über Kopfhörer tauschen sie einem distanzierten Live-Kommentar lauscht.

Performed and devised by/Gespielt und inszeniert von: Johanna Freiburg, Alex Large, Sean Patten, Liane Sommers, Berit Stumpf, Simon Will
Video: Alex Large
Slide Projections/Diaprojektionen: Leigh Haas
Sound: Sebastian Bark
Lighting Design/Lichtgestaltung: Hagen Gottschalck
Technical Management/Technische Leitung: Leigh Haas
Technical Assistant/Technische Assistenz: Berte Neraal
Production management/Produktionsleitung: Christina Runge
Co-Producers/Koproduzenten: Kampnagel Hamburg, D; Podewil Berlin, D; Künstlerhaus Mousonturm, Frankfurt/Main, D; NOW Festival Nottingham, UK. Associated with Kunstherbst Berlin, D

Funded by/Gefördert von: Senatsverwaltung für Wissenschaft, Forschung und Kultur, Berlin, D
Supported by/Mit finanzieller Unterstützung von: Arts Council England, UK; Festspielhaus Hellerau, Dresden, D
First performance/Uraufführung: 15.3.2000 (Kampnagel, Hamburg, D)
Further performances/Weitere Aufführungen: Podewil Berlin, D (2000); NOW Festival Nottingham, UK (2000); „transeuropa2000", Hildesheim, D (2000); Künstlerhaus Mousonturm, Frankfurt/Main, D (2000); Festspielhaus Hellerau, Dresden, D (2000); STUK, Leuven, B (2001); Tramway, Glasgow, UK (2001)

Where Do You Want to Go to Die?

video installation

Videoinstallation

Where: a mini-bus, with video projected onto the windscreen
How long: 53 minutes loop

Wo: ein Minibus mit Videoprojektion auf der Windschutzscheibe
Wie lange: 53-minütiger Loop

A video projection shows a night-time journey around Berlin from the point of view of the front windscreen of a van. Each of eight episodes starts from darkness with just the chattering voices of seven people on a journey. The image of a speeding road appears and out of the banal atmosphere the van pulls up. A passenger appears in the glare of the headlights, and performs a parting gesture till they are abandoned and become a fading image.

Eine Videoprojektion zeigt eine nächtliche Fahrt durch Berlin, gefilmt durch die Windschutzscheibe. Jede der acht Episoden beginnt in Dunkelheit mit den plaudernden Stimmen von sieben Menschen auf einer Reise. Bilder beschleunigter Straßen erscheinen, bis aus der alltäglichen Stimmung heraus der Minibus plötzlich anhält. Ein Passagier erscheint im Scheinwerferlicht, vollzieht eine Geste des Abschieds und wird schließlich allein zurückgelassen.

Performed and devised by/Gespielt und inszeniert von: Johanna Freiburg, Alex Large, Sean Patten, Liane Sommers, Berit Stumpf, Sarah Thom, Simon Will

Video Edit/Videoschnitt: Alex Large
Co-Producers/Koproduzenten: Berliner Kulturveranstaltungs-GmbH, D; Galerie Arndt & Partner Berlin, D
First exhibited/Erstmals ausgestellt: 19.6.2000 (EXPO, Hannover, D)
Further exhibited/Weitere Ausstellungen: Kunstherbst Berlin, D (2000); (M)Art Inn, Helsingborg, SE (2000); Arnolfini, Bristol, UK (2001); Podewil, Berlin, D (2001); NOW Festival, Nottingham, UK (2001); Festival Dia E Vento, Porto, PT (2001); Hull Time Based Arts, Hull, UK (2002); Podewil, Berlin, D (2002); rum 46 Århus, DK (2002); Homo Alibi 3.0 Festival, Riga, LV (2002); Live Culture at Tate Modern, London, UK (2003); Junges Theater Bremen, D (2005)

Are We Nearly There Yet?

internet radio docu-soap
Dokusoap-Hörspiel

Where: internet radio
How long: 10 hours total

Wo: Internetradio
Wie lange: Gesamtlänge 10 Stunden

Originally broadcast weekly on web radio in 18 episodes, listeners were invited to "relieve your boredom with ours", by eavesdropping on a simple tale of a group of friends on a round trip from Berlin to the Baltic sea on a dreary autumn day.

Ursprünglich in 18 Episoden wöchentlich im Webradio ausgestrahlt. Die Hörer sind eingeladen ihre „Langeweile mit unserer zu stillen", indem sie den banalen Unterhaltungen einer Gruppe von Freunden bei ihrer Autofahrt von Berlin bis zur Ostsee und zurück beiwohnen.

Performed and devised by/Gespielt und inszeniert von: Johanna Freiburg, Alex Large, Sean Patten, Liane Sommers, Berit Stumpf, Sarah Thom
Voiceover/Stimme: Rigley Riley
Sound: Martin Cooper
Co-producers/Koproduzenten: The Junction, Cambridge, UK; Mute magazine, UK
First broadcasted/Erstausstrahlung: June/Juni 2000 (Gaia Live web radio)

Further broadcasts/Weitere Ausstrahlungen: Ersatzradio, an ErsatzStadt project, Berlin, D (2003)/Ersatzradio, ein Projekt von ErsatzStadt, Berlin, D (2003)

You Know You Want It (Part 1: The Annie Lennox Project)

durational performance and installation
Live-Installation und Ausstellung

Where: a gallery space
How long: 3-hour performance, followed by installation with video of the event and 5 life-size cut-outs of the artists

Wo: ein Galerieraum
Wie lange: dreistündige Live-Installation, im Anschluss Ausstellung des Raumes (mit Videoloop des Events und 5 lebensgroßen Aufstellfiguren der Künstler)

You Know You Want It

Created for gallery spaces, internationally renowned celebrities are forced to celebrate an occasion of Gob Squad's choice. Part 1: Annie Lennox's Birthday, sees Annie taped into the corner of a gallery. In a grotto of Annie fan mail, Annie drawings, Annie balloons and Annie dolls, fans are able to make and present birthday cards for her under the watchful and caring eye of Gob Squad.

Produziert für Galerieräume, werden international bekannte Persönlichkeiten von Gob Squad dazu gezwungen, einen festlichen Anlass zu begehen. Part 1: Annie Lennox's Birthday zeigt Annie gefesselt in der Ecke eines

Galerieraums. In einem Schrein aus Annie-Fanpost, Annie-Zeichnungen, Annie-Luftballons und Annie-Puppen können Fans unter der aufmerksamen und liebevollen Aufsicht von Gob Squad Geburtstagskarten für Annie herstellen und übergeben.

Performed and devised by/Gespielt und inszeniert von: Johanna Freiburg, Alex Large, Annie Lennox, Sean Patten, Liane Sommers, Berit Stumpf, Simon Will
Sound: Alex Large
First performance/Uraufführung: 9.9.2000 (Galerie Arndt & Partner Berlin, D); Associated Kunstherbst Berlin, D

To@ster
durational performance
Live Installation

Where: outdoors. A large table with six toasters
How long: 5-8 hours

Wo: ein grosser Tisch mit sechs Toastern im Freien
Wie lange: 5–8 Stunden

Large-scale images of famous or infamous people are rendered using 1000 slices of rare, medium and burnt toast – each a piece in a mosaic. As the picture emerges, and the air fills with smoke, the performers chat to their audience and ask them to lend a hand. The conversation inevitably turns from toasted sandwich preferences to the function of art, the history or legacy of the individual being to@sted and whether it is possible to capture ones personality in an image. Tea is served.

Großformatige Bilder berühmter und nicht berühmter Menschen werden aus 1000 Scheiben ungetoasteter, leicht gebräunter und verbrannter Toastscheiben hergestellt – jeder Toast ein Pixel in einem Mosaik. Während sich das Bild allmählich zusammensetzt und die Luft sich mit Rauchschwaden füllt, plaudern die Künstler mit ihrem Publikum und fordern zum Helfen auf. Das Gespräch führt unweigerlich von Toastbelagsvorlieben zur Aufgabe der Kunst im Allgemeinen, der Geschichte und dem Vermächtnis der geto@steten Person und der Frage, ob es möglich ist, Persönlichkeit im

Bild festzuhalten. Es wird Tee serviert.

Performed and devised by/Gespielt und inszeniert von: Sean Patten, Simon Will (2004 joined by/ab 2004 zusammen mit Bastian Trost)
Commissioned by/Im Auftrag von: OK Girl$ Gallery, Berlin, D
First performance/Uraufführung: 8.9. 2000 (OK Girl$ Gallery, Berlin, D)
Further performances/Weitere Aufführungen: Rollende Road Schau, Volksbühne Berlin, D (2001); Trampoline, Nottingham, UK (2002); 100° Festival, Hebbel am Ufer, Berlin, D (2004); pictoplasma conference, Berlin, D (2004)

The Great Outdoors
multimedia performance
Multimediaperformance

Where: a theatre, city streets
How long: 90 minutes

Wo: ein Theater, die Straßen der Stadt
Wie lange: 90 Minuten

To@ster

The Great Outdoors sees its performers leave the artifice of theatre for the "gritty reality" of real life and the here and now. One by one, they make their exits to explore the surrounding city of the host venue, maintaining their presence via mobile phones and video projections, quoting the aesthetics of surveillance cameras. Gradually, they go further and further until they fully disappear.

In The Great Outdoors verlassen die Darsteller den Kunstraum Theater auf der Suche nach der rauhen Wirklichkeit und dem Hier und Jetzt. Einer nach dem anderen nimmt Abschied, um die Stadt des Spielortes zu erkunden. Präsent nur noch über Mobiltelefone und Videoprojektionen, die die Ästhetik von Überwachungskameras zitieren, entfernen sie sich allmählich immer weiter und lassen die Zuschauer schließlich allein zurück.

Performed and devised by/Gespielt und inszeniert von: Johanna Freiburg, Sean Patten, Berit Stumpf, Sarah Thom, Simon Will (2002 joined by Bastian Trost/ ab 2002 zusammen mit Bastian Trost)
With/Mit: Passers-by/Passanten
Video/Multimedia: Miles Chalcraft
Sound: Martin Cooper
Musical consultant/Musikalische Beratung: Daniel Haaksman
Lighting Design/Lichtgestaltung: Susanne Weber
Set Realisation/Bühnenumsetzung: Fanni Halmburger
Technical Management/Technische Leitung: Susanne Weber
Technical Assistant/Technische Assistenz: Leif Alexis
Production management/Produktionsleitung: Christina Runge
Co-producers/Koproduzenten: Podewil Berlin, D; 4 days association Praha, CZ; NOW Festival Nottingham, UK
Funded by/Gefördert von: Hauptstadtkulturfonds Berlin, D, Fonds Darstellende Künste e.V., D
Supported by/Mit Unterstützung von: Ars Electronica Center/Museum of the Future, Linz, A; The British Council
First performance/Uraufführung: 9.10.2001 (Podewil, Berlin, D)
Further performances/Weitere Aufführungen: 4 days in motion Festival, Praha, CZ (2001); NOW Festival, Nottingham, UK (2001); Künstlerhaus Mousonturm, Frankfurt/Main, D (2002); Podewil, Berlin, D (2002)

The Finalists
online performance
Online-Performance

Where: websites and chatrooms
How long: 2 weeks

Wo: Websites und Chatrooms
Wie lange: 2 Wochen

The Finalists are four entities, which reside exclusively in the Internet. The figures make themselves accessible to the user, through their personal homepage, which changes sequentially during the period of 10 days, from their original state to their self-destruction. Chat events and a message board invite interaction. The finale takes place as a simultaneous webstream.

Die „Finalists" sind vier Kreaturen, die ihre Existenz ausschließlich im Internet fristen. Dem User erschließen sich die Figuren von ihrer Entstehung bis hin zur Selbstzerstörung über ihre Personal Homepages, die sich über den Zeitraum von 10 Tagen fortlaufend verändern. Chat-Events und Message-Board laden zur Interaktion ein. Das Finale findet in Form eines simultanen Webstreams statt.

Concept/Konzept: Gob Squad/Miles Chalcraft, Anette Schäfer
Performed and devised by/Gespielt und inszeniert von: Sean Patten, Liane Sommers, Sarah Thom, Simon Will
Technical realisation/Technische Umsetzung: Miles Chalcraft
Webdesign & Graphic design/Webdesign & Grafische Gestaltung: Anette Schäfer
Co-producer/Koproduzent: Winning project of the international competition Webscene, initiated by SpielArt-Festival, Munich, in co-operation with Stadtforum and Medienforum Munich (D) and Ars Electronica, Linz (A)/Siegerprojekt des international ausgeschriebenen Wettbewerbs Webscene, der vom Festival SpielArt München in Kooperation mit dem Stadtforum und dem Medienforum München sowie Ars Electronica, Linz, initiiert wurde
First presented/Uraufführung: 17.11. 2001 (SpielArt-Festival, München, D)
Further presentations/Weitere Aufführungen: Ars Electronica, Linz, A (2001); Blue Rodeo, Podewil Berlin, D (2001)

Welcome to our world... built with you in mind

durational performance and installation
Live-Installation und Ausstellung

Where: a tent in a city
How long: 2–3 hours, followed by installation

Wo: ein Zelt in der Stadt
Wie lange: 2–3 Stunden, im Anschluss Ausstellung

Communicating with each other via walkie-talkies, an explorer and a cartographer work together to discover and model a new world, gathering stories and information from people passing by. The new model of the world is exhibited.

Miteinander über Walkietalkie kommunizierend, entwickeln ein Entdecker und ein Kartograph ein neues Modell der Welt, indem sie Geschichten und Informationen von Passanten sammeln. Das neue Modell der Welt wird ausgestellt.

Concept/Konzept: Gob Squad/Miles Chalcraft in collaboration with/in Zusammenarbeit mit Daniel Belasco Rogers, Sophia New (plan b performance)
Performed and devised by/Gespielt und inszeniert von: Daniel Belasco Rogers, Sophia New, Sarah Thom, Simon Will
Video/Multimedia design: Miles Chalcraft
Production management/Produktionsleitung: Eva Hartmann
Co-producers/Koproduzenten: A-Tipis, initiated by/initiiert von Victoria, Ghent, B; in collaboration with/in Zusammenarbeit mit Oerol Festival, NL; Forma, UK; Parc de la Villette, F
First performance/Uraufführung: 27.9.2002 (work in progress presentation/Präsentation, Nightwalking: Navigating the Unknown, South Bank Centre, London, UK)
Further performances/Weitere Aufführungen: Oerolfestival, Terschelling, NL (2005); Parc de la Villette, Paris, F (2005); Gentse Feesten, Ghent, B (2005)

Room Service (Help me make it through the night)

live interactive film
interaktiver Live-Film

Where: a hotel
How long: 5-6 hours at night time

Wo: ein Hotel
Wie lange: 5–6 Nachtstunden

In the conference room of a hotel the audience watch four performers on monitors. Somewhere in the same hotel they are isolated in four rooms with only a phone and a videocamera for company.

Im Tagungsraum eines Hotels beobachtet das Publikum auf Monitoren vier Darsteller. Irgendwo im gleichen Hotel sind sie in vier Zimmern isoliert, nur ein Telefon und eine Videokamera verbinden sie mit der Außenwelt.

Performed and devised by/Gespielt und inszeniert von: Johanna Freiburg, Sean Patten, Elyce Semenec, Berit Stumpf, Sarah Thom, Bastian Trost, Simon Will
Video/Graphics: Miles Chalcraft
Sound: Sebastian Bark, Jeff McGrory
Technical Management/Technische Leitung: Lars-Egge Müggenburg
Technical Assistant/Technische Assistenz: Leif Alexis
Production management/Produktionsleitung: Eva Hartmann
Administrative Assistant/Assistenz Produktionsleitung: Sofie-Louise Thørner-Andersen
Co-producers/Koproduzenten: Kampnagel Hamburg, D; Podewil Berlin, D
Funded by/Gefördert von: Kulturbehörde der Freien und Hansestadt Hamburg, D; Senatsverwaltung für Wissenschaft, Forschung und Kultur Berlin, D; Fonds Darstellende Künste e.V. Bonn, D
Supported by/Mit Unterstützung von: InterCity Hotel Hamburg, D
Financial assistance by/Mit finanzieller Unterstützung von: Arts Council England, UK (UK Touring)
First performance/Uraufführung: 24.1.2003 (InterCity Hotel Hamburg, D)
Further performances/Weitere Aufführungen: The Britannia Hotel Coventry, The Howard Johnson Hotel, West Bromwich, UK (2003/Jubilee Arts and Fierce-Festival); Hotel Odessa, Varna, BG (2003/Varna Summer-Festival); Mercure Hotel, Berlin, D (2003/Podewil); Hotel Laguna, Zagreb, HR (2004/Festival

eXUrban); Maritim Hotel, Hannover, D (2004/ Festival Theaterformen); nh Hotel, Fribourg, CH (2004/Festival Belluard Bollwerk International); Holiday Inn Hotel, Mannheim, D (2004/Festival Wunder der Prärie); Park Plaza Hotel, Nottingham, UK (2005/co-promoted by Dance 4, Lakeside and Nottingham Playhouse); Great Eastern Hotel, London, UK (2005)

Neukölln sucht den Superstar
karaoke casting show
Karaoke Casting Show

Where: an open-sided truck in Neukölln, a district of Berlin
How long: 2 hours

Wo: ein offener Bauwagen in Neukölln, einem Stadtteil von Berlin
Wie lange: 2 Stunden

Welcome To Our World... Built With You In Mind

Three talent spotters descend on the Berlin district of Neukölln and invite locals to sing their hearts out on an outdoor stage. Rockumentary style interviews are made and the winners of the rough and ready talent contest become local heroes for the evening.

Drei Talentscouts landen im Berliner Stadtteil Neukölln und laden Bewohner ein, sich auf einer Freilichtbühne das Herz aus dem Leib zu singen. Interviews im MTV-Stil verleihen jedem Teilnehmer Glamour, und die Gewinner des improvisierten Talentwettbewerbs werden zu den Stadtteilhelden des Abends.

Performed and devised by/Gespielt und inszeniert von: Sean Patten, Tatjana Turanskyj, Simon Will
Producer/Produzent: Rollende Road Schau, Volksbühne Berlin, D
First performance/Uraufführung: 28.6. 2003 (Rollende Road Schau, Berlin, D)

Super Night Shot
multi-perspective film event
Multiperspektivisches Filmevent

Where: the city streets, a theatre laid out like a cinema
How long: the length of a video tape (60 minutes)

Wo: die Straßen der Stadt, ein Theater als Kino
Wie lange: die Länge einer Videocassette (60 Minuten)

Super Night Shot is a multi-perspective film, shot one hour before it is shown, with no cuts or edits. A gang of four activists declares war on anonymity and ventures onto the city streets to capture a beautiful Hollywood kiss with a stranger on video.

Super Night Shot ist ein multiperspektivischer Film ohne Schnitte, der erst eine Stunde bevor er gezeigt wird auf den Straßen der Stadt entsteht. Eine Truppe von vier Aktivisten erklärt der Anonymität den Krieg und macht sich auf, einen Hollywood-reifen Kuss mit einem Fremden auf Video zu bannen.

Performed and devised by/Gespielt und inszeniert von: Johanna Freiburg, Sean Patten, Elyce Semenec, Berit Stumpf, Sarah Thom, Bastian Trost, Simon Will
With/Mit: Passers-by/Passanten
Sound: Sebastian Bark, Jeff McGrory
Assistant/Assistenz: Nina Tecklenburg
Producer/Produzent: Volksbühne am Rosa-Luxemburg-Platz, Berlin, D
Financial assistance by/Mit finanzieller Unterstützung von: Arts Council England, UK (UK Touring)
First performance/Uraufführung: 5.12.2003 (Volksbühne im Prater, Berlin, D)
Further performances/Weitere Aufführungen: Volksbühne im Prater, D (2004 & 2005); Kampnagel Hamburg, D (2004); ArtRock Festival St. Brieuc, F (2004); West Bromwich, UK (2004); Unithea Festival, Frankfurt/Oder, D (2004); Festival Belluard Bollwerk International, Fribourg, CH (2004); Sommerakademie Mousonturm Frankfurt/M, D (2004); LIFT Festival London, UK (2004); Norwich and Norfolk Festival, UK (2005); Nottingham, UK (co-promoted by Dance 4, Lakeside and Nottingham Playhouse) (2005); „ErsatzStadt" Volksbühne Berlin, D (2005); The Junction, Cambridge, UK (2005); Rollende Road Schau, Berlin, D (2005); Staatstheater Stuttgart (2005); Steirischer Herbst Graz, A (2005)

Who Are You Wearing?
durational performance
Live-Installation

Where: a red carpet
How long: 3 hours

Wo: ein roter Teppich
Wie lange: 3 Stunden

A red-carpet live-TV performance for launch events and gala openings, where every guest is given a celebrity interview and 15 seconds of fame.

Eine Live-TV-Übertragung von einem roten Teppich, der anlässlich von Eröffnungs- und Gala-Events ausgerollt wird. Jedem Gast wird ein Starinterview und 15 Sekunden Ruhm geschenkt.

Performed and devised by/Gespielt und inszeniert von: Sean Patten, Bastian Trost, Simon Will
Video/Graphics: Miles Chalcraft
Sound: Jeff McGrory
Producer/Produzent: Lust Lies Art & Fashion, Berlin (D)
First performance/Uraufführung: 10.1.2004 (Lust Lies Art & Fashion, Berlin, D)
Further performances/Weitere Aufführungen: Volkspalast Eröffnung, Palast der Republik, Berlin, D (2004)

You Wish
workshop series specialising in multimedia performance
Workshopserie für Multimedia-Performance

Where: Aizpute (LV), Krakow (PL), Krems (A), Lodz (PL)
How long: 7 days per workshop (September 2004 till July 2005)

Wo: Aizputè (LV), Kraków (PL), Krems (A), Lodz (PL)
Wie lange: 7 Tage pro Workshop (September 2004 bis Juli 2005)

Lead by/Geleitet von: Sebastian Bark, Miles Chalcraft, Johanna Freiburg, Dariusz Kostyra, Jeff McGrory, Berit Stumpf, Simon Will
Participants/Teilnehmer: Practioners and students in the fields of art, theatre, stage design and media (from Austria, Croatia, Czech Republic, Estonia, Germany, Latvia, Lithuania, Poland, Romania)/Künstler und Studenten aus den Bereichen Bildende Kunst, Theater, Bühnenbild und Medien (aus Deutschland, Estland, Kroatien, Lettland, Litauen, Österreich, Polen, Rumänien,Tschechien)
Production management/Produktionsleitung: Eva Hartmann
Onsite Production Management/Produktionsleitung vor Ort: Agnese Luse (Riga, LV); Jakub Szreder (Kraków, PL); donaufestival Niederösterreich (Krems, A); Katarzyna Wielga (Lodz, PL)
Funded by/Gefördert von: Kulturstiftung des Bundes, D

Prater-Saga 3:
In diesem Kiez ist der Teufel eine Goldmine
play
Inszenierung eines Stücktextes als Castingshow

Where: a theatre set, laid out like a TV studio with a live link to a busy city street
How long: 2 hours

Wo: ein Bühnenbild, einem Fernsehstudio nachempfunden, mit Liveüber-tragung von einer belebten Straße der Stadt
Wie lange: 2 Stunden

Prater Saga 3 (photo: David Baltzer)

Prater-Saga 3 sees Gob Squad work with a written script for the first time. As part of a five part saga written by René Pollesch, Gob Squad cast passers by in the leading roles of the play. Each night outside the theatre they audition, rehearse, and negotiate contracts with their new stars. Cued with head-phones, these "found actors" deliver their lines to cameras in a TV studio set.

Prater-Saga 3 ist die erste Gob-Squad-Arbeit, die einen Text als Ausgangs-punkt hat. Als Teil einer fünfteiligen Saga, geschrieben von René Pollesch, castet Gob Squad Passanten für die Hauptrollen des Stücks. Jede Nacht aufs Neue durchlaufen diese Audition, Probe und Vertragsverhandlung und wer-den zu „echten" Stars. Über Kopfhörer wird den gecasteten Laien Text einge-flüstert, den sie in die Kameras eines Fernsehstudiosets sprechen.

Performed and devised by/Gespielt und inszeniert von: Johanna Freiburg, Sean Patten, Elyce Semenec, Berit Stumpf, Sarah Thom, Bastian Trost, Simon Will
With/Mit: Passers-by/Passanten
Text: René Pollesch
Set design/Bühnenbild: Bert Neumann
Graphics/Video design: Miles Chalcraft
Sound: Jeff McGrory
Assistant/Assistenz: Nina Tecklenburg
Lighting/Licht: Frank Novak
Technical Support, Sound/Tontechnik: Martin Renning/Onnen Bock
Technical Support, Video/Videotechnik: Lisa Böffgen
Props/Requisite: Susann Köppl
Assistant, Set design/Bühnenbildassistenz: Chasper Bertschinger
Assistant, Costume design/Kostümassistenz: Esther Friedemann
Dresser/Garderobe: Jutta Rommel
Producer/Produzent: Volksbühne am Rosa-Luxemburg-Platz, Berlin, D
First performance/Uraufführung: 10.12.2004 (Volksbühne im Prater, Berlin, D)
Further performances/Weitere Aufführungen: Volksbühne im Prater, Berlin, D (2005)

King Kong Club

interactive film event
interaktives Filmevent

Where: a film set/cinema in a theatre space
How long: 2 hours

Wo: ein Filmstudio/Kino im Theaterraum
Wie lange: 2 Stunden

In the cloakroom you don't just leave your coat but also your name and your face. In exchange you receive a new identity as an ape and become part of a cloned society. King Kong Club is a place for encounters, both a film set and a cinema. Visitors attend the making of a strange film and become both its actors and audience.

An der Garderobe gibt der Besucher nicht nur seinen Mantel ab, sondern auch seinen Namen und sein Gesicht. Dafür erhält er seine Identität als Affe und wird zum Teil einer geklonten Gesellschaft. King Kong Club ist ein Ort der Begegnung, ist gleichermaßen Filmset und Kino. Die Besucher wohnen der Entstehung eines skurrilen Films bei und werden gleichermaßen zu dessen Akteuren und Zuschauern.

Performed and devised by/Gespielt und inszeniert von: Miles Chalcraft, Johanna Freiburg, Dariusz Kostyra, Ilia Papatheodorou, Sean Patten, Erik Pold, Berit Stumpf, Sarah Thom, Bastian Trost, Simon Will
Sound: Sebastian Bark, Jeff McGrory
Video: Robert Shaw
Lighting Design/Lichtgestaltung: Micha Lentner-Niyorugira
Technical Management/Technische Leitung: Susanne Weber
Technical Consultant/Beratung Sound- und Videotechnik: Lars Egge Müggenburg
Production management/Produktionsleitung: Eva Hartmann
Assistants/Assistenz: Henriette Huppmann, Nina Thielicke
Costume production/Kostümschneiderei: Kostümwerk, Hamburg, D
Funded by/Gefördert von: Kulturstiftung des Bundes, D; Senatsverwaltung für Wissenschaft, Forschung und Kultur Berlin, D; Kulturbehörde der Freien und Hansestadt Hamburg, D
Co-producers/Koproduzenten: donaufestival Niederösterreich, A; Kampnagel Hamburg, D; Hebbel am Ufer Berlin, D
First performance/Uraufführung: 31.3.2005 (Hebbel am Ufer Berlin, D)
Further performances/Weitere Aufführungen: donaufestival Niederösterreich, A (2005); Kampnagel Hamburg, D (2005)

King Kong Club (photo: Manuel Reinartz)

Selected Publications
Ausgewählte Veröffentlichungen

Arntzen, Knut Ove: „Ambient Theatre and Clubbing. Urban Post Mainstream". In: Trans. Internet-Zeitschrift für Kulturwissenschaften, no./Nr. 9, 2/2001, http://www.inst.at/trans/9Nr/arntzen9.htm

Diez, Georg: „Diese Jahre mit Gob Squad". In: Frankfurter Allgemeine Sonntagszeitung, 5.12.2004

Evert, Kerstin: „Verortung als Konzept. Rimini Protokoll und Gob Squad". In: Klein, Gabriele; Sting, Wolfgang (ed./Hg.): Zeitgenössische Performances. Ästhetische Positionen. Bielefeld 2005 (to be published/in Druck)

Freiburg, Johanna: „Sprechende Räume sind banal". In: Hammerthaler, Ralph; Schweeger, Elisabeth (ed./Hg.): Räumungen. Von der Unverschämtheit, Theater für ein Medium der Zukunft zu halten. Berlin 1999, p./S. 44–53

Gerstmeier, Joachim: „Gob Squad". In: Hünnekens, Ludger; Winzen, Matthias (ed./Hg.): Dissimile. Prospektionen: Junge europäische Kunst. Baden-Baden 2002, p. / S. 60–65 (What Are You Looking At? in Baden-Baden)

„Gob Squad interviewed by exUrban Festival crew". In: „Save as...city.doc" Frakcija Performing Arts Magazine, no./Nr. 33/34, Zagreb 2005

„Gob Squad im Gespräch mit Aenne Quiñones". In: Prater-Saga 1–5 (working title/Arbeitstitel). Berlin 2005 (to be published/in Druck)

Goldberg, RoseLee: Performance: Live Art since the 60's. London 1998, p./S. 86

Henne, Claudia: „Learning by doing. Eine Forschungsreise durch das ‚Live.Performance.Art'-Festival ‚Home & Away' in Hannover". In: Theater Heute, no./Nr. 12, 12/1999, p./S. 32–39

Hoffmann, Jens: "Aperto Performance" In: Flash Art. The World's Leading Art Magazine, vol./Bd. XXXIII, no./Nr. 214, 10/2000, p./S. 49–51 (I can in Berlin)

Keidan, Lois: "Bending the Rules. New British Performance". In: Bridges. The British Council in Deutschland. Autumn/Herbst 1997

Klein, Gabriele: „Gespräch mit Johanna Freiburg und Bastian Trost". In: Klein, Gabriele (publication commissioned by/Hg. im Auftrag des Steirischen Herbstes): Bodies – Cities – Subjects. Die Theatralisierung des städtischen Raumes (working title/Arbeitstitel). Wien 2005 (to be published/in Druck)

Kunstforum International, vol./Bd. 143, 1–2/1999, p./S. 294 (I can in Berlin)

Lehmann, Hans-Thies: Postdramatisches Theater. Frankfurt am Main 1999, p./ S. 25 & 216 f.

Lengers, Birgit; Matzke, Mieke; Arioli, Ann-Marie: „Film und Theater – Produktive Mischverhältnisse und Missverständnisse". In: der dramaturg, 2/2003, p./S. 19–21

Matzke, Annemarie: „‚Come in and look at my live': Selbst-Inszenierung als Versuchsaufbau". In: Forum Modernes Theater, vol./Bd. 17, issue/Heft 1/2002, p./S. 19–27

Matzke, Annemarie: „Touristen, Passanten, Mitbewohner. Strategien des zeitgenössischen Site Specific Theatre". In: Roesner, David; Wartemann, Geesche; Wortmann, Volker (ed./Hg.): Szenische Orte – Mediale Räume. Hildesheim 2005 (to be published/in Druck)

Matzke, Annemarie: „Testen – Spielen – Tricksen – Scheitern. Selbstinszenierung im zeitgenössischen Theater". Hildesheim 2005 (to be published/in Druck)

Roselt, Jens: „Vom Affekt zum Effekt – Schauspielkultur und Popkultur". In: Fischer-Lichte, Erika; Kolesch, Doris; Weiler, Christel (ed./Hg.): Transformationen. Theater der neunziger Jahre. Berlin 1999, p./S. 111–121

Roselt, Jens: „Gob Squad – What are you looking at?" In: HOME & AWAY – Programmheft EXPO 2000, Hannover 1999, p./S. 51–55

Schulz, Christoph; Gob Squad: „Room Service". In: Schnitt. Das Filmmagazin, no./Nr. 32, autumn/Herbst 2003, p./S. 20–21

Siegmund, Gerald: „Die Wahrheit im Ozean der Fälschungen. Befragt: Berit Stumpf und Sean Patten". In: Frankfurter Allgemeine Zeitung, 29.7.1999

Stumpf, Berit: „Der perfekte Moment. Drei Fragen an Berit Stumpf von Gob Squad". In: Tagesspiegel (Spielzeitbeilage), 10/2000

Tiedemann, Kathrin: „,Live is Life'. Berit Stumpf und Sean Patten im Gespräch mit Kathrin Tiedemann". In: TheaterKulturVision. Arbeitsbuch von Theater der Zeit. Ed. by/hg. von Hörnigk, Therese; Masuch, Bettina; Raddatz, Frank M. Berlin 1998, p./S. 34-38

Vnuk, Gordana: "Festival of the Iconoclastic Theatre". In: „Disturbing (the) Image", Frakcija Performing Arts Magazine, no./Nr. 15, Zagreb, 10/1999

Weiler, Christel: „What you see is what you get (Gob Squad, Forced Entertainment, PME)". In: Theater der Zeit, 12/2000, p. / S. 57–59.

Wesemann, Arnd: „Does Dance need Art? How truly beneficial is the crossover between dance and the visual arts?" / „Braucht der Tanz die Kunst? Und wie fruchtbar ist das Crossover zwischen Tanz und Bildender Kunst wirklich?" In: ballettanz, 1/1999, p./S. 26–33

Writers and Photographers
Autoren und Fotografen

Robin Arthur (Berlin, D)
is a member of Forced Entertainment, Sheffield (UK). He saw *Super Night Shot* in Berlin in 2003.
ist ein Mitglied von Forced Entertainment. Er sah *Super Night Shot* 2003 in Berlin.

David Baltzer (Berlin, D)
first photographed Gob Squad in 1998 for *Close Enough to Kiss* in Berlin. He still photographs Gob Squad today, most recently for SAGA 3.
fotografierte Gob Squad zum ersten Mal 1998 bei der Berliner Aufführung von *Close Enough to Kiss*. Heute fotografiert er Gob Squad noch immer, zuletzt bei SAGA 3.

Wonge Bergmann (Frankfurt/Main, D)
met Gob Squad in 1996 when he was the house photographer for the TAT in Frankfurt. He currently works as a freelance photographer and as the company photographer for Jan Fabre/Troubleyn.
lernte Gob Squad als „Hausfotograf" des TAT 1996 in Frankfurt/Main kennen. Er arbeitet heute als freier Fotograf und Companyfotograf von Jan Fabre/Troubleyn.

Philip Bither (Minneapolis, USA)
is Senior Curator for Performing Arts at the Walker Art Center, Minneapolis (USA) and brought Gob Squad to the States, after he saw *Safe* in Edinburgh in 2000.
ist Kurator für Performing Arts am Walker Art Center, Minneapolis (USA), und brachte Gob Squad in die Staaten, nachdem er *Safe* 2000 in Edinburgh gesehen hatte.

Bettina Blümner (Berlin, D)
photographed Gob Squad in 1998 for *What Are You Looking At?* in Berlin. Currently she works as a director and photographer.

fotografierte Gob Squad 1997 in Berlin für *What Are You Looking At?*. Sie arbeitet heute als Regisseurin und Fotografin.

Till Briegleb (Hamburg, D)
was working as an arts editor when he saw *15 Minutes to Comply* in Kassel in 1997. He is currently a freelance author.
war Kulturredakteur, als er 1997 *15 Minutes to Comply* in Kassel sah. Heute arbeitet er als freier Autor.

Daniel Brine (London, UK)
was Combined Arts Officer at the Arts Council of England in 1998 (when he received the business card and Christmas greeting). He attended *Say It Like You Mean It* while he was co-director of the NOW Festival, Nottingham in 2000. He is currently Associate Director of the Live Art Development Agency, London.
war 1998 (als er die Visitenkarte und den Weihnachtsgruß bekam) Combined Arts Officer beim Arts Council of England und besuchte *Say It Like You Mean It* 2000 in Nottingham, als er Ko-Leiter des NOW Festivals war. Heute ist er Ko-Leiter der Live Art Development Agency, London (UK).

Christian Brox (Berlin, D)
first photographed Gob Squad in 1999 for *Safe* while he was recovering from his business management studies. Currently he still takes photographs, applies his business studies and works as a producer.
fotografierte Gob Squad zum ersten Mal 1999 bei *Safe*, während er sich von seinem BWL-Studium erholte. Heute fotografiert er immer noch, wendet sein BWL-Studium an und arbeitet als Producer.

Andrew Caleya Chetty (London, UK)
has known Gob Squad since the very beginning. During the period he worked for the NOW Festival in Nottingham (1995-2001), he commissioned 5 Gob Squad works. Currently he works as a curator for The Public, West

Bromwich, (UK).
kennt Gob Squad seit den Anfängen. Während der Zeit, die er als Künstlerischer Leiter des NOW Festivals in Nottinham gearbeitet hat (1995–2001), koproduzierte er 5 Gob Squad-Arbeiten. Zur Zeit arbeitet er als Kurator für The Public, West Bromwick (UK).

Miles Chalcraft (Berlin, D)
has been around the company since the very beginning in various roles. He took the pressfoto for *The Great Outdoors* (Berlin, 2001) and collaborates with Gob Squad to this Day. He also programmes festivals of digital arts in Berlin and Nottingham (UK).
war für die Gruppe seit den Anfängen in diversen Rollen und Funktionen tätig. Er machte das Pressefoto zu *The Great Outdoors* (Berlin, 2001) und arbeitet noch immer mit Gob Squad zusammen. Außerdem kuratiert er Festivals im Bereich Medienkunst in Berlin und Nottingham (UK).

Simon Cunningham (UK)
in 1995, when he first photographed Gob Squad (*Work*), he had a darkroom on the landing, developed in the bath and rinsed the photos in the sink. These days it's all bigger and older. He puts his head under a cloth prior to exposure.
1995, als er Gob Squad zum ersten Mal fotografierte *(Work)*, hatte er eine Dunkelkammer auf dem Treppenabsatz, entwickelte in der Badewanne und wässerte die Fotos im Waschbecken. Heute ist alles größer und älter. Er steckt seinen Kopf unter ein Tuch bevor er belichtet.

Arno Declair (Hamburg, D)
is a theatre photographer. He first photographed Gob Squad in 1999 for *Safe* in Hamburg.
ist Theaterfotograf. Er fotografierte Gob Squad zum ersten Mal 1999 bei *Safe* in Hamburg.

Georg Diez (Berlin, D)
is a journalist. He saw *Super Night Shot* in 2003 in Berlin.
ist Journalist. Er sah *Super Night Shot* 2003 in Berlin.

Miriam Dreysse (Gießen, D)
is a theatre academic and currently works at the Institut für Angewandte Theaterwissenschaft in Giessen (D). In 1995 she saw the Giessen version of

House. Calling Laika in the TAT, Frankfurt was one of many further Gob Squad works she saw.
ist Theaterwissenschaftlerin und arbeitet zur Zeit am Institut für Angewandte Theaterwissenschaft in Gießen (D). 1995 sah sie die Gießener Version von *House. Calling Laika* im Frankfurter TAT war eine von vielen weiteren Arbeiten, die sie als Zuschauerin verfolgte.

Nikola Duric (Hamburg, D)
is a member of the performance collective Showcase Beat Le Mot, Hamburg/Berlin (D). He saw *What Are You Looking At?* for the first time in Berlin in 1998 and was a guest performer for performances of *What Are You Looking At?* in Berlin and Colchester.
ist ein Mitglied der Performancegruppe Showcase Beat Le Mot, Hamburg/Berlin (D). Er sah *What Are You Looking At?* zum ersten Mal 1998 in Berlin und war 2002 Gastperformer bei Aufführungen von *What Are You Looking At?* in Berlin und Colchester.

Tobias Dusche (Hamburg, D)
is a screenwriter. He saw *Room Service* in 2003 in Hamburg.
ist Drehbuchautor. Er sah *Room Service* 2003 in Hamburg.

Paul Fraser (Nottingham, UK)
is a screenwriter. In 1996 he helped out on *An Effortless Transaction* as a technician.
ist Drehbuchautor. 1996 half er bei *An Effortless Transaction* als Techniker aus.

Daniel Haaksman
is a DJ, music producer and occasional journalist. In 1997, when he saw *15 Minutes to Comply* in Kassel (D) he was a DJ and student.
ist DJ, Musikproduzent und Gelegenheits-Journalist. 1997, als er *15 Minutes to Comply* in Kassel sah, war er DJ und Student.

Jens Hoffmann (London, UK)
worked in 1997 as an organizer of "Theaterskizzen" at the documenta X (Kassel, D) when he saw *15 Minutes to Comply*. He commissioned *I Can* and *What Are You Looking At?* and brought Gob Squad to Sean Kelly Gallery, N.Y. He currently works as Director of Exhibitions at the Institute of Contemporary Arts in London, UK.
arbeitete 1997 als Organisator von Theaterskizzen bei der documenta X (Kassel, D), als er *15 Minutes to Comply* sah. Er gab *I Can* und *What Are You Looking At?*

in Auftrag und brachte Gob Squad in die Sean Kelly Gallery, N.Y. Heute arbeitet er als Kurator am Institute of Contemporary Arts in London, UK.

Gareth Howell (Nottingham, UK)
is an artist. He saw *Where Do You Want to Go to Die?* in Nottingham in 2001.
ist Künstler. Er sah *Where Do You Want to Go to Die?* 2001 in Nottingham.

Falk Hoysack (Berlin, D)
is a cameraman. He photographed Gob Squad in 2001 in Leuven (B) backstage whilst touring with *Say It Like You Mean It.*
ist Kameramann. Er fotografierte Gob Squad 2001 in Leuven (B) bei einem Gastspiel von *Say It Like You Mean It* backstage.

Tashi Iwaoka (Nottingham, UK)
is a theatre-making practitioner (and he'd love to become just a happy ordinary person who does weird things). He is the first person who ever purchased an *I can* (ordered in Nottingham in 2000, received delivery in Berlin in 2001).
ist Theatermacher (und möchte gern ein glücklicher, normaler Mensch werden, der komische Sachen macht). Er war die erste Person, die ein *I Can* erstand (2000 bestellt in Nottingham, erhalten 2001 in Berlin).

Mark Jeffery (Chicago, USA)
is part of Goat Island, Chicago (USA). He saw T*he Great Outdoors* in Prague in 2001.
ist Mitglied der Performancegruppe Goat Island, Chicago (USA). Er sah *The Great Outdoors* 2001 in Prag.

Ina Kaifi (Hamburg, D)
was hanging out a lot in 1997 and thus had time to watch *Close Enough to Kiss* in Berlin. She is currently a freelance author.
hat 1997 viel rumgegammelt und hatte deshalb Zeit, *Close Enough to Kiss* in Berlin zu sehen. Heute ist sie freie Autorin.

Alexander Kelly (Sheffield, UK)
is Co-artistic Director of Third Angel, Sheffield (UK). He saw *Say It Like You Mean It* in 2000 in Hildesheim (D).
ist Ko-Künstlerischer Leiter von Third Angel, Sheffield (UK). Er sah *Say It Like You Mean It* 2000 in Hildesheim (D).

Christiane Kühl (Berlin, D)
was a theatre editor in 2001 when she saw *The Great Outdoors* in Berlin. Currently she works as a freelance journalist for print and radio.
war 2001, als sie *The Great Outdoors* in Berlin sah, Theaterredakteurin und arbeitet heute als freie Journalistin für Print und Hörfunk.

Albrecht Kunze (Frankfurt/Main, D)
makes radio pieces (text, music, direction) and music. He was already doing this in 1998 when he saw *Calling Laika* in Frankfurt/Main. He currently also runs a label for radio pieces.
macht Hörstücke (Text, Musik, Regie) und Musik. Das tat er bereits 1998, als er *Calling Laika* in Frankfurt/Main sah. Heute ist er zusätzlich auch Betreiber eines HörLabels.

Peter Laudenbach (Berlin, D)
is a journalist and theatre critic. He likes writing about business in theatre magazines and theatre in business magazines. In 2000 he imagined that the whole world was a Gob Squad performance.
ist Journalist und Theaterkritiker. Er schreibt am liebsten in Theaterzeitschriften über Wirtschaft und in Wirtschaftszeitschriften über Theater. 2000 stellte er sich vor, daß die Welt eine Gob-Squad-Inszenierung ist.

Armin Linke (Milano, I)
first photographed Gob Squad in 1998 for *What Are You Looking At?* at the Berlin Biennale. He currently lives in Milan, Italy and works as a photographer.
fotografierte Gob Squad erstmals 1998 in Berlin bei *What Are You Looking At?*. Er lebt in Mailand (Italien) und arbeitet als Fotograf.

Mieke Matzke (Berlin, D)
was a student in Giessen and a member of the performance collective She She Pop when she travelled to Nottingham in 1995 to see *Work*. She currently works as a research associate in Berlin and is still a member of She She Pop (Hamburg/Berlin, D)
als sie 1995 nach Nottingham reiste, um *Work* zu sehen, war sie Studentin der Theaterwissenschaft in Gießen und Mitglied der Performancegruppe She She Pop. Heute ist sie wissenschaftliche Mitarbeiterin in Berlin und noch immer Mitglied von She She Pop.

Jordan McKenzie (London, UK)

is a performance artist and a lecturer. He saw *Safe* in 1999 in Nottingham. After toying with the idea of presenting his memories of the piece by sending a fax as himself dressed up as the lead singer of KISS, he decided not be so performance-arsey.

ist Performancekünstler und Dozent. Er sah *Safe* 1999 in Nottingham. Nachdem er eine Weile mit der Idee gespielt hatte, seine Erinnerungen an das Stück darzustellen, indem er ein Fax senden würde, das ihn als Sänger von KISS verkleidet zeigt, entschied er sich nicht, so anzugeben.

Till Müller-Klug (Berlin, D)

is a writer and director. In 1999 he collaborated with Gob Squad on the radio piece *Little White Lies*.

ist Autor und Regisseur. Er arbeitete 1999 mit Gob Squad in Berlin an dem Live-Hörspiel *Little White Lies*.

Aenne Quiñones (Berlin, D)

worked as a curator for theatre/performance at the Podewil in Berlin (D), when, in 1996, she came to Nottingham, watched *An Effortless Transaction* and her relationship with Gob Squad began. When she invited the group to become artist in residence in the Berlin Podewil in 1999, most of the company moved to Berlin. Currently she is a dramaturge at the Volksbühne am Rosa-Luxemburg-Platz, Berlin (D).

arbeitete 1996 als Kuratorin für Theater/Performance am Podewil Berlin (D), als sie *An Effortless Transaction* in Nottingham besuchte und ihre Verbindung mit Gob Squad begann. Auf Grund ihrer Einladung, artist in residence im Berliner Podewil zu werden, zog ein Großteil von Gob Squad 1999 nach Berlin. Heute ist sie Dramaturgin an der Volksbühne am Rosa-Luxemburg-Platz, Berlin (D).

Manuel Reinartz (Leipzig/Berlin, D)

first photographed Gob Squad in 2000 for *You Know You Want It (Part 1: The Annie Lennox Project)*. At the time he studied photography in Leipzig. He currently lives and works in Leipzig and Berlin.

fotografierte Gob Squad zum ersten Mal 2000 für *You Know You Want It (Part 1: The Annie Lennox Project)*. Damals studierte er Fotografie an der HGB Leipzig. Heute lebt und arbeitet er in Leipzig und Berlin.

Johan Reyniers (Brüssel, B)

is artistic director of the Kaaitheater, Brussels (B). He saw *Safe* for the first time in Hamburg in 1999.

ist Künstlerischer Leiter des Kaaitheater, Brüssel (B). Er sah *Safe* zum ersten Mal 1999 in Hamburg.

Antony Rizzi (Frankfurt/Main, D)

is an Italian/American visual performance artist living in Frankfurt/Main, D. When he met Gob Squad in 1996 he was a dancer for the Forsythe Ballet Company. He saw *Say It Like You Mean It* in Frankfurt/Main in 2000.

ist ein Performancekünstler italienisch-amerikanischer Herkunft, der in Frankfurt/Main lebt. Als er 1996 Gob Squad kennen lernte, war er Tänzer beim Forsythe Ballett. Er sah *Say It Like You Mean It* 2000 in Frankfurt/Main.

Anette Schäfer (Berlin, D)

kuratiert Festivals im Bereich Medienkunst in Berlin und Nottingham (UK) und arbeitet als Grafik-Designerin. 2001 gestaltete sie das Bildmaterial für *The Finalists*.

programmes festivals of digital arts in Berlin and Nottingham (UK) and works as a graphic-designer. In 2001 she created the visual graphics for *The Finalists*.

Uta Schnell (Halle, D)

works as a research associate for Kulturstiftung des Bundes (D). When she was worried about Gob Squad in 2000, she worked for the world exhibition Expo in Hannover.

ist Wissenschaftliche Mitarbeiterin der Kulturstiftung des Bundes (D). Als sie sich 2000 um Gob Squad Sorgen machte, arbeitete sie für die Weltausstellung Expo in Hannover.

Janine Schulze (Leipzig, D)

was a PhD student when she saw *Close Enough to Kiss* in Munich in 1997. Currently she is a dance academic and managerial director of the Leipzig Dance Archive e.V.

war 1997, als sie *Close Enough to Kiss* in München sah, Doktorandin. Heute ist sie Tanzwissenschaftlerin und Geschäftsführende Leiterin des Tanzarchivs Leipzig e.V.

Elisabeth Schweeger (Frankfurt/Main, D)
was artistic director of the marstall in Munich (D) when she invited *Calling Laika*.
She is currently director of the Schauspiel Frankfurt/Main (D).
war Künstlerische Leiterin des marstall/München (D), als sie 1998 *Calling Laika*
nach München einlud. Heute ist sie Intendantin des Schauspiel Frankfurt/Main (D).

Emily Shenston (West Bromwich, UK)
works as an administrative assistant at The Public in her home town of West
Bromwich (UK), where she saw *Super Night Shot* in 2004.
arbeitet als Verwaltungsassistentin bei The Public in ihrer Heimatstadt West
Bromwich (UK), wo sie 2004 *Super Night Shot* gesehen hat.

Gerald Siegmund (Gießen/Frankfurt, D)
worked as a freelance theatre and dance critic when he saw *Show & Tell* in
Frankfurt/Main in 1996. Currently he works as a research associate in
Giessen (D) at the Institute for Applied Theatre Studies.
arbeitete als freier Theater- und Tanzkritiker, als er 1996 *Show & Tell* in
Frankfurt/Main sah. Er ist Wissenschaftlicher Mitarbeiter am Institut für Angewandte Theaterwissenschaft in Gießen (D).

Friedemann Simon (Hamburg, D)
first photographed Gob Squad in 2000 for *Say It Like You Mean It* in Hamburg. He
currently works as a theatre photographer in Hamburg.
fotografierte Gob Squad zum ersten Mal 2000 bei *Say It Like You Mean It* in
Hamburg. Arbeitet auch heute noch als Theaterfotograf in Hamburg.

Tom Stromberg (Hamburg, D)
produced Gob Squad's first production in Germany at the TAT, Frankfurt/Main
(D). In 1998, as one of the last works shortly before he left the TAT as artistic
director, he produced *Calling Laika*. He is currently director of the Schauspielhaus in Hamburg (D).
produzierte Gob Squads erste Arbeit in Deutschland am TAT, Frankfurt/Main
(D). 1998, kurz vor seinem Weggang als Künstlerischer Leiter an diesem
Haus produzierte er dort als eine der letzten Arbeiten *Calling Laika*. Zur Zeit ist
er Intendant des Deutschen Schauspielhauses in Hamburg (D).

Ange Taggart (Nottingham, UK)
worked in 1995 as a nursery nurse coordinator, when she saw *Work* in
Nottingham and her life changed. She is currently a performance artist.
arbeitete 1995 als Sozialarbeiterin in einem Familienzentrum, als sie *Work* in
Nottingham sah und sich ihr Leben änderte. Heute ist sie Performancekünstlerin.

Alf Thum (Hildesheim, D)
is a freelance cultural manager and worried about Gob Squad together with
Uta Schnell in 2000.
ist freischaffender politischer Bildner und machte sich 2000 zusammen mit
Uta Schnell um Gob Squad Sorgen.

Kathrin Tiedemann (Düsseldorf, D)
has known Gob Squad since the beginning and from various different contexts (as a journalist, as curator of the Berlin festival reich & berühmt and as
a dramaturg at Kampnagel Hamburg). She is currently the artistic director of
the FFT in Düsseldorf.
kennt Gob Squad bereits seit den Anfängen und aus unterschiedlichen
Zusammenhängen. Als Journalistin, als Kuratorin des reich & berühmt Festivals in Berlin (D) oder als Dramaturgin auf Kampnagel Hamburg (D). Zur Zeit
ist sie Künstlerische Leiterin des FFT in Düsseldorf (D).

Tatjana Turankyj (Berlin, D)
is an artist and self-declared fan. She saw *Where Do You Want to Go to Die?* in 2001
in Berlin.
ist Künstlerin und bezeichnet sich selbst als Fan. Sie sah *Where Do You Want to
Go to Die?* 2001 in Berlin.

Emina Visnic (Zagreb, HR)
is one of the artistic directors of the Urban Festival in Zagreb (HR). She saw
Room Service in 2004 at the Laguna Hotel in Zagreb.
ist Teil des Leitungsteams des Urban Festivals in Zagreb (HR). Sie sah *Room
Service* 2004 im Laguna Hotel in Zagreb.

Gordana Vnuk (Hamburg, D)
met Gob Squad in 1998 when she was artistic director of Chapter Arts Centre
in Cardiff (UK). She has also been the artistic director of the Eurokaz Festival
in Zagreb (HR) since 1987. She is currently the director of Kampnagel in

Hamburg (D).
lernte Gob Squad 1998 kennen, als sie Künstlerische Leiterin des Chapter Arts Centre in Cardiff (UK) war. Seit 1987 ist sie Künstlerische Leiterin des Eurokaz Festival in Zagreb (HR). Zur Zeit ist sie Intendantin von Kampnagel Hamburg (D).

Christina von Haugwitz (Köln/Cologne, D)
first photographed Gob Squad in 1998 in Frankfurt/Main for *Calling Laika*, whilst working as a theatre photographer. She currently works as a freelance photojournalist and author.
fotografierte Gob Squad zum ersten Mal 1998 in Frankfurt/Main für *Calling Laika*, sie arbeitete damals als Theaterfotografin. Heute arbeitet sie als freie Bildjournalistin und Autorin.

Matt Watkins (Nottingham, UK)
is an artist. He came to see *Say It Like You Mean It* in Nottingham in 2000.
ist Künstler. Er besuchte *Say It Like You Mean It* 2000 in Nottingham.

Mark Waugh (Brighton/London, UK)
works as visual arts officer with responsibility for strategic national development of Live Art at the Arts Council of England and as an independent producer and curator. He has written and lectured on an array of subjects from Araki to Warhol. In 2000 he attended *Say It Like You Mean It* in Nottingham.
arbeitet als Visual Arts officer für das Arts Council of England (Schwerpunkt: strategische Entwicklung von Live Art) und als unabhängiger Produzent und Kurator. Er hat über eine Reihe von Themen geschrieben und gelehrt (von Araki bis Warhol). 2000 besuchte er *Say It Like You Mean It* in Nottingham.

Arnd Wesemann (Berlin, D)
is a journalist and editor. He saw *The Great Outdoors* in 2001 in Berlin.
ist Journalist und Redakteur. Er sah *The Great Outdoors* 2001 in Berlin.

List of Photographs
Bildverzeichnis

Key/Schlüssel:
JF = Johanna Freiburg
AL = Alex Large
SP = Sean Patten
LS = Liane Sommers
BS = Berit Stumpf
ST = Sarah Thom
BT = Bastian Trost
SW = Simon Will

Page/Seite 148 Photo: Armin Linke, Hamburg 2000. **l-r:** SW, BS, LS
Page/Seite 149 Photo: Christian Brox, Hamburg 2000. Audience

Page/Seite 150–153 Video stills: Gob Squad, Berlin 2000. AL, JF, SP, BS, LS, SW, ST

Page/Seite 154 Photo: Miles Chalcraft, Berlin 2001. SW

Page/Seite 155 Video stills: Gob Squad, Berlin & Prague 2001. **Top-bottom/oben-unten:** BS, JF, SP

Page/Seite 156 Video stills: Gob Squad, Hamburg 2003. **Top/oben l-r:** BT, BS **bottom/unten:** ST, SP

Page/Seite 157 Video stills: Gob Squad, Hamburg 2003. **Top/oben l-r:** BT, BS **bottom/unten:** SW, ST

Page/Seite 158 Photo: David Baltzer, Berlin 2003. BT & Passer-by/Passant

Page/Seite 159 Photos: David Baltzer, Berlin 2003. **l-r:** JF, SP, ST, Elyce Semenec

Page/Seite 164 top/oben l-r: Photos: Bettina Blümner, Gob Squad, Simon Cunningham, Gob Squad; **bottom/unten l-r:** Photos: Gob Squad, David Baltzer, Gob Squad

Page/Seite 165 Photo: Gob Squad, Nottingham 1992. AL

Page/Seite 168 Photo: Gob Squad, Hamburg 1999. **l-r:** LS, BS, SP, JF, SW, AL & „Tony"

Page/Seite 169 Photo: Gob Squad, Minneapolis (US) 2001

Page/Seite 171 Photo: Falk Hoysack, Leuven (B) 2001. **l-r:** JF, LS, SW, Berte Neraal, SP

Page/Seite 172 Photo: Gob Squad, Berlin 2004. **l-r:** BT, SW, SP

Page/Seite 175 Photo: Gob Squad, Glastonbury (UK) 1995. **l-r:** Stephen

Watson, LS, AL, Leanne Price, SP

Page/Seite 178 Photo: Gob Squad, Glastonbury (UK) 1998. **l-r:** BS, AL, SP, Mat Hand, Gareth Howell, LS

Page/Seite 183 Photo: Gob Squad, Berlin 2004. BT

Page/Seite 186 Photo: Gob Squad, London 2002. ST

Page/Seite 188 Photo: David Baltzer, Berlin 2004. **l-r:** Passer-by as „Bigman"/Passantin als „Bigman", Elyce Semenec, SW

Page/Seite 189 Photo: Manuel Reinartz, Berlin 2005.

Acknowledgements/Danksagungen

Gob Squad couldn't have made it this far without the support of our friends, colleagues and audiences, producers and promoters, funders, ladies and gentlemen of the press, mums, dads, aunties and neighbours, all the van drivers, technicians who worked late when we couldn't agree which scene to cut and our accountants who diligently filed receipts for sparklers as well as videotapes. We'd like to thank you all.

Thank you to those who contributed to the work when we were making it and who have offered continual support over the years. Thanks in particular to our long-term collaborators:
Miles Chalcraft (for his madcap ideas, hairbrained schemes and crazy wiring), Martin Cooper (for his total lack of respect for theatrical tradition eg. playing fart noises as we bow at important festivals), Elyce Semenec (for putting so much of herself into the work), Sebastian Bark (for his sensitivity and perfectionism), Jeff McGrory (for his vast record collection and eternal optimism).

Thanks to our admin staff over the years, Matt Adams, Christina Runge, Eva Hartmann and Nina Thielicke who have had the patience to wait for those interminable "group decisions".

Thanks to all the people that made an appearance in one of our shows or stepped in further down the line as lighting, video or sound operators, in particular Leif Alexis, Sebastian Bark, Miles Chalcraft, Naim Cortazz, Nikola Duric, Michael Egger, Thomas Hall, Mat Hand, Gareth Howell, Sirko Knüpfer, Penny Linfield, Berte Neraal, Mathew Risden, Anette Schäfer, Stephan Trümper, Tatjana Turanskyj, Dennis Waldrop and Susanne Weber.

Our special thanks to all the people contributing their memories, without their effort we couldn't have made this book. All the contributions in text and pictures we received (even though not all could make it into this book, and none of them could be printed full length) brought a smile to our faces. Thank you to the photographers who have generously allowed us to print previous-

Gob Squad hätte es nicht so weit bringen können ohne die Unterstützung unserer Freunde, Kollegen und Zuschauer, Produzenten und Veranstalter, Geldgeber, Damen und Herrren der Presse, Mütter, Väter, Tanten und Nachbarn, all die Transporter-Fahrer, Techniker, die bis spät in die Nacht arbeiteten, wenn wir uns nicht einig wurden, welche Szene wir rausschmeißen sollten, und unsere Buchhalter, die sorgfältig Quittungen für Wunderkerzen und Video-Kassetten ablegten.
Dank an alle, die zu unserer Arbeit beigetragen haben, während sie entstand, und die uns über die Jahre Unterstützung gewährt haben. Ganz besonderen Dank an unsere langjährigen Mitarbeiter:
Miles Chalcraft (für seine größenwahnsinnigen Ideen, haarsträubenden Pläne und beängstigenden Verkabelungen), Martin Cooper (für seinen absoluten Mangel an Respekt für theatrale Traditionen, zum Beispiel Furzgeräusche abzuspielen, wenn wir uns auf wichtigen Festivals verbeugen), Elyce Semenec (dafür, dass sie so viel von sich in die Arbeit eingebracht hat), Sebastian Bark (für seine Sensibilität und seinen Perfektionismus), Jeff McGrory (für seine umfangreiche Plattensammlung und seinen ewigen Optimismus).

Dank an unseren Verwaltungsstab durch die Jahre: Matt Adams, Christina Runge, Eva Hartmann und Nina Thielicke, die die Geduld aufbrachten, die langwierigen „Gruppen-Entscheidungen" abzuwarten.

Dank an all die Leute, die in einer unserer Shows aufgetreten oder auf später eingestiegen sind auch als Licht-, Video- und Tonleute: Leif Alexis, Sebastian Bark, Miles Chalcraft, Naim Cortazz, Nikola Duric, Michael Egger, Thomas Hall, Mat Hand, Gareth Howell, Sirko Knüpfer, Penny Linfield, Berte Neraal, Mathew Risden, Anette Schäfer, Stephan Trümper, Tatjana Turanskyj, Dennis Waldrop und Susanne Weber.

Unser besonderer Dank gilt allen, die ihre Erinnerungen festgehalten haben und ohne deren Bemühungen wir dieses Buch nicht hätten machen können. All die Text- und Bildbeiträge (auch wenn sie nicht alle und in ganzer Länge

ly unseen pictures. Many thanks to everyone who has helped us produce this book:

Robin Arthur, David Baltzer, Wonge Bergmann, Philip Bither, Bettina Blümner, Erin Boberg, Ingo Bousa, Andrew Brader, Till Briegleb, Daniel Brine, Christian Brox, Gion Capeder, Miles Chalcraft, Andrew Caleya Chetty, Paul Clarke, Simon Cunningham, Arno Declair, Georg Diez, Chris Dorley-Brown, Miriam Dreysse, Nikola Duric, Tobias Dusche, Fritz Emslander, Kerstin Evert, Karen Fraser, Paul Fraser, Heike Freiburg, Daniel Haaksman, Eva Hartmann, Martin Heying, Jens Hoffmann, Gareth Howell, Falk Hoysack, Tashi Iwaoka, Claude Jansen, Mark Jeffery, Ina Kaifi, Alexander Kelly, Knut Klaßen, Florian Kollmer, Christiane Kühl, Albrecht Kunze, Live Art Development Agency, Peter Laudenbach, Thomas Leib, Matthias Lilienthal, Kate Ling, Armin Linke, Mieke Matzke, Jordan McKenzie, Judd Morrissey, Harald Müller, Till Müller-Klug, Sophia New, Stéphane Noël, Haiko Pfost, Gwenn Potard, Aenne Quiñones, Manuel Reinartz, Johan Reyniers, Antony Rizzi, Christoph Rodatz, Jens Roselt, Anette Schäfer, Uta Schnell, Felix Schnieder-Henninger, Christoph Schulz, Janine Schulze, Elisabeth Schweeger, Emily Shenston, András Siebold, Gerald Siegmund, Friedemann Simon, Claudia Splitt, Tom Stromberg, Ange Taggart, Nina Thielicke, Alf Thum, Kathrin Tiedemann, Tatjana Turanskyj, Wolfgang Unger, Emina Visnic, Gordana Vnuk, Christina von Haugwitz, Matt Watkins, Mark Waugh, Regina Wenig, Arnd Wesemann, Andrzej Wirth.

in diesem Buch enthalten sein konnten), haben uns glücklich gemacht. Dank an die Fotografen, die uns großzügig erlaubt haben, bisher ungesehene Bilder zu drucken. Vielen Dank an alle, die geholfen haben, dieses Buch zu produzieren:

Robin Arthur, David Baltzer, Wonge Bergmann, Philip Bither, Bettina Blümner, Erin Boberg, Ingo Bousa, Andrew Brader, Till Briegleb, Daniel Brine, Christian Brox, Gion Capeder, Miles Chalcraft, Andrew Caleya Chetty, Paul Clarke, Simon Cunningham, Arno Declair, Georg Diez, Chris Dorley-Brown, Miriam Dreysse, Nikola Duric, Tobias Dusche, Fritz Emslander, Kerstin Evert, Karen Fraser, Paul Fraser, Heike Freiburg, Daniel Haaksman, Eva Hartmann, Martin Heying, Jens Hoffmann, Gareth Howell, Falk Hoysack, Tashi Iwaoka, Claude Jansen, Mark Jeffery, Ina Kaifi, Alexander Kelly, Knut Klassen, Florian Kollmer, Christiane Kühl, Albrecht Kunze, Live Art Development Agency, Peter Laudenbach, Thomas Leib, Matthias Lilienthal, Kate Ling, Armin Linke, Mieke Matzke, Jordan McKenzie, Judd Morrissey, Harald Müller, Till Müller-Klug, Sophia New, Stéphane Noël, Haiko Pfost, Gwenn Potard, Aenne Quiñones, Manuel Reinartz, Johan Reyniers, Antony Rizzi, Christoph Rodatz, Jens Roselt, Anette Schäfer, Uta Schnell, Felix Schnieder-Henninger, Christoph Schulz, Janine Schulze, Elisabeth Schweeger, Emily Shenston, András Siebold, Gerald Siegmund, Friedemann Simon, Claudia Splitt, Tom Stromberg, Ange Taggart, Nina Thielicke, Alf Thum, Kathrin Tiedemann, Tatjana Turanskyj, Wolfgang Unger, Emina Visnic, Gordana Vnuk, Christina von Haugwitz, Matt Watkins, Mark Waugh, Regina Wenig, Arnd Wesemann, Andrzej Wirth.

This book is produced by Gob Squad in cooperation with:
Dieses Buch wurde von Gob Squad produziert in Zusammenarbeit mit:

Volksbühne am Rosa-Luxemburg-Platz Berlin
Kampnagel Hamburg

Gob Squad is a performance art collective whose members are:
Gob Squad ist ein Performancekollektiv, dessen Mitglieder sind:
Johanna Freiburg, Sean Patten, Berit Stumpf, Sarah Thom, Bastian Trost,
Simon Will.
Company Administration/Organisation: Eva Hartmann
Assisted by/Unterstützt von: Nina Thielicke

Impressum:

Synwolt Verlag Berlin

Erstausgabe/First Edition April 2005

© Cover photo/Titelfoto: Gob Squad (from/aus *What Are You Looking At?*)

© Inside cover/Innencover: Mark Jeffery remembers/erinnert *The Great Outdoors*

© Gob Squad
www.gobsquad.com

© 2005 Synwolt Verlag Berlin (svb)
Oderberger Straße 40, 10435 Berlin
mail@synwolt-verlag.de
www.synwolt-verlag.de

Editors/Herausgeber: Gob Squad, Johanna Freiburg und Aenne Quiñones
Translations by/Übersetzungen von: Daniel Belasco Rogers, Sophia New,
Ilia Papatheodorou
English copy editor/Korrektor für englische Sprache: Mat Hand
Project Administration/Projektorganisation: Nina Thielicke
Layout/Satz: LSD (www.lsd-berlin.com)
With special thanks to/Mit herzlichen Dank an Jeanne-Marie Katajew
Photos/Fotos © photographers/Fotografen

Printed in Germany, April 2005

ISBN 3-937065-06-7

All I still seem to remember is laughing, and laughing – laughing so hard – yet now all I seem to remember is how sad they left, why did they escape, how fragile they all were in their 'lost outdoors' of discovering. Their attempt to find a new space of zero gravity, in going outdoors, in going outside.

I remember in the gut a celebration. Deep in the gut that allowed a release of a trapped bird to escape into the night sky. A smiling toothed mouth released into the nightsky. An escape. upwards, mobile. away. UP. UP. AWAY. Yet now I wish to cry, to cry, to cry, to cry to cry, to cry, to cry, to cry, to cry, to

That there was still haunting us as we sat
that night in our seats. You see the present
that we knew had just the previous month
fallen down in front of us on many tv
screens.

What they yearned in their departures we
could see. this is somewhat where we
wanted. To go back to a before land. To
recover and put back together the fallen
down land.

We were there because we were attempting
an aftermath. They seemed to be there to leave
us, to depart, to report from a REMOTE, im
leaving through a wooden door. Along a
thread like stream each one reported

Contents

Ch 8

Positioning is the first body of thought that comes to grips with the difficult problem of getting heard in our overcommunicated society.

How positioning got started

If one word can be said to have marked the course of advertising in the past decade, the word is "positioning."

Positioning has become a buzzword among advertising, sales, and marketing people. Not only in America, but around the world. Teachers, politicians, and editorial writers are using the word.

Most people think positioning got started in 1972 when we wrote a series of articles entitled "The Positioning Era" for the trade paper *Advertising Age*.

Since then, we have given more than 1000 speeches on positioning to advertising groups in 21 different countries around the world. And we have given away more than 150,000 copies of our "little orange booklet" which reprints the *Advertising Age* articles.

Positioning has changed the way the advertising game is being played today.

"We're the third largest-selling coffee in America," say the Sanka radio commercials.

The third largest? Whatever happened to those good old advertising words like "first" and "best" and "finest"?

Well, the good old advertising days are gone forever and so are the words. Today you find comparatives, not superlatives.

"Avis is only No. 2 in rent-a-cars, so why go with us? We try harder."

"Seven-Up: the uncola."

Along Madison Avenue, these are called positioning slogans. And the advertising people who write them spend their time and research money looking for positions, or holes, in the marketplace.

But positioning has stirred up interest well beyond Madison Avenue. With good reason.

Anyone can use positioning strategy to get ahead in the game of life. And look at it this way: If you don't understand and use the principles, your competitors undoubtedly will.

What positioning is all about

How did a hard-sell concept like positioning become so popular in a business noted for its creativity?

In truth, the past decade might well be characterized as a "return to reality." White knights and black eye patches gave way to such positioning concepts as "Lite Beer from Miller. Everything you always wanted in a beer. And less."

Poetic? Yes. Artful? Yes. But also a straightforward, clearly defined explanation of the basic positioning premise.

To be successful today, you must touch base with reality. And the only reality that counts is what's already in the prospect's mind.

To be creative, to create something that doesn't already exist in the mind, is becoming more and more difficult. If not impossible.

The basic approach of positioning is not to create something new and different, but to manipulate what's already up there in the mind, to retie the connections that already exist.

Today's marketplace is no longer responsive to the strategies that worked in the past. There are just too many products, too many companies, and too much marketing noise.

The question most frequently asked by positioning skeptics is, "Why?" Why do we need a new approach to advertising and marketing?

The overcommunicated society

The answer is that we have become an overcommunicated society. The per-capita consumption of advertising in America today is $376.62 a year. (That compares with $16.87 in the rest of the world.)

If you spend $1 million a year on advertising, you are bombarding the average consumer with less than a half cent of advertising, spread out over 365 days—a consumer already exposed to $376.61½ worth of other advertising.

In our overcommunicated society, to talk about the "impact" of your advertising is to seriously overstate the potential effectiveness of your message. Advertising is not a sledgehammer. It's more like a light fog, a very light fog that envelops your prospects.

In the communication jungle out there, the only hope to score big is to be selective, to concentrate on narrow targets, to practice segmentation. In a word, "positioning."

The mind, as a defense against the volume of today's communications, screens and rejects much of the information offered it. In general, the mind accepts only that which matches prior knowledge or experience.

Millions of dollars have been wasted trying to change minds with advertising. Once a mind is made up, it's almost impossible to change it. Certainly not with a weak force like advertising. "Don't confuse me with the facts, my mind's made up." That's a way of life for most people.

The average person will sit still when being told something which he or she knows nothing about. (Which is why "news" is an effective advertising approach.) But the average person cannot tolerate being told he or she is wrong. Mind-changing is the road to advertising disaster.

The oversimplified mind

The only defense a person has in our overcommunicated society is an oversimplified mind.

Not unless they repeal the law of nature that gives us only 24 hours in a day will they find a way to stuff more into the mind.

The average mind is already a dripping sponge that can only soak up more information at the expense of what's already there. Yet we continue to pour more information into that supersaturated sponge and are disappointed when our messages fail to get through.

Advertising, of course, is only the tip of the communication iceberg. We communicate with each other in a wide variety of bewildering ways. And in a geometrically increasing volume.

The medium may not be the message, but it does seriously affect the message. Instead of a transmission system, the medium acts like a filter. Only a tiny fraction of the original material ends up in the mind of the receiver.

Furthermore, what we receive is influenced by the nature of our overcommunicated society. "Glittering generalities" have become a way of life in our overcommunicated society. We oversimplify because that's the only way to cope.

Technically, we are capable of increasing the volume of communication at least tenfold. We're experimenting with direct television broadcasting from satellites. Every home would have 100 channels or so to choose from.

North American Philips has just introduced a 3½-inch compact disc that holds 600 megabytes of data, more than enough to store the entire *Encyclopaedia Britannica*.

Terrific. But who is working on a compact disc for the mind? Who is trying to help the prospect cope with complexity that so overwhelms the mind that the average reaction to the wealth of information today is to tighten the intake valve? To accept less and less of what is so freely available? Communication itself is the communication problem.

The oversimplified message

The best approach to take in our overcommunicated society is the oversimplified message.

In communication, as in architecture, less is more. You have to sharpen your message to cut into the mind. You have to jettison the ambiguities, simplify the message, and then simplify it some more if you want to make a long-lasting impression.

People who depend on communication for their livelihood know the necessity of oversimplification.

Let's say you are meeting with a politician whom you are trying to get elected. In the first 5 minutes, you'll learn more about your political product than the average voter is going to learn about that person in the next 5 years.

Since so little material about your candidate is ever going to get into the mind of the voter, your job is really not a "communication" project in the ordinary meaning of the word.

It's a selection project. You have to select the material that has the best chance of getting through.

The enemy that is keeping your messages from hitting pay dirt is the volume of communication. Only when you appreciate the nature of the problem can you understand the solution.

When you want to communicate the advantages of a political candidate or a product or even yourself, you must turn things inside out.

You look for the solution to your problem not inside the product, not even inside your own mind.

You look for the solution to your problem inside the prospect's mind.

In other words, since so little of your message is going to get through anyway, you ignore the sending side and concentrate on the receiving end. You concentrate on the perceptions of the prospect. Not the reality of the product.

"In politics," said John Lindsay, "the perception is the reality." So, too, in advertising, in business, and in life.

But what about truth? What about the facts of the situation?

What is truth? What is objective reality? Every human being seems to believe intuitively that he or she alone holds the key to universal truth. When we talk about truth, what truth are we talking about? The view from the inside or the view from the outside?

It does make a difference. In the words of another era, "The customer is always right." And by extension, the seller or communicator is always wrong.

It may be cynical to accept the premise that the sender is wrong and the receiver is right. But you really have no other choice. Not if you want to get your message accepted by another human mind.

Besides, who's to say that the view from the inside looking out is any more accurate than the view from the outside looking in?

By turning the process around, by focusing on the prospect rather than the product, you simplify the selection process. You also learn principles and concepts that can greatly increase your communication effectiveness.

2

The assault on the mind

As a nation we have fallen in love with the concept of "communication." (In some grade schools "show and tell" is now being called "communication.") We don't always appreciate the damage being done by our overcommunicated society.

In communication, more is less. Our extravagant use of communication to solve a host of business and social problems has so jammed our channels that only a tiny fraction of all messages actually gets through. And not necessarily the most important ones either.

The transmission traffic jam

Take advertising, for example. With only 6 percent of the world's population, America consumes 57 percent of the world's advertising. (And you thought our use of energy was extravagant. Actually, we consume only 33 percent of the world's energy.)

Advertising, of course, is only a small channel in the communication river.

Take books. Each year some 30,000 books are published in America. Every year another 30,000. Which doesn't sound like a lot until you realize it would take 17 years of reading 24 hours a day just to finish one year's output.

Who can keep up?

Take newspapers. Each year American newspapers use more than 10 million tons of newsprint. Which means that the average person consumes 94 pounds of newsprint a year.

There's some question whether the average person can digest all this information. The Sunday edition of a large metropolitan newspaper like *The New York Times* weighs about 4½ pounds and contains some 500,000 words. To read it all, at an average reading speed of 300 words per minute, would take almost 28 hours. Not only would your Sunday be shot, but also a good part of the rest of the week too.

How much is getting through?

Take television. A medium barely 35 years old. A powerful and pervasive medium, television didn't replace radio or newspapers or magazines. Each of the three older media is bigger and stronger than it ever was.

Television is an additive medium. And the amount of communication added by television is awesome.

Ninety-eight percent of all American homes have at least one television set. (A third have two or more.)

Ninety-six percent of all television households can receive four or more TV stations. (A third can receive ten or more.)

The average American family watches television more than 7 hours a day. (More than 51 hours a week.)

Like motion pictures, the TV picture is really a still picture which changes 30 times a second. Which means the average American family is exposed to some 750,000 television pictures a day.

Not only are we being pictured to death, we are being papered to death. Take that Xerox machine down the hall. American business processes 1.4 trillion pieces of paper a year. That's 5.6 billion every working day.

Down the halls at the Pentagon, copy machines crank out 350,000 pages a day for distribution throughout the Defense Department. Equal to 1000 good-sized novels.

"World War II will end," said Field Marshal Montgomery, "when the warring nations run out of paper."

Take packaging. An 8-ounce package of Total breakfast cereal contains 1268 words of copy on the box. Plus an offer for a free booklet on nutrition. (Which contains another 3200 words.)

The assault on the mind takes place in many different ways. The U.S. Congress passes some 500 laws a year (that's bad enough), but regulatory agencies promulgate some 10,000 new rules and regulations in the same amount of time.

And the regulatory agencies are not stingy with their words either. Consider this: The Lord's Prayer contains 56 words; the Gettysburg Address, 266; the Ten Commandments, 297; the Declaration of Independence, 300; and a recent U.S. government order setting the price of cabbage, 26,911.

At the state level, over 250,000 bills are introduced each year. And 25,000 pass the legislatures to disappear into the labyrinths of the law.

Ignorance of the law is no excuse. Ignorance of the lawmakers apparently is. Our legislators continue to pass thousands of laws that you can't possibly keep track of. And even if you could, you couldn't possibly remember how a law might differ from one of our 50 states to another.

Who reads, sees, or listens to all this outpouring of communication?

There's a traffic jam on the turnpikes of the mind. Engines are overheating. Tempers are rising.

George Bush, Ted Kennedy, and Chevrolet

How much do you know about George Bush? Most people know just three things: (1) He's good-looking. (2) He's from Texas. (3) He's Vice President of the United States.

Not much for a person who's been in public service for a good part of his adult life. Yet that might be just enough to make Mr. Bush President of the United States in 1988.

Actually there are many people who don't know Mr. Bush as well as you might think. A *People* magazine poll showed that

44 percent of supermarket shoppers didn't know who George Bush was, even though he had been Vice President for 4 years.

On the other hand, 93 percent of the consumers recognized Mr. Clean, the genie on the bottle of the Procter & Gamble cleaner of the same name. They recognized Mr. Clean, even though he hadn't been seen on television in 10 years, which shows the power of advertising to register a simple message.

What do you know about Ted Kennedy? Probably a lot more than you know about George Bush. And probably enough to keep him from being the next President of the United States.

At best, communication in an overcommunicated society is difficult. Yet you are often better off if communication doesn't take place. At least until you are ready to position yourself for the long term. You never get a second chance to make a first impression.

What do the following names mean to you: Camaro, Cavalier, Celebrity, Chevette, Citation, Corvette, and Monte Carlo?

Automobile model names, right? Would you be surprised to learn that these are all Chevrolet models?

Chevrolet is one of the most heavily advertised products in the world. In a recent year, General Motors spent more than $178 million to promote Chevrolet in the United States. That's $487,000 a day, $20,000 an hour.

What do you know about Chevrolet? About Chevrolet engines, transmissions, tires? About the seats, upholstery, steering?

Be honest. How many Chevrolet models are you familiar with? And do you know the differences between them? Confusing, isn't it?

The only answer to the problems of an overcommunicated society is the positioning answer. To cut through the traffic jam in the prospect's mind, you must use Madison Avenue techniques.

Nearly half the jobs in the United States can be classified as information occupations. More and more people are trying to cope with the problems of our overcommunicated society.

Whether you have an information job or not, you can benefit from learning the lessons of Madison Avenue. At home and in the office.

The media explosion

Another reason our messages keep getting lost is the number of media we have invented to serve our communication needs.

There is television. Commercial, cable, and pay.

There's radio. AM and FM.

There's outdoor. Posters and billboards.

There are newspapers. Morning, evening, daily, weekly, and Sunday.

There are magazines. Mass magazines, class magazines, enthusiast magazines, business magazines, trade magazines.

And, of course, buses, trucks, streetcars, subways, and taxicabs. Generally speaking, anything that moves today is carrying a "message from our sponsor."

Even the human body has become a walking billboard for Adidas, Gucci, Benetton, and Gloria Vanderbilt.

Take advertising again. Just after World War II, the per-capita consumption of advertising in the United States was about $25 a year. Today it's 15 times as much. (Inflation accounts for part of this increase, but volume is also up substantially.)

Do you know 15 times as much about the products you buy? You may be exposed to much more advertising, but your mind can't absorb any more than it used to. There's a finite limit to how much you can take in, and advertising, even at $25 a year, was already way over the limit. That 1-quart container that sits on top of your neck can hold just so much.

At $376 per person, the average American consumer is already exposed to twice as much advertising per year as the average Canadian. Four times as much as the average English person. And five times as much as the average French person.

While no one doubts the advertiser's financial ability to dish it out, there's some question about the consumer's mental ability to take it all in.

Each day, thousands of advertising messages compete for a share of the prospect's mind. And make no mistake about it, the mind is the battleground. Between 6 inches of gray matter is where the advertising war takes place. And the battle is rough, with no holds barred and no quarter given.

Advertising is a brutal business where mistakes can be costly. But out of the advertising wars, principles have been developed to help you cope with our overcommunicated society.

The product explosion

Another reason our messages keep getting lost is the number of products we have invented to take care of our physical and mental needs.

Take food for example. The average supermarket in the United States has some 12,000 individual products or brands on display. For the consumer, there's no relief in sight. In fact, the product explosion could get worse. In Europe they are building super-supermarkets (called hypermarkets) with room for several times as many products. Biggs in Cincinnati, the first hypermarket in America, stocks 60,000 products.

The packaged-goods industry obviously expects the proliferation to continue. Those scratch marks on the side of most grocery boxes, the Universal Product Code, represent 10 digits. (Your social security number has only 9. And the system is designed to handle more than 200 million people.)

And this same situation holds in the industrial field. The Thomas Register, for example, lists 80,000 companies. There are 292 manufacturers of centrifugal pumps, 326 builders of electronic controls, to take two categories at random.

There are half a million active trademarks registered at the U.S. Patent Office. And 25,000 new ones get added every year. (Hundreds of thousands of products are sold without trademarks too.)

In a typical year, the 1500 companies listed on the New York Stock Exchange introduce more than 5000 "significant" new products. And presumably a lot more than that were insignificant. Not to mention the millions of products and services marketed by America's 5 million other corporations.

Take drugs. There are some 100,000 prescription drugs on the U.S. market. While many of these are specialized and used almost exclusively by medical specialists, the general practitioner still has a herculean job to keep informed about the multitude of drug products available.

Herculean? No, it's an impossible job. Even Hercules himself could not have kept up with more than a small fraction of these drugs. To expect more is to be totally ignorant of the finite capacity of even the most brilliant mind.

And how does the average person cope with the product and media explosions? Not very well. Studies on the sensitivity of the human brain have established the existence of a phenomenon called "sensory overload."

Scientists have discovered that a person is capable of receiving only a limited amount of sensation. Beyond a certain point, the brain goes blank and refuses to function normally. (Dentists have been toying with some of these discoveries. Earphones are placed on the patient, and the sound level is turned up until the sensation of pain no longer is felt.)

The advertising explosion

Ironically, as the effectiveness of advertising goes down, the use of it goes up. Not just in volume, but in the number of users.

Doctors, lawyers, dentists, accountants are dipping their toes into the advertising pool. Even institutions like churches, hospitals, and government have begun to advertise. (In a recent year the U.S. government spent $228,857,200 on advertising.)

Professional people used to consider advertising beneath their dignity. But as competition heats up, lawyers, dentists, optometrists, accountants, and architects are starting to promote themselves.

Cleveland-based Hyatt Legal Services is spending $4.5 million a year on television advertising. Jacoby & Meyers is another big legal advertiser.

Advertising is likely to start soon in the medical profession for a simple reason: Our overcommunicated society is in the process of becoming an overmedicated one too. A study for the Department of Health and Human Services predicts a surplus of about 70,000 doctors by 1990.

How will these excess doctors find patients to practice on? By advertising, of course.

But the professionals who are opposed to advertising say it downgrades their profession. And it does. To advertise effectively today, you have to get off your pedestal and put your ear to the ground. You have to get on the same wavelength as the prospect.

3

Getting into the mind

In our overcommunicated society, the paradox is that nothing is more important than communication. With communication going for you, anything is possible. Without it, nothing is possible. No matter how talented and ambitious you may be.

What's called luck is usually an outgrowth of successful communication. Saying the right things to the right person at the right time. Finding what the NASA people in Houston call a window in space.

Positioning is an organized system for finding a window in the mind. It is based on the concept that communication can only take place at the right time and under the right circumstances.

The easy way into the mind

The easy way to get into a person's mind is to be first. You can demonstrate the validity of this principle by asking yourself a few simple questions.

What's the name of the first person to fly solo across the North Atlantic? Charles Lindbergh, right?

Now, what's the name of the second person to fly solo across the North Atlantic?

Not so easy to answer, is it?

What's the name of the first person to walk on the moon? Neil Armstrong, of course.

What's the name of the second?

What's the name of the highest mountain in the world? Mount Everest in the Himalayas, right?

What's the name of the second highest mountain in the world?

What's the name of the first person you ever made love with?

What's the name of the second?

The first person, the first mountain, the first company to occupy the position in the mind is going to be awfully hard to dislodge.

Kodak in photography, Kleenex in tissue, Xerox in plain-paper copiers, Hertz in rent-a-cars, Coca in cola, General in electric.

The first thing you need to "fix your message indelibly in the mind" is not a message at all. It's a mind. An innocent mind. A mind that has not been burnished by someone else's brand.

What's true in business is true in nature too.

"Imprinting" is the term animal biologists use to describe the first encounter between a newborn animal and its natural mother. It takes only a few seconds to fix indelibly in the memory of the young animal the identity of its parent.

You might think all ducks look alike, but even a day-old duckling will always recognize its mother, no matter how much you mix up the flock.

Well, that's not quite true. If the imprinting process is interrupted by the substitution of a dog or cat or even a human being, the duckling will treat the substitute as its natural mother. No matter how different the creature looks.

Falling in love is a similar phenomenon. While people are more selective than ducks, they're not nearly as selective as you might think.

What counts most is receptivity. Two people must meet in a situation in which both are receptive to the idea. Both must have open windows. That is, neither is deeply in love with some-one else.

Marriage, as a human institution, depends on the concept of first being better than best. And so does business.

If you want to be successful in love or in business, you must appreciate the importance of getting into the mind first.

You build brand loyalty in a supermarket the same way you build mate loyalty in a marriage. You get there first and then be careful not to give them a reason to switch.

The hard way into the mind

And what if your name is not Charles or Neil or Kleenex or Hertz? What if someone else got into your prospect's mind first?

The hard way to get into a person's mind is second. Second is nowhere.

What's the largest-selling book ever published? (Also the first book ever printed with movable type?) The Bible, of course.

And the second largest-selling book ever published? Who knows?

New York is the largest cargo port in the United States. But which one is second? Would you believe Hampton Roads, Virginia? It's true.

Who was the second person to fly solo across the North Atlantic? (Amelia Earhart was not the second person to fly the North Atlantic solo, although she was the first woman to do it. Now then, who was the second woman?)

If you didn't get into the mind of your prospect first (personally, politically, or corporately), then you have a positioning problem.

In a physical contest, the odds favor the fastest horse, the strongest team, the best player. "The race isn't always to the swift, nor the battle to the strong," said Damon Runyan, "but that's the way to bet."

Not so in a mental contest. In a mental battle the odds favor the first person, the first product, the first politician to get into the mind of the prospect.

In advertising, the first product to establish the position has an enormous advantage. Xerox, Polaroid, Bubble Yum, to name a few more examples.

In advertising, it's best to have the best product in your particular field. But it's even better to be first.

Love might be wonderful the second time around, but nobody cares who the second person to fly solo across the North Atlantic was. Even if that person was a better pilot.

There are positioning strategies to deal with the problem of being No. 2 or No. 3 or even No. 203. (See Chapter 8, "Repositioning the competition.")

But first make sure you can't find something to be first in. It's better to be a big fish in a small pond (and then increase the size of the pond) than to be a small fish in a big pond.

Advertising learns the lesson

The advertising industry is learning the Lindbergh lesson the hard way.

With the magic of money and enough bright people, some companies feel that any marketing program should succeed.

The wreckage is still washing up on the beach. DuPont's Corfam, Gablinger's beer, the Convair 880, Vote toothpaste, Handy Andy cleaner.

The world will never be the same again, and neither will the advertising business.

Not that a lot of companies haven't tried. Every drugstore and supermarket is filled with shelf after shelf of "half successful" brands. The manufacturers of these me-too products cling to the hope that they can develop a brilliant advertising campaign which will lift their offspring into the winner's circle.

Meanwhile, they hang in there with coupons, deals, point-of-purchase displays. But profits are hard to come by, and that "brilliant" advertising campaign, even if it comes, doesn't ever seem to turn the brand around. No wonder management people turn skeptical when the subject of advertising comes up.

It's enough to drive an advertising person into the soft ice cream business.

The chaos in the marketplace is a reflection of the fact that advertising just doesn't work the way it used to. But old traditional ways of doing things die hard. "There's no reason why advertising can't do the job," say the defenders of the status quo, "as long as the product is good, the plan is sound, and the commercials are creative."

But they overlook one big, loud reason. The marketplace itself. The noise level today is far too high.

Messages prepared in the old, traditional ways have no hope of being successful in today's overcommunicated society.

To understand how we got to where we are today, it might be helpful to take a quick look at recent communication history.

The product era

Back in the fifties, advertising was in the product era. In a lot of ways, these were the good old days when the "better mousetrap" and some money to promote it were all you needed.

It was a time when advertising people focused their attention on product features and customer benefits. They looked for, as Rosser Reeves called it, the "Unique Selling Proposition."

But in the late fifties, technology started to rear its ugly head. It became more and more difficult to establish that "USP."

The end of the product era came with an avalanche of me-too products that descended on the market. Your "better mousetrap" was quickly followed by two more just like it. Both claiming to be better than the first one.

Competition was fierce and not always honest. It got so bad that one product manager was overheard to say, "Wouldn't you know it. Last year we had nothing to say, so we put 'new and improved' on the package. This year the research people came up with a real improvement, and we don't know what to say."

The image era

The next phase was the image era. Successful companies found that reputation, or image, was more important in selling a product than any specific product feature.

The architect of the image era was David Ogilvy. As he said in his famous speech on the subject, "Every advertisement is a long-term investment in the image of a brand." And he proved the validity of his ideas with programs for Hathaway shirts, Rolls-Royce, Schweppes, and others.

But just as the me-too products killed the product era, the me-too companies killed the image era. As every company tried to establish a reputation for itself, the noise level became so high that relatively few companies succeeded.

And of the ones that made it, most did it primarily with spectacular technical achievements, not spectacular advertising. Xerox and Polaroid, to name two.

The positioning era

Today it has become obvious that advertising is entering a new era—an era where creativity is no longer the key to success.

The fun and games of the sixties and seventies have given way to the harsh realities of the eighties.

To succeed in our overcommunicated society, a company must create a position in the prospect's mind, a position that takes into consideration not only a company's own strengths and weaknesses, but those of its competitors as well.

Advertising is entering an era where strategy is king. In the positioning era, it's not enough to invent or discover something. It may not even be necessary. You must, however, be first to get into the prospect's mind.

IBM didn't invent the computer. Sperry-Rand did. But IBM was the first company to build a computer position in the mind of the prospect.

What Amerigo discovered

The Sperry-Rand of the fifteenth century was Christopher Columbus.

As every schoolchild knows, the man who discovered America was poorly rewarded for his efforts. Christopher Columbus made the mistake of looking for gold and keeping his mouth shut.

Amerigo Vespucci didn't. The IBM of the fifteenth century, Amerigo was 5 years behind Christopher. But he did two things right.

First, he positioned the New World as a separate continent, totally distinct from Asia. This caused a revolution in the geography of his day.

Second, he wrote extensively of his discoveries and theories. Especially significant are the five letters of his third voyage. One (Mundus Novus) was translated into 40 different languages over a 25-year period.

Before he died, Spain granted him Castilian citizenship and gave him a major state post.

As a result, the Europeans credited Amerigo Vespucci with the discovery of America and named the place after him.

Christopher Columbus died in jail.

What Michelob discovered

The great copywriters of yesterday, who have gone to the big ad agency in the sky, would die all over again if they saw some of the campaigns currently running.

Take beer advertising, for example. In the past a beer copywriter looked closely at the product to find a copy platform. And he or she found product features like "real-draft" Piels and "cold-brewed" Ballantine.

And even further back a beer copywriter searched for just the right words to paint a picture of quality, taste, and appetite appeal.

"Just a kiss of the hops."

"From the land of sky blue waters."

Today, however, poetry in advertising is as dead as poetry in poetry.

One of the biggest advertising successes of recent times is the campaign for Michelob. The brand was launched with a campaign that is as poetic as a stop sign. And just as effective.

"First class is Michelob" positioned the brand as a premium-priced American-made beer. In a few years, Michelob became one of the largest-selling beers in the United States. At premium prices too.

Was Michelob the first premium-priced domestic beer? No, of course not. But Michelob was the first to build the position in the beer-drinker's mind.

What Miller discovered

Notice how the poetry in the old Schlitz beer slogan hides the positioning.

"Real gusto in a great, light beer."

Did anyone out there in the neighborhood bar and grill believe that Schlitz was any lighter than Budweiser or Pabst? No, the Schlitz slogan made as much sense to the Joe Sixpacks of this world as the lyrics in an Italian opera.

But over at the Miller Brewing Company, they apparently asked themselves what would happen if they really positioned a beer as a light beer.

So Miller introduced "Lite" beer. And the rest is history. A runaway success that spawned a host of me-too brands. Including, ironically, Schlitz Light. (Presumably to be promoted as: "Real gusto in a great, light, light beer.")

For many people or products today, one roadway to success is to look at what your competitors are doing and then subtract the poetry or creativity which has become a barrier to getting the message into the mind. With a purified and simplified message, you can then penetrate the prospect's mind.

For example, there's an imported beer whose positioning strategy is so crystal-clear that those old-time beer copywriters probably wouldn't even accept it as advertising.

"You've tasted the German beer that's the most popular in America. Now taste the German beer that's the most popular in Germany." This is how Beck's beer effectively positioned itself against Lowenbrau.

Advertising like this made Beck's beer popular in America too. Sales kept going up year after year. Lowenbrau, on the other hand, gave up the struggle and became a domestic brand.

Strange things have been happening in American advertising. It's becoming less poetic—and more effective.

Those little ladders in your head

To better understand what your message is up against, let's take a closer look at the ultimate objective of all communication: the human mind.

Like the memory bank of a computer, the mind has a slot or position for each bit of information it has chosen to retain. In operation, the mind is a lot like a computer.

But there is one important difference. A computer has to accept what you put into it. The mind does not. In fact, it's quite the opposite.

The mind rejects new information that doesn't "compute." It accepts only that new information which matches its current state of mind. It filters out everything else.

You see what you expect to see

Take any two abstract drawings. Write the name Schwartz on one and the name Picasso on the other. Then ask someone for an opinion. You see what you expect to see.

Ask two people of opposite persuasion, say, a Democrat and a Republican, to read an article on a controversial subject. Then ask each one if the article changed his or her opinion.

You'll find that the Democrat gets out of the article facts to support one point of view. The Republican gets out of the same article facts to support the opposite point of view. Very little mind changing takes place. You see what you expect to see.

Pour a bottle of Gallo into an empty 50-year-old bottle of French Burgundy. Then carefully decant a glass in front of a friend and ask for an opinion.

You taste what you expect to taste.

Blind taste testings of champagne have often ranked inexpensive California brands above French ones. With the labels on, this is unlikely to happen.

You taste what you expect to taste.

Were it not so, there would be no role for advertising at all. Were the average consumer rational instead of emotional, there would be no advertising. At least not as we know it today.

One prime objective of all advertising is to heighten expectations. To create the illusion that the product or service will perform the miracles you expect. And presto, that's exactly what the advertising does.

But create the opposite expectation and the product is in trouble. The introductory advertising for Gablinger's beer created a feeling that because it was a diet product, it would taste bad.

And sure enough, the advertising worked! People tried it and were easily convinced that it did taste bad. You taste what you expect to taste.

An inadequate container

Not only does the human mind reject information which does not match its prior knowledge or experience, it doesn't have much prior knowledge or experience to work with.

In our overcommunicated society, the human mind is a totally inadequate container.

According to Harvard psychologist Dr. George A. Miller, the average human mind cannot deal with more than seven units at a time. Which is why seven is a popular number for lists that have to be remembered. Seven-digit phone numbers, the

Seven Wonders of the World, seven-card stud, Snow White and the Seven Dwarfs.

Ask someone to name all the brands he or she remembers in a given product category. Rarely will anyone name more than seven. And that's for a high-interest category. For low-interest products, the average consumer can usually name no more than one or two brands.

Try listing all ten of the Ten Commandments. If that's too difficult, how about the seven danger signals of cancer? Or the four horsemen of the Apocalypse?

In one newspaper survey, 80 out of 100 Americans couldn't name a single member of the President's Cabinet.

If our mental storage bowl is too small to handle questions like these, how in the world are we going to keep track in our mind of all those brand names which have been multiplying like rabbits over the years?

Thirty years ago the six leading cigarette companies between them offered the American smoker 17 different brands. Today they sell more than 175. (A vending machine built to hold all these brands would have to be 30 feet long.)

"Modelitus" has struck every industry, from automobiles to beer to zoom lenses. Detroit currently sells 290 different models in a bewildering variety of styles and sizes. Caravelle, Capri, Cimarron, Camaro, Calais, Cutlass. Let's see, is it a Chevrolet Caravelle or a Plymouth Caravelle? The public is confused.

To cope with complexity, people have learned to simplify everything.

When asked to describe an offspring's intellectual progress, a person doesn't usually quote vocabulary statistics, reading comprehension, mathematical ability, etc. 'He's in seventh grade" is a typical reply.

This ranking of people, objects, and brands is not only a convenient method of organizing things but also an absolute necessity to keep from being overwhelmed by the complexities of life.

The product ladder

To cope with the product explosion, people have learned to rank products and brands in the mind. Perhaps this can best be visualized by imagining a series of ladders in the mind. On each step is a brand name. And each different ladder represents a different product category.

Some ladders have many steps. (Seven is many.) Others have few, if any.

A competitor that wants to increase its share of the business must either dislodge the brand above (a task that is usually impossible) or somehow relate its brand to the other company's position.

Yet too many companies embark on marketing and advertising programs as if the competitor's position did not exist. They advertise their products in a vacuum and are disappointed when their messages fail to get through.

Moving up the ladder in the mind can be extremely difficult if the brands above have a strong foothold and no leverage or positioning strategy is applied.

An advertiser who wants to introduce a new product category must carry in a new ladder. This, too, is difficult, especially if the new category is not positioned against the old one. The mind has no room for what's new and different unless it's related to the old.

That's why if you have a truly new product, it's often better to tell the prospect what the product is not, rather than what it is.

The first automobile, for example, was called a "horseless" carriage, a name which allowed the public to position the concept against the existing mode of transportation.

Words like "off-track" betting, "lead-free" gasoline, and "sugar-free" soda are all examples of how new concepts can best be positioned against the old.

The "against" position

In today's marketplace the competitor's position is just as important as your own. Sometimes more important. An early success in the positioning era was the famous Avis campaign.

The Avis campaign will go down in marketing history as a classic example of establishing the "against" position. In the case of Avis, this was a position against the leader.

"Avis is only No. 2 in rent-a-cars, so why go with us? We try harder."

For 13 years in a row, Avis lost money. Then they admitted that they were No. 2 and Avis started to make money.

The first year Avis made $1.2 million. The second year, $2.6 million. The third year, $5 million. Then the company was sold to ITT.

Avis was able to make substantial gains because they recognized the position of Hertz and didn't try to attack them head-on.

To better understand why the Avis program was so successful, let's look into the mind of the prospect and imagine we can see a product ladder marked "rent-a-cars."

On each rung of the product ladder is a brand name. Hertz on top. Avis on the second rung. National on the third.

Many marketing people have misread the Avis story. They assume the company was successful because it tried harder.

Not at all. Avis was successful because it related itself to Hertz. (If trying harder were the secret of success, Harold Stassen would have been President many times over.)

As an indication of how far the advertising business has come in its acceptance of comparative ads, *Time* magazine originally rejected the "We try harder" line as being too competitive with Hertz. Other magazines followed the *Time* lead.

So the account executive panicked and agreed to change the line to "We try damned hard." (A curse word presumably being less offensive than a comparative word.)

Only after the ad was canceled did *Time* change its mind and agree to accept the original version. (The account executive was fired.)

Establishing the "against" position is a classic positioning maneuver. If a company isn't the first, then it has to be the first to occupy the No. 2 position. It's not an easy task.

But it can be done. What Avis is doing in rent-a-cars, Burger King is doing in fast foods, and Pepsi is doing in colas.

The "uncola" position

Another classic positioning strategy is to worm your way onto a ladder owned by someone else. As 7-Up did. The brilliance of this idea can only be appreciated when you comprehend the enormous share of mind enjoyed by Coke and Pepsi. Almost two out of every three soft drinks consumed in the United States are cola drinks.

By linking the product to what was already in the mind of the prospect, the "uncola" position established 7-Up as an alternative to a cola drink. (The three rungs on the cola ladder might be visualized as: One, Coke. Two, Pepsi, And three, 7-Up.)

To prove the universality of positioning concepts, McCormick Communications took beautiful-music radio station WLKW, an also-ran in the Providence (Rhode Island) market, and made it number one. Their theme: WLKW, the unrock station.

To find a unique position, you must ignore conventional logic. Conventional logic says you find your concept inside yourself or inside the product.

Not true. What you must do is look inside the prospect's mind.

You won't find an "uncola" idea inside a 7-Up can. You find it inside the cola drinker's head.

The F.W.M.T.S. trap

More than anything else, successful positioning requires consistency. You must keep at it year after year.

Yet after a company has executed a brilliant positioning coup, too often it falls into what we call the F.W.M.T.S. trap: "Forgot what made them successful."

Shortly after the company was sold to ITT, Avis decided it was no longer satisfied with being No. 2. So it ran ads saying, "Avis is going to be No. 1."

That's advertising your aspirations. Wrong psychologically. And wrong strategically.

Avis was not destined to be No. 1 unless it could find a weakness in Hertz to exploit.

Furthermore, the old campaign not only related No. 2 Avis to No. 1 Hertz on the product ladder in the prospect's mind, but also capitalized on the natural sympathy people have for the underdog.

The new campaign was just conventional brag-and-boast advertising.

Be honest. In the last 20 years, Avis has run many different advertising campaigns: "The wizard of Avis." "You don't have to run through airports."

But what is the single theme that leaps into your mind when someone mentions Avis?

Of course, "Avis is only No. 2, etc." Yet Avis in the last few years has consistently ignored the only concept it really owns in the mind. Someday when National Rent-A-Car passes Avis in sales, Avis will appreciate the value of the No. 2 concept it lost.

If you want to be successful today, you can't ignore the competitor's position. Nor can you walk away from your own. In the immortal words of Joan Didion, "Play it as it lays."

5
You can't get there from here

There's an old story about a traveler who asked a farmer for directions to a nearby town.

The farmer replied, "Well, you go down the road for a mile, turn left at the fork. No, that won't work."

"You turn around and drive for half a mile till you hit a stop sign, then turn right," the farmer continued. "No, that won't work either." After a long pause, the farmer looked at the confused traveler and said, "You know what, son, you can't get there from here!"

That just happens to be the fate of many people, politicians, and products today. They happen to be in a position where "they can't get there from here."

Avis is not going to be No. 1. Wishing won't make it so. And neither will massive amounts of advertising.

The "can do" spirit refuses to die

In many ways our country's Vietnam experience was a typical example of American "can do" spirit. Anything is possible if only you try hard enough. But no matter how hard we tried, no matter how many soldiers and how much money we poured in, the problem could not be solved by an outside force.

We couldn't get there from here.

In spite of hundreds of Vietnam examples to the contrary, we live in a "can do" environment. Yet many things are not possible, no matter how hard you try.

Take the 55-year-old executive vice president who is never going to get the top job. When the chief executive retires in a few years at age 65, the board appoints a 48-year-old successor.

The 55-year-old is out of phase for the president's job. To have a chance for promotion, he or she must be at least a decade younger than the current holder.

In the battle for the mind, the same thing often happens to the product that's out of phase.

Today a company can have a great product, a great sales force, a great advertising campaign and still fail miserably if it happens to be in a position in which "you can't get there from here." No matter how many millions it is prepared to spend.

And the best example is what happened to RCA in the computer business.

The handwriting on the wall

In 1969 we wrote an article for *Industrial Marketing* magazine using RCA as one of the prime examples. Entitled "Positioning Is a Game People Play in Today's Me-Too Marketplace," the article pulled no punches. It named names and made predictions, all based on the rules of a game called positioning. (It was the first time anyone had used the word "positioning" to describe the process of coping with the mental position that a larger, more established competitor occupies.)

One prediction, in particular, turned out to be strikingly accurate. As far as the computer industry was concerned, we wrote, "A company has no hope to make progress head-on against the position that IBM has established."

The operative word, of course, was "head-on." And while it's possible to compete successfully with a market leader (the article suggested several approaches), the rules of positioning say it can't be done "head-on."

Back in 1969 this raised a few eyebrows. Who were we to say that a powerful, multibillion-dollar company like RCA couldn't find happiness in the computer business if it so desired?

So as 1970 rolled around, it was full speed ahead at RCA. The incredible story was told in the pages of the business press.

"RCA fires a broadside at No. 1," said the headline of an article in the September 19, 1970, issue of *Business Week*.

"RCA goes head-to-head with IBM," said the headline of a news item in the October 1970 issue of *Fortune*.

"RCA computer push is head-on slash at IBM," said the headline of a story in the October 26, 1970, issue of *Advertising Age*.

And just to make sure there was no mistaking the company's intentions, Robert W. Sarnoff, chairman and president, made a prediction that by the end of 1970, RCA would be in a "firm No. 2 position" in the computer industry. Pointing out that his company had already invested "far more to develop a strong position in the computer industry than we have ever put into any previous business venture," including color TV, Mr. Sarnoff said that the goal had been development of a solid profit position in the early seventies.

The "can do" spirit dies

Less than a year later, the roof fell in. "The $250 million disaster that hit RCA," said the headline of a story in the September 25, 1971, issue of *Business Week*.

That's a lot of dough. Someone figured out that if you took that much money in one-hundred-dollar bills and put it on the sidewalk in Rockefeller Center, the stack would go right past Bob Sarnoff's window on the 53rd floor of the RCA Building.

Those were bad times for computer manufacturers. In May 1970, after years of unprofitable computer operations, General Electric threw in the sponge by selling the mess to Honeywell.

With two major computer manufacturers folding one right after another, the urge to say "I told you so" was irresistible.

So later in the year 1971, we came back with "Positioning Revisited: Why Didn't GE and RCA Listen?" (The article appeared in the November 1971 issue of *Industrial Marketing*.)

How do you advertise and market against a company like IBM? The two positioning articles made some suggestions.

How to go against an IBM

The computer business has often been referred to as "Snow White and the Seven Dwarfs." Snow White has established a position unrivaled in the history of marketing.

IBM has 70 percent of the mainframe computer business vs. less than 10 percent for the largest of the dwarfs.

How do you go against a company with a position like IBM?

Well, first you have to recognize it. Then you don't do the thing that too many people in the computer field try to do. Act like IBM.

A company has no hope to make progress head-on against the position that IBM has established. And history, so far, has proved this to be true.

The small companies in the field probably recognize this. But the big companies seem to think they can take their strong positions against IBM. Well, as one unhappy executive was heard to say, "There just isn't enough money in the world." You can't get there from here.

"Fight fire with fire" is the old cliché. But as the late Howard Gossage used to say, "That's silly. You fight fire with water."

A better strategy for IBM's competitors would be to take advantage of whatever positions they already own in the minds of their prospects and then relate them to a new position in computers. For example, how should RCA have positioned its computer line?

Our 1969 article made a suggestion: "RCA is a leader in communications. If they positioned a computer line that related to their business in communications, they could take advantage of their own position. Even though they would be ignoring a great deal of business, they would be establishing a strong beachhead."

Take General Electric, a company that is a big user of computers. Time sharing was the big technological topic of the day. If GE had concentrated on time-sharing computers, they too might have succeeded in the computer field. (Actually, the only computer operation General Electric didn't sell to Honeywell was their time-sharing network, which remains profitable to this day.)

Take NCR, a company with a strong position in cash registers.

NCR has made great progress in the computer business by concentrating its efforts on retail data entry systems. Computerized cash registers, if you will.

Where the situation is hopeless, however, the effort in finding a valid position is probably wasted. Much better to concentrate on other areas of a company's business. As Charlie Brown said, "No problem is too big to run away from."

In truth, outright failure is often preferable to mediocre success.

An also-ran can easily be tempted to think that the answer to the problem is trying harder. A company stuck with a losing position is not going to benefit much from hard work.

The problem is not what, but when, The extra effort, if it is going to be of much help, should be applied early to establish the precious posture of product leadership.

With it, everything is possible. Without it, the going is going to be rough indeed. (As the Eskimo remarked, the lead dog is the only one who enjoys a change of view.)

Smith and Jones at General Electric

One example might help illustrate the principle. Two gentlemen had their eyes on the top job at General Electric. One was named Smith. The other was named Jones.

Smith was your typical "can do" corporate executive. So when he was given the computer operation to run, he accepted the assignment with relish.

Jones, on the other hand, was realistic. He knew that GE hadn't gotten into the computer business early enough to dominate it. At this late stage of the game, it was going to cost the company too much to catch up to IBM. If it ever could.

After Smith failed to turn the computer business around, Jones got a chance to participate. He recommended that General Electric get out of the computer business, which it eventually did by selling the operation to Honeywell.

That's one reason why Reginald H. Jones wound up as chief executive of the General Electric Company. And J. Stanford Smith wound up at International Paper.

In a nutshell, the hierarchy in the computer business is duplicated in almost every other industry. Invariably, every industry has a strong leader (IBM in computers, Xerox in copiers, and General Motors in automobiles) and a host of also-rans.

If one can understand the role of positioning in the computer industry, then one can transfer this knowledge to almost any other situation.

What works for computers will also work for cars and for colas.

Or vice versa.

Positioning of a leader

Companies like Avis and Seven-Up found viable alternative positions to marketing leaders.

But most companies don't want to be an also-ran, successful or not. They want to be a leader like Hertz or Coke.

So how do you get to be the leader? Actually it's quite simple. Remember Charles Lindbergh and Neil Armstrong?

You just get there firstest with the mostest.

Establishing leadership

History shows that the first brand into the brain, on the average, gets twice the long-term market share of the No. 2 brand and twice again as much as the No. 3 brand. And the relationships are not easily changed.

The leader brand in category after category outsells the number two brand by a wide margin. Hertz outsells Avis, General Motors outsells Ford, Goodyear outsells Firestone, McDonald's outsells Burger King, General Electric outsells Westinghouse.

Many marketing experts overlook the enormous advantages of being first. Too often they attribute successes like Kodak and IBM and Coke to "marketing acumen."

The failures of leaders

Yet when the shoe is on the other foot, when a marketing leader isn't first in a new category, the new product is usually an also-ran.

Coca-Cola is a gigantic company compared with Dr. Pepper. Yet when Coke introduced a competitive product, Mr. Pibb, even the immense resources of the Atlanta giant couldn't put much of a dent in Dr. Pepper's sales. Mr. Pibb remains a poor second.

IBM is a much bigger company than Xerox and has awesome resources of technology, work force, and money. Yet what happened when IBM introduced a line of copiers competitive with those of Xerox?

Not much. Xerox still has a share of the copier market several times that of IBM.

And supposedly Kodak was going to cream Polaroid when the Rochester colossus got into the instant camera business. Far from it. Kodak managed to take only a small share, at the expense of a substantial loss in its conventional camera business.

Almost all the advantages accrue to the leader. In the absence of any strong reasons to the contrary, consumers will probably select the same brand for their next purchase as they selected for their last purchase. Stores are more likely to stock the leading brands.

The larger, more successful companies usually have the first pick of outstanding college graduates. In fact, they usually attract more and better employees.

At almost every step of the way, the leading brand has the advantage.

On an airplane flight, for example, the airline will often stock one brand of cola, one brand of ginger ale, one brand of beer, etc.

On your next flight, see if the three brands aren't Coke, Canada Dry, and Budweiser, the three leading brands of cola, ginger ale, and beer.

The instability of equality

It's true that in some categories the two leading brands run neck and neck.

What's equally true is that these categories are inherently unstable. Sooner or later, you can expect one brand to get the upper hand and open a lead which eventually will reach a stable 5 to 3 or 2 to 1 ratio.

Consumers are like chickens. They are much more comfortable with a pecking order that everybody knows about and accepts.

Hertz and Avis.

Harvard and Yale.

McDonald's and Burger King.

When two brands are close, one or the other is likely to get the upper hand and then dominate the market for years to come.

Between 1925 and 1930, for example, Ford and Chevrolet were locked in a head-to-head battle. Then Chevrolet took the lead in 1931.

In the model years since, including dislocations caused by depression and wars, Chevrolet has lost the lead only four times to Ford.

The time for extra effort is clearly when the situation is in doubt. When neither side has a clearcut superiority. Winning the battle for sales leadership in a single year will often clinch the victory for decades to come.

It takes 110 percent of rated power for a jet to get its wheels off the ground. Yet when it reaches 30,000 feet, the pilot can throttle back to 70 percent of power and still cruise at 600 miles per hour.

Strategies for maintaining leadership

Question: Where does the 800-pound gorilla sleep? Answer: Anywhere he wants to.

Leaders can do anything they want to. Short-term, leaders are almost invulnerable. Momentum alone carries them along.

(Old wrestling expression: You can't get pinned when you're on top.)

For General Motors, Procter & Gamble, and the leaders of this world, the worries are never about this year or next. Their worries are long-term. What's going to happen 5 years from now? 10 years from now?

Leaders should use their short-term flexibility to assure themselves of a stable long-term future. As a matter of fact, the marketing leader is usually the one who moves the ladder into the mind with his or her brand nailed to the one and only rung. Once there, what should leaders do and not do?

What not to do

As long as a company owns the position, there's no point in running advertisements that repeat the obvious. "We're No. 1" is a typical example.

Much better is to enhance the product category in the prospect's mind. IBM's advertising usually ignores competition and sells the value of computers. All computers, not just the company's types.

Why isn't it a good idea to run advertising that says, "We're No. 1"?

The reason is psychological. Either the prospect knows you are No. 1 and wonders why you are so insecure that you have to say so. Or the prospect doesn't know you are No. 1. If not, why not?

Maybe you have defined your leadership in your own terms and not the prospect's terms. Unfortunately, that just won't work.

You can't build a leadership position on your own terms. "The best-selling under-$1000 high-fidelity system east of the Mississippi."

You have to build a leadership position in the prospect's terms.

What to do

"The real thing." This classic Coca-Cola advertising campaign is a strategy that can work for any leader.

The essential ingredient in securing the leadership position is getting into the mind first. The essential ingredient in keeping that position is reinforcing the original concept. Coca-Cola is the standard by which all others are judged. In contrast, everything else is an imitation of "the real thing."

This is not the same as saying "We're No. 1." The largest brand could be the largest seller because it has a lower price, it is available in more outlets, etc.

But "the real thing," like a first love, will always occupy a special place in the prospect's mind.

"We invented the product." A powerful motivating force behind Xerox copiers. Polaroid cameras. Zippo lighters.

Covering all bets

Unfortunately, leaders often read their own advertising so avidly they end up thinking they can do no wrong. So when a competitor introduces a new product or a new feature, the tendency is to pooh-pooh the development.

Leaders should do the opposite. They should cover all bets. This means a leader should swallow his or her pride and adopt every new product development as soon as it shows signs of promise.

General Motors spent $50 million to cover the Wankel engine when it was offered to the automotive industry. Money down the drain? Not necessarily.

General Motors probably looks on the $50 million spent to buy a Wankel license as cheap insurance to protect an $84 billion-a-year business.

Suppose the Wankel had become the automotive engine of the future. And Ford or Chrysler had been the first to buy the rights. Where would General Motors be now?

Right where Kodak and 3M are in office copiers. When these two leaders in coated-paper copiers had a chance to cover by buying rights to Carlson's xerography process, they declined.

"Nobody would pay 5 cents for a plain-paper copy when they could get a coated-paper copy for a cent and a half." Logical enough. But the essence of covering is protection against the unexpected.

And the unexpected did happen. Haloid took a chance on the Carlson patents, and today the company (successively Haloid Xerox and then Xerox) is a $9 billion giant. Bigger than 3M and only a step behind Kodak. *Fortune* calls the Xerox 914 plain-paper copier "probably the single most profitable product ever manufactured in the United States."

And what did Xerox do for an encore?

Almost nothing. The spectacular success of the 914 was followed by one failure after another. Most notably in computers.

Power from the product

"Only when our office copying success has been repeated, not once, but several times," said the Xerox chairman early on in the company's diversification game, "can we fairly reach the conclusion that this organization has the kind of power that can be relied upon again and again."

This is the classic mistake made by the leader. The illusion that the power of the product is derived from the power of the organization.

It's just the reverse. The power of the organization is derived from the power of the product, the position that the product owns in the prospect's mind.

Coca-Cola has power. The Coca-Cola Company is merely a reflection of that power.

Outside the cola field, the Coca-Cola Company has to earn its power the hard way—either by getting into the mind first, by establishing a strong alternative position, or by repositioning the leader.

So Coca-Cola's Mr. Pibb runs a poor second to Dr. Pepper, and all the power of the Coca-Cola Company can't do much about it.

So, too, with Xerox. The power is in the position that Xerox owns in the mind. Xerox means copier. Xerox owns the copier position because it got into the mind first and then exploited that copier position by a massive marketing program.

But in computers, office duplicators, word processors, and other products, Xerox starts at ground zero. Xerox has obviously tried to duplicate its copier success in other fields. But it has apparently forgotten one essential element of the 914 program. It was the first to fly the plain-paper copier ocean.

Covering with multibrands

Most leaders should cover competitive moves by introducing another brand. This is the classic "multibrand" strategy of Procter & Gamble.

It may be a misnomer to call it a multibrand strategy. Rather it's a single-position strategy.

Each brand is uniquely positioned to occupy a certain location in the mind of the prospect. When times change, when new products come and go, no effort is made to change the position. Rather a new product is introduced to reflect changing technologies and changing tastes.

In other words, Procter & Gamble recognizes the enormous difficulty of moving an established position. When you have one already established, why change it? It may be cheaper and more effective in the long run to introduce a new product. Even if you eventually have to kill off an old, established name.

Ivory was a soap. It still is. When heavy-duty laundry detergents became available, the pressure was probably on to introduce Ivory Detergent. But this would have meant changing the position of Ivory in the prospect's mind.

A much better solution was Tide. Now the new detergent concept had a new name to match. And Tide became an enormous success.

And when Procter & Gamble introduced a dishwasher detergent, they didn't call it Dishwasher Tide. They called it Cascade.

Each leading Procter & Gamble brand has its own separate identity: Joy, Crest, Head & Shoulders, Sure, Bounty, Pampers, Comet, Charmin, and Duncan Hines. Not a Plus, Ultra, or Super in the lot.

So a multibrand strategy is really a single-position strategy. One without change. Ivory has been going strong for 99 years.

Covering with a broader name

What dethrones a leader, of course, is change.

The New York Central Railroad was not only the leading railroad in the twenties, it was also the bluest of blue-chip stocks. Several mergers later, the Penn Central (as it is called today) is an anemic relic with scarcely a trace of its former glory.

American Airlines, on the other hand, is flying high.

The covering move for the New York Central, of course, would have been to open an airline division at an early stage in the game.

"What? You want us to start an airline to take business away from our railroad? Over my dead body we will."

The pure covering move is often difficult to sell internally. Management often sees the new product or service as a competitor rather than as an opportunity.

Sometimes a name change will help bridge the gap from one era to the next. By broadening the name, you can allow the company to make the mental transition.

Sales Management changed its name to *Sales & Marketing Management* to encompass the fast-growing function of marketing. At some point in the future the publication could drop the other shoe and change again. To *Marketing Management*.

From Haloid to Haloid Xerox to Xerox is the general pattern.

You know, of course, how the Kodak Company got its name. From Eastman to Eastman Kodak to Kodak, right?

Well, they haven't dropped the other shoe yet. So the official name is still the Eastman Kodak Company.

The Direct Mail Association changed its name a number of years ago to Direct Mail-Marketing Association—a recognition of the fact that mail was only one of the ways for a company to do direct marketing.

So recently they changed again, to the Direct Marketing Association.

While a New York Central Transportation Company might not have been a success either, there is plenty of evidence to indicate that people take names very literally. (Eastern Airlines, for example.)

Government agencies are usually very good at the game of broadening the name. The Department of Housing and Urban Development, for example. (It used to be the Housing and Home Finance Agency.) By broadening the name, a government agency can enlarge its scope of operations, increase its staff, and naturally justify a larger budget.

Oddly enough, one agency that missed a bet was the Federal Trade Commission. A broader name would be Consumer Protection Agency, a name that would also take advantage of a current hot topic.

Leaders can also benefit by broadening the range of applications for their products. Arm & Hammer has done a good job in promoting the use of baking soda in the refrigerator.

The Florida Citrus Commission promotes orange juice, the largest-selling fruit drink, for lunch snacks, with meals, etc. "It isn't just for breakfast anymore," say the commercials.

Business Week, the leading business magazine, has successfully promoted itself as a good publication for consumer advertising. Today roughly 40 percent of its advertising volume is in consumer products.

Leadership is not the end of a positioning program. It's only the start. Leaders are in the best position to exploit opportunites as they arise.

Leaders should constantly use the power of their leadership to keep far ahead of the competition.

7 Positioning of a follower

What works for a leader doesn't necessarily work for a follower. Leaders can often cover a competitive move and retain their leadership.

But followers are not in the same position to benefit from a covering strategy. When a follower copies a leader, it's not covering at all. It's better described as a me-too response. (Usually phrased more diplomatically as "keeping in tune with the times.")

Why products fail

Most products fail to achieve reasonable sales goals because the accent is on "better" rather than "speed." That is, the No. 2 company thinks the road to success is to introduce a me-too product, only better.

It's not enough to be better than the competitor. You must introduce your product before someone else has a chance to establish leadership. With a more massive advertising and promotion launch. And a better name. (More on this point later.)

Yet the opposite normally occurs. The me-too company wastes valuable time on improving the product. Then the launch is made with a smaller advertising budget than the leader's. And then the new product is given the house name, because that's the easy way to ensure a quick share of market. All deadly traps in our overcommunicated society.

How do you find an open position in the prospect's mind?

Cherchez le creneau

The French have a marketing expression that sums up this strategy rather neatly.

Cherchez le creneau. "Look for the hole."

Cherchez le creneau and then fill it.

That advice goes against the "bigger and better" philosophy ingrained into the American spirit.

Another typically American attitude makes positioning thinking difficult. Ever since childhood, we have been taught to think in a certain way.

"The power of positive thinking," Norman Vincent Peale called it. An attitude which may sell a lot of books but which can destroy a person's ability to find a creneau.

To find a creneau, you must have the ability to think in reverse, to go against the grain. If everyone else is going east, see if you can find your creneau by going west. A strategy that worked for Christopher Columbus can also work for you.

Let's explore some strategies for finding creneaus.

The size creneau

For years, Detroit automakers were on a longer, lower kick. Each model year, cars became more streamlined, better looking.

Enter the Volkswagen Beetle. Short, fat, and ugly.

The conventional way to promote the Beetle would have been to minimize the weaknesses and maximize the strengths.

"Let's get a fashion photographer who can make the car look better than it is. Then we'll play up the reliability angle," is your ordinary strategy.

But the creneau was size. The most effective ad Volkswagen ever ran was the one which stated the position clearly and unequivocally.

"Think small."

With two simple words, this headline did two things at once. It stated the Volkswagen position, and it challenged the prospect's assumption that bigger is necessarily better.

The effectiveness of this approach, of course, depends on the existence of an open creneau in the prospect's mind. Not that there weren't other small cars on the market at the time the Beetle was introduced. There were, but no one else had preempted the small-car position.

Integrated circuits and other electronic devices make the "small-size" creneau technically feasible in many product categories. Only time will tell which companies will be able to capitalize on electronics to build valuable positions based on miniaturization.

The opposite presents opportunities too. There are opportunities to build positions in projection television sets and other products based on large size.

The high-price creneau

The classic example is Michelob. The people at Anheuser-Busch found an untapped market for a premium-priced domestic beer. And they moved into the mind with the Michelob name.

High-price creneaus seem to be opening up in many product categories. As our throwaway society sees the urgent need for conversation, there's a new appreciation of a quality product designed to last.

Which is one reason behind the success of $40,000 automobiles like the BMW 635-CS and $50,000 cars like the Mercedes-Benz 500-SEL.

And S. T. Dupont (nice name) lighters at, as the ads say, "$1500 and down."

Price is an advantage, especially if you're the first in the category to establish the high-price creneau.

Some brands base almost their entire product message on the high-price concept.

"There is only one Joy, the costliest perfume in the world."

"Why you should invest in a Piaget, the world's most expensive watch."

High price is effective not only for luxury items like cars, perfume, and watches, but also mundane products like Whitney's Yogurt and Orville Redenbacher's Gourmet Popping Corn.

Mobil 1 synthetic engine lubricant at $3.95 a quart is another example. Even traditional low-priced products like flour, sugar, and salt represent positioning opportunities.

Too often, however, greed gets confused with positioning thinking. Charging high prices is not the way to get rich. Being the first to (1) establish the high-price position (2) with a valid product story (3) in a category where consumers are receptive to a high-priced brand is the secret of success. Otherwise, your high price just drives prospective customers away.

Furthermore, the place to establish the high price is in the ads, not in the store. The price (high or low) is as much a feature of the product as anything else.

If you do your positioning job right, there should be no price surprises in the store. Your ads don't have to quote exact prices, although sometimes that's a good thing to do. What they should do, however, is to clearly position your brand in a particular price category.

The low-price creneau

Instead of high price, the opposite direction can also be a profitable tack to take.

In evaluating price as a possible creneau, keep in mind that the low-price creneau is often a good choice for new products like facsimile equipment and videotape players. Products customers believe they are taking a chance on. (If the thing doesn't work right, I'm not out that much money.)

The high-price creneau is often a good choice for old, established products like automobiles, watches, and television sets. Especially those products for which customers are not happy with existing repair services.

The recent introduction of generic ("no name") food brands is an attempt to exploit the low-price creneau in the supermarket. (Although retailer emphasis on sales and low prices over the years have pretty much wiped out the opportunities in that direction.)

When you combine all three price strategies (high, standard, and low), you normally have a strong marketing approach. As Anheuser-Busch has done with Michelob, Budweiser, and Busch (their low-priced beer).

The weakest brand, of course, is Busch because of the poor name and lack of a strong positioning concept. Why would the owner of the place put his name only on his lowest-priced product?

A better name for a low-priced beer is Old Milwaukee, which leads its category in sales.

Other effective creneaus

Sex is one. Marlboro was the first national brand to establish a masculine position in cigarettes, one reason why Phillip Morris's Marlboro brand has climbed steadily in sales. From fifth place in sales to first place in a 10-year period.

Timing is critical. In 1973 Lorillard tried to introduce its own masculine brand called Luke. The name was terrific, the packaging was great, the advertising was brilliant. "From Kankakee to Kokomo along comes Luke movin' free and slow."

The only thing wrong was the timing. About 20 years too late. Luke really was movin' slow, so Lorillard killed him.

In positioning a product, there's no substitute for getting there first.

What masculinity did for Marlboro, femininity did for Virginia Slims, a brand that carved out a substantial share with the opposite approach. But Eve, a me-too brand that also tried the feminine approach, was a failure. Eve was too late.

When you use sex to segment a product category and establish a position, the obvious approach isn't always the best.

Take perfume, for example. You'd think that the more delicate and feminine the brand, the more successful it would be. So what's the largest-selling brand of perfume in the world?

No, it's not Arpege or Chanel No. 5. It's Revlon's Charlie. The first brand to try a masculine name complete with pantsuit ads.

The knockoff brand, "Just Call Me Maxi," was not only poorly done but reportedly cost the president of Max Factor his job.

The Charlie success story illustrates the paradox of established product categories like perfume. The bulk of the business is in one direction (feminine brand names), but the opportunity lies in the opposite (a masculine brand name).

Age is another positioning strategy to use. Geritol tonic is a good example of a successful product aimed at older folks.

Aim toothpaste is a good example of a product aimed at children. Aim has carved out 10 percent of the toothpaste market. A tremendous accomplishment in a market dominated by two powerful brands, Crest and Colgate.

Time of day is also a potential positioning possibility. Nyquil, the first night-time cold remedy, is one example.

Distribution is another possibility. L'eggs was the first hosiery brand to be distributed in supermarkets and mass merchandise outlets. L'eggs now is the leading brand, with sales in the hundreds of millions.

Another possibility is the heavy-user position. "The one beer to have when you're having more than one" positioned Schaefer as the brand for the heavy beer drinker.

The factory creneau

One common mistake in looking for creneaus is filling a hole in the factory rather than one in the mind.

Ford's Edsel is the classic example. In the laughter that followed the demise of poor Edsel, most people missed the point.

In essence, the Ford people got switched around. The Edsel was a beautiful case of internal positioning to fill a hole between

Ford and Mercury on the one hand and Lincoln on the other hand.

Good strategy inside the factory. Bad strategy outside where there was simply no position for this car in a category already cluttered with heavily chromed, medium-priced cars.

If the Edsel had been tagged a "high-performance" car and presented in a sleek two-door, bucket-seat form and given a name to match, no one would have laughed. It could have occupied a position that no one else owned, and the ending of the story might have been different.

Another "fill-the-factory" mistake was the *National Observer,* the first national weekly newspaper.

Dow Jones, the *Observer's* proud parent, also publishes *The Wall Street Journal,* but only 5 days a week. Voilà, you can hear somebody say. Let's fill the factory with a weekly newspaper. That way, we get free use of those expensive *Journal* presses.

But where was the hole in the prospect's mind? He or she could already subscribe to *Time, Newsweek, U.S. News & World Report,* and other news magazines.

Aah, you say. But the *National Observer* is a weekly newspaper, not a magazine. But that's playing semantic games. Prospects didn't differentiate between the two.

The technology trap

Even a great technical achievement of a research laboratory will fail if there is no creneau in the mind.

In 1971 Brown-Forman Distillers launched Frost 8/80, the first "dry, white whisky."

Frost 8/80 should have been a big success. There was a big hole there. There was no other dry, white whisky. As Brown-Forman president William F. Lucas said, "It was greeted with great applause by our people and a gnashing of teeth by our competitors."

Yet less than 2 years later, Frost 8/80 was dead. A multi-million-dollar failure. Volume had totaled just 100,000 cases, one-third of the company's projections.

What went wrong? Look at the positioning claim from the prospect's point of view.

The first white whisky? Not true. There are at least four others. Their names are gin, vodka, rum, and tequila.

As a matter of fact, Frost 8/80 ads encouraged the prospect to look at the new whisky as a substitute for other distilled spirits. According to the ads, Frost 8/80 could be used like vodka or gin in martinis, like scotch or bourbon in manhattans and whisky sours.

Don't try to trick the prospect. Advertising is not a debate. It's a seduction.

The prospect won't sit still for the finer points of verbal logic. As the politician said, "If it looks like a duck and walks like a duck, I say it's a duck."

The everybody trap

Some marketing people reject the "cherchez le creneau" concept. They don't want to be tied down to a specific position because they believe it limits their sales. Or their opportunities.

They want to be all things to all people.

Years ago, when there were a lot fewer brands and a lot less advertising, it made sense to try to appeal to everybody.

In politics it used to be suicide for a politician to take a strong position on anything. Don't step on anybody's toes.

But today in the product arena and in the political arena, you have to have a position. There are too many competitors out there. You can't win by not making enemies, by being everything to everybody.

To win in today's competitive environment, you have to go out and make friends, carve out a specific niche in the market. Even if you lose a few doing so.

Today the everybody trap may keep you afloat if you're already in office or already own a substantial share of market. But it's deadly if you want to build a position from nowhere.

8 Repositioning the competition

There comes a time when you can't find a creneau. With hundreds of variations in each product category on the market, the chances of finding an open hole today are very slim.

For example, take your average supermarket, with 12,000 different products or brands on display. That means a young person has to sort out and catalog 12,000 different names in his or her head.

When you consider that the average college graduate has a speaking vocabulary of only 8000 words, you can see the problem.

The kid spends 4 years in a university and ends up 4000 words down.

Creating your own creneau

With a plethora of products in every category, how does a company use advertising to blast its way into the mind? The basic underlying marketing strategy has got to be "reposition the competition."

Because there are so few creneaus to fill, a company must create one by repositioning the competitors that occupy the positions in the mind.

In other words, to move a new idea or product into the mind, you must first move an old one out.

"The world is round," said Christopher Columbus. "No, it's not," said the public, "it's flat."

To convince the public otherwise, fifteenth century scientists first had to prove that the world wasn't flat. One of their more convincing arguments was the fact that sailors at sea were first able to observe the tops of the masts of an approaching ship, then the sails, then the hull. If the world were flat, they would see the whole ship at once.

All the mathematical arguments in the world weren't as effective as a simple observation the public could verify themselves.

Once an old idea is overturned, selling the new idea is often ludicrously simple. As a matter of fact, people will often actively search for a new idea to fill the void.

Never be afraid to conflict either. The crux of a repositioning program is undercutting an existing concept, product, or person.

Conflict, even personal conflict, can build a reputation overnight. Where would Sam Ervin have been without Richard Nixon?

For that matter, where would Richard Nixon have been without Alger Hiss?

And Ralph Nader got famous not by saying anything about Ralph Nader but by going out and attacking the world's largest corporation single-handedly.

People like to watch the bubble burst.

Repositioning aspirin

Tylenol went out and burst the aspirin bubble.

"For the millions who should not take aspirin," said Tylenol's ads. "If your stomach is easily upset . . . or you have an ulcer . . . or you suffer from asthma, allergies, or iron-deficiency anemia, it would make good sense to check with your doctor before you take aspirin.

"Aspirin can irritate the stomach lining," continued the Tylenol ad, "trigger asthmatic or allergic reactions, cause small amounts of hidden gastrointestinal bleeding.

"Fortunately, there is Tylenol . . . "

Sixty words of copy before any mention of the advertiser's product.

Sales of Tylenol acetaminophen took off. Today Tylenol is the No. 1 brand of analgesic. Ahead of Anacin. Ahead of Bayer. Ahead of Bufferin. Ahead of Excedrin. A simple but effective repositioning strategy did the job.

Against an institution like aspirin. Amazing.

Repositioning Lenox

For a repositioning strategy to work, you must say something about your competitor's product that causes the prospect to change his or her mind, not about your product, but about the competitor's product.

"Royal Doulton. The china of Stoke-on-Trent, England vs. Lenox. The china of Pomona, New Jersey."

Note how Royal Doulton is repositioning Lenox china, a product that many buyers thought was an imported one. (Lenox. Sounds English, doesn't it?)

Royal Doulton credits a 6 percent gain in market share to this one advertisement.

The late Howard Gossage used to say that the objective of your advertising should not be to communicate with your consumers and prospects at all, but to terrorize your competition's copywriters, and there's some truth in that.

Repositioning American vodkas

"Most American vodkas seem Russian," said the ads. And the captions said: "Samovar: Made in Schenley, Pennsylvania. Smirnoff: Made in Hartford, Connecticut. Wolfschmidt: Made in Lawrenceburg, Indiana.

"Stolichnaya is different. It is Russian," continued the ad. And the bottle is labeled, "Made in Leningrad, Russia."

Stolichnaya sales began to soar as a result. Needless to say.

But why the need to disparage the competition? Couldn't PepsiCo, the importers of the Stolichnaya brand, have simply advertised it as the "Russian vodka?"

They could have, of course. But that presumes a degree of product interest on the part of the vodka buyer that just doesn't exist.

How many times have you picked up a bottle of liquor and read the label to find out where it was made? Furthermore, the names themselves (Samovar, Smirnoff, Wolfschmidt, Popov, Nikolai) imply a Russian origin. It's this latter factor alone that was responsible for much of Stolichnaya's astounding success.

People like to see the high and mighty exposed. Note how other vodka ads play into Stolichnaya's hands.

> It was the Golden Age of Russia. Yet in this time when legends lived, the Czar stood like a giant among men. He could bend an iron bar on his bare knee. Crush a silver ruble with his fist. And had a thirst for life like no other man alive. And his drink was Genuine Vodka. Wolfschmidt Vodka.

Then the reader turns the page to find the Stolichnaya ad, where he sees that Wolfschmidt is made in Lawrenceburg, Indiana.

Along comes Afghanistan and suddenly Stolichnaya is in trouble. But only temporarily. After a few months, the storm blew over and Stolichnaya came back bigger than ever.

Repositioning Pringle's

What happened to Pringle's potato chips? Introduced with a $15 million fanfare from Procter & Gamble, the "new-fangled" potato chips rapidly gobbled up 18 percent of the market.

Then the old-fangled brands like Borden's Wise struck back with a classic repositioning strategy.

They read the two labels on television. "In Wise, you find: Potatoes. Vegetable oil. Salt. In Pringle's, you find: Dehydrated potatoes. Mono- and diglycerides. Ascorbic acid. Butylated hydroxy-anisole.''

Sales of Pringle's came tumbling down. From a respectable 18 percent of the potato chip market to 10 percent. A far cry from P & G's goal of 25 percent.

Oddly enough, research isolated another problem. The most common complaint against Pringle's is that they "taste like cardboard.''

It's exactly what you might expect from a consumer exposed to words like "diglycerides" and "butylated hydroxy-anisole." Taste, esthetic or gustatory, is in the mind. Your eyes see what you expect to see. Your tongue reacts the way you expect it to react.

If you were forced to drink a beaker of dihydrogen oxide, your response would probably be negative. If you asked for a glass of water, you might enjoy it.

That's right. There's no difference on the palate. The difference is in the brain.

Recently the Cincinnati giant changed its strategy. Pringle's would become an "all natural" product.

But the damage had already been done. In politics or packaged goods, the rule is once a loser, always a loser. It would be as hard to bring Pringle's back as to bring Jimmy Carter back.

In some small corner of the brain is a penalty box marked "loser." Once your product is sent there, the game is over.

Go back to square one and start all over again. With a new product and a new game.

Of all companies, Procter & Gamble should have known the power of repositioning. And should have taken steps in advance to protect Pringle's.

Repositioning Listerine

One of P & G's most powerful programs is the one for Scope mouthwash. P & G used two words to reposition Listerine, the King of Halitosis Hill.

"Medicine breath.''

These two words were enough to torpedo Listerine's highly successful "the taste you hate, twice a day" theme.

The Scope attack carved a few share points out of market leader Listerine and firmly established Scope in second place.

The Listerine/Scope battle caused the usual casualties. Micrin and Binaca folded. Lavoris saw its market share wither away.

But let's face it. Scope has not become the market success it should be, based on theory.

Why? Look at the name again.

Scope? It sounds like a board game from Parker Brothers. Not like a good-tasting mouthwash that will make you a big hit with the opposite sex. If Scope had been given a name like Close-Up toothpaste, it could have parlayed its brilliant repositioning strategy with sales success to match.

Repositioning vs. comparative ads

The success of the Tylenol, Scope, Royal Doulton, and other repositioning programs has spawned a host of similar advertising. Too often, however, these copycat campaigns have missed the essence of repositioning strategy.

"We're better than our competitors" isn't repositioning. It's comparative advertising and not very effective. There's a psychological flaw in the advertiser's reasoning which the prospect is quick to detect. "If your brand is so good, how come it's not the leader?"

A look at comparative ads suggests why most of them aren't effective. They fail to reposition the competition.

Rather, they use the competitor as a benchmark for their own brand. Then they tell the reader or viewer how much better they are. Which, of course, is exactly what the prospect expects the advertiser to say.

"Ban is more effective than Right Guard, Secret, Sure, Arrid Extra Dry, Mitchum, Soft & Dry, Body All, and Dial," said a recent Ban ad. The reader looks at an ad like this and asks, "What else is new?"

Is repositioning legal?

If disparagement were illegal, every politician would be in jail. (And many husbands and wives would be in deep trouble too.)

Actually, the Federal Trade Commission deserves much of the credit for making repositioning ads possible—at least on television.

In 1964 the National Broadcasting Company dropped its ban on comparative advertising. But nothing much happened. Commercials are expensive to produce, a few advertisers wanted to produce two versions. One to run on NBC and one to run on the other two networks.

So in 1972 the FTC prodded the American Broadcasting Company and the Columbia Broadcasting System to allow commercials that named rival brands.

In 1974 the American Association of Advertising Agencies issued new comparative ad guidelines which represented a complete turnaround from previous policy. Traditionally, the 4A's had discouraged the use of comparative ads by its member agencies.

In 1975 the Independent Broadcasting Authority, which controls radio and television in Britain, gave the green light for "knocking" ads in the U.K.

So repositioning has been "legal" for at least a decade.

Is repositioning ethical?

In the past advertising was prepared in isolation. That is, you studied the product and its features, and then you prepared advertising which communicated to your customers and prospects the benefits of those features. It didn't make much difference whether the competition offered those features or not.

In the traditional approach, you ignored competition and made every claim seem like a preemptive claim. Mentioning a competitive product, for example, was considered not only bad taste but poor strategy as well.

In the positioning era, however, the rules are reversed. To establish a position, you must often not only name competitive names but also ignore most of the old advertising rules as well.

In category after category, the prospect already knows the benefits of using the product. To climb on his or her product ladder, you must relate your brand to the brands already in the prospect's mind.

Yet repositioning programs, even though effective, have stirred up a host of complaints. Many advertising people deplore the use of such tactics.

An old-time advertising man put it this way. "Times have changed. No longer are advertisers content to huckster their own wares on their own merits. Their theme now is how much better their product is than any other. It is a deplorable situation, with TV as the worst offender, where competitive products are pictured and denigrated before the eyes of millions. There should be some kind of regulation to restrict that type of unethical marketing."

"Comparative advertising is not against the law," said the chairman of a top 10 agency, "nor should it be. But to practice it as we do today makes a mockery of pretensions to culture and refinement and decent corporate behavior."

You can't have it both ways. If you want culture and refinement, you produce operas. If you want to make money, you produce movies.

Culture and refinement may be admirable qualities, but not in advertising.

Is society sick when people are ready to believe the worst about a product or person, but balk about believing the best?

Are newspapers wrong to put the bad news on the front page and the good news in the back along with the society columns? (If they print any at all.)

The communication industry is like gossip. It feeds on the bad news, not the good.

It may not be your idea of the way things should be. It just happens to be the way things are.

To be successful in this overcommunicated society of ours, you have to play the game by the rules that society sets. Not your own.

Don't be discouraged. A little disparagement may be preferable in the long run to a lot of conventional "brag and boast."

Done honestly and fairly, it keeps the competition on their toes.

The power
of the name

The name is the hook that hangs the brand on the product ladder in the prospect's mind. In the positioning era, the single most important marketing decision you can make is what to name the product.

Shakespeare was wrong. A rose by any other name would not smell as sweet. Not only do you see what you want to see, you also smell what you want to smell. Which is why the single most important decision in the marketing of perfume is the name you decide to put on the brand.

Would "Alfred" have sold as well as "Charlie?" Don't bet on it.

And Hog Island in the Caribbean was going nowhere until they changed the name to Paradise Island.

How to choose a name

Don't look to the past for guidance and pick the name of a French racing car driver (Chevrolet) or the daughter of your Paris representative (Mercedes).

What worked in the past won't necessarily work now or in the future. In the past when there were fewer products, when the volume of communication was lower, the name wasn't nearly as important.

Today, however, a lazy, say-nothing name isn't good enough to cut into the mind. What you must look for is a name that begins the positioning process, a name that tells the prospect what the product's major benefit is.

Like Head & Shoulders shampoo, Intensive Care skin lotion, and Close-Up toothpaste.

Or like DieHard for a longer-lasting battery. Shake 'n Bake for a new way to cook chicken. Edge for a shaving cream that lets you shave closer.

A name should not go "over the edge," though. That is, become so close to the product itself that it becomes generic, a general name for all products of its class rather than a trade name for a specific brand.

"Lite beer from Miller" is a typical product name that went over the line. So now we have Schlitz Light, Coors Light, Bud Light, and a host of other light beers. The public and the press quickly corrupted the name to "Miller Lite," and so Miller lost its right to exclusive use of "light" or its phonetic equivalent as a trademark for beer.

For years to come, trademark attorneys will be using Lite as an example of the danger of using descriptive words as trademarks. (Lawyers love coined names like Kodak and Xerox.)

Choosing a name is like driving a racing car. To win, you have to take chances. You have to select names that are almost, but not quite, generic. If once in a while you go off the track into generic territory, so be it. No world champion driver has made it to the top without spinning out a few times.

A strong, generic-like, descriptive name will block your me-too competitors from muscling their way into your territory. A good name is the best insurance for long-term success. *People* is a brilliant name for the gossip-column magazine. It's a runaway success. The me-too copy, *Us* magazine, is in trouble.

How not to choose a name

On the other hand. *Time* is not as good a name for a newsweekly as the more generic *Newsweek*.

Time was the first into the newsweekly pool and is an obvious success. But *Newsweek* isn't far behind. (As a matter of fact, *Newsweek* sells more pages of advertising each year than does *Time*.)

Many people think *Time* is a great name for a magazine. And in a way, it is. Short, catchy, memorable. But it's also subtle and tricky. (*Time* could be a trade magazine for the watch industry.)

Fortune is another name cut out of the same cloth. (*Fortune* could be a magazine for stockbrokers, commodity traders, or gamblers. It's not clear.) *Business Week* is a much better name. Also a more successful magazine.

Names also get out of date, opening up creneaus for alert competitors.

Esquire was a great name for a magazine for the young-man-about-town. When young-men-about-town used to sign their names John J. Smith, Esq. But *Esquire* lost its leadership to *Playboy.* Everybody knows what a playboy is and what he's interested in. Girls, right? But what's an esquire? And what's he interested in?

For many years, *Yachting* has been the leading publication in the marine field. But today how many esquires own yachts? So every year *Sail Magazine* keeps getting closer in sales to *Yachting.*

When virtually all advertising was in newspapers and magazines, *Printer's Ink* was a good name for a magazine directed to the advertising field. But today radio and television are just as important as print. So *Printer's Ink* is dead and *Advertising Age* reigns supreme.

One of the strongest publications in the world today is *The Wall Street Journal.* It has no real competitors. But *The Wall Street Journal* is a weak name for a daily business newspaper. The name implies a narrow, financial orientation. But the publication covers business generally.

Of such observations are opportunities fashioned.

Engineers and scientists in love with their own creations are responsible for some of the really bad names. Names like XD-12, for example. (Presumably standing for "experimental design number 12.") These are inside jokes that have no meaning in the mind of the prospect.

Take Mennen E, for example. People are literal and they take things literally. Mennen E deodorant was doomed to failure in spite of a $10 million advertising launch. The trouble was the name on the can. The introductory ad even admitted that the idea was a little unusual. "Vitamin E, incredibly, is a deodorant."

It is incredible. That is, unless they were appealing to people who want the strongest, best-fed, healthiest armpits in the country. Mennen E didn't last very long.

And what about Breck One and Colgate 100? Brand names like these are meaningless.

With marginal differences in many product categories, a better name can mean millions of dollars difference in sales.

When to use a coined name

What about the obvious success of companies with coined names like Coca-Cola, Kodak, and Xerox?

One of the things that makes positioning thinking difficult for many people is the failure to understand the role of timing.

The first company into the mind with a new product or new idea is going to become famous. Whether the name is Lindbergh or Smith or Rumplestiltskin.

Coca-Cola was first with a cola drink. Kodak was first with low-cost photography. Xerox was first with the plain-paper copier.

Take the word "Coke." Because of the success of Coca-Cola, the nickname Coke has acquired what the semanticists call a secondary meaning.

Would you name a soft drink after the word for "the residue of coal burned in the absence of air"? Or the street name for a narcotic cocaine?

So strong is the secondary meaning of the word Coke that the Coca-Cola Company has nothing to fear from these negative connotations.

But choosing a coined name like Keds, Kleenex, and Kotex for a new product is dangerous, to say the least. Only when you are first in the mind with an absolutely new product that millions of people are certain to want can you afford the luxury of a mean-nothing name.

Then, of course, any name would work.

So stick with common descriptive words (Spray 'n Wash) and avoid the coined words (Qyx).

As a guide, the five most common initial letters are S, C, P, A, and T. The five least common are X, Z, Y, Q, and K. One out of eight English words starts with an S. One out of 3000 starts with an X.

Negative names can be positive

Technology continues to create new and improved products. Yet they often are scarred at birth with second-class imitation names.

Take margarine, for example. Even though the product has been around for decades, it is still perceived as imitation butter. (It's not nice to fool Mother Nature.)

A better choice of name at the beginning would have helped. What should margarine have been called? Why "soy butter," of course—a name in the peanut butter tradition.

The psychological problem with a name like "margarine" is that it is deceptive. It hides the origin of the product.

Everyone knows that butter is made from milk. But what's margarine made from? Because the origin of the product is hidden, the prospect assumes there must be something basically wrong with margarine.

Bringing the product out of the closet

The first step in overcoming negative reactions is to bring the product out of the closet. To deliberately polarize the situation by using a negative name like soy butter.

Once this is done, it allows the development of a long-term program to sell the advantages of soy butter vs. cow butter. An essential ingredient of such a program is "pride of origin" which the soy name connotes.

The same principle is involved in the shift from colored to Negro to black.

"Negro" is a margarine name, forever relating Negroes to second-class citizenship. "Colored" doesn't sufficiently polarize the situation. The implication is, the less colored the better.

"Black" is a much better choice. It allows the development of "pride of blackness," an essential first step to long-term equality. (You might prefer to be white, but I prefer to be black.)

In naming people or products, you should not let your competitors unfairly preempt words that you need to describe your own products. Like butter in the case of margarine. Or like sugar in the case of corn syrup.

A number of years ago, scientists found a way to make sweeteners out of corn starch. Result: products called dextrose, corn syrup, and high-fructose corn syrup.

With names like "high-fructose corn syrup," it's no wonder that even in the trade the products were considered imitation or second-class in comparison with sucrose or "real sugar." So Corn Products, one of the major suppliers of corn syrups, decided to call its sweeteners "corn sugars." This move allowed the company to put corn on an equal footing with cane and beet.

"Consider all three types of sugar," say the ads. "Cane, beet, and corn."

Marketing people should know that the Federal Trade Commission is the keeper of the generics for many industries. But the FTC can be persuaded. "If we can't call it sugar, can we put corn syrup in a soft drink and call the product 'sugar-free'?"

Special-interest groups recognize the power of a good name. The "Right to Life" movement and "fair trade" laws are two examples.

And what senator or representative would dare oppose a bill called the "Clean Air Act?"

In working against an established concept like "fair trade," it's important not to try to rename the competition. All you cause is confusion among your audience.

To counter the widespread consumer acceptance of fair trade laws, the opposition tried to call it "price maintenance" legislation. It was many, many years before fair trade laws were repealed by the many states that had enacted them.

A better tactic is to turn the name around. That is to reposition the concept by using the same words to turn the meaning inside out. "Fair to the trade, but unfair to the consumer" is an example of this tactic.

Even better is to rename the opposition before the powerful name takes root. "Price manitenance" would probably have worked as a blocking strategy, but only early in the game. Another example of the importance of being first.

David and Michael and Hubert and Elmer

In spite of the common belief that it's "only a name," there is a growing body of evidence that a person's name plays a significant role in the game of life.

Two psychology professors, Dr. Herbert Harari and Dr. John W. McDavid, were trying to find out why elementary school students made fun of classmates with unusual names.

So they experimented with different names attributed to compositions supposedly written by fourth and fifth graders. Two sets of names, in particular, illustrate the principle.

There were two popular names (David and Michael) and two unpopular names (Hubert and Elmer) on some of the compositions. Each composition was given to a different group of elementary school teachers to grade. (The teachers that participated in the experiment had no reason to believe they weren't grading ordinary school papers.)

Would you believe that compositions bearing the names of David and Michael averaged a letter grade higher than the same compositions attributed to Elmer and Hubert? "Teachers know from past experience," say the professors, "that a Hubert or an Elmer is generally a loser."

What about famous people with odd first names? Hubert Humphrey and Adlai Stevenson, for example. Both losers to men with the popular names of Richard and Dwight.

What if Richard Humphrey had run against Hubert Nixon? Would America have elected a Hubert Nixon?

Jimmy, Jerry, Richard, Lyndon, John, Dwight, Harry, Franklin. Not since Herbert have we had a "loser" name in the White House.

And who did Herbert Hoover beat in 1928? Another man with a loser name, Alfred.

In 1932, when Herbert ran against a "winner" name like Franklin, he lost. And he lost big.

What would you expect from someone named Edsel? Edsel was a loser name before Ford introduced the Edsel car. And the name contributed to the marketing disaster.

Take Cyril and John. According to psychologist David Sheppard, people who don't know anyone with these names nevertheless expect a Cyril to be sneaky and a John to be trustworthy.

You see what you expect to see. And a bad or inappropriate name sets up a chain reaction that only serves to confirm your initial unfavorable opinion.

Elmer is a loser. See, he's not doing that job very well. I told you, Elmer is a loser.

A true story. An account officer at a New York bank was named Young J. Boozer. Once when a customer asked to speak to "Young Boozer," he was told by the switchboard operator, "We have a lot of them around here. Which one do you want to talk to?"

Hubert and Elmer in the sky

The name is the first point of contact between the message and the mind.

It's not the goodness or badness of the name in an esthetic sense that determines the effectiveness of the message. It's the appropriateness of the name.

Take the airline industry, for example. The four largest domestic carriers are United, American, Delta and . . .

Well, do you know the name of the "second largest passenger carrier of all the airlines in the free world," to use one of the airline's advertising slogans?

That's right. Eastern Airlines.

Like all airlines, Eastern has had its ups and downs. Unfortunately, more downs than ups. Among the four largest domestic airlines, Eastern consistently ranks fourth on passenger surveys.

Why? Eastern has a regional name that puts it in a different category in the prospect's mind than big nationwide names like American and United.

The name Eastern puts the airline in the same category with Piedmont, Ozark, and Southern.

You see what you expect to see. The passenger who has a bad experience on American or United says, "It was just one of those things." An exception to the good service he or she was expecting.

The passenger who has a bad experience on Eastern says, "It's that Eastern Airlines again." A continuation of the bad service he or she was expecting.

It's not that Eastern hasn't tried. A number of years ago, Eastern brought in some big-league marketing people and pulled out the throttle. Eastern was among the first to "paint the planes," "improve the food," and "dress up the flight attendants" in an effort to improve its reputation.

And Eastern hasn't been bashful when it comes to spending money. Year after year, it has one of the biggest advertising budgets in the industry. In a recent year, Eastern spent more than $70 million on advertising.

For all the money, what do you think of Eastern? Where do you think they fly? Up and down the East Coast, to New York, Boston, Philadelphia, Washington, Miami, right?

Well, Eastern also goes to St. Louis, New Orleans, Atlanta, Denver, Los Angeles, Seattle, Acapulco, Mexico City.

You can't hang "the wings of man" on a regional name. When prospects are given a choice, they are going to prefer the national airline, not the regional one.

The airline's problem is typical of the difficulty people have in separating reality from perception. Many experienced marketing people look at the Eastern situation and say, "It's not the name that gets Eastern into trouble. It's the poor service, the food, the baggage handling, the surly flight attendants." The perception is the reality.

What do you think of Piedmont Airlines? How about Ozark Airlines? And what about Allegheny?

Allegheny, of course, has thrown in the towel and become USAir. Even North Central and Southern gave up and merged to become Republic Airlines. Both airlines are doing quite well.

The Akron twins

Another common name problem is represented by two companies headquartered in Akron, Ohio.

What does a company do when its name (Goodrich) is similar to the name of a larger company in the same field (Goodyear)?

Goodrich has problems. Research indicates that they could reinvent the wheel and Goodyear would get most of the credit.

Not surprisingly, B. F. Goodrich recognizes the problem. This is how they expressed it a number of years ago in an advertisement:

> The curse of Benjamin Franklin Goodrich. His name. It's one of fate's cruel accidents that our biggest competitor's name turns out to be almost identical to our founder's. Goodyear. Goodrich. Awfully confusing.

At the bottom of the ad, it says: "If you want Goodrich, you'll just have to remember Goodrich."

In other words, it's not Goodrich's problem at all. It's your problem.

B. F. Goodrich was the first domestic company to market steel-belted radial-ply tires in the United States. Yet several years later when tire buyers were asked which company makes steel-belted radials, 56 percent named Goodyear, which didn't make them for the domestic market. Only 47 percent said Goodrich, which did.

As they say in Akron, "Goodrich invents it. Firestone develops it. Goodyear sells it."

Every year Goodyear increases its lead. Today it outsells Goodrich 3 to 1. So the rich get richer. Fair enough.

But what is odd is that the loser's advertising continues to get all the publicity. "We're the other guys" got a lot of favorable attention in the press. But not a lot of favorable attention from the tire-buying public. Its name alone forever condemns Goodrich to eat the dust of its bigger competitor.

The Toledo triplets

If the Akron twins seem confusing, consider the predicament of the Toledo triplets. Owens-Illinois, Owens-Corning Fiberglas and Libbey-Owens-Ford.

These are not small outfits either. Owens-Illinois is a $3.5 billion company. Owens-Corning Fiberglas is a $3 billion company. And Libbey-Owens-Ford is a $1.75 billion company.

Look at the confusion problem from the point of view of Owens-Corning Fiberglas.

Owens, of course, is usually connected with Illinois. Owens-Illinois is a larger company with a stronger claim to the Owens name.

And Corning is usually linked with glass. In nearby Corning, New York, is the Corning Glass Works, a $1.7 billion company. It has succeeded in firmly linking the Corning name to the glass concept.

So what's left for Owens-Corning Fiberglas?

Fiberglas.

Which is probably why the company runs ads that say "Owens-Corning is Fiberglas." In other words, if you want Fiberglas, you'll just have to remember Owens-Corning.

It would be a lot easier if the company changed its name to the Fiberglas Corporation. Then if you want fiberglass (with a lowercase "f"), all you have to remember is Fiberglas (with an uppercase "F"). This step would help focus the attention on the company's primary objective, to turn fiberglass from a generic name back into a brand name.

What should you do if your name is Hubert or Elmer or Eastern or Goodrich or Owens-Corning Fiberglas? Change it.

But name changing is rare, in spite of the logic. Most companies are convinced they have too much equity in their present name. "Our customers and employees would never accept a new name."

What about Olin and Mobil and Uniroyal and Xerox? And how about Exxon Corporation? It was only a few years ago that Exxon changed its name from. . . .

Well, do you even remember what Exxon's old name was? No, it wasn't Esso and it wasn't Humble Oil or Enjay, although the company did use these names in its marketing operations.

The old name of Exxon Corporation was Standard Oil of New Jersey. Amazing what a few years and a few dollars can do.

There is only negative equity in a bad name. When the name is bad, things tend to get worse. When the name is good, things tend to get better.

Continental confusion

Do you know the difference between a $4.6 billion company called The Continental Group, Inc., and a $4 billion company called The Continental Corporation? Not too many people do until they find out that The Continental Group is the world's largest maker of cans and Continental Corporation is the big insurance company.

"Ah, yes. Continental Can and Continental Insurance. Now I know the companies you meant."

Why would a company drop "can" and "insurance" in favor of the anonymity of "group" and "corporation"? The obvious answer is that these two companies sell more than cans and insurance.

But is it possible to build an identity on a nothing name? Unlikely, especially when you consider the existence of other companies with claims on the Continental name. There is Continental Oil, Continental Telephone, Continental Grain, and Continental Illinois Corp. (All billion dollar companies, by the way.)

Or how about the secretary whose boss says, "Get me Continental on the phone." In Manhattan alone, there are 235 listings in the telephone directory starting with Continental.

The
no-name
trap

10

"I'm going to L.A.," the corporate executive will say. "And then I have to make a trip to New York." Why is Los Angeles often called L.A., but New York is seldom called N.Y.?

"I worked for GE for a couple of years and then went to Western Union." Why is General Electric often called GE, but Western Union is seldom called WU?

General Motors is often GM, American Motors is often AM, but Ford Motor is almost never FM.

Phonetic shorthand

The principle at work here is phonetic shorthand.

Ra-di-o Cor-po-ra-tion of A-mer-i-ca is 12 syllables long. No wonder most people use R-C-A, three syllables long.

Gen-er-al E-lec-tric is six syllables long, so most people use G-E, two syllables.

Gen-er-al Mo-tors is often GM. A-mer-i-can Mo-tors is often AM. But Ford Mo-tor is almost never referred to as FM. The single syllable Ford says it all.

But where there's no phonetic advantage, most people won't use initials. New York and N.Y. are both two syllables long. So while the initials N.Y. are often written, they are seldom spoken.

Los An-ge-les is four syllables long, so L.A. is frequently used. Note, too, that San Fran-cis-co, a four-syllable word, is seldom shortened to "S.F." Why? There's a perfectly good two-syllable word (Frisco) to use a shorthand for San Francisco. Which is why people say "Jer-sey" for New Jersey instead of "N.J."

When they have a choice of a word or a set of initials, both equal in phonetic length, people will invariably use the word, not the initials.

Phonetic length can sometimes fool you. The initials WU look a lot shorter than the name Western Union. But phonetically they are exactly the same length. Dou-ble-U U. West-ern Un-ion. (Except for W, every other English language letter is just one syllable.)

While customers refer to companies phonetically, the companies they talk about have a different way of looking at themselves. Companies are visually oriented. They go to a lot of trouble making sure the names look right without considering how it sounds.

Visual shorthand

Business people also fall into the same trap. The first thing to go is the given name. When young Edmund Gerald Brown starts up the executive ladder at General Manufacturing Corporation, he instantly becomes E. G. Brown from GMC on internal letters and memos.

But to be well known, you've got to avoid using initials—a fact known by most politicians. Which is why E. M. Kennedy and J. E. Carter bill themselves as Ted Kennedy and Jimmy Carter.

As a matter of fact, the new wave of politicians don't use either middle names or initials. Jack Kemp, Gary Hart, Bill Bradley, George Bush, Ronald Reagan.

What about FDR and JFK? The irony of the situation is that once you get to the top, once you are well known, then initials can be used without ambiguity. Franklin Delano Roosevelt and

John Fitzgerald Kennedy could use initials only after they became famous. Not before.

The next thing to go is the name of the company. What starts out as visual shorthand to conserve paper and typing time ends up as the monogram of success.

IBM, AT&T, GE, 3M. Sometimes it seems that membership in the Fortune 500 depends upon having a readily recognized set of initials. The moniker that tells the world you have made it.

So today, we have such monikers as AM International, AMAX, AMF, AMP, BOC, CBI Industries, CF Industries, CPC International, EG&G, FMC, GAF, IC Industries, ITT, LTV, MEI, NCR, NL Industries, NVF, PPG Industries, SCM, TRW, and VF.

These are not two-bit companies. All are currently on *Fortune's* list of the 500 largest industrial companies. The smallest company on the list, AM International, had sales of $598 million in a recent year and more than 10,000 employees. (You might recognize them as the former Addressograph Multigraph Corp.)

If you select the company next up in size from every initial company on the Fortune 500 list, you will find the following: Allegheny International, American Motors, Amstar, Bristol-Myers, Celanese, Cluett Peabody, Consolidated Foods, Data General, Gannett, Hartmarx, H. J. Heinz, Hewlett-Packard, Inspiration Resources, Lever Brothers, Louisiana Land & Exploration, Mohasco, National Cooperative Refinery Association, North American Philips, Procter & Gamble, G. D. Searle, Weirton Steel, and Westmoreland Coal.

Which list of companies is better known? The name companies, of course.

Some of the initial companies like ITT and NCR are well known, to be sure. But like FDR and JFK, these companies were well known before they dropped their names in favor of initials.

Which companies are likely to grow faster? Again, the name companies.

To test this point, we conducted a survey of both "name" and "initial" companies using a *Business Week* subscriber list. The results show the value of a name.

The average awareness of the "initial" companies was 49 percent. The average awareness of a matched group of "name" companies was 68 percent, 19 percentage points higher.

What drives big companies into committing corporate suicide? For one thing, the top executives have seen the company's initials on internal memos for so long they just naturally assume that everybody knows good old VF. Then, too, they misread the reasons for the success of companies like IBM and GE.

No shortcuts to success

A company must be extremely well known before it can use initials successfully. Apparently the use of the initials "GE" triggers the words "General Electric" inside the brain.

Invariably, people must know the name first before they will respond to initials. The Federal Bureau of Investigation and the Internal Revenue Service are extremely well known. So we respond instantly to FBI and IRS.

But HUD is not recognized nearly so quickly. Why? Because most people don't know the Department of Housing and Urban Development. So if HUD wants to become better known, the department must first make the name Housing and Urban Development better known. Taking a shortcut by using only the initials HUD won't help very much.

Similarly, General Aniline & Film was not a very well known company. When they changed their name to GAF, they made certain that they were never going to become very well known. Now that GAF has legally changed its name to initials, presumably there's no way to expose the prospect to the original name.

Yet alphabet soup seems to be on the corporate menu of many companies today. They fail to think through the process of positioning themselves in the mind. So they fall victim to the fad of the day.

And, no question about it, today's fad is "initialitus." Look at RCA. Everyone knows that RCA stands for Radio Corporation of America. So the company could use the initials to trigger the "Radio Corporation of America" words buried deep inside the mind.

But now that RCA is legally RCA, what will happen next? Nothing. At least in the next decade or so. The words are already buried in the minds of millions of people. And they'll stay there indefinitely.

But what about the next generation of prospects? What will they think when they see those strange initials, RCA?

Roman Catholic Archdiocese?

Positioning is like the game of life. A long-term proposition. Name decisions made today may not bear fruit until many, many years in the future.

The mind works by ear

The primary reason name selection errors are so common is that executives live in an ocean of paper. Letters, memos, reports. Swimming in the Xerox sea, it's easy to forget that the mind works aurally. To utter a word, we first translate the letters into sounds. Which is why beginners move their lips when they read.

When you were a child, you first learned to speak and then to read. And you learned to read slowly and laboriously by saying the words out loud as you forced your mind to connect the written word with the aural sound stored in the brain.

By comparison, learning to speak requires much less effort than learning to read. We store sounds directly and then play them back in various combinations as our mental dexterity improves.

As you grow up, you learn to translate written words into the aural language needed by the brain so rapidly that you are unaware the translation process is taking place.

Then you read in the paper that 80 percent of learning takes place through the eyes. Of course it does. But reading is only a portion of the learning process. Much learning occurs from visual clues which do not involve reading in the conventional sense at all. As when you learn the emotional state of another person by "reading" body clues.

When words are read, they are not understood until the visual/verbal translator in your brain takes over to make aural sense out of what you have seen.

In the same way, a musician learns to read music and hear the sound in his or her head, just as if someone were actually playing the tune on an instrument.

Try to memorize a poem without reading it out loud. It's far easier to memorize written material if we reinforce the aural component, the working language of the brain.

Which is why not only names but also headlines, slogans, and themes should be examined for their aural qualities. Even if you plan to use them in printed material only.

Did you think that Hubert and Elmer were bad names? If so, you must have translated the printed words into their aural equivalents. Because Hubert and Elmer don't look bad. They just sound bad.

In a way, it's a shame that the print media (newspapers, magazines, outdoor advertising) came first and radio second. Radio is really the primal media. And print is the higher-level abstraction.

Messages would "sound better" in print if they were designed for radio first. Yet we usually do the reverse. We work first in print and then in the broadcast media.

Name obsolescence

Another reason companies drop their names for initials is the obsolescence of the name itself. RCA sells a lot of things besides radios.

And how about United Shoe Machinery? The company had become a conglomerate. Furthermore, the domestic shoe machinery market was drying up as imports continually increased their share. What to do? They took the easy way out.

United Shoe Machinery changed its name to USM Corporation. And lived anonymously ever after.

Smith-Corona-Marchant is another company which has lost its corporate identity. The result of mergers, Smith never did make coronas or marchants. So it decided to shorten the name to SCM Corporation.

Presumably, both SCM and USM made the change to escape the obsolete identity of the past. Yet the fact is that the exact opposite occurred.

The mind can't remember USM without dredging United Shoe Machinery from it subconscious.

At least RCA, USM, and SCM had phonetic shorthand going for them. Without it, the difficulties are greater. Much, much greater. When Corn Products Company changed its name to CPC International, it found little recognition of the CPC name. The initials CPC are not phonetically shorter than Corn Products. Both are three syllables long, so the CPC initials were seldom used until the name change was made. Ask people in the business if they are familiar with CPC International. See if they don't say, "Oh, you mean Corn Products Company?"

In our initial-happy society, the first question the mind normally asks itself is, "What do those initials stand for?"

The mind sees the letters AT&T and says, "Ah, American Telephone & Telegraph."

But what reply does the mind get when it sees TRW? Obviously, there are a fair number of people who remember the Thompson Ramo Wooldridge Corporation. And TRW is a $6 billion company, so it gets a lot of press and does a lot of advertising. But would those advertising dollars work harder if TRW had a "name" name instead of an initial name?

Some companies put sets of initials in series. How about trying to remember the D-M-E Corporation, a subsidiary of VSI Corporation?

We're not trying to suggest that companies shouldn't change their names. Quite the contrary. Nothing remains the same for very long. Times change. Products become obsolete.

Markets come and go. And mergers are often necessary. So the time comes when a company must change its name.

U.S. Rubber was a worldwide corporation that marketed many products not made of rubber. Eaton Yale & Towne was the result of a merger that produced a big company with a complicated name. Socony-Mobil was saddled with a first name that originally stood for Standard Oil Company of New York.

All of these names have been changed for sound marketing reasons. The traditional "foot-in-the-past" approach could have produced USR Corporation, EY&T Company, and SM Inc. Three marketing monstrosities.

Instead, "forgetting the past" created three new modern corporate identities—Uniroyal, Eaton, and Mobil. The marketing strengths of these names speak for themselves. These companies successfully forgot the past and positioned themselves against the future.

The confusion between cause and effect

In spite of the drawbacks, companies are lured to initials like moths to a candle. The success of the IBMs of this world seems to be proof that initials are effective. It's the classic confusion between cause and effect.

International Business Machines became so rich and famous (the cause) that everyone knew what company you were talking about when you used its initials (the effect).

When you try to reverse the procedure, it doesn't work. You can't use the initials of a company that is only modestly successful (the cause) and then expect it to become rich and famous (the effect).

It's like trying to become rich and famous by buying limousines and corporate jets. First, you have to become successful in order to have the money to buy the fringe benefits.

In some ways, the rush to adopt initials represents a desire to look accepted even at the cost of a loss in communications. It also represents the copycat thinking prevalent in some management circles. The success of IBM encouraged word processing competitors like CPT and NBI to use initials in their names.

The success of AT&T encouraged MCI to also market their long distance service with an initial name.

And look at the contrasting name strategies of two different airlines.

Pan A-mer-i-can Air-lines (seven syllables) has a phonetically long name. So they shortened it to Pan Am, two syllables. Much better than the initials PAA, which would be difficult to remember.

Trans World Air-lines (four syllables) is actually phonetically shorter than the T-Dou-ble-U-A they are using, But isn't TWA well known? Yes, it is, thanks to $70 million worth of advertising a year.

Although TWA spends about as much on advertising as its larger American and United competitors, surveys show that TWA has half the passenger preference of the other two. The inefficiency of the initials TWA is one reason.

What name should Trans World Airlines use?

"Trans World," of course. Only two syllables long, Trans World is short and graphic.

Acronyms and phone directories

Some companies are lucky. Their initials, either by design or by accident, form acronyms. For example: Fiat (Federation International Automobiles Torino) and Sabena (*Société Anonyme Belge d'Exploitation de la Navigation Aeriènne*).

Often organizations will select carefully names that form meaningful acronyms. Two examples: CARE (Committee for Aid and Rehabilitation in Europe) and MADD (Mothers Against Drunk Drivers).

Other companies aren't so lucky. When General Aniline & Film changed its name to GAF, it chose to overlook the fact that the acronym sounds like "clumsy error." GAF is a gaffe in more ways than one.

The other thing people tend to forget when they pick a name is the problem of finding it in the telephone directory. Since you seldom look up your own name in a phone book, you might not realize how hard it is to locate.

Take MCI, for example. In the Manhattan telephone directory, you might expect to find MCI somewhere between McHugh and McKensie. But of course, it's not there. MCI Tele-communications is 48 pages away where it has to compete with seven other companies that incorporate MCI in their names. (Following standard rules of alphabetizing a list of names, the phone company puts all initial names up front.)

Take USM Corporation, for example. In the Manhattan telephone directory, there are seven pages of listings starting with "US." So you ought to be able to find USM somewhere between US Luggage & Leather Products and *US News & World Report.*

But, of course, it's not there. Those US listings stand for "United States," as in United States Luggage. The US in USM doesn't stand for anything. So again the name goes up front with the rest of the "pure" initial companies.

Many companies are saddled with obsolete names through no fault of their own. But before you throw away a name in favor of meaningless initials, see if you can find another "name" that will do the job you want done.

With a good name, your positioning job is going to be a lot easier.

The free-ride trap

Take a product called Alka-Seltzer Plus. Let's see if we can visualize how Alka-Seltzer Plus might have gotten its name.

A bunch of the boys are sitting around a conference table trying to name a new cold remedy designed to compete with Dristan and Contac.

"I have it," says Harry. "Let's call it Alka-Seltzer Plus. That way we can take advantage of the $20 million a year we're already spending on the Alka-Seltzer name."

"Good thinking, Harry," and another money-saving idea is instantly accepted, as most money-saving ideas usually are.

But lo and behold, instead of eating into the Dristan and Contac market, the new product turns around and eats into the Alka-Seltzer market.

Every so often the makers of Alka-Seltzer Plus redesign the label. The "Alka-Seltzer" gets smaller and smaller, and the "Plus" gets bigger and bigger.

A better name for the product would have been Bromo-Seltzer Plus. That way they could have taken business away from the competition.

The conglomeration of the corporation

In the product era life was simpler. Each company specialized in a single line. The name told it all.

Standard Oil, U.S. Steel, U.S. Rubber, United Airlines, Pennsylvania Railroad.

But technological progress created opportunities. So companies started branching into new fields.

Enter the conglomerate. The company that specializes in nothing. By development or acquisition, the conglomerate is prepared to enter any field in which it thinks it can make a buck.

Take General Electric. GE makes everything from jet engines to nuclear power plants to plastics.

RCA is in satellite communications, solid-state electronics, and rent-a-cars.

Many people pooh-pooh the conglomerate. Companies should "stick to their knitting," they say. But conglomerates have provided the capital to sustain vigorous competition in the marketplace. If it weren't for the conglomerates, we would be a nation of semimonopolies.

Take copiers, for example. Xerox, the pioneer in the plain-paper field, now faces competition from the computer manufacturer (IBM), from a photo company (Kodak), and from a postage-meter company (Pitney Bowes).

Even when conglomerates grow by acquisition (RCA's purchase of Hertz, ITT's purchase of Avis), they provide the money needed to sustain growth and competition.

Otherwise, when the original founders retired or died, the tax bite would leave the company too weak to defend its turf.

The typical life cycle of a corporation starts with an entrepreneur with an idea. If successful, you can count on two things, death and taxes, to ensure that the operation will end up as part of a conglomerate.

Two different strategies

Because companies grow by two different strategies (internal development or external acquisition), two different "name" strategies evolved. Corporate egos dictate the strategies.

When a company develops a product internally, it usually puts the corporate name on the product. For example, General Electric computers.

When the company develops a product by external acquisition, it usually keeps the existing name. RCA kept the Hertz name. ITT kept the Avis name.

But not always.

When Sperry-Rand developed a computer line internally, they called the product Univac. When Xerox went into computers by external acquisition, they changed the name from Scientific Data Systems to Xerox Data Systems.

Corporate egos aside, when should a company use the house name and when should they select a new name? (You can't really disregard corporate egos. Try telling General Electric not to put the GE name on a new product and you'll begin to appreciate the enormity of the corporate ego problem.)

One reason why the principles of name selection remain so elusive is the Charles Lindbergh syndrome.

If you get into the mind first, any name is going to work.

If you didn't get there first, then you are flirting with disaster if you don't select an appropriate name.

Divide and conquer

To illustrate the advantages of separate names rather than house names, compare the strategies of Procter & Gamble with those of Colgate-Palmolive.

You'll find many house names in the Colgate-Palmolive line. To name a few: Colgate toothpaste, Colgate toothbrushes, Palmolive Rapid Shave, Palmolive dishwashing liquid, Palmolive soap.

You won't find any house names in the Procter & Gamble lineup. Procter & Gamble carefully positions each product so that it occupies a unique niche in the mind. For example: Tide makes clothes "white." Cheer makes tham "whiter than white." And Bold makes them "bright."

With fewer brands Procter & Gamble does twice as much business and makes five times as much profit as Colgate-Palmolive.

While it's fashionable on Madison Avenue these days to pooh-pooh Procter & Gamble advertising, it's interesting to note that Procter & Gamble makes more money every year than all of America's 6000 advertising agencies combined.

A new product needs a new name

When a really new product comes along, it's almost always a mistake to hang a well-known name on it.

The reason is obvious. A well-known name got well known because it stood for something. It occupies a position in the prospect's mind. A really well-known name sits on the top rung of a sharply defined ladder.

The new product, if it's going to be successful, is going to require a new ladder. New ladder, new name. It's as simple as that.

Yet the pressures to go with the well-known name are enormous. "A well-known name has built-in acceptance. Our customers and prospects know us and our company, and they will be more likely to accept our new product if we have our name on it." The logic of line extension is overwhelming and sometimes very difficult to refute.

Yet history has destroyed this illusion.

Xerox spent almost a billion dollars for a profitable computer company with a perfectly good name, Scientific Data Systems. Then what did Xerox do? Of course, they changed the name of the company from Scientific Data Systems to Xerox Data Systems.

Why? Obviously because Xerox was the better and more widely known name. And not only better known, but Xerox had a marketing mystique. A corporate Cinderella, Xerox could do no wrong.

The teeter-totter principle

When you look into the prospect's mind, you can see what went wrong.

It's the teeter-totter principle. One name can't stand for two distinctly different products. When one goes up, the other goes down.

Xerox means copier, not computer. (If you asked your secretary to get you a Xerox copy, you'd be upset if you got a reel of mag tape.)

Even Xerox knew this. "This Xerox machine can't make a copy," said the headline of one of their computer ads.

You knew that any Xerox machine that couldn't make a copy was headed for trouble. When Xerox folded its computer operations, it wrote off an additional $84.4 million.

What's a Heinz? It used to mean pickles. Heinz owned the pickle position and got the largest share.

Then the company made Heinz mean ketchup. Very successfully too. Heinz is now the No. 1 brand of ketchup.

But what happened to the other side of the teeter-totter? Why, of course, Heinz lost its pickle leadership to Vlasic.

To be successful, Xerox would have had to make Xerox mean computers.

Does this make sense for a company like Xerox that owns the copier position? A company that gets most of its volume from copiers?

Xerox is more than a name. It's a position. Like Kleenex, Hertz, and Cadillac, Xerox represents a position of enormous long-term value.

It's bad enough when someone tries to take your position away. It's tragic when you do it to yourself.

Anonymity is a resource

One reason why companies keep looking for a free ride is that they underestimate the value of anonymity.

In politics, in marketing, in life, anonymity is a resource, easily squandered by too much publicity.

"You can't beat somebody with a nobody," goes the old political saying. But today you can.

The rapid rise of a "nobody" like Gary Hart is proof that politics is a different game today. The old maxims are no longer valid.

Richard Nixon may be the best-known political name in the world. But almost any nobody could beat him.

Publicity is like eating. Nothing kills the appetite quite as much as a hearty meal. And nothing kills the publicity potential of a product or a person quite as much as a cover story in a national magazine.

The media are constantly looking for the new and different, the fresh young face.

In dealing with media, you must conserve your anonymity until you are ready to spend it. And then when you spend it, spend it big. Always keeping in mind that the objective is not publicity or communication for its own sake, but publicity to achieve a position in the prospect's mind.

An unknown company with an unknown product has much more to gain from publicity than a well-known company with an established product.

"In the future everyone will be famous for 15 minutes," Andy Warhol once predicted.

When your 15 minutes arrive, make the most of every second.

12 The line-extension trap

When the marketing history of the past decade is written, the single most significant trend will have to be line extension. That is, taking the name of an established product and using it on a new one. (The free-ride trap carried to its ultimate conclusion.)

Dial soap, Dial deodorant.

Life Savers candy. Life Savers gum.

Kleenex tissue. Kleenex towels.

Line extension has swept through the advertising and marketing community like Sherman through Georgia. And for some very sound reasons.

Logic is on the side of line extension. Arguments of economics. Trade acceptance. Consumer acceptance. Lower advertising costs. Increased income. The corporate image.

Inside-out thinking

Logic is on the side of line extension. Truth, unfortunately, is not.

Line extension is a result of clear, hard-headed, inside-out thinking that goes something like this:

"We make Dial soap, a great product that gets the biggest share of the bar-soap market. When our customers see Dial deodorant, they'll know it comes from the makers of the great Dial soap."

"Furthermore," and this is the clincher, "Dial is a deodorant soap. Our customers will expect us to produce a high-quality underarm deodorant." In short, Dial soap customers will buy Dial deodorants.

Notice, however, how the rationale changes when the line extension is in the same category.

Bayer "invented" aspirin and marketed the leading brand of analgesic for many years. The people at Bayer couldn't fail to notice the progress made by the "anti-aspirin" approach used by Tylenol.

So Bayer introduced an acetaminophen product called "Bayer nonaspirin pain reliever." Presumably people who had been buying Tylenol and other acetaminophen products would now switch back to Bayer, the leading name in headache remedies.

But neither strategy worked.

Dial has a large share of the soap market and a very small share of the deodorant market.

And Bayer nonaspirin never got more than a tiny share of the acetaminophen market.

Outside-in thinking

Let's look at line extension from the point of view of the prospect and work backward.

Both Dial and Bayer hold strong positions inside the prospect's mind.

But what does it mean to own a position in the mind? Simply this: The brand name becomes a surrogate or substitute for the generic name.

"Where is the Bayer?"

"Hand me the Dial."

The stronger the position, the more often this substitution takes place. Some brands are so strong they are practically generic. Fiberglas, Formica, Jell-O, Kleenex, Band-Aid, Sanka.

"Generic" brand names are, of course, close to the edge, so they have to be handled carefully or Uncle Sam will take your goodies away.

From a communication point of view, the generic brand name is very efficient. One word serves in place of two. When you have a generic brand name, you can afford to ignore the brand and promote the category.

"Coffee keeps you awake? Drink Sanka."

"Serve your family low-calorie Jell-O instead of cake or pie."

From the prospect's point of view, line extension works against the generic brand position. It blurs the sharp focus of the brand in the mind. No longer can the prospect say "Bayer" if he or she wants aspirin. Or "Dial" for soap.

In a sense, line extension educates the prospect to the fact that Bayer is nothing but a brand name. It destroys the illusion that Bayer is a superior form of aspirin. Or that Dial is deodorant soap rather than just a brand name for a deodorant soap.

JCPenney vs. DieHard

What actually gets driven into the mind is not the product at all but the "name" of the product, which the prospect uses as a hook to hang attributes on.

So if the name of the automobile battery is the DieHard and Sears tells you that it will last 48 months, you have a hook (DieHard) to hang the long-lasting idea on.

But if the name of the battery is the JCPenney battery and the retailer tells you it never needs water, you have a very weak hook (JCPenney) to hang this feature on.

In a physical sense, the name is also like the point of a knife. It opens up the mind to let the message penetrate. With the right name, the product fills the creneau and stays there.

So why would JCPenney call it the JCPenney battery? Presumably there were other communicative words like DieHard available.

It's easy to see why if you apply "inside-out" thinking. "We're the JCPenney company. We're highly respected among all kinds of buyers including battery buyers. We'll put our own name on the product so that everyone will instantly know who made it and that it's an exceptionally good product."

Then the clincher. "With the JCPenney name on the battery, the prospect will know where to buy it."

"Terrific thinking, J. C." And another logical inside-out decision is made.

But when the tables are turned, the name makes no sense because the mind of the prospect is organized differently. The prospect thinks in terms of products.

It should come as no surprise that in terms of brand preference (the battery ladder in the mind of the prospect) the DieHard sits on the top rung and JCPenney is way down the line.

But doesn't a big retailer like JCPenney sell a lot of batteries? Of course, but as everyone knows, many products with the wrong name are sold "in spite of" rather than "because of."

On the other hand, doesn't the prospect have difficulty remembering that the DieHard battery can only be bought at Sears? Yes, it is a problem for Sears and not everyone who might want to buy the DieHard will be able to make the connection. But it's better to establish a position in the prospect's mind first and then worry about how to establish a retail connection later.

In positioning, the shortest distance between two points is not necessarily the best strategy. The obvious name isn't always the best name.

Inside-out thinking is the biggest barrier to success. Outside-in thinking is the best aid.

Two ways of looking at the name

The consumer and the manufacturer see things in totally different ways.

Would you believe that to the folks down in Atlanta, Coca-Cola is not a soft drink? To the manufacturer, Coca-Cola is a company, a brand name, an institution, and a great place to work.

But to the consumer, Coca-Cola is a sweet, dark, carbonated beverage. What's in the glass is Coke. It's not a cola drink manufactured by a company called Coca-Cola.

The tablets in a bottle of aspirin are Bayer. Not aspirin manufactured by a company called Bayer. (The company name, of course, is Sterling Drug, not Bayer. So Bayer nonaspirin could just as logically have been called Sterling nonaspirin.)

The great strength of a generic brand name is this close identification with the product itself. In the consumer's mind, Bayer is aspirin and every other aspirin brand becomes "imitation Bayer."

The Coca-Cola slogan, "The real thing," capitalizes on the tendency of the prospect to put the first product into the mind on a pedestal and to treat the me-too products as somehow inferior to the original.

If Coke or Kleenex or Bayer is not available or if other brands are cheap enough, then the prospect might buy something else. But Bayer would still own a strong position in the mind.

But notice what happens when the same customer is asked to buy a product called "Bayer nonaspirin." If Bayer is aspirin, how can Bayer also be nonaspirin?

Bayer timed-release aspirin, Bayer decongestant cold tablets, Bayer nonaspirin pain reliever. Each extension of the Bayer line undercuts the brand's aspirin position.

As you might expect, Bayer's total share of the analgesic market keeps falling.

What's a Protein 21?

Perhaps the classic example of the line-extension trap is what happened to Protein 21 shampoo.

A number of years ago the Mennen company introduced a combination shampoo/conditioner called Protein 21, which rapidly carved out a 13 percent share of the shampoo market.

Then Mennen hit the line-extension lure. In rapid succession, the company introduced Protein 21 hairspray in regular and extra hold, scented and unscented. Also Protein 21 conditioner (in two formulas) and Protein 21 concentrate. And to make sure you can't remember what to put on your hair, Mennen also markets Protein 29. For men.

No wonder Protein 21's share of the shampoo market has fallen from 13 percent to 2 percent. And the decline is bound to continue.

But as incredible as it may seem, line extensions continue to sweep the packaged goods field.

What's a Scott?

Take the position of Scott in paper products. Scott has the lion's share of the billion-dollar market for towels, napkins, toilet tissues, and other consumer paper products. But Scott was weak where they thought they were strong.

ScotTowels, ScotTissue, Scotties, Scotkins, even BabyScott diapers. All of these names undermine the Scott foundation. The more products hung on the Scott name, the less meaning the name has to the average consumer.

Take ScotTissue, for example. ScotTissue was the No. 1 brand in the toilet-tissue market. Then Mr. Whipple and his tissue squeezers at Procter & Gamble moved in. Now ScotTissue is second to Charmin.

In Scott's case, a large share of market didn't mean they owned the position. More important is a large share of mind. The consumer could write "Charmin, Kleenex, Bounty, and Pampers" on a shopping list and we'd know exactly what products he or she was going to get. "Scott" on a shopping list has no meaning.

The actual brand names aren't much help either. Which brand, for example, is engineered for the nose, Scotties or ScotTissue?

In positioning terms, the name Scott exists in limbo. It isn't firmly ensconced on any product ladder.

Scott has begun to see the error of its ways. Viva paper towels, a Scott brand, is a winner. So is Cottonelle bathroom tissue.

What's a Life Saver?

Life Savers gum is another example of line extension that went nowhere.

Again, the logic is on the side of line extension. In an article in *The New York Times,* Life Savers' executive vice president explained the strategy:

"I am convinced that one way to improve the odds is by transferring an existing strong name to a new product requiring similar attributes."

Then he explains the attributes of Life Savers candy: "Our consumer dialogue indicates that the Life Savers brand name conveys more than merely the candy with the hole. It also means excellence in flavor, outstanding value, and dependable quality."

Not exactly. How many people would have said "Life Savers" if you asked them, "What brand means excellence in flavor, outstanding value, and dependable quality?" None.

Now what if you ask them "What's the name of the candy with the hole?"

Most people would say "Life Savers."

So what happened to Life Savers gum? The product never got more than a few percent of the market. One of those brands you won't see anymore because it was quietly killed.

As the television commercials used to say, "It's a great product, but where's the hole?"

The hole, of course, is not in the product at all. It's in the marketing strategy.

Ironically, Life Savers, Inc. has a big success in the gum field. The bubble gum field.

No, it wasn't Life Savers bubble gum.

It's Bubble Yum. The first brand of soft bubble gum. (The advantage of being first plus the advantage of not using a line-extension name.)

Bubble Yum is a runaway success. Sales already exceed those of Life Savers candy.

Not only is Bubble Yum the largest-selling brand of bubble gum, it's likely to become the largest-selling brand of chewing gum of any type.

What's an Eveready?

Many companies find themselves in rough water when new technologies rock their boats.

Eveready, a product of Union Carbide, dominated the battery market when flashlights were the principal application. Then came the transistor and with it a host of new products including tape recorders and more powerful radios. And, of course, the longer-lasting alkaline batteries.

P. R. Mallory saw the opportunity and introduced the Duracell alkaline battery in a distinctive black and gold case.

The folks at Union Carbide pooh-poohed the idea of a new name. "We've already got the best name in the battery business," they said.

But to hedge their bets, the Union Carbide people copied the Duracell black and gold color scheme. And gave the words "alkaline power cell" more prominence than the Eveready trademark.

The Duracell battery just says Duracell in bold type. It doesn't need to say "alkaline power cell" because Duracell means alkaline power cell.

This, of course, is the essence of positioning. To make your brand name stand for the generic. So the prospect freely uses the brand name for the generic.

Finally the Union Carbide people gave up and decided to copy the Duracell approach. The Eveready alkaline power cell became the Energizer which finally is giving Duracell a run for its money.

Line extension seems so intuitively right that company after company falls into the trap. Examples are not hard to find. They're a saga of opportunities missed.

The 100-mm dud

What's the name of the first extra-long, 100-mm cigarette?

Benson & Hedges, right? It's the best-known and largest-selling 100-mm brand.

"The disadvantages of Benson & Hedges" launched the brand and burned the name into the mind of the cigarette smokers.

Benson & Hedges became known as the first, the original, the inventor of the 100-mm concept.

But, of course, it wasn't. The first 100-mm cigarette was Pall Mall Gold, but Pall Mall fell into the line-extension trap.

Then Benson & Hedges moved in and preempted the long-cigarette position.

You'd think the missed opportunity represented by Pall Mall Gold would have discouraged them.

But it didn't. As we said, the logic in favor of line extension is overwhelming.

So now we have Pall Mall Menthol, Pall Mall Extra Mild, and Pall Mall Light 100s. The confusion has detracted from sales of the basic Pall Mall brand.

Take Pall Mall Menthol, for example. Again, the logic is unassailable to the manufacturer. "Menthol cigarettes like Kool and Salem are getting a larger and larger share of the market. . . . If we had a menthol brand, we could capture a share of that growing market."

Introducing Pall Mall Menthol. Which never achieved more than 7 percent of the volume of Kool.

In 1964 Pall Mall was the No. 1 cigarette brand in the United States.

In 1965 Pall Mall line-extended for the first time. They also fell to second place in sales. Every year since, Pall Mall's share of the American cigarette market has declined.

From 14.4 percent in 1964 to 3.8 percent today.

Line-extension logic in cigarettes should work two ways. Since regular brands represent a large share of the market, would you introduce a Kool nonmenthol?

Of course not. Kool was the original menthol cigarette. Kool means menthol. Like Bayer means aspirin.

Today a well-stocked tobacco shop will carry well over 100 different brands (including line extensions) out of an industry that produces in the neighborhood of 175 brands. It boggles the mind.

Naturally, the two leading brands, Marlboro and Winston, have long since line-extended the lights, 100-mm, and menthol. So according to the theory, can you expect to see the Marlboro and Winston brands follow in Pall Mall's steps? Perhaps. But in the land of the blind, the one-eyed man is king.

What brands are left to challenge the leaders? Almost all major cigarette brands have been line-extended to death.

Confusion in corn oils

What's the name of the first corn-oil margarine?

Fleischmann's is the leading brand of corn-oil margarine and the biggest seller.

But the first corn-oil margarine was Mazola. A classic example of logic leading you astray.

Mazola was the name of the leading brand of liquid corn oil. What more logical choice for a corn-oil margarine than Mazola? Mazola corn oil. Mazola corn-oil margarine. And the rest is history.

Fleischmann's is the No. 1 brand today.

Oddly enough, Fleischmann's margarine, if you want to get technical, is a line-extended name. Remember Fleischmann's yeast? Fortunately for Fleischmann's, few people do because few people bake their own bread today.

And then there is Fleischmann's gin, vodka, and whisky, also from the same company. The confusion factor is minimized because of the mental distance between a liquor product and a margarine. (Who really believes that Cadillac dog food is made by General Motors?)

The coffee-cup caper

Another missed opportunity took place in the freeze-dried coffee field. Today Taster's Choice is the leading brand and the largest seller.

But what was the name of the first freeze-dried coffee? Maxim. So why isn't Maxim the No. 1 brand? It's a story of intrigue and courage that might be worth telling in more detail.

With its Maxwell House brand, General Foods owned the coffee market. The company got the largest share and made the most money. Then it invented a new process called "freeze-dried instant."

On the surface this seemed to be a way for General Foods to increase its share of the coffee market.

Or was it?

General Foods' opening move was good news for competition. By using the name Maxim, a spinoff of the Maxwell House name, the company instantly became vulnerable. (Maxim, Maxwell, get it? Most people didn't.) Maxim is a meaningless word that doesn't connote a benefit.

The Nestlé counterattack was named Taster's Choice. Not only was the strategic choice of the name superb, but Nestlé's advertising was just about perfect.

"Tastes like ground roast," said the Taster's Choice ads, relating the freeze-dried coffee brand to the standard of excellence, ground-roasted coffee.

Taster's Choice is the big winner in the coffee-cup caper. In spite of the fact that General Foods invented the freeze-dried category and was first on the scene, Taster's Choice outsells Maxim 2 to 1.

The fickle-fingers affair

Another missed opportunity is known in hand lotion circles as "the fickle-fingers affair." The story starts with Jergens, the No. 1 brand with the dominant share of market.

First, the company introduced Jergens Extra Dry, a cream-like product in an era of liquidlike lotions. Jergens Extra Dry was really a significant innovation smothered by the similarity of names. The prospect didn't recognize the difference.

But the competition did.

Chesebrough-Pond's introduced Intensive Care. Now for the first time, the new creamlike lotion had a name which positioned the product clearly in the consumer's mind. And the product took off.

Of course, when Jergens realized what was happening, they countered with a brand called Direct Aid.

But it was the old story of too little and too late because the marketing victory went to Intensive Care. Today Intensive Care is the No. 1 brand. It outsells Jergens, Jergens Extra Dry, and Direct Aid combined.

But isn't the brand really called "Vaseline Intensive Care," a line-extended name?

True, but customers call the product Intensive Care, not Vaseline. In the mind of the prospect Vaseline is petroleum jelly; Intensive Care is a hand lotion.

Reverse line extension

While line extension is usually a mistake, the reverse can work. Reverse line extension is called "broadening the base." One of the best examples is Johnson's baby shampoo.

By promoting the mildness of the product to the adult market, the company has made Johnson's baby shampoo one of the leading brands of adult shampoo.

Notice the characteristics of this broadening-the-base strategy. Same product, same package, same label. Only the application has changed.

If Johnson & Johnson had line-extended the product and introduced Johnson's adult shampoo, the product would not have been nearly as successful.

Another example of broadening the base is Blue Nun, a white wine being promoted as equally good with meat courses as with fish.

But aren't these examples of the "everybody trap"? Not exactly. Johnson's baby shampoo is the first and only baby shampoo being promoted as an adult product too. And Blue Nun is the only white wine being advertised as good with meat as well as fish.

If other brands tried the same approach, they wouldn't be nearly as successful as these two.

And then there is Arm & Hammer baking soda, being promoted as good for refrigerators and drains. Very successfully too. But what happened when the same company line-extended with Arm & Hammer, the baking soda deodorant?

Very little. As Phyllis Diller says, "It only works if you're standing in the refrigerator."

When line extension can work

13

Line extension is popular. No doubt about it.

At one point in time, professional baseball, football, basketball, and tennis teams in the New York City area were known as the Mets, Jets, Nets, and Sets.

The city's off-track betting offices put up posters featuring the New York Bets. If the city had a gym team, presumably they would be called the New York Sweats.

Why stop there? A street gang could be the New York Ghetts. City planners, the New York Debts.

Fortunately for one's sanity, the trend seems to be in the other direction. The tennis team changed its name from the New York Sets to the New York Apples.

Short-term advantages

One of the reasons for the continuing popularity of line extension is that in the short term, line extension has some advantages.

Let's say there was going to be a professional swimming team in New York. "Here come the Wets" might be a typical newspaper headline announcing the event. With one word, "Wets," we know it's (1) a professional sports team, (2) located in the metropolitan New York area, and (3) involved in some kind of water sport.

But that's only in the short term. As the original announcement fades in the mind, confusion sets in.

Is there really a swimming team called the Wets? Or have I confused them with a basketball team called the Nets? Or was I thinking about a tennis team called the Sets? Now let's see, the Nets changed their name to the Apples. Or was it the Sets that changed their name to the Apples?

Because the line-extension name is related to the original name, it achieves an instant flash of understanding. "Ah, yes, Diet Coca-Cola."

It also generates an instant flash of sales. When Alka-Seltzer announces a new product like Alka-Seltzer Plus, everybody stocks up on it. Consumers aren't necessarily buying it, but retailers are.

So the early sales figures look good. (To book $1 million worth of business, you only have to sell $35 worth to every supermarket.)

Business looks great the first 6 months as you fill the pipelines. But when the reorders don't come in, all of a sudden things turn dark.

Long-term disadvantages

After the initial recognition of a line-extension brand, the prospect is never quite sure there is such a product.

Schlitz Light, Pall Mall Extra Mild, Jergens Extra Dry. Brand names like these slide into (and out of) the mind effortlessly. They require almost no mental work on the part of the prospect.

Easy come, easy go. Line-extension names are forgettable because they have no independent position in the mind. They are satellites to the original brand name. Their only contribution is to blur the position occupied by the original name. Often with catastrophic results.

Way back in the thirties, the Ralston Purina Company was running radio commercials for "Ralston 1, 2, 3." One was Shredded Ralston. Two was Regular Ralston. Three was Instant Ralston.

One, two, three, they're all gone.

And the legendary David Ogilvy broke his pencil writing advertisements combining Rinso White with Rinso Blue.

Sara Lee tried to get into the frozen dinner field with products like Sara Lee Chicken & Noodles Au Gratin and Sara Lee Beef & Pepper Stew.

Sara Lee owns the dessert position. Nobody doesn't like Sara Lee, but there were a lot of people out there who didn't like the chicken & noodles au gratin. And didn't buy it. Especially with the name Sara Lee on it.

So the kitchens of Sara Lee came in out of the frozen entree field. After dropping some $8 million on the project.

Almost everybody has tried line extension. *Saturday Review Magazine* tried to publish in four different flavors—*The Arts, Science, Education, The Society.* A $17 million loss.

Levi Strauss and Brown Shoe tried to launch, would you believe, "Levi's for Feet." Levi is, by far, the market leader in jeans, but this time they booted it.

Then there is Avis flowers, Zenith watches, Old Grand-Dad tobacco, Bic pantyhose, Kleenex diapers.

Also Pierre Cardin wine. In both red and white, of course. And Chanel for Men.

"Two" seems to be a popular line-extension concept. We have Alka-2, Dial 2, Sominex 2, as well as Jaws 2. (Almost never has a motion picture sequel generated as much business as the original.)

Even advertising agencies have jumped into twos. Ogilvy & Mather 2, Doyle Dane Bernbach 2, N. W. Ayer 2, and Grey 2, to name a few twos.

But the most shocking announcement of all came from Procter & Gamble. After decades of resisting the line-extension fad, P&G spend $50 million to introduce Liquid Tide. "We expect Liquid Tide to be the No. 1 liquid," said a P&G spokesperson.

But Liquid Tide is unlikely to topple the industry leader, Wisk. Furthermore, the new product is sure to cannibalize Tide powder.

The shopping-list test

The classic test for line extension is the shopping list.

Just list the brands you want to buy on a piece of paper and send your spouse to the supermarket: Kleenex, Bayer, and Dial.

That's easy enough. Most husbands or wives would come back with Kleenex tissue, Bayer aspirin, and Dial soap.

Line extensions like Kleenex towels, Bayer non-aspirin, and Dial antiperspirants have not destroyed the brands' original positions. Yet. But give them enough time to hang themselves.

How about this list: Heinz, Scott, Kraft.

Will your spouse bring back Heinz pickles or ketchup (or perhaps baby food)? Scott tissue or towels? Kraft cheese, mayonnaise, or salad dressing?

The confusion caused when one name stands for more than one product is slowly but surely sapping the strength of brands like Scott and Kraft.

Like a star that's overexpanded, the brand eventually becomes a burned-out hulk. An enormous marketing white elephant. What makes line extension so insidious is that the disease takes many years to exact its toll. Many years of slow, debilitating existence.

Take Kraft. A famous name which suffers from terminal line extension.

What's a Kraft? It's everything and yet it's nothing. In almost no categories is the Kraft brand number one. In mayonnaise, Kraft is second to Hellmann's. In salad dressing, Kraft is second to Wishbone.

Where Kraftco has the leading brand in a category, they don't call it Kraft.

In cream cheese, it's Philadelphia, not Kraft.

In ice cream, it's Sealtest, not Kraft.

In margarine, it's Parkay, not Kraft.

Where is the strength of the Kraft name? It's too diffuse. Kraft means everything and nothing. Line extension is a weakness, not a strength.

What about cheese? Surely Kraft is a strong name in cheese. And it is.

"America," say the ads, "spells cheese K-R-A-F-T." Terrible spelling and terrible strategy.

Marketing is like horse racing. The winning horse is not necessarily a good horse. It all depends on the ability of the horses in the race. In a claiming race, the winner is the best of the worst. In a stakes race, the best is the best.

Kraft has been successful in cheese. Now, name all the other cheese brands you known.

Kraft is a winner in a claiming race.

Where there are no brands or weak brands, you can line-extend. But as soon as strong competition arrives, you're in trouble.

The bartender test

In addition to the shopping list test, there's the bartender test. What do you get when you order the brand by name?

"J&B on the rocks" should get you scotch. "A Beefeater martini" should arrive with gin. And "a bottle of Dom Perignon" will definitely get you champagne.

What about "Cutty on the rocks"? You'll get scotch, of course, but will you get Cutty Sark or the more expensive 12-year-old Cutty 12?

Cutty 12 is a typical example of twisted thinking. Combine a well-known name (Cutty) with a descriptive adjective (12). Very logical from the point of view of the distillery. But what about the point of view of the drinker?

When you order "Chivas on the rocks," you let everyone know you want the best. Chivas Regal.

To get Cutty 12, you can't just say "Cutty." And when you add the "12," you're never quite sure whether the bartender heard you or, just as important, whether the people around you heard the "12."

Nor does the promotion of Cutty 12 help the original Cutty Sark brand. It's a constant reminder to the Cutty Sark drinker that he or she is drinking a lower-quality product.

Cutty 12 got into the ball game after Chivas Regal, so we shouldn't have expected much. But there was a 12-year-old brand of scotch in the U.S. market well before Chivas.

Johnnie Walker Black Label.

Today, of course, Chivas Regal outsells Johnnie Walker Black Label by a considerable margin.

"Give me a Johnnie Walker with a splash, bartender."

"Black Label or Red Label, sir?"

"Aaaaaaaaaaah . . . the hell with it. Make it a Chivas."

Cutty 12 and Johnnie Walker Black Label are step-up examples of line extension. They usually result in anemic sales at the higher-priced end. (Who wants to pay premium prices for a low-price name?)

What's a Packard?

The step-down problem is just the reverse. Step-down products are often instantly successful. The hangover comes later.

Before World War II Packard was the premier American automobile. More so even than Cadillac, it was a status symbol esteemed all over the world.

Heads of state bought armored Packards. One was made for Franklin Roosevelt. Like Rolls-Royce, Packard loftily declined the annual model-change policy of lesser makers. They positioned themselves above the pack.

Then in the middle thirties, Packard introduced their first step-down model, the relatively inexpensive Packard Clipper.

The Packard Clipper was the most successful car Packard ever built. Sales were terrific, but it killed the company. (Or more precisely, it killed Packard's prestige position, which in turn killed the company.)

Packard drifted along until 1954 when Studebaker absorbed the company. The end of the road came years later.

What's a Cadillac?

What do you know about Cadillac? How long is it? What colors does it come in? What's the horsepower of the engine? What options are available?

To the average automobile prospect, General Motors has succeeded in communicating almost nothing about Cadillac. Except its position as the top-of-the-line, domestic luxury automobile.

But even General Motors sometimes forgets that for every product there are two points of view. And most line-extension mistakes are made because the marketer did not appreciate this fact.

What's a Cadillac? This might surprise you, but from General Motors' point of view, a Cadillac is not an automobile at all. It's a division. As a matter of fact, it's one of GM's most profitable divisions.

But from the buyer's point of veiw, Cadillac is a big luxury car. You can see the problem.

Because of the gasoline situation, Cadillac is worried. So to maintain that profitability, General Motors has introduced a small Cadillac, the Cimarron. But in the long-term a mini-Cadillac conflicts with the big-car position that Cadillac owns in the mind.

So the prospect looks at the Cimarron and asks, "Is it or isn't it a Cadillac?"

Long-term, the Cimarron gets in the way of the most effective answer to the challenge of smaller luxury cars like Mercedes and BMW. To establish a small luxury brand, General Motors needs a separate high-price name and a separate dealer organization.

What's a Chevrolet?

For automobiles as well as other products, you can ask yourself that age-old question and you'll know if you have a positioning problem.

What is it?

For example, what's a Chevrolet? It's a car that's fallen into the everybody trap. By trying to appeal to everybody, a product winds up appealing to nobody.

What's a Chevrolet? We'll tell you what a Chevrolet is. It's a big, small, cheap, expensive car.

O.K., how come Chevy is still No. 1? How come they haven't lost their leadership to Ford?

To which we reply, "What's a Ford?" Same problem. Ford is also a big, small, cheap, expensive car.

Ford has another problem. Not only is Ford an automobile brand. Ford is also a company.

A Ford Ford might be all right, but there is a real problem for the company in selling Ford Mercurys or Ford Lincolns. (One reason why the Ford Motor Company has always had a hard time selling higher-priced cars.)

What's a Volkswagen?

A line-extension tragedy usually moves to its inevitable conclusion in three acts.

Act One is the big success, the big breakthrough. Usually the result of finding a wide-open creneau and then exploiting it brilliantly.

Volkswagen invented the small-car position and moved rapidly to exploit the breakthrough. "Think small," perhaps the most famous single advertisement every run, stated the position in no uncertain terms.

Very quickly, the Volkswagen Beetle established an exceptionally strong position in the automotive market. Like most classic success stories, Volkswagen became more than a brand name for a product.

"I drive a Volkswagen" says more than who made the automobile the person owns. "I drive a Volkswagen" says something about the owner's way of life. A no-nonsense, practical person, self-confident about his or her status in life. A simple, functional piece of transportation equipment.

The Volkswagen owner is a reverse snob. He or she loves to put down the car buyer who loves to impress the neighbors. "The 1970 Volkswagen will stay ugly longer" expresses this attitude perfectly.

Act Two is fueled by greed and visions of unending successes. So Volkswagen extends Volkswagen reliability and quality to bigger, more expensive cars. To buses and jeep-type vehicles.

Act Three is the denouement. Is it possible that eight models won't sell as well as one? It's not only possible, it happened.

From first place in imported cars, Volkswagen fell to fourth. Behind Toyota, Datson, and Honda. And just barely ahead of Mazda and Subaru.

The pattern of early success followed by line extension followed by disillusionment is fairly common. After all, you can't expect companies like Scott and Volkswagen to rest on their laurels. You'd expect them to find new fields to conquer. So how do they go about finding them? One way is obvious. They develop a new concept or a new product with a new position and a new name to match.

A name is a rubber band

It will stretch, but not beyond a certain point. Furthermore, the more you stretch a name, the weaker it becomes. (Just the opposite of what you might expect.)

How far should you stretch a name? This is an economics call as much as a judgment call.

Let's say you have a line of canned vegetables. Do you have a brand name for peas, another for corn, and still a third for string beans? Probably not. Economically, it wouldn't make sense.

So Del Monte is probably right to use the same brand name on its line of canned fruits and vegetables. But notice what happens when a competitor zeroes in on a single product. The Dole line of canned pineapple.

Dole vs. Del Monte in pineapple is no contest. Dole wins every time.

So what does Dole do next? It puts the Dole name on fresh bananas. The Dole banana.

Let's say Dole is successful in making Dole mean bananas. So what happens to pineapple? It's the teeter-totter principle with bananas on one side and pineapple on the other.

But can't Dole do what Del Monte did? Become a full-line supplier of canned and fresh food products?

Sure, but only at the expense of sacrificing its valuable pineapple franchise. And with the added disadvantage of being the last to line-extend.

Rules of the road

We call line extension a "trap," not a mistake. Line extension can work if. . . .

But it's a big if. If your competitors are foolish. If your volumn is small. If you have no competitors. If you don't expect to build a position in the prospect's mind. If you don't do any advertising.

The truth is, many products are sold, few are positioned.

That is, the customer will pick up a can of peas without having a going-in preference, or position, for a brand of peas. In this case, any well-known brand name is going to do better than any unknown name.

And if you work for a company with thousands of small-volume products (3M is a typical example), you obviously cannot have a new name for every one.

So we offer some rules of the road that will tell you when to use the house name and when not to.

1. **Expected volume.**   Potential winners should not bear the house name. Small-volume products should.

2. **Competition.**   In a vacuum, the brand should not bear the house name. In a crowded field, it should.

3. **Advertising support.**   Big-budget brands should not bear the house name. Small-budget brands should.

4. **Significance.**   Breakthrough products should not bear the house name. Commodity products such as chemicals should.

5. **Distribution.**   Off-the-shelf items should not bear the house name. Items sold by sales reps should.

14 Positioning a company: Xerox

You can position anything. A person, a product, a politician. Even a company.

Why would anyone want to position a company? Who buys a company? And why would a company want to sell itself? To whom? (To protect themselves against unfriendly takeovers, most companies would like to be invisible.)

The buying and selling of companies

Actually, a lot of buying and selling of companies is going on. Only it's called different names.

When a new employee accepts a job, he or she "buys" the company. (With its recruiting programs, a company is actually selling itself.)

Who would you rather work for, General Electric or the Schenectady Electrical Works?

Every year companies across the country compete for top graduates at the nation's leading universities. Who do you think gets the cream of the crop?

That's right. The companies that occupy the best positions in the minds of the prospective employee. The General Electrics, the Procter & Gambles.

And when investors buy a share of stock, what they are really paying for is a piece of that company's position, now and in the future.

How much a person is willing to pay for that stock (six or sixty times earnings) depends on the strength of that position in the buyer's mind.

Positioning a company effectively has lots of advantages if you happen to be an officer or director of that corporation. It's not easy, though.

The name problem again

First of all, the name. Especially the name. Would you believe that Pullman doesn't happen to be much of a factor in the railroad car business anymore?

And that bus revenues represent only a small part of Greyhound's total sales.

Both Pullman and Greyhound have changed drastically. Yet the way they are perceived by the public has scarcely changed at all. Their names have locked them to their past reputations.

Yet they have tried. Especially Greyhound, which has spent millions of dollars telling the financial community that it is "more than a bus company."

But as long as those buses with the long slim dogs on the side go zipping up and down the interstate highways, the corporate advertising is an expensive mistake. If Greyhound wants to be more than a bus company, it needs a new name. A "more than a bus company" name.

But even with the right name, the corporate positioning job isn't done. Your company's name ought to stand for something within your industry.

Standing for something

Consider Ford. Everyone knows that Ford is an automobile company. But what kind of car is a Ford?

Ford can't build a corporate position on a specific kind of car, because it builds them in all types and all sizes, including trucks. (Whether it should or not is another matter.)

So the positioning question boils down to some quality to be found across the board in all vehicles.

The company has settled on "innovation" as the key attribute in a vehicle from Ford. Result: the "Ford has a better idea" campaign.

Not bad, but many corporate programs settle on a mundane and hackneyed approach. Of which the most mundane and hackneyed, perhaps, is one based on people.

"Our people are our greatest resource."

"Gulf people: Meeting the challenge."

"Grumman: We're proud of the many products we make. We're prouder of the people who make them."

Are there no differences in quality between the people in one company and those in another?

Of course there are. But it's quite another matter to build a position based on better people.

Most people think that the bigger, more successful companies have the better people. And the smaller, less successful companies have the leftovers.

So if your company occupies the top rung of the product ladder in the prospect's mind, you can be sure that the prospect will also think that your company has the best people.

If you're not on top and you tell the prospect you have the better people. . . . Well, that's one of those inconsistencies that doesn't usually get resolved in your favor.

If Ford really has the better ideas, why doesn't it use them in the marketplace to overtake General Motors instead of using them in its advertising to impress the public?

This is not a question of fact. (Ford could have the better ideas and still be in second place.) This is just a question that springs up in the prospect's mind.

And your advertising, to be successful, must answer this question.

Diversification is not the answer

Next to "people," the most common corporate positioning theme is "diversification." Companies want to become known as diversified manufacturers of a wide range of high-quality products.

But diversification is not effective as a corporate advertising approach. As a matter of fact, the two concepts of positioning and diversification are poles apart.

It's a fact of life that strong positions in the prospect's mind are built on major achievements. Not on broad product lines.

General Electric is known as the world's largest electrical manufacturer. Not as a diversified maker of industrial, transportation, chemical, and appliance products.

Even through General Electric makes thousands of consumer and industrial products, most of its successful products have been electrical ones. Most of its unsuccessful ones have been nonelectrical products. Computers being a typical example.

General Motors is known as the world's largest builder of automobiles. Not as a diversified maker of industrial, transportation, and appliance products.

IBM has a reputation as the world's largest computer manufacturer. Not as a worldwide manufacturer of many types of office machines.

A company may be able to make more money by diversifying. It should think twice, however, about trying to build a position based on that concept.

Even the stock market consistently undervalues conglomerates like ITT and Gulf & Western. (Many companies are worth more broken into parts than they are worth whole.)

Sometimes companies think they are concentrating their communication efforts when they are really not. The positioning concept becomes so broad that it is almost meaningless.

Which company used to call itself "a developer and supplier of information systems for work, education, and entertainment?"

Would you believe Bell & Howell? That's right, Bell & Howell.

How do you develop an effective position for a company? Let's look at Xerox, a company that seems to already have a position.

What's in Xerox's mind?

Why would Xerox want a position? Xerox has a position. Xerox is the Coca-Cola of copiers.

Quick, name another copier company? Nothing jumps into the mind, does it? Sure, after a while, you probably can remember that Sharp, Savin, Ricoh, Royal, and Canon make copiers. Even IBM and Kodak make copiers.

But nobody owns the copier position the way Xerox does. This is an enormous advantage in selling copiers. When you think your company needs another copier, your first thought is Xerox and your first telephone call is most likely to Xerox.

So what's the problem? Xerox sees the office market moving toward systems, expecially computer-based information systems. So Xerox bought Scientific Data Systems and subsequently changed the name to Xerox Data Systems.

"Our objective in acquiring SDS," said the chairman, "was to offer broader-based information systems. We feel that to really seize the opportunities around the world for supplying information, we had to broaden out from graphics, as IBM is broadening out into graphics. People in the seventies who can say to a customer, 'We can handle all your information needs, whether fascimile transmission, graphics, or whatever,' will have an enormous advantage."

Six years later, Xerox Data Systems folded. But the loss of XDS didn't stop Xerox from trying to broaden the company's product line. Xerox was still committed to the concept of going beyond copiers.

In the years to come, Xerox introduced a parade of office automation products. The XTEN network, the Ethernet network, the Star workstation, the 820 personal computer. "Now the industry will know our secret for certain," declared a Xerox vice president. "We want to be No. 1 in this market."

What's in the prospect's mind?

If Xerox would look into the minds of its prospects, it would quickly see that moving into office information systems is not in the cards.

The trade publication *Information Week* recently surveyed a sample of its subscribers. (The magazine has 100,000 subscribers, 80 percent of whom represent companies with 1000 or more employees. It would seem that this is the heart of the office automation market.)

Here are the answers given when subscribers were asked, "Which manufacturers of office information systems are you most interested in?"

IBM	81%
Wang	40%
Digital Equipment	36%
AT&T	22%
Hewlett-Packard	21%

Xerox didn't make the charts.

What can Xerox do? Our message to Xerox is to stop fighting copiers. You can't change what's in the prospect's mind.

Start using copiers. They could be your strongest asset. An asset in a strategic war with IBM and AT&T.

The "third-leg" strategy

It's a way for Xerox to take advantage of its heritage. As with many strategies, it's helpful to step back and get a sense of what has been going on in the marketplace.

Let's look first at the office of the past. Things were simple then. To put yourself in business, you got a telephone from AT&T, a typewriter from IBM, and a copier from Xerox.

Now look at the office of the present. All the action has been in the typewriter leg. Typewriters have been supplanted by computers. The telephone and copier legs have hardly changed at all.

What about the office of the future? If you believe everything you read, the office of the future will have a single leg consisting of an office automation system supplied by a single vendor. IBM, of course, is everyone's bet.

As a result, every manufacturer worth its computer is chasing this "single vendor" idea.

But systems don't always sell. The high-fidelity audio system was never supplied by one vendor as consumers picked the receivers and turntables and tape players they wanted.

The same went for the home entertainment center and the dream that GE had to sell all the major appliances in the kitchen. The woman of the house picked her favorite brands.

Furthermore, even if the office of the future should turn out to be one big system supplied by one big manufacturer, it's unlikely that Xerox would be a major factor.

Therefore, Xerox has nothing to lose and everything to gain by betting on a different scenario.

The "third-leg" scenario is a different view of the office of the future. It's a view that sees the office of the future as still having three legs. The telephone leg of AT&T becomes a communication leg with the addition of voice mail and facsimile equipment.

The typewriter leg of IBM becomes an input or processing leg with the addition of computers, workstations, and networks.

The question is what will Xerox add to the copier leg?

Some "cross-leg" difficulties

There's a good deal of evidence that the merging of legs is not the way of the future. History points to the difficulty of many "cross-leg" activities.

Take Xerox vs. IBM. (1) Xerox has not been very successful with computers, workstations, or local area networks, all of which belong to the leg owned by IBM. (2) On the other hand, IBM has not been very successful with copiers, a leg, or position, owned by Xerox.

Take Xerox vs. AT&T. (1) Nobody, including Xerox, has done very well with facsimile equipment, a leg owned by AT&T. (2) Voice mail and facsimile will take off as soon as AT&T gets behind them.

Take AT&T vs. IBM. (1) AT&T won't do well with computers, a leg owned by IBM. (2) On the other hand, IBM and Rolm won't do very well with telephones, a leg owned by AT&T. (Satellite Business Systems is losing $100 million a year.)

Even since Scientific Data Systems, Xerox has been trying to bridge the copier/computer gap. Instead of being an obstacle, the copier/computer gap in the long run could turn out to be Xerox's strongest ally.

"Third-leg" opportunities

If AT&T's telephone leg has become the communication leg and IBM's typewriter leg has become the input and processing leg, then what has Xerox's copier leg become?

The obvious answer is the output leg. There are many "third-leg" opportunities for Xerox as offices add computer printers, scanners, and storage devices to complement their copiers.

Furthermore, a hot new technology is moving into the output side of the office. That technology is the laser. There are laser printers, laser typesetters, laser memory systems.

Furthermore, the laser is making a name for itself in many other places. In communication, the laser is beginning to replace satellites. In the hospital, the laser is revolutionizing heart surgery. In the supermarket, you find laser check-out counters.

McDonnell/Douglas talks about a laser that is "capable of transmitting the entire contents of a 24-volume set of encyclopedia in a single second." United Telecom is setting up a nationwide laser network. AT&T is laying down a transatlantic laser link. GTE is bouncing laser beams off the moon.

In the consumer field, there is the laser videodisk player. The laser audiodisk player. And the laser everything disk which can play both video and audio.

No self-respecting rock show would end without a laser light show. Even Ronald Reagan's "star wars" satellites would be equipped with nuclear-powered laser weapons.

The fourth technology

In the past 30 years, three technologies have roared through the office and into the dictionary. The first was *thermography* by 3M, a photocopying process that uses infrared rays to produce a copy on a special type of paper.

The second was *xerography* by Xerox, a copying process that uses the action of light to produce a copy on plain paper.

The third is the *microprocessor* technology that computer companies like IBM have dominated.

There's an opportunity for Xerox to put another technological word in a yet to be published edition of Webster's Dictionary.

The fourth technology would be called "lasography." It could be defined as the process of communicating, printing, scanning, and storing optical or printed messages with the use of laser beams and optical fibers.

One word can say a lot

Xerox is a $9 billion company with more than 100,000 employees. It ought to be impossible to position an enterprise as big and diverse as Xerox with a single word.

But in an overcommunicated society there is only so much room in the mind. Today Xerox means just one word—copiers. Tomorrow Xerox could use lasography to create a broader mental position.

Lasography says new and different, and the business world loves things that are new and different.

Lasography sounds like a basic technology somehow related to xerography. In other words, it connects with Xerox's last big technology.

Lasography from Xerox, the company that's perceived to be in the "ography" business.

Lasography uses lasers, which are perceived to be on the leading edge of technology.

Lasography is the one concept that takes advantage of Xerox's position and broadens it to include the next generation of products.

In the positioning game you can't sit still. You must constantly be alert to keep your position targeted to today's problems and today's markets.

15

Positioning a country: Belgium

With the advent of relatively inexpensive airfare, we're fast becoming a world of tourists.

In days gone by, international travel was limited to the older, more affluent person. Today that's all changed. There was a time when the flight attendants were young and the travelers old. Now the travelers are young and the flight attendants are old.

The Sabena situation

One of the many North Atlantic carriers jockeying for these international travelers is an airline called Sabena Belgian World Airlines. But all competitors don't compete on an equal basis. TWA and Pan Am, for example, have for some time had a long list of gateway cities in both the United States and Europe.

But Sabena flies nonstop from North America to only one city in Europe: Brussels. Unless there was a hijacker aboard, every Sabena plane was going to land in Belgium.

While Sabena captured the lion's share of the traffic to Belgium, they were on a very meager diet. Not too many people were flying to this little country. Only one out of 50 North Atlantic passengers fly to Belgium.

On the country ladder in the prospective traveler's mind, Belgium was on one of the bottom rungs. If it was on the ladder at all.

One look at the situation and it was easy to tell what was wrong with Sabena's advertising. Sabena was using classic airline strategy. Sell the food and the service.

"Do I have to be a bon vivant to fly Sabena?" said a typical ad. But all the terrific food in the world won't induce you to fly an airline that isn't going where you want to go.

Position the country, not the airline

Sabena's most productive strategy was obviously not to position the airline but to position the country. In other words, do what KLM had done for Amsterdam.

Sabena had to make Belgium a place where a traveler would want to spend some time. Not a place you traveled through to get to somewhere else.

Furthermore, there's a moral here that shines through loud and clear. Whether you're selling colas, companies, or countries. Out of mind, out of business.

Most Americans knew very little about Belgium. They thought Waterloo was a suburb of Paris and the most important product of Belgium was waffles. Many didn't even know where the country was.

"If it's Tuesday, this must be Belgium," was the title of a popular motion picture.

But how do you find a position for a country? Well, if you think about it, the most successful countries all have strong mental images.

Say "England" and people think of pageantry, Big Ben, and the Tower of London.

Say "Italy" and they think of the Coliseum and St. Peter's and works of art.

Say "Amsterdam" and it's tulips, Rembrandt, and those wonderful canals.

Say "France" and it's food and the Eiffel Tower and the dazzling Riviera.

Your mind sees cities and countries as mental picture postcards. In your mind, New York is probably a skyline of tall buildings. San Francisco is cable cars and the Golden Gate Bridge. Cleveland is a gray place with a lot of industrial smokestacks.

Obviously, London, Paris, and Rome are all top-of-the-ladder destinations that are most popular with first-time travelers to Europe. Sabena had little chance to get these travelers.

But in the United States there is a large segment of seasoned travelers looking to visit the next tier of destinations. Countries like Greece with its ruins. Switzerland with its mountains.

Once the objective became clear, finding a position wasn't that difficult.

Beautiful Belgium

Belgium is a beautiful country with many of the things that appeal to the seasoned European traveler. Like interesting cities, historical palaces, museums, and art galleries.

Oddly enough, many Belgian people don't have a high opinion of their own country as a tourist attraction. That attitude is perhaps epitomized by a sign that used to be at the Brussels airport. Among other things it said, "Welcome to Belga country. Weather: mild, but rains 220 days a year, on average."

As the result, Belgium's favorite tourist strategy was to promote the central location of Brussels as a "gateway" city and the ease of getting somewhere else. Like London, Paris, and Rome. (If you want to visit New York, fly to Philadelphia because it's close by.)

There's an important lesson here. The perceptions of people living in a place are often different from those visiting it.

Many New Yorkers fail to see New York as a tourist attraction. They remember the garbage strikes and forget the Statue of Liberty. Yet New York attracts 16 million visitors a year who all want to see those "big buildings."

Three-star cities

But while "beautiful" was a good position, it wasn't really enough as a tourist promotion theme. To position a country as a destination, you need attractions that will keep the traveler around for at least a few days.

Nobody considers Monaco much of a destination because its number one attraction, Monte Carlo, can be seen in an evening.

Obviously, size is an important factor. Big countries have lots of attractions. Small countries are at a disadvantage. (If the Grand Canyon ran through Belgium, you wouldn't have much land left to look at.)

We found the answer to the overall positioning problem in one of those Michelin Guides. You may not know that Michelin rates cities as well as restaurants.

Michelin's Benelux edition lists six three-star "worth a special journey" cities. Five were in Belgium: Bruges, Ghent, Antwerp, Brussels, and Tournai.

But what was really surprising was the fact that the big tourist attraction to the North, Holland, had only one three-star city, Amsterdam.

The ad that resulted was headlined, "In beautiful Belgium, there are five Amsterdams." The illustration was comprised of five beautiful four-color pictures of Belgium's three-star cities.

This advertisement generated an enormous number of inquiries about a country many travelers had seen only through the train window as they traveled from Amsterdam to Paris.

One of the inquiries came in the form of a call from the minister of tourism in Holland to his counterpart in Belgium. Needless to say, there was one irate Dutchman who wanted that advertisement killed, along with the people who created it.

The "three-star city" strategy had three important things going for it.

First, it related Belgium to a destination that was already in the mind of the traveler, Amsterdam. In any positioning program, if you can start with a strongly held perception, you'll be that much ahead in your efforts to establish your own position.

Second, the Michelin Guide, another entity already in the mind of the traveler, gave the concept credibility.

Finally, the "five cities to visit" made Belgium a bona fide destination.

Eventually the "three-star cities of beautiful Belgium" concept was moved into television. The response was substantial.

A television commercial with its ability to communicate in sight and sound can drive pictures of a country into the mind much more quickly than a print advertisement.

There's also a danger of misusing the medium of television. This happens when your visuals are similar to visuals being used by other countries.

Think about those islands in the Caribbean you've seen advertised. Can you keep those palm trees and beaches separate in your mind? Do you conjure up the same mental postcard when someone says Nassau, the Virgin Islands, or Barbados? If there's no difference, the mind will simply dump all those visuals in a slot marked "Islands in the Caribbean" and tune out.

The same thing can happen with those quaint European villages. Or the smiling residents waving mugs of beer at you. We solved the problem by using the Michelin "stars" as if they were church bells which rang out as they were superimposed on the Belgium city scenes.

What happened?

Now you might be wondering why, after all this, you haven't seen much about Belgium and its three-star cities.

A number of events kept this program from getting off the ground. All of which holds a lesson for anyone embarked on a positioning program.

New management not committed to the program arrived on the scene, and when headquarters in Brussels wanted to change the strategy, they quickly acquiesced.

The lesson here is that a successful positioning program requires a major long-term commitment by the people in charge. Whether it's the head of a corporation, a church, an airline, or a country.

In a constantly changing political environment, this is difficult to accomplish.

16 Positioning an island: Jamaica

When Edward Seaga replaced socialist Michael Manley as Jamaican prime minister, he proclaimed an open door for capitalist investment.

David Rockefeller was so impressed, he formed a group of 25 American corporate chiefs specifically for the purpose of developing Jamaica. In the due course of events the Jamaicans, encouraged by the Rockefeller committee, hired us to develop a position for the island of Jamaica.

Investment or tourism?

Jamaica at the time needed both. But which should come first?

Obviously, investments won't do much for tourism, but many tourists work for big companies. If they come back from Jamaica with favorable impressions, they just might encourage their companies to invest in the island. Executives at those same companies like to invest in places that are fun to visit. Which is why you see so little investment in Alaska and so much in the Caribbean.

Who wants to go to Fairbanks in the wintertime to check out the plant?

The competition

Looking at the Caribbean from a tourist's point of view, there are four major competitors to Jamaica: the Bahamas, Puerto Rico, the U.S. Virgin Islands, and Bermuda. Each of these destinations draws more visitors a year than Jamaica.

What springs to mind when you mention any of these Caribbean islands? With one exception, the consistent visual image is the couple in the bathing suits on the beach, underneath the palm trees. (This sea, sand, and surf picture has become a visual cliché for the Caribbean.)

The exception, of course, is Bermuda. Years of advertising those motorbikes parked beside the pink sand have put a strong visual in the mind.

Effective, too. Our research shows that in terms of perceptions, Bermuda is second in desirability to the U.S. Virgin Islands. If it weren't for the weather factor (Bermuda is considerably north of the other islands), Bermuda would have been in first place.

Jamaica's positioning problem is similar to the problem of Belgium. How to put a mental picture postcard into the mind of the Caribbean prospect?

The search for the postcard

The first approach is to sort through thousands of postcards to find the one perfect picture of the island of Jamaica. But it can't be found.

There's a good reason. If there were one image that captured the essense of the island, someone would have noticed it already and used it. In other words, there would have been an image already burned into at least a few minds.

The second approach is to visit Jamaica and shoot hundreds or thousands of pictures trying to capture that illusive mental picture postcard. Not surprisingly, nothing totally right turns up.

The third approach is the one that should have been used first. It's to look into the mind of the prospect to see what mental images already exist. And then select one you can tie Jamaica into.

What is the verbal essence of Jamaica? An old advertisement said, "Jamaica is the big green island in the Caribbean that has deserted beaches, cool mountains, country pastures, open plains, rivers, rapids, waterfalls, ponds, good drinking water, and a jungly interior."

Does that sound familiar? Does it remind you of a very popular tourist destination in the Pacific?

The Hawaiian connection

That's right. Hawaii. Most people have a mental picture of the big green volcanic mountains coming down to the blue sea.

It's a view that you can also see as you approach the island of Jamaica, the Hawaii of the Caribbean.

The Hawaii of the Caribbean becomes an even more powerful concept when you compare Jamaica with its four biggest competitors. This chart lists the highest point of each destination.

Bermuda	259 feet
Bahamas	400 feet
U.S. Virgin Islands	1556 feet
Puerto Rico	4389 feet
Jamaica	7402 feet

At 7402 feet, Blue Mountain in Jamaica is higher than any point in the United States east of the Mississippi River.

Another important comparison is the size of each destination. This chart gives the length of the largest island in each destination.

Bermuda	4 miles
Bahamas	8 miles
U.S. Virgin Islands	7½ miles
Puerto Rico	50 miles
Jamaica	62½ miles

Again, Jamaica is considerably larger than any of its competitors. Jamaica has hundreds of miles of beaches and two volcanic mountain ranges with a towering peak over 7000 feet. This supports the "More to see, more to do" advantages that are also implicit in the Hawaiian connection.

Conceptually, this approach says to tourists that the things they travel a great distance to Hawaii for (natural beauty, big green mountains, beautiful beaches, wonderful year-round weather) can be found a lot closer to home, down in the Caribbean.

Jamaica could even copy one of the most successful of Hawaii's marketing ploys: meeting tourists with flowers at the airport.

Jamaica has beautiful flowers and this gesture, above all, would say that Jamaica is a friendly place as well as a beautiful one.

Benefits of the "Hawaiian" position

"The Hawaii of the Caribbean" provides a quick visual analogy. Jamaica doesn't have the luxury of building that visual image over the years. Transferring Hawaii's mental picture postcards will save enormous amounts of time and money.

Furthermore, the concept strongly differentiates Jamaica from the other Caribbean destinations.

A poster entitled "A cartographer's view of the Caribbean" made this point very graphically. It showed each of the destinations drawn to scale. (You need a magnifying glass to find Bermuda.)

Another major benefit of the Hawaiian analogy is the platform it provides for European programs. If you live on the Continent, Hawaii is a long way away.

If you're wondering why you haven't heard much about the Hawaii of the Caribbean, you'll have to ask Mr. Seaga. He is widely viewed as a Caribbean Ronald Reagan, but "he is really the Jimmy Carter of Jamaica," a Rockefeller aide told *The Wall Street Journal*. "He's the person who gets involved in every detail and agonizes over every issue."

Presumably he is still agonizing over this one.

17 Positioning a product: Milk Duds

The brand is Milk Duds, a product of Switzer Clark. Milk Duds is a candy product that comes in a little yellow and brown box. It had a reputation as a "movie" candy for teenagers, but the company wanted to broaden its Milk Duds business to include the younger crowd.

Looking into the mind

The first step in any positioning program is to look inside the mind of the prospect.

And who is the prospect for Milk Duds? It's not some little kid who doesn't know the score. Research indicates that the best Milk Duds prospect is a sophisticated candy buyer. He or she has been in and out of candy stores several hundred times at least.

The average Milk Duds prospect is 10 years old. A cautious, suspicious, shrewd purchasing agent who is always on the lookout for value received.

Most positioning programs are nothing more or less than a search for the obvious. Yet the obvious is easy to miss if you zero in too quickly on the product itself. (As with the "purloined letter" of Edgar Allan Poe, the obvious is often hard to find because it's too easy to see. It's too obvious.)

What's in the prospect's mind when the subject of candy comes up? Not Milk Duds, even though the average 10-year-old kid might be vaguely aware of the brand.

For most 10-year-olds, the candy urge immediately conjures up the concept of candy bars.

Candy bars like Hersheys, Nestlés, Mounds, Almond Joys, Reeses, Snickers, Milky Ways. Put there, of course, by the millions of dollars' worth of advertising spent on these and other candy bar brands.

Repositioning the competition

Since Milk Duds was getting only a small fraction of that kind of advertising money, it would have been hopeless to try to build a separate identity for the brand. The only way to drive Milk Duds into the kid's mind was to find a way to reposition the candy bar category.

In other words, find a way to make the millions of dollars spent by the competition work for Milk Duds by setting up the brand as an alternative to the candy bar. (Little would be gained by just putting another candy name in an overloaded mind.)

Fortunately, there was a glaring weakness in the candy bar competition that could be exploited. And the weakness is obvious once you look at the size and shape and price of today's Hershey bar.

A candy bar just doesn't last very long. A kid can go through a 50-cent Hershey bar in 2.3 seconds flat.

There exists a strong undercurrent of dissatisfaction among America's candy eaters. As the candy bar has shrunk in size, this discontent has grown.

"My allowance doesn't last very long when it comes to candy bars."

"Either I'm eating faster or candy bars are getting smaller."

"You can suck up a candy bar awfully fast these days!"

This is the soft, chocolaty underbelly of the candy bar competition.

Milk Duds are different. They come in a box instead of a package. They give the kid 15 individual slow-eating chocolate-covered caramels.

Compared with a candy bar, a box of Milk Duds will last a long time. (If you try to stuff a whole box in your mouth, it will cement your jaws shut.) Which is exactly why the product has been so popular in movie theaters.

So what is Milk Duds' new position?

The long-lasting alternative

Why, it's America's long-lasting alternative to the candy bar.

If this seems like the obvious answer to you, it wasn't to the people who used to do the Milk Duds advertising. In some 15 years of Milk Duds' television commercials, there wasn't one reference to the long-lasting idea.

Let's take a mental walk through a 30-second television commercial to see how the long-lasting idea was sugarcoated for the benefit of the 10-year-old.

1. Once there was a kid who had a big mouth . . . (A kid is standing next to an enormous mouth.)

2. . . . that loved candy bars. (The kid is shoveling candy bars one right after another into the mouth.)

3. . . . but they didn't last very long. (The kid runs out of candy bars and the mouth gets very upset.)

4. Then he discovered chocolaty caramel Milk Duds. (The kid holds up the Milk Duds, and the mouth starts to lick its chops.)

5. The mouth loved the Milk Duds because they last a long time. (The kid rolls the Milk Duds one by one up the mouth's tongue.)

6. (Then the kid and the mouth sing a duet together, which is the campaign song.) When a candy bar is only a memory, you'll still be eating your Milk Duds.

7. Get your mouth some Milk Duds. (Big smiles on both the kid and the mouth.)

Did it work?

Not only did the television advertising reverse a downward sales trend, but in the ensuing months the company sold more Milk Duds than it ever did in its history.

If there is one important lesson to be learned from the Milk Duds example, it's this: The solution to a positioning problem is usually found in the prospect's mind, not in the product.

18 Positioning a service: Mailgram

What's the difference between the positioning of a product (like Milk Duds) and the positioning of a service (like Western Union's Mailgram)?

Not much, especially from a strategic point of view. Most of the differences are in techniques.

Visual vs. verbal

In a product ad, the dominant element is usually the picture, the visual element. In a service ad, the dominant element is usually the words, the verbal element. (So if you saw an advertisement with a big picture of an automobile, you would assume the car was being advertised, not a car rental service.)

With a product like Milk Duds, the primary medium was television, a visually oriented vehicle.

With a service like Mailgram, the primary medium was radio, a verbally oriented vehicle.

Naturally, there are a lot of exceptions to these principles. If everyone knows what the product looks like, there is no advantage in using print, television, or other forms of visual media.

Conversely, if a service can make effective use of a visual symbol (O. J. Simpson for Hertz, for example), then visual media can often be productive.

In spite of the exceptions, it's surprising how often these visual/verbal generalities hold up. In a four-way test of newspapers, magazines, radio, and television for Mailgram, the most effective medium was radio. But the essence of the Mailgram story is strategy, not media. Before discussing strategy, it may be helpful to take a look at how the system works.

Electronic mail

Developed jointly with the U.S. Postal Service and inaugurated on a limited experimental basis in 1970, Mailgram is the nation's first electronic mail.

To send a Mailgram, you call Western Union, which transmits the message electronically to a post office near the recipient. The Mailgram is delivered the next business day.

In addition to sending Mailgrams by telephone, the customer can also send them by telex, TWX, magnetic tape, computer, facsimile equipment, or communicating typewriters.

Why belabor the technicalities? Why discuss the complex details of the Mailgram system?

To make an important point. Most advertising programs never go beyond the details of the product or service which is offered for sale. And the more interesting and complex the service is, the more likely this will happen. The marketing people who are responsible for introducing the product get all wrapped up in the service and forget all about the customer. As a matter of fact, the traditional approach would have been to introduce Mailgram as a "new, automated, computerized electronic communication service" or something of that sort. (Western Union spent millions on computer programming alone, not to mention the enormous expense of earth stations, satellites, etc.)

The low-cost telegram

Regardless of how much money you spend, regardless of how technologically interesting your service is, to get inside the prospect's mind, you have to relate to what's already there. You can't walk away from your existing position in the prospect's mind.

And what's up there in the prospect's mind? The Telegram, of course.

Anytime you mention the word "Western Union," the average mind conjures up the most famous yellow message in the history of the world. And the "gram" part of the Mailgram name only reinforces this perception.

So what's the difference between the new gram and the old gram?

Well, the main difference is price. Both have the same telegraphic format. Both demand immediate attention. But the yellow Telegram message is three times the price of the blue and white Mailgram message.

So the positioning theme developed for Mailgram was simple: "Mailgram: Impact of a Telegram at a fraction of the cost."

At this point, someone said "Wait a minute. Why position Mailgram against the Telegram, also a Western Union service? Why take business away from ourselves?

"Furthermore, the Telegram is a declining business. Why compare a new, modern service like Mailgram with an old service past its prime? The Telegram still has an important role to play, but it is not a growth business."

The logic is impeccable. But as often happens, logic is not necessarily the best strategy for dealing with human minds. Still, the logic was so sound, it was worthwhile rethinking the concept. Especially since there was another positioning strategy that also had merit.

The high-speed letter

Actually the Mailgram name itself suggests a second positioning approach. We could relate the Mailgram to the U.S. mail.

Then, too, if Western Union wanted the Mailgram to take business away from another service, the numbers suggest it would be much better to position the service against regular mail.

In a recent year, 68 billion first-class letters were dropped into the nation's letter boxes. That's 815 first-class letters per household per year.

The Telegram generates only a tiny fraction of that kind of volume.

So a second theme was developed: "Mailgram: A new high-speed service for important messages."

Which is the better approach? In spite of the negatives, positioning theory suggests that the "low-cost Telegram" is a better direction than the "high-speed letter." Yet Mailgram was too important to Western Union to make a decision based on judgment alone. So both campaigns were test-marketed using computer data to track results.

Low cost vs. high speed

The test itself was a massive one. No tiny markets like Peoria were even considered. The six Mailgram test cities were Boston, Chicago, Houston, Los Angeles, Philadelphia, and San Francisco. All big, important communication centers.

Who won? Actually both campaigns were effective. Here are the data for Mailgram volume increases in the test cities during the 13-week program.

High-speed letter cities	plus 73%
Low-cost Telegram cities	plus 100%

These numbers alone were enough to prove the superiority of the "low-cost Telegram" position. But what really decided the issue were the product awareness levels in the test cities, which were measured both before the program ran and afterward.

Here are the figures on how many people could correctly describe what a Mailgram was before the print and broadcast advertising began.

High-speed letter cities	27%
Low-cost Telegram cities	23%

Statistically, not much difference. This indicates that the test market cities were pretty evenly matched. In other words, about one-fourth of the market already knew about the Mailgram service.

After the advertising ran, however, there was a big difference in the two groups of cities. Here are the Mailgram awareness levels 13 weeks later.

High-speed letter cities	25%
Low-cost Telegram cities	47%

As unbelievable as it may seem, awareness in the high-speed letter cities actually declined. From 27 percent to 25 percent. (Not really statistically significant.)

Then where did the increased volume come from in the high-speed letter cities? Obviously from people who knew what a Mailgram was and were reminded to use the service by the advertising.

It was a totally different story in the low-cost Telegram cities. Mailgram awareness more than doubled. From 23 percent to 47 percent.

Not only was this a big jump, but the numbers suggest that Mailgram volume increases were likely to continue over a long period of time.

Western Union also measured Telegram volume in the test cities before, during, and after the advertising. They found that volume held fairly stable. In fact, the company felt that advertising the Mailgram as the low-cost Telegram helped rather than hurt Telegram volume.

And what has happened to Mailgram since the development of this advertising strategy? The volume numbers tell the story.

1972	. . . . 6 million	1977	. . . . 28 million
1973	. . . . 11 million	1978	. . . . 33 million
1974	. . . . 20 million	1979	. . . . 37 million
1975	. . . . 23 million	1980	. . . . 39 million
1976	. . . . 25 million	1981	. . . . 41 million

After 10 years of success, Western Union decided to change the Mailgram strategy. Instead of "impact," the new strategy would emphasize "next-day delivery." So they hired a new advertising agency to develop the new program.

Again, the volume numbers tell the story.

1981	. . . . 41 million
1982	. . . . 37 million
1983	. . . . 30 million
1984	. . . . 22 million

Rarely can you find such a clearcut example of the difference between good advertising strategy and bad. (Most examples are clouded by other factors.) But in the Mailgram case, the minute the strategy was changed, volume declined.

Your problem is not just one of developing a good strategy. Equally important is the courage you will need to keep hammering at the same theme, year after year.

Positioning a Long Island bank

Like Western Union, banks sell a service and not a product. Unlike a Mailgram, however, which is a national service, banking is still a regional service.

In fact, positioning a bank is much like positioning a department store, an appliance store, or any other kind of retail establishment. To successfully position a retail outlet, you must know the territory.

The Long Island banking situation

To understand how we developed a position for the Long Island Trust Company, you should know a little bit about the territory.

For many years Long Island Trust was the leading bank on the Island. It was the largest bank, it had the most branches, and it made the most money.

In the seventies, however, the bank battlefield on Long Island changed dramatically. A new law permitted unrestricted branch banking throughout New York State.

Since then, many of the big New York City banks have become firmly entrenched in the Long Island area. Banks like Citibank, Chase Manhattan, and Chemical Bank.

Also, a good number of Long Island's residents commute to New York City everyday and do part of their banking at these same banks.

However, the intrusion of the big city banks into Long Island Trust's territory was only part of the problem. The territory that really counts is in the mind of the banking prospect. And a little research turned up a lot of bad news.

Mapping the prospect's mind

By now you can appreciate the importance of knowing what's in the prospect's mind. Not only about your product or service, but about competitive offerings as well.

Often the insights are intuitive. Nobody needs a $20,000 research project to know that Western Union is strongly identified with the Telegram. Nor was much research needed to determine the positions of Milk Duds, Belgium, and Xerox.

More often than not, however, it can be exceedingly helpful to map the prospect's mind by means of formal positioning research. Helpful not only in developing a strategy, but in selling the strategy to top management. (The chief executive who has spent 30 years with one company will obviously see that company differently than a prospect whose total exposure over the same 30 years can be measured in minutes or even seconds.)

"Mapping the prospect's mind" is normally done with a research technique called "semantic differential." This was the procedure used to develop a positioning program for the Long Island Trust Company.

In semantic differential research, the prospect is given a set of attributes and then asked to rank each competitor on a scale, generally from 1 to 10.

For example, price might be one of the attributes. In automobiles, it's obvious that Cadillac would be ranked at the high end and Chevette at the low end.

In banking, there is almost no price perception, so other attributes were selected. The ones chosen were these: (1) many branches, (2) full range of services, (3) quality of service, (4) large capital, (5) helps Long Island residents, and (6) helps Long Island economy.

The first four attributes are the traditional reasons for doing business with a particular bank. The last two are unique to the Long Island situation.

As far as the traditional reasons were concerned, the situation was bleak for the Long Island Trust. Prospects rated them last on all four attributes.

Many branches

Chemical	7.3
National Bank of North America	6.7
European American	6.6
Chase Manhattan	6.4
Citibank	6.1
Long Island Trust	5.4

Full range of services

Chemical	7.7
Citibank	7.7
Chase Manhattan	7.6
National Bank of North America	7.4
European American	7.3
Long Island Trust	7.0

Quality of service

Chemical	7.2
Citibank	7.0
National Bank of North America	7.0
Chase Manhattan	6.9
European American	6.8
Long Island Trust	6.7

Large capital

Chemical	8.2
Chase Manhattan	8.2
Citibank	8.1
National Bank of North America	7.8
European American	7.7
Long Island Trust	7.1

The positions were reversed, however, when the attributes concerned Long Island itself.

Here is how the respondents ranked the six banks on the Long Island attributes.

Helps Long Island residents

Long Island Trust	7.5
National Bank of North America	6.6
European American	5.2
Chemical	5.1
Chase Manhattan	4.7
Citibank	4.5

Helps Long Island economy

Long Island Trust	7.3
National Bank of North America	6.7
European American	5.4
Chemical	5.4
Citibank	5.3
Chase Manhattan	4.9

When the attributes concerned Long Island, the Long Island Trust Company went right to the top. A not too surprising result, considering the power of the name.

Developing the strategy

What approach should Long Island Trust take? Conventional wisdom says you accept your strengths and work on improving your weaknesses. In other words, run ads telling the prospects about the great service, friendly tellers, etc.

Conventional wisdom is not positioning thinking. Positioning theory says you must start with what the prospect is already willing to give you.

And the only thing the prospect gave Long Island Trust was the "Long Island position." Accepting this position allowed the bank to repel the invasion of the big city banks. The first ad stated the theme.

Why send your money to the city if you live on the Island?

It makes sense to keep your money close to home. Not at a city bank. But at Long Island Trust. Where it can work for Long Island.

After all, we concentrate on developing Long Island.

Not Manhattan Island. Or some island off Kuwait.

Ask yourself, who do you think is most concerned about Long Island's future?

A bank-come-lately with hundreds of other branches in the greater metropolitan area plus affiliates in five continents?

Or a bank like ours that's been here for over 50 years and has 33 offices on Long Island.

A second ad had a photo of palm trees in front of a building with a Citibank N.A. sign.

To a big city bank, a branch in Nassau isn't necessarily your Nassau.

Chances are it will turn out to be in the Bahamas. It's one of the favorite locations of the big city banks. In fact, the multinational institutions have some $75 billion in loans booked in the Bahamas and Cayman Islands.

Nothing wrong with that. Except it doesn't do much for you if Long Island is your home.

Long Island is not only our favorite location, it's our only location. We have 18 branches in Nassau (County, that is) and 16 in Queens and Suffolk.

And we've been here a long time, over a half century. We're involved financially to the extent that 95 percent of our loans and services go to Long Islanders and their homes, schools, and businesses.

Other ads in the campaign had similar themes:

"The city is a great place to visit, but would you want to bank there?"

"To a city bank, the only island that really counts is Manhattan." (A tiny drawing of Long Island is dwarfed by an enormous drawing of Manhattan.)

"If times get tough, will the city banks get going? (Back to the city.)"

Fifteen months later the same research was repeated. Notice how Long Island Trust's position improved in every attribute.

Many branches

Long Island Trust	7.0
National Bank of North America	6.8
Chemical	6.6
Citibank	6.5
Chase Manhattan	6.1
European American	6.1

From last to first place in "many branches." In spite of the fact that Chemical Bank, for example, has more than twice as many branches on Long Island.

Full range of services

Citibank	7.8
Chemical	7.8
Chase Manhattan	7.6
Long Island Trust	7.3
National Bank of North America	7.3
European American	7.2

In "full range of services" Long Island Trust moved up two spots. From sixth to fourth place.

Quality of service

Citibank	7.8
Chemical	7.6
Chase Manhattan	7.5
Long Island Trust	7.1
National Bank of North America	7.1
European American	7.0

In "quality of service" Long Island Trust also moved from sixth to fourth place.

Large capital

Long Island Trust	7.0
Chemical	6.7
Citibank	6.7
National Bank of North America	6.6
Chase Manhattan	6.6
European American	6.4

In "large capital" Long Island Trust moved from last to first place.

Results were seen not only in the research but in the branches too. "With the assistance of the advertising agency which pioneered the widely accepted concept of positioning," said the bank's annual report, "our lead bank, Long Island Trust, assumed the mantle of the Long Island Bank for Long Islanders. Acceptance of the campaign was immediate and gratifying."

You might think that a bank promoting the area that it serves is an obvious idea. And it is.

But the best positioning ideas are so simple and obvious that most people overlook them.

Positioning a New Jersey bank

The bank is United Jersey with 116 branches in the state of New Jersey.

United Jersey is not in the same situation as Long Island Trust. (There is no one positioning approach that will work everywhere.) There are many differences between the two banks, the most important being that unlike Long Island Trust, United Jersey is not the biggest local bank in its marketing territory. (That distinction belongs to First Fidelity with Midlantic in second place and United Jersey in third.)

Finding a viable banking position

One thing that United Jersey has in common with Long Island Trust is its marketing environment. Both operate in the shadows of Citibank, Chase Manhattan, Chemical, Manufacturers Hanover, and the other big New York City banks. That's at the north end of the territory.

In the south, United Jersey operates in the shadows of the big Philadelphia banks (Mellon, First Pennsylvania).

The problem of finding a viable banking position is complicated by the fact that the services offered by United Jersey are similar to those of its competitors. Federal and state regulations see to that.

The only approach that will work is the Tylenol approach. You don't find the answer to the problem of positioning the bank by studying the bank. You find it by studying the competition, as Tylenol did by studying the problems of aspirin.

At one end of the scale, United Jersey competes in the marketing jungle known as metropolitan New York City.

And it really is a banking jungle. In Manhattan alone, there are 389 banks. Not to mention Brooklyn, Queens, the Bronx, Staten Island, and the entire state of New Jersey.

The King and Queen of the jungle are Citibank and Chase Manhattan. These are big banks. In Manhattan alone Citibank has 74 branches.

How do you find weakness in Citibank, which has almost as many vice presidents as United Jersey has employees?

The disadvantage of large size

The problem of finding a meaningful advantage for United Jersey can be approached by looking at the disadvantages of its big-city competitors.

Why position United Jersey against the big banks? Why not take on the score of small financial institutions? The reason to go against the big banks is because they are the ones in the minds of the prospects. Positioning is always a question of dealing with what's in the mind.

The disadvantage of large size is slow service. As an Avis ad once said, "Rent from us. The line at our counter is shorter." Banks shouldn't hold up people, either. We developed a positioning strategy for United Jersey called the "fast-moving bank." This strategy had two key aspects.

A. Exploit the only real weakness of the big metropolitan New York banks: their slow reaction time.

B. Encourage United Jersey management to make sure the bank's performance matches the advertising's promise. That took the form of seven key commitments.

1. **Decentralized decisions.** United Jersey pushed decision making down to the local level. (One of their lending teams can approve a $10 million loan, and that team meets daily.) In 10 commercial banking centers throughout the state, other officers on site can make business loans quickly.

2. **Cross training.** United Jersey trains its people in all their banking services, not just in one specialty. So when a customer has a question, he or she doesn't have to wait for an answer while the question is referred to another person.

3. **Commitment to electronics.** United Jersey's system of statewide ATMs (Automatic Teller Machines) is the largest private network in the state. United Jersey's corporate customers can be on line directly with the bank's computers for balance inquiries and other daily questions.

4. **Speedy lock box service.** United Jersey people pick up checks six times a day during the workweek, four times on the weekend. Its Newark lock box has its own private ZIP Code. United Jersey empties lock boxes and fills up customer accounts as fast as it can.

5. **FACT terminals.** (Fast Authorization of Cashless Transactions.) With these terminals now in place, merchants enjoy the benefit of rapid electronic approvals. And faster approvals with minimized risk mean improved cash flow.

6. **Responsiveness.** Whether it's being first with a new product or matching the competition's rates, United Jersey is committed to being responsive to the customer's financial needs.

7. **Central location.** United Jersey built its new corporate headquarters in Princeton. From the geographic center of the state, United Jersey is less than an hour away from any of its business customers by car, even less by helicopter.

Advertising the fast-moving bank

When the bank's performance matched the promises the advertising was going to make, the advertising started to make the promises. Focusing on the weakness of the competition, naturally.

Each television spot contrasted United Jersey bankers with their counterparts at the whimsically named "Lethargic National Bank." In one spot, approval for a business loan at Lethargic National seemed to take forever. A second spot showed a Lethargic banker disappearing when a customer needed a quick answer to his questions. And in the third spot, a husband and wife found the bankers at Lethargic moving in slow motion on a simple installment loan.

The humorous vignettes drove home the point that United Jersey "values your time as much as your money."

Print advertisements also carried the "fast-moving bank" theme. "Haste makes money" and "Banks shouldn't hold up people," were two typical headlines.

"Time Is Money" desk signs were given to all United Jersey bank officers, a not-so-subtle reminder not to keep the customer sitting next to their desk waiting.

Did it work?

By all measurements the fast-moving bank strategy was a big success for United Jersey. Unaided awareness, for example, almost tripled in just over a year.

Business and profits went up. A year after the program started, United Jersey announced earnings were up $30 million, an increase of 26 percent over the previous year.

An even more important barometer of change was the attitude of employees. One United Jersey officer reported, "The image advertising is great, but the best thing I've seen happen is that our people, line officers, etc., are striving to live up to Fast Moving . . . and they are! I've seen a tremendous change in attitude since the campaign began. Approvals come faster. People don't sit on things."

The essence of a good positioning strategy is that it transcends every aspect of a company. You know you have a winner when you run it up the corporate flagpole and everybody salutes.

Positioning a ski resort: Stowe

There are over a thousand "name" ski areas in America. Since the mind of the average skier can hold only a fraction of those names, the problem of positioning a ski resort can be difficult.

If your name is Stowe, the problem is greatly simplified. Stowe is already well known. "Stowe is for me the essential Eastern ski village," said *Advertising Age* columnist James Brady, "the way Aspen is out west or Val d'Isere is in France or Kitzbühel is in Austria."

Why a position for Stowe?

With that kind of reputation, why does Stowe need a position? Isn't it enough to advertise Stowe and let the skier conjure up the Stowe image?

To a certain extent, this is true. The reputation of a product like Steinway or a place like Stowe creates word of mouth which carries the reputation along from year to year. But proper positioning can enhance the word of mouth and contribute to the process. In essence, the positioning supplies the material to talk about.

What do skiers talk about? James Brady put it best. They talk about places to ski, places like Aspen, Val d'Isere, and Kitzbühel.

With this background in mind, the search began for a position for Stowe. The situation seemed to call for the outside expert, the person who could supply the credibility to bring a comparison claim to life.

The top 10 ski resorts in the world

The noted ski and travel writer, Abby Rand, supplied the credibility. Writing in *Harper's Bazaar,* she selected the top 10 ski resorts in the world. One was Stowe, Vermont. The others were: Aspen, Colorado; Courchevel, France; Jackson Hole, Wyoming; Kitzbühel, Austria; Portillo, Chile; St. Christoph, Austria; St. Moritz, Switzerland; Sun Valley, Idaho; and Vail, Colorado. (Not a bad list.)

The positioning advertisements for Stowe used shoulder patches to illustrate the ski areas. "Of the world's top 10 ski resorts," said the ad, "only one is in the East."

"You don't have to go to the Alps or the Andes or even to the Rockies to experience the ski vacation of a lifetime," continued the ad. "You need only head for the Ski Capital of the East: Stowe, Vermont."

Skiers responded to the new Stowe strategy. They requested thousands of brochures in response to the advertising. They also broke all attendance records at the ski resort.

You might think it would be easy to increase business at a place like Stowe, but competition has one major advantage. Places like Stratton, Sugarbush, Big Bromley, and Mt. Snow are all located south of Stowe. So the skier driving from the major population center (New York City) has to drive an hour or two longer to get to Stowe. One of the functions of the advertising is to promise the skier a reward for the longer drive.

"One of the top 10 ski resorts in the world" is a classic positioning strategy. It takes advantage of the mind's tendency to "make a list" when trying to cope with complexity. "The seven wonders of the world" is one of the earliest examples of this approach.

Furthermore, the "top 10" strategy can conceivably be used indefinitely. There's no reason to change. What better strategy can there be than having your place or product included in a list of the world's best?

When you use a recognized authority to give your product or service credibility, you are tapping a fundamental aspect of human nature. There's security in not having to trust your own judgment.

The dark side of this tendency to defer to authority was explored by Allen Funt, creator of *Candid Camera*. "The worst thing, and I see it over and over," said Mr. Funt, "is how easily people can be led by one kind of authority or even the most minimal signs of authority."

"We put up a sign on the road, *Delaware Closed Today*," reported Mr. Funt. "Motorists didn't question it. Instead they asked, 'Is Jersey open?'"

22 Positioning the Catholic Church

This book could have been written about religion just as well as about advertising.

A farfetched idea?

Not really. The essence of any religion is communication. From divinity to clergy to congregation.

The problems arise not with a perfect divinity or an imperfect congregation but with the clergy.

How the clergy applies communication theory to the practice of religion will have a major influence on the way religion affects the congregation.

An identity crisis

Some years ago, positioning thinking was applied to the Catholic Church. In other words, communication problems of this enormous institution were treated as if they belonged to a major corporation.

This request did not come from the Pope or a committee of bishops. It came from a group of laity who were deeply concerned about what one renowned theologian dubbed a "certain crisis of identity" that had followed in the wake of the reforms of Vatican II.

It was quickly apparent that communication in the Catholic Church was haphazard at best.

While much effort had been expended in improving techniques, the programs lacked a strong central theme or any continuity. (An especially serious problem in an era of electronic overcommunication.)

It was like General Motors with no overall corporate advertising programs. All communication came from the local dealers. Some of it good, much of it bad.

A large measure of the problems could be traced to Vatican II.

Prior to that "opening of the windows," the institutional Church had a clearly perceived position in the minds of the faithful. To most, the Church was the teacher of the law. Much emphasis was placed on rules, rewards, and punishment. The Church was consistent in its approach to old and young alike.

Vatican II moved the Catholic Church away from this posture of law and order. Many rules and regulations were dismissed as unnecessary. Changes in liturgy and style became commonplace. Flexibility took the place of rigidity.

Unfortunately, there was no advertising manager in Rome when these momentous changes were being made. No one to distill what had transpired and produce a program in simple language that explained the new directions.

After years of not needing a "corporate" communication program, it's understandable that the Catholic Church failed to recognize the scope of the problem on its hands.

Losing its influence

What was painfully lacking was a clear presentation of what the new church was about.

The faithful quietly asked, "If you are not the teacher of the law, what are you?"

In the years since Vatican II, there has been no simple answer forthcoming. No attempt to reposition the church in the minds of the laity. Even in the minds of the clergy, for that matter.

And with no answers, confusion walked in and many people walked out.

For the first time, regular Mass attendance dropped below 50 percent of the Catholic population. This amounts to a 20 percent drop, while Protestant attendance has remained remarkably stable.

There are 20 percent fewer priests, nuns, and brothers today than there were 10 years ago. Vocations have dropped by 60 percent.

One final set of statistics is especially significant. The Catholic Church is presently the "largest community of moral authority in American society." (A title bestowed upon it by the Protestant theologian Peter Berger.)

Yet when a group of 24,000 highly influential executives were asked by *U.S. News & World Report* to rate the influence of major institutions, the Church and other organized religions came in dead last.

The moral authority of the Catholic Church was obviously not being communicated very well.

What role for the Church?

"What is the role of the Catholic Church in the modern world?"

This question was asked of clergy, bishops, laity. Never was the same answer received twice.

Some say there is no simple answer. Some say there's more than one answer. (Recognize the everybody trap.)

Corporate executives usually have answers to questions like this. If you ask the top executives at General Motors, they will more than likely see their role as being the world's largest manufacturer of automobiles. Companies spend millions finding and communicating the essence of their products with words like "Whiter than white" or "Fighting cavities is what Crest is all about."

The Church had to answer this unanswered question in simple, definitive terms. And it had to put this answer into a totally integrated communication program. Then it had to take this program to the flock in a new and dramatic way.

Working out an identity program for a corporation usually entails a retracing of steps until you discover the basic business of a company. This requires poring over old plans and programs. Seeing what worked and what didn't.

In the case of the Catholic Church, you have to go back 2000 years and retrace the steps of the Church. Instead of old annual reports, you have to rely on Scripture.

In the search for a simple, direct expression of the role of the Church, two explicit statements in the Gospel could hold the answer.

First, during Christ's ministry on earth, God, as reported in Matthew's Gospel, instructed man to listen to the words of his Son, the Beloved (Matt. 17:23).

Then Christ, as he departed from earth, instructed his followers to go and teach all nations what they had heard from him (Matt. 28:19).

Teacher of the word

It's apparent from the Scriptures that Christ saw the role of the Church as "teacher of the word."

Because he was "the Son of God," it must be assumed that his word is a word for all ages. Christ's parables were not just for the people of his time, but also for now.

Hence they must have in their construction a universality which would never become dated. They are simple and deep. In them Jesus gives to people of all ages food for thought and action.

So it can be assumed that those who proclaim the message today can and should transmit the old message in a new form in their own locality, in their own time, in their own way.

Thus the retracing of steps led to defining the role of the Church as that of keeping Christ alive in the minds of each new generation and relating his word to the problems of their time.

In many ways Vatican II seemed to point the Church backward rather than forward. From "teacher of the law" to "teacher of the word."

This may seem like a very simplistic, almost obvious answer to a complicated problem.

And it is. Experience has shown that a positioning exercise is a search for the obvious. Those are the easiest concepts to communicate because they make the most sense to the recipient of a message.

Unfortunately, obvious concepts are also the most difficult to recognize and to sell.

The human mind tends to admire the complicated and dismiss the obvious as being too simplistic. (For example, many clerics in the Catholic Church admire the definition of the role of the Church put forth by a noted theologian named Avery Dulles. His answer: The Church hasn't one role. It has six different roles to play.)

Implementing the position

Once the obvious concept had been isolated, the next thing to be done was to develop the techniques for implementing it.

First and foremost was pulpit training. To fulfill the role of "teacher of the word," the clergy had to become far better speakers and to give far better sermons. (Your best religious speakers today can be found not in church but on Sunday morning television.)

In addition to pulpit training, an introductory film entitled *Return to the Beginning* was proposed.

The start of any major communication effort often needs some drama to get people's attention. The emotion of the film medium is ideal for this kind of effort. (Which is also why television is so powerful a tool for new product introductions.)

A wide range of other program elements was suggested, all carefully constructed around the role of the church as "teacher of the word."

The point here is that once a positioning strategy has been developed, it sets the direction for all the activities of the organization. Even one as large and multifaceted as the Catholic Church.

What happened?

Nothing.

It has been very difficult to convince the management of the Catholic Church to implement this solution to their problems.

Not only do bishops resist having lay people tell them how to run their Church, but the solution appears to be much too obvious for them to accept. Simplicity is not as attractive as complexity.

And as with most big problems, they don't go away. If you've been reading the newspapers, you've probably noted that the Pope is in the process of convening another synod to evaluate the results of Vatican II. The Vatican newspaper *L'Osservatore Romano* said that the synod's purpose was to resolve confusion that has arisen over Vatican II in the 20 years since it ended.

Will they at long last acknowledge the confusion problems? Will they solve their "crisis of identity" and come up with a communications program that repositions the Church in the modern world? Will this program reconcile the widening gulf between liberal and conservative Catholics?

Don't hold your breath.

23

Positioning yourself and your career

If positioning strategies can be used to promote a product, why can't they be used to promote yourself?

No reason at all.

So let's review positioning theory as it might apply to your own personal career.

Define yourself

What are you? People suffer from the same disease as products. They try to be all things to all people.

The problem with this approach is the mind of the prospect. It's difficult enough to link one concept with each product. It's almost impossible with two or three or more concepts.

The most difficult part of positioning is selecting that one specific concept to hang your hat on. Yet you must, if you want to cut through the prospect's wall of indifference.

What are you? What is your own position in life? Can you sum up your own position in a single concept? Then can you run your own career to establish and exploit that position?

Most people aren't ruthless enough to set up a single concept for themselves. They vacillate. They expect others to do it for them.

"I'm the best lawyer in Dallas."

Are you? How often would your name be mentioned if we took a survey of the Dallas legal community?

"I'm the best lawyer in Dallas" is a position that can be achieved with some talent, some luck, and a lot of strategy. And the first step is to isolate the concept that you are going to use to establish that long-term position. It's not easy. But the rewards can be great.

Make mistakes

Anything worthwhile doing is worthwhile doing lousy. If it wasn't worthwhile doing, you shouldn't have done it at all.

On the other hand, if it is worthwhile doing and you wait until you can do it perfectly, if you procrastinate, you run the risk of not doing it. Ever.

Therefore, anything worthwhile doing is worthwhile doing lousy.

Your reputation will probably be better within the company if you try many times and succeed sometimes than if you fear failure and only try for sure things.

People still remember Ty Cobb, who stole 96 bases out of 134 tries (70 percent). But they have forgotton Max Carey, who stole 51 bases out of 53 (96 percent).

Eddie Arcaro, perhaps the greatest jockey who ever rode a horse, had 250 straight losers before he rode his first winner.

Make sure your name is right

Remember Leonard Slye? Few people did, until he changed his name to Roy Rogers, an important first step in becoming a motion picture star.

How about Marion Morrison? A little feminine for a he-man cowboy, so he changed it to John Wayne.

Or Issur Danielovitch? First changed to Isadore Demsky and then to Kirk Douglas.

"Fate tried to conceal him," said Oliver Wendell Holmes, Jr., "by naming him Smith."

Common law grants you the right to adopt any name you want as long as you're not trying to defraud or be deceptive. So don't change your name to McDonald and open up a hamburger stand.

Also, if you're a politician, don't bother to change your name to "None of the Above." Luther D. Knox, a candidate in a Louisiana gubernatorial primary, had his name legally changed to just that. However, a federal judge had Mr. None of the Above's name taken off the ballot because the move was deceptive.

Avoid the no-name trap

Many business people fall victim to initialitus personally as well as corporately.

As young executives, they notice that top managers usually use initials: J. S. Smith, R. H. Jones. So they do the same. On memos and in letters.

It's a mistake. You can afford to do that only if everyone knows who you are. If you're on your way up, if you're trying to burn your name into the minds of top management, you need a name, not a set of initials. For exactly the same reasons your company does.

Write your name and look at it. Roger P. Dinkelacker.

What a name like this says psychologically to management is: We are such a big company and you have such an insignificant job that you must use the "P" to differentiate yourself from the other Roger Dinkelackers on the staff.

Not likely.

It is possible, if your name is something like John Smith or Mary Jones, that you actually do need a middle initial to differentiate yourself from the other John Smiths or Mary Joneses.

If so, what you really need is a new name. Confusion is the enemy of successful positioning. You can't "burn in" a name that's too common. How are other people going to differentiate between John T. Smith and John S. Smith?

They won't bother. They'll just forget you along with the rest. And the no-name trap will have claimed another victim.

Avoid the line-extension trap

If you had three daughters, would you name them Mary 1, Mary 2, and Mary 3? As a matter of fact, would you name them Mary, Marian, and Marilyn? Either way, you're creating a lifetime of confusion.

When you hang a junior on your son's name, you do him no favor. He deserves a separate identity.

In show business, where you must burn a clearcut identity in the mind of the public, even a famous last name should probably not be used.

Today Liza Minnelli is a bigger star than her mother, Judy Garland, ever was. As Liza Garland, she would have started with a handicap.

Frank Sinatra, Jr., is an example of the most difficult kind of line-extension name. He literally started with two strikes against him.

With a name like Frank Sinatra, Jr., the audience says to itself, "He's not going to be able to sing as well as his father."

Since you hear what you expect to hear, of course he doesn't.

Find a horse to ride

Some ambitious, intelligent people find themselves trapped in situations where their future looks bleak. So what do they generally do?

They try harder. They try to compensate by long hours of hard work and effort. The secret of success is to keep your nose to the grindstone, do your job better than the next person, and fame and fortune will come your way, right?

Wrong. Trying harder is rarely the pathway to success. Trying smarter is the better way.

It's the story of the shoemaker's children all over again. Too often, management people don't know how to manage their own careers.

Their own promotional strategy is often based on the naive assumption that ability and hard work are all that counts. And so they dig in and work harder, waiting for the day that someone will tap them on the shoulder with the magic wand.

But that day seldom comes.

The truth is, the road to fame and fortune is rarely found within yourself. The only sure way to success is to find yourself a horse to ride. It may be difficult for the ego to accept, but success in life is based more on what others can do for you than on what you can do for yourself.

Kennedy was wrong. Ask not what you can do for your company. Ask what your company can do for you. Therefore, if you want to take maximum advantage of the opportunities that your career has to offer, you must keep your eyes open and find yourself a horse to do the job for you.

The first horse to ride is your company.   Where is your company going? Or more impolitely, is it going anywhere at all?

Too many good people have taken their good prospects and locked them into situations that are doomed to failure. But failure at least gives you a second chance. Even worse is the company with less than average chances for growth.

No matter how brilliant you are, it never pays to cast your lot with a loser. Even the best officer on the Titanic wound up in the same lifeboat as the worst. And that's if he was lucky enough to stay out of the water.

You can't do it yourself. If your company is going nowhere, get yourself a new one. While you can't always pick an IBM or a Xerox, you ought to be able to do considerably better than average.

Place your bets on the growth industries. Tomorrow-type products like computers, electronics, optics, communications.

And don't forget that soft services of all types are growing at a much faster rate than hard products. So look at banks, leasing, insurance, medical, financial, and consulting service companies.

Don't forget that your experience with yesterday-type products can blind you to opportunities in totally different product areas. And especially services.

And when you change jobs to join one of those tomorrow-type companies, don't just ask how much they are going to pay you today.

Also ask how much they are likely to pay you tomorrow.

The second horse to ride is your boss.   Ask yourself the same questions about your boss as you asked yourself about your company.

Is he or she going anywhere? If not, who is? Always try to work for the smartest, brightest, most competent person you can find.

If you look at biographies of successful people, it's amazing to find how many crawled up the ladder of success right behind someone else. From their first assignment in some menial job to their last as president or CEO of a major company.

Yet some people actually like to work for incompetents. I suppose they feel that a fresh flower stands out better if it's surrounded by wilted ones. They forget the tendency of top management to throw the whole bunch out if they become dissatisfied with an operation.

Two types of individuals come in looking for jobs.

One is inordinately proud of his or her specialty. He or she will often say, "You people really need me around here. You're weak in my specialty."

The other type says just the opposite. "You're strong in my specialty. You do a terrific job, and I want to work with the best."

Which type is more likely to get the job? Right. The latter person.

On the other hand, strange as it might seem, top management people see more of the other type. The person who wants to be an expert. Preferably with a big title and salary to match.

"Hitch your wagon to a star," said Ralph Waldo Emerson. Good advice then. Even better advice now.

If your boss is going places, chances are good that you are too.

The third horse to ride is a friend. Many business people have an enormous number of personal friends but no business friends. And while personal friends are awfully nice to have and can sometimes get you a deal on a TV set or braces for the kids, they're usually not too helpful when it comes to finding a better job.

Most of the big breaks that happen in a person's career happen because a business friend recommended that person.

The more business friends you make outside of your own organization, the more likely you are to wind up in a big, rewarding job.

It's not enough just to make friends. You have to take out that friendship horse and exercise it once in a while. If you don't you won't be able to ride it when you need it.

When an old business friend you haven't heard from in 10 years calls you and wants to have lunch, you know two things will happen: (1) you're going to pay for the lunch, and (2) your friend is looking for a job.

When you need a job, it's usually too late to try that type of tactic. The way to ride the friendship horse is to keep in touch regularly with all your business friends.

Send them tear sheets of articles they may be interested in, clips of publicity items, and congratulatory letters when they get promoted.

And don't assume people always see stories that might have mentioned them. They don't. And they always appreciate it when someone sends them an item they may have missed.

The fourth horse to ride is an idea. On the night before he died, Victor Hugo wrote in his diary, "Nothing, not all the armies of the world, can stop an idea whose time has come."

Everyone knows that an idea can take you to the top faster than anything else. But people sometimes expect too much of an idea. They want one that is not only great, but one that everyone else thinks is great too.

There are no such ideas. If you wait until an idea is ready to be accepted, it's too late. Someone else will have preempted it.

Or in the in-out vocabulary of a few years ago: Anything definitely in is already on its way out.

To ride the "idea" horse, you must be willing to expose yourself to ridicule and controversy. You must be willing to go against the tide.

You can't be first with a new idea or concept unless you are willing to stick your neck out. And take a lot of abuse. And bide your time until your time comes.

"One indication of the validity of a principle," according to psychologist Charles Osgood, "is the vigor and persistence with which it is opposed." "In any field," says Dr. Osgood, "if people see that a principle is obvious nonsense and easy to refute, they tend to ignore it. On the other hand, if the principle is difficult to refute and it causes them to question some of their own basic assumptions with which their names may be identified, they have to go out of their way to find something wrong with it."

Never be afraid of conflict.

Where would Winston Churchill have been without Adolf Hitler? We know the answer to that one. After Adolf Hitler was disposed of, at the very first opportunity the British public promptly turned Winston Churchill out of office.

And you remember what Liberace said about the bad reviews one of his concerts received. "I cried all the way to the bank."

An idea or concept without an element of conflict is not an idea at all. It's motherhood, apple pie, and the flag, revisited.

The fifth horse to ride is faith.   Faith in others and their ideas. The importance of getting outside of yourself, of finding your fortune on the outside, is illustrated by the story of a man who was a failure most of his life.

His name was Ray Kroc, and he was a lot older than most

people and a failure to boot when he met two brothers who changed his life.

For the brothers had an idea, but no faith. So they sold their idea as well as their name to Ray Kroc for relatively few dollars.

Ray Kroc became one of the richest people in America. Worth hundreds of millions of dollars.

The brothers? They were the McDonald brothers, and every time you eat one of their hamburgers, remember it was the vision, courage, and persistence of the outsider who made the McDonald's chain a success. Not two guys named McDonald.

The sixth horse to ride is yourself.   There is one other horse. An animal that is mean, difficult, and unpredictable. Yet people often try to ride it. With very little success.

That horse is yourself. It is possible to succeed in business or in life all by yourself. But it's not easy.

Like life itself, business is a social activity. As much cooperation as competition.

Take selling, for example, You don't make a sale all by yourself. Somebody also has to buy what you're selling.

So remember, the winningest jockeys are not necessarily the lightest, the smartest, or the strongest. The best jockey doesn't win the race.

The jockey that wins the race is usually the one with the best horse.

So pick yourself a horse to ride and then ride it for all it's worth.

Positioning
your business

How do you get started on a positioning program?

It's not easy. The temptation is to work on the solution without first thinking through the problem. Much better to think about your situation in an organized way before leaping to a conclusion.

To help you with this thinking process, here are six questions you can ask yourself to get your mental juices flowing.

Don't be deceived. The questions are simple to ask but difficult to answer. They often raise soul-searching issues that can test your courage and your beliefs.

1. What position do you own?

Positioning is thinking in reverse. Instead of starting with yourself, you start with the mind of the prospect.

Instead of asking what you are, you ask what position you already own in the mind of the prospect.

Changing minds in our overcommunicated society is an extremely difficult task. It's much easier to work with what's already there.

In determining the state of the prospect's mind, it's important not to let corporate egos get in the way. You get the answer to the question "What position do we own?" from the market-place, not from the marketing manager.

If this requires a few dollars for research, so be it. Spend the money. It's better to know exactly what you're up against now than to discover it later when nothing can be done about it.

Don't be narrow-minded. You must look at the big picture, not the details.

Sabena's problem is not Sabena, the airline, but Belgium, the country.

Seven-Up's problem is not the prospect's attitude toward lemon/lime drinks, but the overwhelming share of mind occupied by the colas. "Get me a soda," to many people, means a Coke or a Pepsi.

Looking at the big picture helped Seven-Up develop its successful uncola program.

Most products today are like 7-Up before the uncola campaign. They have weak or nonexistent positions in the minds of most prospects.

What you must do is to find a way into the mind by hooking your product, service, or concept to what's already there.

2. What position do you want to own?

Here is where you bring out your crystal ball and try to figure out the best position to own from a long-term point of view. "Own" is the key word. Too many programs set out to communicate a position that is impossible to preempt because someone else already owns it.

Ford failed to position the Edsel successfully. One reason was there simply was no room in the mind of the auto buyer for another heavily chromed, medium-priced car.

On the other hand, when Richardson Merrill was trying to position an entry in the cold-remedy field against Contac and Dristan, it wisely avoided a direct confrontation. Leaving these two to fight it out in the daylight hours, Richardson Merrill chose to preempt the "nightmare cold remedy" position for Nyquil.

Nyquil turned out to be the most successful new product they have introduced in recent years.

Sometimes you can want too much. You can want to own a position that's too broad. A position that can't be established in the prospect's mind. And even if it could, it couldn't be defended against the assaults of narrowly based products like Nyquil.

This, of course, is the everybody trap, and one example is a famous campaign for a beer called Rheingold. This brewery wanted to preempt New York City's working class. (Not a bad objective when you consider the large number of heavy beer drinkers in this group.)

So they produced some marvelous commercials featuring Italians drinking Rheingold, Blacks drinking Rheingold, Irish drinking Rheingold, Jews drinking Rheingold, and so on.

Well, rather than appeal to everybody, they ended up appealing to nobody. The reason was simple. Prejudice being a basic human commodity, the fact that one ethnic group drank Rheingold sure didn't impress another ethnic group.

In fact, all the campaign did was alienate every ethnic group in New York.

In your own career, it's easy to make the same mistake. If you try to be all things to all people, you wind up with nothing. Better to narrow the focus of your expertise. To establish a unique position as a specialist, not as a jack-of-all-trades generalist.

The job market today belongs to the people who can define and position themselves as specialists.

3. Whom must you outgun?

If your proposed position calls for a head-to-head approach against a marketing leader, forget it. It's better to go around an obstacle rather than over it. Back up. Try to select a position that no one else has a firm grip on.

You must spend as much time thinking about the situation from the point of view of your competitors as you do thinking about it from your own.

Prospects don't buy, they choose. Among brands of automobiles. Among brands of beer. Among brands of computers. The merit, or lack of merit, of your brand is not nearly as important as your position among the possible choices.

Often to create a viable position, you must reposition another brand or even an entire category of product. As Tylenol did to aspirin, for example.

Notice what happens when you fail to deal with the competition. Bristol-Myers spent $35 million to launch Nuprin, and American Home Products spent $40 million to launch Advil. Both products contain ibuprofen, an analgesic new to America.

But both campaigns failed to reposition Tylenol, the dominant headache remedy on the market. As a result, neither product has been able to carve out more than a tiny market share.

Coming to grips with the competition is the main problem in most marketing situations.

4. Do you have enough money?

A big obstacle to successful positioning is attempting to achieve the impossible. It takes money to build a share of mind. It takes money to establish a position. It takes money to hold a position once you've established it.

The noise level today is fierce. There are just too many me-too products and too many me-too companies vying for the mind of the prospect. Getting noticed is getting tougher.

During the course of a single year, the average human mind is exposed to some 200,000 advertising messages. When you remember that a 30-second $500,000 Super Bowl commercial can make only one of those 200,000 impressions, the odds against an advertiser today must be seen as enormous.

This is why a company like Procter & Gamble is such a formidable competitor. When it bets on a new product, it will slide

$50 million on the table, look around at the competition, and say, "Your bet."

If you don't spend enough to get above the noise level, you allow the Procter & Gambles of this world to take your concept away from you. One way to cope with the noise-level problem is to reduce the geographic scope of your problem. To introduce new products or new ideas on a market-by-market basis rather than nationally or even internationally.

With a given number of dollars, it's better to overspend in one city than to underspend in several cities. If you become successful in one location, you can always roll out the program to other places. Provided the first location is appropriate.

If you can become the No. 1 scotch in New York (the No. 1 scotch-drinking area of the country), you can roll out the product to the rest of the U.S.A.

5. Can you stick it out?

You can think of our overcommunicated society as a constant crucible of change. As one idea replaces another in bewildering succession.

To cope with change, it's important to take a long-range point of view. To determine your basic position and then stick to it.

Positioning is a concept that is cumulative. Something that takes advantage of advertising's long-range nature.

You have to hang in there, year after year. Most successful companies rarely change a winning formula. How many years have you seen those Marlboro men riding into the sunset? Crest has been fighting cavities for so long they're into their second generation of kids. Because of change, a company must think even more strategically than it did before.

With rare exceptions, a company should almost never change its basic positioning strategy. Only its tactics, those short-term maneuvers that are intended to implement a long-term strategy.

The trick is to take that basic strategy and improve it. Find new ways to dramatize it. New ways to avoid the boredom factor. In other words, new ways to have Ronald McDonald end up eating a hamburger.

Owning a position in the mind is like owning a valuable piece of real estate. Once you give it up, you might find it's impossible to get it back again.

The line-extension trap is a good example. What you are really doing when you line-extend is weakening your basic position. And once that's gone, you are adrift without an anchor.

Levi's line-extended into casual clothes. And then found its basic position in jeans undermined by "designer label" jeans.

6. Do you match your position?

Creative people often resist positioning thinking because they believe it restricts their creativity.

And you know what? It does. Positioning thinking does restrict creativity.

One of the great communication tragedies is to watch an organization go through a careful planning exercise, step by step, complete with charts and graphs and then turn the strategy over to the "creatives" for execution. They, in turn, apply their skills and the strategy disappears in a cloud of technique, never to be recognized again.

An institution like this would have been much better off running the flip-chart with the strategy on it rather than the ad with thousands of dollars worth of creativity applied.

"Avis is only No. 2 in rent-a-cars, so why go with us? We try harder." This doesn't sound like an ad. It sounds like the presentation of the marketing strategy. In truth, it's both.

Do your advertisements for yourself match your position? Do your clothes, for example, tell the world that you're a banker or a lawyer or an artist?

Or do you wear creative clothes that undermine your position?

Creativity by itself is worthless. Only when it is subordinated to the positioning objective can creativity make a contribution.

The role of the outsider

The question sometimes arises: Do we do it ourselves or do we hire someone to position us?

The someone that often gets hired is an advertising agency. An ad agency? Who needs help from those Madison Avenue hucksters?

Everybody. But only the rich can afford to hire an advertising agency. All the others have to learn how to do it themselves. Have to learn how to apply the invaluable ingredient only available from the outsider.

And what does the outsider supply? An ingredient called ignorance. In other words, objectivity.

By not knowing what goes on inside a company, the outsider is better able to see what is happening on the outside. In the mind of the prospect.

The outsider is naturally attuned to outside-in thinking, while the insider is more comfortable with inside-out thinking.

Objectivity is the key ingredient supplied by the advertising or marketing communication or public relations agency.

What the outsider doesn't supply

In a word, magic. Some business managers believe that the role of an advertising agency is to wave a magic wand which causes prospects to immediately rush out and buy the product.

The wand, of course, is called "creativity," a commodity much sought after by the neophyte advertiser.

The popular view is that the agency "creates." And that the best agencies are filled with a substance called "creativity" which they liberally apply to their advertising solutions.

In advertising circles, the story is told about an advertising agency that was very creative. So creative, in fact, it could take straw and spin it into gold.

Now you might have heard of them because they had a very creative name. Rumplestiltskin, Inc.

The legend lives on. Even today, some people think agencies are so creative that they can spin straw into gold.

Not true. Advertising agencies can't spin straw into gold. If they could, they'd be in the straw-spinning business and not the advertising business.

Today, creativity is dead. The name of the game on Madison Avenue is positioning.

25 Playing the positioning game

Some people have trouble playing the positioning game because they are hung up on words.

They assume, incorrectly, that words have meanings. They let Mr. Webster rule their life.

You must understand the role of words

As general semanticists have been saying for decades, words don't contain meanings. The meanings are not in the words. They are in the people using the words.

Like a sugar bowl which is empty until someone fills it with sugar, a word has no meaning until someone uses it and fills it with meaning.

If you try to add sugar to a leaky sugar bowl, you won't get anywhere. So, too, if you try to add meaning to a leaky word. Much better to discard that leaky word and use another.

The word "Volkswagen" won't hold the concept of a medium-sized luxury car, so you discard that sugar bowl and use another, "Audi," which holds the concept better. You don't insist that because it's made in a Volkswagen factory, it must be a Volkswagen. Mental rigidity is a barrier to successful positioning.

(While Volkswagen faltered in the American market, Audi boomed. Currently Audi outsells BMW and is breathing down the neck of Mercedes-Benz.)

To be successful today at positioning, you must have a large degree of mental flexibility. You must be able to select and use words with as much disdain for the history book as for the dictionary.

Not that conventional, accepted meanings are not important. Quite the contrary. You must select the words which trigger the meanings you want to establish.

But is this ethical? Remember, words have no meaning. They are empty containers until you fill them with meaning. If you want to reposition a product, a person, or a country, you often have to first change the container.

In a sense, every product or service is "packaged goods." If it isn't sold in a box, the name becomes the box.

You must know how words affect people

Words are triggers. They trigger the meanings which are buried in the mind.

Of course, if people understood this, there would be no advantage in renaming a product or selecting emotional words like Mustang for an automobile.

But they don't. Most people are "unsane." They're not completely sane and they're not completely insane. They're somewhere in between.

What's the difference between sane people and insane people? What exactly do insane people do? Alfred Korzybski, who developed the concept of general semantics, explains that insane people try to make the world of reality fit what is in their heads.

The insane person who thinks he is Napoleon makes the outside world fit that notion.

The sane person constantly analyzes the world of reality and then changes what's inside his or her head to fit the facts.

That's an awful lot of trouble for most people. Besides, how many people want to constantly change their opinions to fit the facts?

It's a whole lot easier to change the facts to fit your opinions.

Unsane people make up their minds and then find the facts to "verify" their opinion. Or even more commonly, they accept the opinion of the nearest "expert," and then they don't have to bother with the facts at all.

So you see the power of the psychologically right name. The mind makes the world of reality fit the name. A Mustang looks sportier, racier, and faster than if the same car had been called the Turtle.

Language is the currency of the mind. To think conceptually, you manipulate words. With the right choice of words, you can influence the thinking process itself. (As proof that the mind "thinks with words" and not abstract thoughts, consider how a language is learned. To be really fluent in a foreign language, say French, you must learn to think in French.)

But there are limits. If a word is so far out of touch with reality, the mind just refuses to use the word. It says "large" on the tube that everyone except the manufacturer calls a "small" toothpaste tube. It says "economy" on the tube that everyone calls "large."

The People's Republic of China is usually called "Red China" because no one believes it is a "people's republic." (Inside the country, the People's Republic of China is undoubtedly an effective name.)

You must be careful of change

The more things change, the more they remain the same. Yet people today are caught up in the illusion of change. Every day, the world seems to be turning faster.

Years ago a successful product might live 50 years or more before fading away. Today a product's life cycle is much shorter. Sometimes it can be measured in months instead of years.

New products, new services, new markets, even new media are constantly being born. They grow to adulthood and then slide to oblivion. And a new cycle starts again.

Yesterday the way to reach the masses was the mass magazines. Today it's network TV. Tomorrow it could be cable. The only permanent thing today seems to be change. The kaleidoscope of life clicks faster and faster. New patterns emerge and disappear.

Change has become a way of life for many companies. But is change the way to keep pace with change? The exact opposite appears to be true.

The landscape is littered with the debris of projects that companies rushed into in attempting to keep pace. Singer trying to move into the boom in home appliances. RCA moving into the boom in computers. General Foods moving into the boom in fast-food outlets. Not to mention the hundreds of companies that threw away their corporate identities to chase the passing fad to initials.

Meanwhile the programs of those who kept at what they did best and held their ground have been immensely successful. Maytag selling its reliable appliances. Walt Disney selling the world of fantasy and fun. Avon calling.

You need vision

Change is a wave on the ocean of time. Short-term, the waves cause agitation and confusion. Long-term, the underlying currents are much more significant. To cope with change, you have to take a long-range point of view. To determine your basic business and stick with it.

Changing the direction of a large company is like trying to turn an aircraft carrier. It takes a mile before anything happens. And if it was a wrong turn, getting back on course takes even longer.

To play the game successfully, you must make decisions on what your company will be doing not next month or next year but in 5 years, 10 years. In other words, instead of turning the wheel to meet each fresh wave, a company must point itself in the right direction.

You must have vision. There's no sense building a position based on a technology that's too narrow. Or a product that's becoming obsolete. Or a name that's defective.

Most of all, you have to be able to see the difference between what works and what doesn't work.

Sounds simple, but it's not. When the tide is rising, everything seems to be working. When the tide is falling, nothing seems to be working.

You have to learn how to separate your efforts from the general movement of the economy. Many marketing experts are blessed with a generous supply of luck. Be wary. Today's hula-hoop marketing genius could be tomorrow's welfare recipient.

Be patient. The sun shines tomorrow on those who have made the right decisions today.

If a company has positioned itself in the right direction, it will be able to ride the currents of change, ready to take advantage of those opportunities that are right for it. But when an opportunity arrives, a company must move quickly.

You need courage

When you trace the history of how leadership positions were established, from Hershey in chocolate to Hertz in rent-a-cars, the common thread is not marketing skill or even product innovation. The common thread is seizing the initiative before the competitor has a chance to get established. The leader usually poured in the marketing money while the situation was still fluid.

Hershey, for example, established a position in chocolate so strong that Hershey felt it didn't need to advertise at all. This conviction was a luxury that competitors like Mars couldn't afford.

Finally Hershey decided to advertise. But not in time. Today the Hershey milk chocolate bar is not the largest seller. It's not even in the top 5.

You can see that establishing a leadership position depends not only on luck and timing but also on a willingness to pour it on when others stand back and wait.

You need objectivity

To be successful in the positioning era, you must be brutally frank. You must try to eliminate all ego from the decision-making process. It only clouds the issue.

One of the most critical aspects of positioning is being able to evaluate products objectively and see how they are viewed by customers and prospects.

You also have to remember that you can't play basketball without a backboard. You need someone to bounce your ideas off. As soon as you think you have found that simple idea that is the solution to your problem, you have lost something.

You have lost your objectivity. You need the other person to take a fresh look at what you have wrought. And vice versa.

Like Ping-Pong, positioning is a game best played by two people. It's no accident that this book was written by two people. Only in a give-and-take atmosphere can ideas be refined and perfected.

You need simplicity

Only an obvious idea will work today. The overwhelming volume of communication prevents anything else from succeeding.

But the obvious isn't always so obvious. "Boss" Kettering had a sign which he placed on the wall of the General Motors Research Building in Dayton: "This problem when solved will be simple."

"Raisins from California. Nature's candy."

"Moist and meaty Gainesburgers. The canned dog food without the can."

"Bubble Yum. Number yum in bubble gum."

These are the kinds of simple ideas that work today. Simple concepts expressed with simple words used in a straightforward way.

Often the solution to a problem is so simple that thousands of people have looked at it without seeing it. When an idea is clever or complicated, however, we should be suspicious. It probably won't work because it's not simple enough.

The history of science is a history of the Ketterings of this world who found simple solutions to complex problems.

The head of an advertising agency once insisted that his account executives paste down the marketing strategy on the back of each layout.

Then when the client asked what the ad was supposed to do, the account person could turn the layout over and read the strategy.

But an ad should be simple enough so that it is the strategy.

The agency made a mistake. It ran the wrong side of the layout.

You need subtlety

Beginners who play the positioning game often remark, "How easy this is. You just find a position you can call your own."

Simple, yes. But easy, no.

The difficulty is finding an open position that's also effective. In politics, for example, it's easy to establish a position to the far right (a conservative position) or the far left (a socialist position). You will undoubtedly preempt either position.

You will also lose.

What you must do is to find an opening near the center of the spectrum. You must be slightly conservative in a field of liberals or slightly liberal in a field of conservatives.

This calls for great restraint and subtlety. The big winners in business and in life are those people who have found open positions near the center of the spectrum. Not at the edge.

You can sometimes have a positioning success and a sales failure. This might be termed "Rolls-Royce thinking."

"We're the Rolls-Royce of the industry" is a claim you often hear in business today.

Do you know how many Rolls-Royces are sold in America every year?

About a thousand, or 0.01 percent of the market. Cadillac, on the other hand, sells more than 300,000.

Both Cadillac and Rolls-Royce are luxury cars, but the gulf between them is enormous. To the average automobile buyer, the Rolls-Royce at $100,000 and up is out of reach.

Cadillac, like Michelob and other premium products, is not. The secret to establishing a successful position is to keep two things in balance: (1) A unique position with (2) an appeal that's not too narrow.

You must be willing to sacrifice

The essence of positioning is sacrifice. You must be willing to give up something in order to establish that unique position.

Nyquil, the nighttime cold medicine, gave up the daytime market.

The focus of most marketing operations is just the opposite. They look for ways to broaden their markets by line extension, by size and flavor proliferation, by multiple distribution. All these things tend to produce short-term sales increases and long-term positioning erosion.

In positioning, smaller may be better. It is usually better to look for smaller targets that you can own exclusively rather than a bigger market you have to share with three or four other brands.

You can't be all things to all people and still have a powerful position.

You need patience

Very few companies can afford to launch a new product on a nationwide scale.

Instead they look for places to make the brand successful. And then roll it out to other markets.

The geographic roll-out is one way. You build the product in one market and then move on to another. From east to west. Or vice versa.

The demographic roll-out is another. Philip Morris built Marlboro into the No. 1 cigarette on college campuses long before it became the No. 1 brand nationwide.

The chronologic roll-out is the third way. You build the brand among a specific age group and then roll it out to others. "The Pepsi Generation" helped Pepsi-Cola build the product among the younger set and then reap the benefits as they grew up.

Distribution is another roll-out technique. The Wella line was first sold through beauty salons. After the products were established, they were sold through drugstores and supermarkets.

You need a global outlook

Don't overlook the importance of worldwide thinking. A company that keeps its eye on Tom, Dick, and Harry is going to miss Pierre, Hans, and Yoshio.

Marketing is rapidly becoming a worldwide ballgame. A company that owns a position in one country now finds that it can use that position to wedge its way into another. IBM has some 60 percent of the German computer market. Is this fact surprising? It shouldn't be. IBM earns more than 50 percent of its profits outside the United States.

As companies start to operate on a worldwide basis, they often discover they have a name problem.

A typical example is U.S. Rubber, a worldwide company that marketed many products not made of rubber. Changing the name to Uniroyal created a new corporate identity that could be used worldwide.

What you don't need

You don't need a reputation as a marketing genius. As a matter of fact, this could be a fatal flaw.

All too often, the product leader makes the fatal mistake of attributing its success to marketing skill. As a result, it thinks it can transfer that skill to other products and other marketing situations.

Witness, for example, the disappointing record of Xerox in computers.

And the mecca of marketing knowledge, International Business Machines Corporation, hasn't done much better. So far, IBM's plain-paper copier hasn't made much of a dent in Xerox's business. Touché.

The rules of positioning hold for all types of products. In the packaged-goods area, for example, Bristol-Myers tried to take on Crest toothpaste with Fact (killed after $5 million was spent on promotion). Then they tried to go after Alka-Seltzer with Resolve (killed after $11 million was spent). Then they tried to unseat Bayer with Dissolve, another financial headache.

The suicidal bent of companies that go head-on against established competition is hard to understand.

Hope springs eternal in the human breast. Nine times out of ten, the also-ran that sets out to attack the leader head-on is headed for disaster.

To repeat, the first rule of positioning is: To win the battle for the mind, you can't compete head-on against a company that has a strong, established position. You can go around, under or over, but never head to head.

The leader owns the high ground. The No. 1 position in the prospect's mind. The top rung of the product ladder. To move up the ladder, you must follow the rules of positioning.

In our overcommunicated society, the name of the game today is positioning.

And only the better players are going to survive.

Index